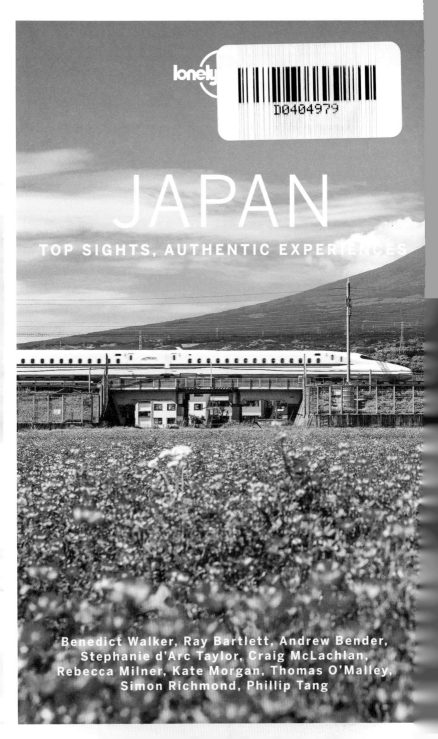

JAPAN

TOP SIGHTS, AUTHENTIC EXPERIENCES

Benedict Walker, Ray Bartlett, Andrew Bender,
Stephanie d'Arc Taylor, Craig McLachlan,
Rebecca Milner, Kate Morgan, Thomas O'Malley,
Simon Richmond, Phillip Tang

Contents

Plan Your Trip

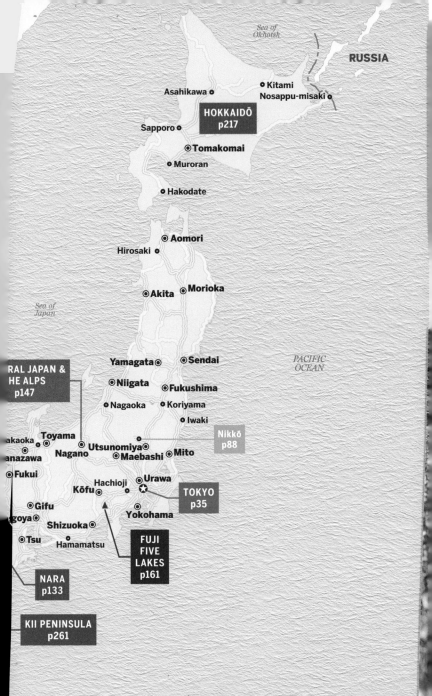

Sea of
Okhotsk

RUSSIA

○ Kitami
Asahikawa ○
Nosappu-misaki ○

HOKKAIDŌ
p217

Sapporo ○
●**Tomakomai**
○ **Muroran**

○ **Hakodate**

●**Aomori**
Hirosaki ○

●**Akita** ●**Morioka**

Sea of
Japan

Yamagata ○   ●**Sendai**

PACIFIC
OCEAN

●**Niigata**   ●**Fukushima**

Nagaoka ○   ○ **Koriyama**

○ **Iwaki**

**RAL JAPAN &
HE ALPS
p147**

Toyama   Utsunomiya ○   ○
akaoka ○ ●   **Nagano**   ●**Maebashi**   ○ **Mito**   **Nikkō
p88**
anazawa ○

○**Fukui**   Hachioji ○   ○ **Urawa**
Kōfu ○   ☆   **TOKYO
p35**
○**Gifu**
goya ○   ○ **Yokohama**
○**Tsu**   **Shizuoka** ○
Hamamatsu ○

**FUJI
FIVE
LAKES
p161**

**NARA
p133**

**KII PENINSULA
p261**

N   0   400 km
     0   200 miles

Welcome to Japan

Japan is truly timeless, a place where ancient traditions are fused with modern life as if it were the most natural thing in the world.

There's an intoxicating buzz to Japan's urban centres, with their vibrant street life, glowing streetscapes, 24-hour drinking-and-dining scenes, architectural wonders that redefine what buildings – and cities – should look like. Leave them behind and you've got a country that is more than two-thirds mountains, with bubbling hot springs at every turn. In the warmer months there is excellent hiking, through cedar groves and fields of wildflowers, up to soaring peaks and ancient shrines (the latter founded by wandering ascetics). Come winter, all this is covered with snow and the skiing is world class. (And if you've never paired hiking or skiing with soaking in onsen you don't know what you've been missing.)

Travelling the country offers numerous opportunities to connect with Japan's traditional culture. Spend the night in a ryokan (traditional inn), sleeping on futons and tatami mats, and padding through well-worn wooden halls to the bathhouse (or go one step further and sleep in an old farmhouse). Chant with monks or learn how to whisk bitter *matcha* (powdered green tea) into a froth. From the splendour of a Kyoto geisha dance to the spare beauty of a Zen rock garden, Japan has the power to enthral even the most jaded traveller.

Chant with monks or learn how to whisk bitter matcha *into a froth.*

Mt Fuji (p164)
BLANSCAPE / SHUTTERSTOCK ©

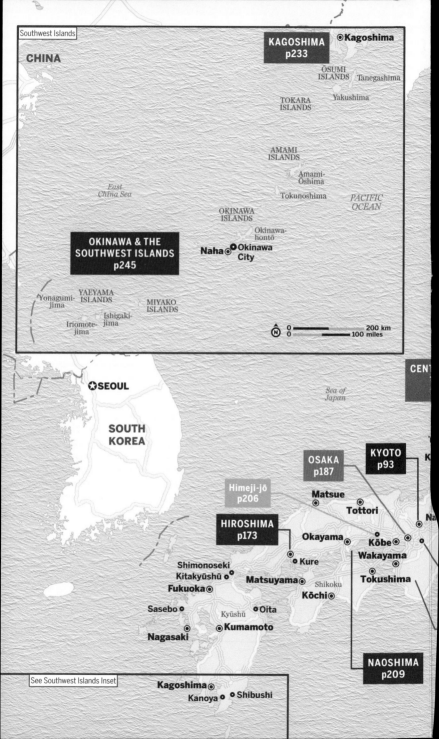

Southwest Islands

CHINA

⊙**Kagoshima**

ŌSUMI
ISLANDS   Tanegashima

TOKARA   Yakushima
ISLANDS

AMAMI
ISLANDS

Amami-
Ōshima

*East
China Sea*

Tokunoshima   *PACIFIC
OCEAN*

OKINAWA
ISLANDS

Okinawa-
hontō

Naha⊙○**Okinawa
City**

Yonagumi-   YAEYAMA
jima   ISLANDS   MIYAKO
                         ISLANDS
Iriomote-   Ishigaki-
jima   jima

Ⓝ 0 ┣━━━━━━┫ 200 km
    0 ┣━━━━━━┫ 100 miles

⊗**SEOUL**

*Sea of
Japan*

CENT

**SOUTH
KOREA**

K

Matsue
⊙

⊙
Tottori

Na

Okayama⊙   ⊙
                Kōbe⊙ ⊙
⊙   ⊙
Kure   **Wakayama**
                        ⊙

Shimonoseki
Kitakyūshū o°   **Matsuyama**⊙   *Shikoku*   **Tokushima**
Fukuoka⊙   **Kōchi**⊙

Sasebo o   *Kyūshū* ○**Oita**
          ⊙**Kumamoto**
Nagasaki

See Southwest Islands Inset

Kagoshima⊙
Kanoya ○ ○**Shibushi**

Jizō statue (p91)

Plan Your Trip
Japan's Top 12

Tokyo

Planet earth's unrivalled 24/7 megalopolis

Tokyo (p35) is one of the world's reigning cities of superlatives – the dining, drinking and shopping are all top class. It's a city always in flux, which is one of its enduring charms, forever sending up breath-taking new structures and dreaming up new culinary delights. It truly has something for everyone, whether your ideal afternoon is spent in an art museum or racing through the streets of Akihabara in a go-kart. From left: Shibuya Crossing (p59); tempura

1

GUITAR PHOTOGRAPHER / SHUTTERSTOCK ©

SEAN PAVONE / SHUTTERSTOCK ©

Kyoto

National reasures, temples and modern-day geisha

There are said to be more than 1000 Buddhist temples in Kyoto
(p93), Japan's imperial capital for over 1000 years. The city is a
showroom of Japanese religious architecture, which produced both
the glittering Kinkaku-ji (Golden Pavilion) and the stark Zen garden at
Ryōan-ji. But don't equate religiosity with temperance here: Kyoto is
also the city where geisha entertained in lantern-lit teahouses (and
still do). Top: Yasaka Pagoda from Sannen-zaka; Bottom: Ryōan-ji (p103)

Central Japan & the Alps

Traditional life away from the crowds

Crowned by the Japan Alps (p147), the nation's geographical and spiritual heart, Chūbu (Central Japan) has year-round appeal. In the green season, hike historic roads through alpine valleys before soaking your weary bones in hot springs. You'll find photo ops galore, friendly farmers in traditional villages, and one of Japan's best preserved castles. Come winter, explore some of the best terrain that powder-hounds could dream of. Above: Shirakawa-gō (p150)

Nara

The Great Buddha of the ancient capital

Nara (p133) was Japan's first permanent capital in the 8th century, and is the site of the country's first monumental building spree. You will find numerous grand temples here, older even than those in Kyoto. The highlight is Nara's Daibutsu (Great Buddha), which is among the largest gilt-bronze effigies in the world; the temple that houses it, Tōdai-ji, is one of the world's largest wooden structures.
Right: Daibutsu

Fuji Five Lakes

Spectacular sleeping giant: Japan's most cherished mountain

Even from a distance, the perfectly symmetrical cone of Japan's highest peak will take your breath away. Fuji-san is among Japan's most revered and timeless attractions. Dawn from the summit? Pure magic. Hundreds of thousands of people climb it every year, but those who'd prefer picture-perfect views can do so from the less-daunting vantage points in the foothills and hot springs of the scenic Fuji Five Lakes district (p161). Right: Fuji-san

Osaka

The friendly metropolis of food and fun

Something magical happens when the sun sets in the Land of the Rising Sun: the grey city streets turn into crackling canyons of neon. Nowhere is this light show more dramatic than along Osaka's Dōtombori-gawa. In fact, just about everything seems to be turned up a notch in Japan's third-largest city (p187). It's a city that loves to let loose and lives to eat – the perfect stop for your urban Japan fix. Above: Dōtombori-gawa

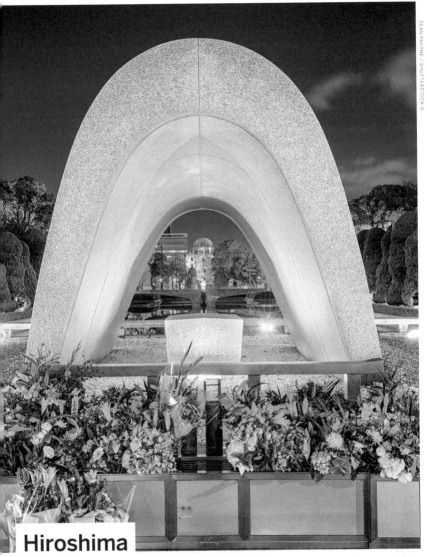

Hiroshima

Heartbreaking history with a message of hope

It's not until you visit the Peace Memorial Museum that the extent of human tragedy wrought by the atomic bomb in 1945 becomes clear. A visit to Hiroshima (p173) is a sobering history lesson and the park around the museum offers many opportunities for reflection. But the city's spirit of determination – as well as its food – will ensure that you'll have good memories to take away with you. Above: Cenotaph Memorial (p179), designed by Kenzō Tange

Kagoshima

Friendly folks and a very vocal volcano

Kagoshima (p233), roughly 1000km southwest of Tokyo, is an urban outpost with a distinctly different, rugged feel. Lording over the city is the smoking (quite literally) volcano Sakurajima. Kagoshima is also the jumping-off point for the island of Yakushima, which, with its ancient cedars, tangled vines and seaside springs, looks more like a *Star Wars* set than planet Earth. If you're after something a little different, this is the place for you.

Right: Sakurajima (p241)

KITINUT JINAPUCK / SHUTTERSTOCK ©

OSAMU WATANABE ©

Naoshima

A living island of interactive art

Naoshima (p209) is Japan's top destination for contemporary art and architecture. An island in the Inland Sea, it functions as one big open-air museum, with buildings and installations from leading international creators – all designed to enhance the glorious natural scenery. Much of what visitors find so compelling, however, is the blend of avant-garde and rural Japan: there are villages here that remain a vital part of the island's artistic renaissance. From left: Seto Inland Sea; Yayoi Kusama's *Pumpkin* sculpture, Benesse Art Site Naoshima (p212)

Hokkaidō

Pristine nature and outdoor adventures galore

Hokkaidō (p217), Japan's northernmost island, is an untamed land-scape of mountains that is pock-marked with crystal-blue caldera lakes and sulphur-rich hot springs. This is 'big mountain and snow' country, where skiers carve snow drifts reaching several metres in depth. In the green season, hikers and cyclists are drawn to the island's wide open spaces and dramatic topography. Clockwise, this page: flower fields; Yuki Matsuri (p22) in Sapporo; Noboribetsu Onsen (p226)

GLOWIMAGES / GETTY IMAGES ©

Okinawa & the Southwest Islands

Spectacular beaches, vibrant diving and 'island time'

Okinawa and the Southwest Islands (p245) are characterised by flat farmlands rolling on to palm-fringed beaches with turquoise waters. Iriomote, the most remote, is covered in primeval forest. Okinawa adds mountains, resorts and capital city Naha, with a multicultural vibe that has emerged from a tragic past. Above: Ishigaki-jima (p248)

Kii Peninsula

Trace the footsteps of holy pilgrims

Not far from Osaka but a world away, this mountainous peninsula (p261) puts you in touch with ancient Japan. Visit the temple complex Kōya-san, with its moss-covered stupas and chanting monks. Then head deeper into the peninsula where you can walk trails known as the Kumano Kodō, a network laid down centuries ago by mountain ascetics, seeking spiritual enlightenment in what must have felt like the ends of the earth. Above: Oku-no-in (p266)

Plan Your Trip
Need to Know

When to Go

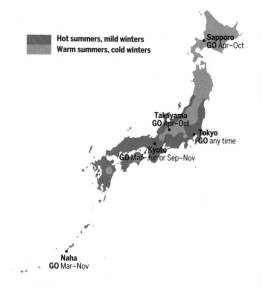

Hot summers, mild winters
Warm summers, cold winters

Sapporo
GO Apr–Oct

Takayama
GO Apr–Oct

Tokyo
GO any time

Kyoto
GO Mar–Jun or Sep–Nov

Naha
GO Mar–Nov

High Season (Apr & May, Aug)

o Cherry-blossom season (late March to early April), Golden Week (early May) and O-Bon (mid-August): sights, trains and hotels packed and prices sky-high.

o City folk head to the cool of the mountains in August; also summer vacation and festival season.

Shoulder (Jun & Jul, Sep–Nov)

o Autumn foliage draws leaf-peepers from October and November, dependant on elevation and latitude.

Low Season (Dec–Mar)

o Ski season kicks off in the mountains, but crowds dwindle elsewhere. Accommodation is at its cheapest.

o Many businesses close over the New Year period (end of December to early January).

Currency
Yen (¥)

Language
Japanese

Visas
Visas are issued on arrival for most nationalities for stays of up to 90 days.

Money
In cities, credit cards are widely accepted; rural areas are hit and miss. Post offices and most convenience stores have international ATMs.

Mobile Phones
Japan operates on the 3G and 4G (LTE) networks. Prepaid data-only SIM cards (for unlocked smartphones only) are widely available at the airport or electronics stores.

Time
Japan Standard Time (GMT/UTC plus nine hours)

Daily Costs

Budget: Less than ¥8000

- Dorm bed: ¥3000
- Bowl of noodles: ¥750
- Happy-hour beer: ¥500
- City one-day subway pass: ¥600
- One temple or museum entry: ¥500

Midrange: ¥8000–20,000

- Double room at a business hotel: ¥10,000
- Dinner for two at an *izakaya* (Japanese pub-eatery): ¥6000
- Half-day cycling tour or cooking class: ¥5000
- Temple and museum entries: ¥1500

Top End: More than ¥20,000

- Double room in a nice hotel: from ¥25,000
- Dinner for two at a good sushi restaurant: from ¥15,000
- Taxi ride between city sights: ¥2500

Useful Websites

Lonely Planet (www.lonelyplanet.com/japan) Destination information, hotel bookings, traveller forum and more.
Japan National Tourism Organization (www.jnto.go.jp) Official tourist site with planning tools and events calendar.
Japan Meteorological Agency (www.jma.go.jp) Up-to-the-minute weather advisories and disaster alerts.

Opening Hours

Note that some outdoor attractions (such as gardens) may close earlier in winter. Standard opening hours:
Banks 9am to 3pm (some to 5pm) Monday to Friday
Bars 6pm to late, with no fixed closing hour
Department stores 10am to 8pm
Museums 9am or 10am to 5pm; often closed Monday
Post offices 9am to 5pm Monday to Friday; some open Saturday
Restaurants lunch 11.30am to 2pm; dinner 6pm to 10pm; last orders taken about half an hour before closing

Arriving in Japan

Narita Airport (Tokyo) Express trains and buses run frequently to central Tokyo (around ¥3000; one to two hours) between 7am and 10.30pm. Taxis cost approximately ¥22,000 plus tolls.
Haneda Airport (Tokyo) Trains and buses (¥400 to ¥1200, 30 to 45 minutes) to central Tokyo run frequently from 5.30am to midnight; times and costs depend on your destination in the city. There are only a couple of night buses. For a taxi budget between ¥6000 and ¥8000.
Kansai International Airport (Osaka) Express trains run frequently to Kyoto (from ¥2850, 75 minutes) and Osaka (¥1430, 40 minutes). Buses cost ¥1050 to ¥1550 to central Osaka (50 minutes), ¥2550 to Kyoto (90 minutes). Trains and buses stop running close to midnight. A shared taxi service to Kyoto costs ¥4200; a standard taxi to Osaka starts at ¥14,000.

Getting Around

Train Fast, reliable and with discount rail passes, very affordable – trains can get you just about anywhere.

Ferry Good for getting to far-flung islands and for fans of slow travel.

Bus The cheapest way to make long-haul journeys and the only way to get to some mountain and rural destinations.

Car rental Roads are well-maintained and foreign-language GPS navigation is ubiquitous. Especially recommended in Hokkaidō, Kyūshū and Okinawa. Drive on the left.

Air A good option for long distances or time-pressed itineraries.

For more on **getting around**, see p309 ➡

Plan Your Trip
Hot Spots For...

Japanese Cuisine
Eating is one of the great pleasures of visiting Japan. Discover just how varied Japanese cuisine is, from region to region and season to season.

SITTIPONG CHANANITHITHAM / SHUTTERSTOCK ©

Kyoto (p93)
Japan's ancient imperial capital is the birthplace of *kaiseki* (haute cuisine; pictured) and the tea ceremony.

Roan Kikunoi
A creative approach to traditional *kaiseki* cuisine (p120).

Osaka (p187)
Colourful Osaka is Japan's capital of street food: fierce competition turns humble dishes to high art.

Wanaka Honten
Top for *tako-yaki* (octopus dumplings; p192).

Central Japan & the Alps (p147)
Dishes like *hoba-miso* (miso grilled on a magnolia leaf) are unique to the Hida region of the Japan Alps.

Kyōya
Woody, rustic Kyōya is a Takayama institution (p156).

Art & Architecture
Japan has a sublime artistic tradition that transcends gallery walls, the pages of books and the kabuki stage to seep into everyday life.

YOSHIO511 / SHUTTERSTOCK ©

Tokyo (p35)
Art museums, theatres and the creations of Japan's 20th-century architects.

Tokyo National Museum
World's largest collection of Japanese art (pictured; p40).

Naoshima (p209)
An island of contemporary art, including several museums designed by Japanese architect Ando Tadao.

Art House Project
A village setting for art installations (p212).

Osaka (p187)
An urban sprawl that lacks Tokyo's well-planned grace but offers unexpected delights amid the chaos.

Abeno Harukas
Japan's tallest building (300m, 60 storeys; p195).

Outdoor Adventure
Japan is a year-round destination for walkers keen for gentle strolls or serious peaks. In winter, it's all about going down the mountains.

KANUMAN / SHUTTERSTOCK ©

Fuji Five Lakes (p161)
Iconic Mt Fuji is the main draw, but the pretty lake district offers gentler hikes through the foothills, too.

Mt Fuji
Japan's highest, most iconic summit (pictured; p164).

Hokkaidō (p217)
Japan's northernmost island is largely undeveloped and is a playground for outdoor enthusiasts.

Niseko United
Niseko offers excellent skiing and snowboarding (p220).

Central Japan & the Alps (p147)
All but one of Japan's 30 highest peaks are found in this glorious alpine region – a year-round destination.

Kamikōchi
Check out the region's amazing scenery (p154).

Historic Sites
See the sights where Japan's history – the samurai warrior, the wandering ascetic and the farmer bent over their rice paddies – is brought to life.

MIRKO KUZMANOVIC / SHUTTERSTOCK ©

Nara (p133)
The nation's first capital hosts Buddhist art, architecture and historic relics from the 8th century.

Tōdai-ji
Home of Nara's Daibutsu statue (p136).

Hiroshima (p173)
This city has numerous monuments to the day that changed history for Japan and the world.

Peace Memorial Museum
Evocative account of the bomb's aftermath (p179).

Okinawa & the Southwest Islands (p245)
Swim with manta rays or enjoy an idyllic beach; previously these islands saw much carnage in WWII.

Okinawa Peace Memorial
Remembering the US invasion (pictured; p254).

Plan Your Trip
Essential Japan

Activities

Highly volcanic Japan bubbles with onsen (hot springs). The Japanese have turned the simple act of bathing into a folk religion and the country is dotted with temples and shrines to this most relaxing of faiths. Many believe the waters to have curative properties; depending on the mineral content they might be hailed a positive effect on one's skin, circulation or digestion. At the very least, you will sleep very, very well after a soak.

Shopping

Tokyo is the fashion trendsetter for all of Japan; Osaka, the shopping capital of western Japan, has a street-smart style of its own. Kyoto is the place to pick up traditional goods such as anything tea and tea-ceremony related. Around the country are pottery towns and others famous for local crafts.

Eating

As visitors to Japan quickly discover, people here are absolutely obsessed with food. You'll find that every island and region of Japan has its own *meibutsu* (local speciality) that is a point of pride. Japan's larger cities have a good spread of cuisines, so you can take your pick from restaurants specialising in different Japanese dishes or Chinese, Thai, French, Italian and more. Look to food courts in department stores and train stations for easy options.

In rural areas, the top foodie meals are often served at ryokan (traditional Japanese inns), where the dishes make ample use of local ingredients. Given the choice, most Japanese travellers book meals at their lodgings. As this is the case, be warned that in many rural or resort areas there may be few restaurants open for dinner.

J. HENNING BUCHOLZ / SHUTTERSTOCK ©

Drinking & Nightlife

Any Japanese city of reasonable size will have a *hankagai* (繁華街), a lively commercial and entertainment district. Famous ones include: Tokyo's Kabukichō, Osaka's Dōtombori and Sapporo's Susukino. Such districts are stocked, often several storeys high, with a medley of drinking options that include *izakaya* (traditional pub-eateries), cocktail bars, Western-style pubs, jazz cafes, nightclubs and more – all awash in the neon lights that form Japan's urban signature.

You can't visit Japan without getting in a round of karaoke (カラオケ; pronounced kah-rah-oh-kay) – a popular local pastime. In Japan, karaoke is sung in a private room among friends. Admission is usually charged per person per half-hour. Food and drinks (ordered by phone) are brought to the room. To choose a song, use the touchscreen device to search by artist or title; most have an English function and plenty of English songs to choose from.

★ Best Markets

Tsukiji (p56), Tokyo

Nishiki (p106), Kyoto

Kuromon Ichiba (p197), Osaka

Ameya-yokochō (p42), Tokyo

Farmer's Market @UNU (p73), Tokyo

Entertainment

Sumo is Japan's national sport. Tournaments take place in January, May and September in Tokyo and in March in Osaka. While sumo has its devout followers, it's baseball that is the fan favourite. It's worth getting tickets while in Japan just to see the perfectly choreographed cheers. Local baseball has a culture all its own, as spectators chomp on dried squid and buy beer from *uriko,* young women with kegs strapped to their backs, who work the aisles with tireless cheer.

From left: *Wagyū* sushi; Tokyo sumo tournament

Month by Month

January

✾ Shōgatsu (New Year)

Families come together to eat and drink to health and happiness. The holiday is officially 1 to 3 January, but many businesses and attractions close the whole first week.

February

February is the coldest month and the peak of Japan's ski season.

✾ Setsubun

The first day of spring is 3 February in the traditional lunar calendar, a shift once believed to bode evil. As a precaution, people visit Buddhist temples, toss roasted beans and shout *'Oni wa soto! Fuku wa uchi!'* ('Devil out! Fortune in!').

✾ Yuki Matsuri

Two million visitors head to Sapporo's annual snow festival in early February. Highlights include the international snow-sculpture contest, ice slides and mazes for kids. Book way ahead.

March

Spring begins in fits and starts. The Japanese have a saying: *sankan-shion* – three days cold, four days warm.

☆ Anime Japan

The world's largest animation festival (www.anime-japan.jp) takes place in Tokyo in late March.

April

Warm weather and blossoming trees makes April the favoured month to visit Japan, but places like Kyoto can get very crowded.

✾ Cherry-Blossom Viewing

When the cherry blossoms burst into bloom, the Japanese hold rollicking *hanami* (blossom-viewing) parties. The blossoms are fickle and hard to time: on average, they hit their peak in Tokyo or Kyoto between 25 March and 7 April.

MARVIN MINDER / SHUTTERSTOCK ©

May

May is lovely: it's warm and sunny in most places and the fresh green in the mountains is stunning. Be wary of the travel crush during Golden Week (29 April to 5 May).

🎏 Sanja Matsuri

The grandest Tokyo festival of all, this three-day event, held over the third weekend of May, attracts around 1.5 million spectators to Asakusa, for a rowdy parade of *mikoshi* (portable shrines) carried by men and women in traditional dress.

🎏 Roppongi Art Night

The galleries of Tokyo's chic Roppongi district stay open day and night for this weekend-long art extravaganza (www.roppongiartnight.com).

June

By mid-June *tsuyu* (the rainy season) sets in, lasting until mid-July.

★ Best Festivals

Cherry-Blossom Viewing, April

Gion Matsuri, July

Yuki Matsuri, February

Rōsoku Matsuri, August

Sanja Matsuri, May

July

Japanese summers are hot and humid; head to Hokkaidō or the Japan Alps to escape the heat. Festivals dominate the calendar and fireworks punctuate the night skies.

🧗 Mt Fuji Climbing Season

Mt Fuji officially opens to climbing on 1 July, and the months of July and August are ideal for climbing the peak.

From left: *Hanami* party, Maruyama Park, Kyoto; Sanja Matsuri

♣ Gion Matsuri

Japan's most vaunted festival is held on 17 and 24 July in Kyoto, when huge, elaborate floats are paraded through the streets. Three evenings prior, locals stroll through street markets dressed in beautiful *yukata* (light cotton kimonos). Accommodation is expensive and difficult to find.

♣ Tenjin Matsuri

Held in Osaka on 24 and 25 July, this massive festival draws home-proud, traditionally attired Kansai folk onto the streets for lively processions of *mikoshi* destined for hundreds of boats on the river, all culminating in fireworks.

☆ Fuji Rock Festival

Japan's biggest music festival takes place over one long (and often wildly muddy and fun) weekend at a mountain resort in late July, with some of music's biggest names and emerging artists.

August

School holidays mean beaches and cooler mountain areas get crowded. Many Japanese return to their home towns (or take a holiday) around O-Bon, so public transport is hectic and shops may close.

♣ O-Bon (Festival of the Dead)

Three days in mid-August are set aside to honour the dead, when their spirits are said to return to the earth. Graves are swept, offerings are made, and lanterns are floated down rivers, in lakes or the sea to help guide spirits on their journey.

♣ Daimon-ji Gozan Okuribi

Huge fires in the shape of Chinese characters and other symbols are set alight in the hills around Kyoto during this festival, which forms part of the O-Bon rites.

♣ Rōsoku Matsuri

Kōya-san's already deeply atmospheric Oku-no-in is lit with some 100,000 candles on 13 August for Rōsoku Matsuri during O-Bon.

♣ Peace Memorial Ceremony

On 6 August, a memorial service is held in Hiroshima for victims of the WWII atomic bombing of the city. Thousands of paper lanterns are floated down the river.

September

Days are still warm, but less humid – though the odd typhoon rolls through this time of year, which can ruin hiking plans.

♣ Moon Viewing

Full moons in September and October call for *tsukimi* (moon-viewing gatherings). People eat *tsukimi dango* – *mochi* (pounded rice) dumplings shaped round like the moon.

October

♣ Asama Onsen Taimatsu Matsuri

In early October, groups of men, women and children parade burning bales of hay through the narrow streets of this Matsumoto district, Asama Onsen, in this rowdy and spectacular fire festival.

♣ Kurama-no-hi Matsuri

On 22 October, this festival sees loin-clothed men carrying huge flaming torches through the streets of the sacred hamlet of Kurama in the mountains outside Kyoto.

November

Crisp and cool days with snow falling in the mountains. Autumn foliage peaks around Tokyo and Kyoto, which can draw crowds.

December

December is cold across most of Japan. Many businesses shut down from 29 or 30 December for the New Year holiday.

✕ Toshikoshi Soba

Eating buckwheat noodles on New Year's Eve, a tradition called *toshikoshi soba,* is said to bring luck and longevity.

♣ Joya-no-kane

Temple bells around Japan ring 108 times at midnight on 31 December, a purifying ritual.

Plan Your Trip
Get Inspired

Read

Shōgun (James Clavell; 1975) A historic tale based on the true story of a Brit who visited Japan in 1600.

The Temple of the Golden Pavilion (Mishima Yukio; 1956) A fictitious take on the actual burning of Kinkaku-ji by a Buddhist acolyte in 1950.

Norwegian Wood (Murakami Haruki; 1987) Coming-of-age story set in 1960s Tokyo, by Japan's most popular living writer.

The Book of Tokyo: A City in Short Fiction (Edited by Michael Emmerich, Jim Hinks and Matsuie Masashi; 2015) Ten stories by contemporary Japanese writers.

Watch

Rashomon (Kurosawa Akira; 1950) Psychological classic set in feudal-era Japan, from the master auteur of Japanese cinema.

Spirited Away (Miyazaki Hayao; 2001) Academy Award–winning animation, and highest-grossing Japanese film to date.

Afterlife (Kore-eda Hirokazu; 1998) A heartwarming exploration of the Japanese notion of reincarnation.

Lost in Translation (Sofia Coppola; 2003) Disorienting, captivating Tokyo through the eyes of two Americans.

Your Name (Shinkai Makoto; 2016) Popular anime where a city boy and country girl swap places.

Listen

Shimanchu nu Takara (Begin) Love song to Okinawa with *eisa* (Okinawan folk-style) chanting.

Hanamizuki (Hitoto Yō) Tender ode to love and loss and a perennial karaoke favourite.

Tokyo, Mon Amour (Pizzicato Five) Moody lounge track from the '90s Shibuya indie scene.

Fujiyama (Dave Brubeck) Mournful meditation on Japan's iconic mountain, from the late composer's *Jazz Impressions of Japan*.

Five-Day Itineraries

Kansai in Depth

Japan often feels like a destination that requires a long trip and lots of advance planning, but it needn't be. The Kansai region is packed with top attractions – such as beautiful Kyoto and lively Osaka – all within an hour of each other by train.

Kyoto (p93) Spend two or three days in this magical city exploring the centuries-old temples and gardens.
🚊 40 min to Nara

Osaka (p187) Eat till you burst in Japan's capital of street food.
🚊 40 min to Gokurakubashi, then 🚊 5 min to Kōya-san

Nara (p133) See the splendid Daibutsu (Great Buddha) and stroll through Nara-kōen.
🚊 40 min to Osaka

Kii Peninsula (p261) Spend your last night in a Buddhist temple in the other-wordly mountaintop monastery Kōya-san.

Tokyo & Mt Fuji

Between Tokyo and the attractions in its orbit, you can cover a lot of varied terrain, taking in both contemporary and traditional Japan with very little fuss. Base yourself in the capital taking advantage of its excellent dining scene and transit links.

Nikkō (p88) 17th-century World Heritage–listed shrines and temples.
🚌 2 hrs to Tokyo, then 🚌 2 ½ hrs to Mt Fuji

Fuji Five Lakes (p161) In summer climb Mt Fuji, catching dawn from the summit. The rest of the year, visit these placid lakes for mountain views.

Tokyo (p35) Museums, markets and parks by day; great food and nightlife after dark.
🚌 2 hrs to Nikkō

FROM LEFT: SEAN PAVONE / SHUTTERSTOCK ©; IAMDOCTOREGG / SHUTTERSTOCK ©

Plan Your Trip
10-Day Itinerary

The Grand Tour

This is a classic route for first-time visitors. It hits many of Japan's star attractions, from shrines to cities, and can be done year-round. Plus, it takes advantage of the excellent value and seamless travel offered by a Japan Rail Pass.

Himeji (p206) Spend a morning touring Japan's best-preserved castle. 🚊 1 hr to Hiroshima

Hiroshima (p173) Bear witness to the momentous history of the 20th century at Hiroshima's Peace Memorial Park. 🚢 40 min to Miyajima

Miyajima (p184) Watch the sun set over the island's floating *torii* (shrine gate) and then bed down in a ryokan (traditional Japanese inn).

RIGHT: RICHIE CHAN / SHUTTERSTOCK ©

Kyoto (p93) Immerse yourself in Japan's traditional side, among the temples and shrines of the old Imperial capital. 🚄 40 min to Nara

Tokyo (p35) Get your bearings and a taste for urban Japan. 🚄 2 hrs to Kyoto

Nara (p133) Hop over to Nara to see the Daibutsu (Great Buddha). 🚄 40 min to Osaka

Osaka (p187) Budget an evening for the bright lights and big flavours of this fun-loving city. 🚄 40 min to Himeji

FROM LEFT: LUCIANO MORTULA - LGM / SHUTTERSTOCK ©, H. YASUI / GETTY IMAGES ©

Two-Week Itinerary

Urban & Rural Adventures

This itinerary gives you four very different snapshots of Japan: the ultramodern city in Tokyo; the Japan of old in Kyoto; the mountain heartland in the Japan Alps; and slower island life on Okinawa and the Southwest Islands. Take your sense of adventure!

Tokyo (p35) Take in the highlights of the capital – the night views, the pop culture and more. 🚃 3 hrs to Nakatsugawa (for Magome)

Japan Alps (p147) Hike through the Kiso Valley, then rent a car to head to mountain hamlets and hot springs. 🚃 2 hrs to Kyoto

Kyoto (p93) Dive deep into Japan's storehouse of traditional culture. ✈ 2½ hrs to Okinawa (Ishigaki), from Kansai International Airport

Okinawa (p245) Explore the beaches, jungles, picturesque villages and cuisine of the remote – and stunning – Yaeyama Islands.

Plan Your Trip
Family Travel

Japan for Kids

Safe, clean and full of mod cons, Japan is a great place to travel with kids. The downside is that many cultural sights (shrines, temples and museums) may bore them; work in plenty of activities to keep things fresh. Teens will love the pop culture and neon streetscapes.

Planning

Very little special planning is required for travellers with children, but do bring any necessary medicines from home, as Japanese pharmacies don't sell foreign medications (though similar ones can be found). The *shinkansen* (bullet train) is very smooth, but if your child is very sensitive you might consider preventative measures; winding mountain roads are as nausea-inducing as anywhere. The only other thing you might want to pack are small forks and spoons, as not all restaurants have these on hand.

Sleeping

Most hotels can provide a cot for an extra fee, providing there's enough room for one. Some hotels have triple rooms, but quads or rooms with two queen-sized beds are rare. Hostels often have family rooms (or at worst, a four-person dorm room that you can book out). These also often have kitchen facilities.

Local families often stay in traditional accommodation (ryokan and *minshuku*) with large tatami rooms that can hold up to five futons, laid out in a row.

Eating

Local families take a lot of meals at 'family restaurants' (ファミレス; *famiresu*), chains like Gusto, Jonathan's, Saizeriya and Royal Host, which have kids' meals, high chairs, big booths and nonsmoking sections. High chairs are not as common as in the West. Supermarkets, bakeries, fast-food restaurants and convenience stores stock

PRINN CHANSINGTHONG / SHUTTERSTOCK ©

sandwiches and other familiar foods; supermarkets carry baby food.

If you plan to stay at a ryokan with a meal plan, discuss any menu modifications when you book; places that regularly get foreign tourists should be accommodating. You can also book a stay without meals.

Getting Around

Children between the ages of six and 11 ride for half-price on trains (including bullet trains), while those aged under six ride for free. Most train stations and buildings in larger cities have lifts; however, some attractions, such as temples and castles, may not have ramps. You won't get much sympathy if you get on a crowded train during morning rush hour (7am to 9.30am) with a pram. If you must, children under 12 can ride with mums in the less-crowded women-only carriages.

★ Best for Kids

Skiing at Niseko United (p220)

Animation at Ghibli Museum (p57)

Disney à la Japan at Tokyo Disney Resort (p80)

Movie magic at Universal Studios Japan (p198)

Beware that side streets often lack pavements, though fortunately traffic is generally orderly in Japan.

Travelling by car is often a good strategy for families, as it makes child- and luggage-wrangling easier. Most destinations outside the major cities are good for driving.

Child seats in taxis are generally not available, but most car-rental agencies will provide one if you ask in advance.

From left: Skiing at Niseko (p220); Ryokan, Kawaguchi-ko (p168)

Edo Market Place at Haneda Airport (p82)

Arriving in Tokyo

Tokyo is the main gateway to Japan. Most travellers will be arriving from Narita Airport in neighbouring Chiba Prefecture, but Haneda Airport, closer to the city centre, is now seeing an increasing number of international flights. Both airports have smooth, hassle-free entry procedures, and are connected to the city centre by public transport.

Where to Stay

The busy western hub of Shinjuku is a traveller favourite; Asakusa, in the east, is the backpacker district. If you're here for the nightlife, consider staying in Shibuya or Roppongi. Ueno and Marunouchi (Tokyo Station) have direct train access to Narita.

For more information on the best neighbourhoods to stay in, see p87.

YULIA GRIGORYEVA / SHUTTERSTOCK ©

Shopping in Harajuku

Harajuku is the gathering point for Tokyo's eccentric fashion tribes: teens who hang out on Takeshita-dōri, polished divas who strut up and down Omote-sandō, and trendsetters and peacocks who haunt the side streets.

Great For...

☑ Don't Miss

The narrow streets on either side of Omote-sandō, known as Ura-Hara ('back' Harajuku).

Takeshita-dōri

Tokyo's famously outré fashion bazaar **Takeshita-dōri** (竹下通り; Map p62; Jingūmae, Shibuya-ku; ☒JR Yamanote line to Harajuku, Takeshita exit) is a pilgrimage site for teens from all over Japan. Here trendy duds sit alongside the trappings of decades of fashion subcultures (plaid and safety pins for the punks; colourful tutus for the decora; Victorian dresses for the Gothic Lolitas).

Laforet

A beacon of cutting-edge Harajuku style for decades, **Laforet** (ラフォーレ; Map p62; www.laforet.ne.jp; 1-11-6 Jingūmae, Shibuya-ku; ⏱11am-9pm; ☒JR Yamanote line to Harajuku, Omote-sandō exit) has lots of quirky, cult-favourite brands that still cut their teeth here (you'll find some examples at the ground-floor boutique, Wall).

Cat Street

Harajuku

ℹ Need to Know

Take JR Yamanote line to Harajuku, or Chiyoda and Fukutoshin lines to Meiji-jingūmae subway station.

✕ Take a Break

Grab a bite at Harajuku Gyōza-rō (p71).

★ Top Tip

Avoid weekends when Harajuku gets very crowded.

KiddyLand

Multistorey toy emporium **KiddyLand** (キデイランド; Map p62; ☎03-3409-3431; www.kiddyland.co.jp; 6-1-9 Jingūmae, Shibuya-ku; ⏰11am-9pm Mon-Fri, 10.30am-9pm Sat & Sun; 🚃JR Yamanote line to Harajuku, Omote-sandō exit) is packed to the rafters with character goods, including all your Studio Ghibli, Sanrio and Disney faves. It's not just for kids either; you'll spot plenty of adults on a nostalgia trip down the Hello Kitty aisle.

Cat Street

Had enough of crowded Harajuku? Exit stage right for **Cat Street** (キャットストリート; Map p62; 🚃JR Yamanote line to Harajuku, Omote-sandō exit), a winding car-free road lined with a mishmash of boutiques, where there's more room to move.

House @Mikiri Hassin

Hidden deep in Ura-Hara (Harajuku's backstreet area), **House** (ハウス@ミキリハッシン; Map p62; http://house.mikirihassin.co.jp; 5-42-1 Jingūmae, Shibuya-ku; ⏰noon-9pm Thu-Tue; 🚇Ginza line to Omote-sandō, exit A1) stocks experimental Japanese fashion brands. Contrary to what the cool merch might suggest, the sales clerks are polite and friendly.

6% Doki Doki

Tucked away on an Ura-Hara backstreet in a bubblegum-pink building, **6% Doki Doki** (ロクパーセントドキドキ; Map p62; www.dokidoki6.com; 2nd fl, 4-28-16 Jingūmae, Shibuya-ku; ⏰noon-8pm; 🚃JR Yamanote line to Harajuku, Omote-sandō exit) sells bright accessories that are part raver, part schoolgirl and, according to the shop's name, 'six percent exciting'. Anyway, it's 100% Harajuku.

COWARDLION / SHUTTERSTOCK ©

Tokyo National Museum

If you visit only one museum, make it this one. Established in 1872, this collection of Japanese art covers ancient pottery, Buddhist sculpture, samurai swords, colourful ukiyo-e (woodblock prints), gorgeous kimonos and more.

Great For...

☑ Don't Miss

For a couple of weeks in spring and autumn, the back garden, home to five vintage teahouses, opens to the public.

Honkan (Japanese Gallery)

The museum is divided into several buildings, the most important of which is the Honkan, which houses the collection of Japanese art. Visitors with only an hour or two should focus on the galleries here. The building itself is in the imperial style of the 1930s, with art deco flourishes throughout. Allow two hours to take in the highlights, a half-day to do the Honkan in depth or a whole day to take in everything else as well.

Gallery of Hōryū-ji Treasures

Next on the priority list is the enchanting Gallery of Hōryū-ji Treasures, which displays masks, scrolls and gilt Buddhas from Hōryū-ji (in Nara Prefecture, dating from 607) in a spare, elegant, box-shaped contemporary building (1999) by Taniguchi Yoshio. Nearby, to the west of the main

Honkan (Japanese Gallery)

❶ Need to Know

東京国立博物館, Tokyo Kokuritsu Hakubut-sukan; Map p66; ☑03-3822-1111; www.tnm. jp; 13-9 Ueno-kōen, Taitō-ku; adult/child ¥620/free; ⏰9.30am-5pm Tue-Thu, to 9pm Fri & Sat, to 6pm on Sun; ⓇJR lines to Ueno, Ueno-kōen exit

✕ Take a Break

There are restaurants in the Gallery of Hōryū-ji Treasures and in the Tōyōkan.

★ Top Tip

Get the brochure *Highlights of Japanese Art* from Room 1-1 on the Honkan's 2nd floor.

gate, is the **Kuro-mon** (Black Gate), transported from the Edo-era mansion of a feudal lord. On weekends it opens for visitors to pass through.

Tōyōkan & Heiseikan

Visitors with more time can explore the three-storied Tōyōkan (Gallery of Asian Art), with its collection of Buddhist sculptures from around Asia and delicate Chinese ceramics. The Heiseikan, accessed via a passage on the 1st floor of the Honkan, houses the Japanese Archaeology Gallery, full of pottery, talismans and articles of daily life from Japan's palaeolithic and neolithic periods. Temporary exhibitions (which cost extra) are held on the 2nd floor of the Heiseikan; these can be fantastic, but sometimes lack the English signage found throughout the rest of the museum.

Kuroda Memorial Hall

Kuroda Seiki (1866–1924) is considered the father of modern Western-style painting in Japan. The **Kuroda Memorial Hall** (黒田記念室; Map p66; ☑03-5777-8600; www. tobunken.go.jp; ⏰9.30am-5pm Tue-Sun) **FREE**, an annexe to the Tokyo National Museum, has some of his works, including key pieces such as *Maiko Girl* and *Wisdom, Impression and Sentiment*, a striking triptych of three nude women on canvases coated with ground gold.

What's Nearby?

Nezu-jinja   Shinto Shrine

(根津神社; Map p66; ☑03-3822-0753; www. nedujinja.or.jp; 1-28-9 Nezu, Bunkyō-ku; ⏰6am-5pm; ⓈChiyoda line to Nezu, exit 1) Not only is this one of Japan's oldest shrines, it is also easily the most beautiful in a district packed with attractive religious buildings. The vermilion-and-gold structure, which dates from the early 18th century, is one of the city's miraculous survivors and is offset by a long corridor of small red *torii* (gates) that makes for great photos.

Ueno-kōen   Park

(上野公園; Map p66; www.ueno-bunka.jp; Ueno-kōen, Taitō-ku; ℝJR lines to Ueno, Ueno-kōen or Shinobazu exit) Best known for its profusion of cherry trees that burst into blossom in spring – making this one of Tokyo's top *hanami* (blossom-viewing spots) – sprawling Ueno-kōen is also the location of the city's highest concentration of museums. At the southern tip is the large scenic pond, **Shinobazu-ike** (不忍池; ⑤JR lines to Ueno, Shinobazu exit), choked with lotus flowers in summer.

Ueno Tōshō-gū   Shinto Shrine

(上野東照宮; Map p66; ☎03-3822-3455; www.uenotoshogu.com; 9-88 Ueno-kōen, Taitō-ku; adult/child ¥500/200; ⊘9am-5.30pm Mar-Sep, to 4.30pm Oct-Feb; ℝJR lines to Ueno, Shinobazu exit) This shrine inside Ueno-kōen was built in honour of Tokugawa Ieyasu, the warlord who unified Japan. Resplendent in gold leaf and ornate details, it dates to 1651 (though it has had recent touch-ups). You can get a pretty good look from outside the gate, if you want to skip the admission fee.

Ameya-yokochō   Market

(アメヤ横町; Map p66; www.ameyoko.net; 4 Ueno, Taitō-ku; ⊘10am-7pm, some shops close Wed; ℝJR lines to Okachimachi, north exit) Step into this partially open-air market paralleling and beneath the JR line tracks, and ritzy, glitzy Tokyo feels like a distant memory. It got its start as a black market, post-WWII, when American goods (which included *ameya* – candy and chocolates)

Yanaka Ginza

were sold here. Today you can pick up everything from fresh seafood to vintage jeans and bargain sneakers.

Asakura Museum of Sculpture, Taitō
Museum

(朝倉彫塑館; Map p66; ☎03-3821-4549; www. taitocity.net/taito/asakura; 7-16-10 Yanaka, Taitō-ku; adult/child ¥500/250; ☉9.30am-4.30pm Tue, Wed & Fri-Sun; 🚃JR Yamanote line to Nippori, north exit) Sculptor Asakura Fumio (artist name Chōso; 1883–1964) designed this atmospheric house himself. It combined his original Japanese home and garden with a large studio that incorporated vaulted ceil-

---

★ **Did You Know?**

The pretty neighbourhood of Yanaka is popular with artists for its dozens of temples. Begin exploring at the Asakura Museum of Sculpture, Taitō.

MADSOLAR / SHUTTERSTOCK ©

ings, a 'sunrise room' and a rooftop garden with wonderful neighbourhood views. It's now a reverential museum with many of the artist's signature realist works, mostly of people and cats, on display.

Yanaka Ginza
Area

(谷中銀座; Map p66; www.yanakaginza.com; 🚃JR Yamanote line to Nippori, north exit) Yanaka Ginza is pure, vintage mid-20th-century Tokyo, a pedestrian street lined with butcher shops, vegetable vendors and the like. Most Tokyo neighbourhoods once had stretches like these (until supermarkets took over). It's popular with Tokyoites from all over the city, who come to soak up the nostalgic atmosphere, plus the locals who shop here.

SCAI the Bathhouse
Gallery

(スカイザバスハウス; Map p66; ☎03-3821-1144; www.scaithebathhouse.com; 6-1-23 Yanaka, Taitō-ku; ☉noon-6pm Tue-Sat; 🚇Chiyoda line to Nezu, exit 1) **FREE** This 200-year-old bathhouse has for several decades been an avant-garde gallery space, showcasing Japanese and international artists in its austere vaulted space. Closed between exhibitions.

Ueno Zoo
Zoo

(上野動物園, Ueno Dōbutsu-en; Map p66; ☎03-3828-5171; www.tokyo-zoo.net; 9-83 Ueno-kōen, Taitō-ku; adult/child ¥600/free; ☉9.30am-5pm Tue-Sun; 🚃JR lines to Ueno, Ueno-kōen exit) Japan's oldest zoo, established in 1882, is home to animals from around the globe, but the biggest attractions are the giant pandas that arrived from China in 2011 – Rī Rī and Shin Shin. Following several disappointments, the two finally had a cub, Xiang Xiang, in 2017. There's also a whole area devoted to lemurs, which makes sense given Tokyoites' love of all things cute.

Tokyo National Museum

HISTORIC HIGHLIGHTS

It would be a challenge to take in everything the sprawling Tokyo National Museum has to offer in a day. Fortunately, the Honkan (Japanese Gallery) is designed to give visitors a crash course in Japanese art history from the Jōmon era (13,000–300 BC) to the Edo era (AD 1603–1868). The works on display here are rotated regularly, to protect fragile ones and to create seasonal exhibitions, so you're always guaranteed to see something new.

Buy your ticket from outside the main gate then head straight to the Honkan with its sloping tile roof. Stow your coat in a locker and take the central staircase up to the 2nd floor, where the exhibitions are arranged chronologically. Allow two hours for this tour of the highlights.

The first room on your right starts from the beginning with **ancient Japanese art** ❶. Pick up a free copy of the brochure *Highlights of Japanese Art* at the entrance to the first room on your right. The exhibition starts here with the **Dawn of Japanese Art**, covering the most ancient periods of Japan's history.

Continue to the **National Treasure Gallery** ❷. 'National Treasure' is the highest distinction awarded to a work of art in Japan. Keep an eye out for more National Treasures, labelled in red, on display in other rooms throughout the museum.

Moving on, stop to admire the **courtly art gallery** ❸, the **samurai armour and swords** ❹ and the ***ukiyo-e* and kimono** ❺.

Next, take the stairs down to the 1st floor, where each room is dedicated to a different decorative art, such as lacquerware or ceramics. Don't miss the excellent examples of **religious sculpture** ❻, and folk art and **Ainu and Ryūkyū cultural artefacts** ❼.

Finish your visit with a look inside the enchanting **Gallery of Hōryū-ji Treasures** ❽.

Ukiyo-e & Kimono (Room 10)

Chic silken kimono and lushly coloured *ukiyo-e* (woodblock prints) are two icons of the Edo-era (AD 1603–1868) *ukiyo* – the 'floating world', or world of fleeting beauty and pleasure.

Japanese Sculpture (Room 11)

Many of Japan's most famous sculptures, religious in nature, are locked away in temple reliquaries. This is a rare chance to see them up close.

MUSEUM GARDEN

Don't miss the garden if you visit in spring and autumn during the few weeks it's open to the public.

Heiseikan & Japanese Archaeology Gallery

Research & Information Centre

❽

Hyōkeikan

Kuro-mon

Main Gate

Gallery of Hōryū-ji Treasures

Surround yourself with miniature gilt Buddhas from Hōryū-ji, one of Japan's oldest Buddhist temples, founded in 607. Don't miss the graceful Pitcher with Dragon Head, a National Treasure.

Courtly Art (Room 3-2)

Literature works, calligraphy and narrative picture scrolls are displayed alongside decorative art objects, which allude to the life of elegance led by courtesans a thousand years ago.

Samurai Armour & Swords (Rooms 5 & 6)

Glistening swords, finely stitched armour and imposing helmets bring to life the samurai, those iconic warriors of Japan's medieval age.

Honkan (Japanese Gallery) 2nd Floor

National Treasure Gallery (Room 2)

A single, superlative work from the museum's collection of 88 National Treasures (perhaps a painted screen, or a gilded, hand-drawn sutra) is displayed in a serene, contemplative setting.

Museum Garden & Teahouses

Honkan (Japanese Gallery)

Tōyōkan (Gallery of Asian Art)

Honkan (Japanese Gallery) 1st Floor

GIFT SHOP

The museum gift shop, on the 1st floor of the Honkan, has an excellent collection of Japanese art books in English.

Dawn of Japanese Art (Room 1)

The rise of the imperial court and the introduction of Buddhism changed the Japanese aesthetic forever. These clay works from previous eras show what came before.

Ainu and Ryūkyū Collection (Room 16)

See artefacts from Japan's historical minorities – the indigenous Ainu of Hokkaidō and the former Ryūkyū Empire, now Okinawa.

Meiji-jingū's *torii*

BEIBAOKE / SHUTTERSTOCK ©

Meiji-jingū

Tokyo's largest and most-famous Shintō shrine feels a world away from the city. The grounds are vast, enveloping the classic wooden shrine buildings and a landscaped garden in a thick coat of green.

Meiji-jingū is dedicated to the Emperor Meiji and Empress Shōken, whose reign (1868–1912) coincided with Japan's transformation from isolationist, feudal state to modern nation. The shrine is undergoing renovation in preparation for its centennial in 2020; some structures may be under wraps, but as a whole it will remain open.

The Gates

Several wooden *torii* mark the entrance to Meiji-jingū. The largest, created from a 1500-year-old Taiwanese cypress, stands 12m high. It's the custom to bow upon passing through a *torii,* which marks the boundary between the mundane world and the sacred one.

Great For...

☑ **Don't Miss**

Meiji-jingū Gyoen when the irises bloom in June.

Visitors purify themselves at the *temizuya* (font)

NAPAT PHOTOGRAPHY / SHUTTERSTOCK ©

❶ Need to Know

明治神宮; Map p62; www.meijijingu.or.jp; 1-1 Yoyogi Kamizono-chō, Shibuya-ku; ⏱dawn-dusk; 🚃JR Yamanote line to Harajuku, Omotesandō exit; FREE

✕ Take a Break

Coffee shop **Mori no Terrace** (杜のテラス; Map p62; ☎03-3379-9222; 1-1 Yoyogi Kamizono-chō, Shibuya-ku; coffee & tea from ¥400; ⏱9am-dusk) is on the gravel path leading into the grounds.

★ Top Tip

Come at 8am or 2pm for the *nikkusai* (offering of food and prayers to the gods).

The Font

Before approaching the main shrine, visitors purify themselves by pouring water over their hands at the *temizuya* (font). Dip the ladle in the water and first rinse your left hand then your right. Pour some water into your left hand and rinse your mouth, then rinse your left hand again. Make sure none of this water gets back into the font!

Main Shrine

Constructed in 1920 and destroyed in WWII air raids, the shrine was rebuilt in 1958; however, unlike so many of Japan's postwar reconstructions, Meiji-jingū has an authentic old-world feel. The main shrine is made of cypress from the Kiso region of Nagano. To make an offering, toss a ¥5 coin in the box, bow twice, clap your hands twice and then bow again. To the right, you'll see kiosks selling *ema* (wooden plaques on which prayers are written) and *omamori* (charms).

Meiji-jingū Gyoen

The shrine itself occupies only a small fraction of the sprawling forested grounds, which contain some 120,000 trees collected from all over Japan. Along the path towards the main shrine, is the entrance to **Meiji-jingū Gyoen** (明治神宮御苑, Inner Garden; ¥500; ⏱9am-4.30pm, to 4pm Nov-Feb), a landscaped garden. It once belonged to a feudal estate; however, when the grounds passed into imperial hands, the emperor himself designed the iris garden to please the empress.

Pop Culture in Akihabara

With its neon-bright electronics stores, retro arcades and cosplay (costume play) cafes 'Akiba' – as it's known to locals – is equal parts sensory overload, cultural mind-bender and just plain fun.

Great For...

☑ Don't Miss

See anime fans dressed as their favourite characters on Chūō-dōri on Sunday afternoons.

Manga & Anime

When *otaku* (geeks) dream of heaven, it probably looks a lot like **Mandarake Complex** (まんだらけコンプレックス; ☎03-3252-7007; www.mandarake.co.jp; 3-11-12 Soto-Kanda, Chiyoda-ku; ⊘noon-8pm; ℞JR Yamanote line to Akihabara, Electric Town exit). Eight storeys are piled high with comic books and DVDs, action figures and cell art just for starters. The 5th floor, in all its pink splendour, is devoted to women's comics, while the 4th floor is for men.

Electric Town

Before Akihabara became *otaku*-land, it was Electric Town – the place for discounted electronics and where early computer geeks tracked down obscure parts for home-built machines. **Akihabara Radio Center** (秋葉原ラジオセンター;

www.radiocenter.jp; 1-14-2 Soto-Kanda, Chiyoda-ku; ⊙generally 10am-6pm; ☒JR Yamanote line to Akihabara, Electric Town exit), a warren of stalls under the train tracks, keeps the tradition alive.

Retro Arcades

On the 5th floor of **Super Potato Retro-kan** (スーパーポテトレトロ館; ☑03-5289-9933; www.superpotato.com; 1-11-2 Soto-kanda, Chiyoda-ku; ⊙11am-8pm Mon-Fri, from 10am Sat & Sun; ☒JR Yamanote line to Akihabara, Electric Town exit), a store specialising in used video games, there's a retro video arcade where you can get your hands on some old-fashioned consoles at a bargain ¥100 per game.

Go-Karting

We're not sure how this is legal but rest assured (at least at the time of research)

it is: *cosplay* go-karting on city streets. Sign up in advance with **Akiba Kart** (アキバカート; ☑03-6206-4752; www.akibanavi.net; basement, 2-4-6 Soto-kanda, Chiyoda-ku; 1/2/3hr ¥2700/3800/5400; ⊙10am-8pm; ☒JR Yamanote line to Akihabara, Electric Town exit); you'll need an international driver's licence.

Live Performances

Shows by the girl group Kamen Joshi – singing and dancing young women wearing cute outfits and hockey masks – are all the rage at **P.A.R.M.S** (☑03-3505-8066; www.alice-project.biz/kamenjoshi; 7th fl, Pasela Resorts Akiba, 1-1-10 Soto-Kanda, Chiyoda-ku; cover charge incl 1 drink Mon-Fri ¥1500, Sat & Sun ¥3500; ⊙shows 5.30pm & 8.15pm Mon-Fri, 10.30am & 6pm Sat & Sun; ☒JR Yamanote line to Akihabara, Electric Town exit), a live-music show in the Pasela Resort's karaoke emporium. It's a chance to swing around a light sabre (handed out to audience members) in a thoroughly Akiba night out.

Sensō-ji

According to legend, in AD 628, two fishermen brothers pulled out a golden image of Kannon (the bodhisattva of compassion) from the nearby Sumida-gawa. Sensō-ji, the capital's oldest temple, was built to enshrine it.

Great For...

☑ Don't Miss

All the traditional snack food sold along Nakamise-dōri.

Kaminari-mon

The temple precinct begins at the majestic Kaminari-mon, which means Thunder Gate. An enormous *chōchin* (lantern), which weighs 670kg, hangs from the centre. On either side are a pair of ferocious protective deities: Fūjin, the god of wind, on the right; and Raijin, the god of thunder, on the left. Kaminari-mon has burnt down countless times over the centuries; the current gate dates to 1970.

Nakamise-dōri Shopping Street

Beyond Kaminari-mon is the bustling shopping street, Nakamise-dōri. With its lines of souvenir stands it is very touristy, though that's nothing new: Sensō-ji has been Tokyo's top tourist sight for centuries, since travel was restricted to religious pilgrimages

during the feudal era. In addition to the
usual T-shirts, you can find Edo-style crafts
and oddities (such as wigs done up in traditional hairstyles). There are also numerous
snack vendors serving up crunchy *sembei*
(rice crackers) and *age-manju* (deep-fried
anko – bean-paste – buns).

Hōzō-mon

At the end of Nakamise-dōri is Hōzō-mon
(蔵門), another gate with fierce guardians.
On its rear are a pair of 2500kg, 4.5m-tall
waraji (straw sandals) crafted for Sensō-
ji by some 800 villagers in northern
Yamagata Prefecture. These are meant to
symbolise the Buddha's power, and it's
believed that evil spirits will be scared off
by the giant footwear.

Hondō (Main Hall)

In front of the grand Hondō, with its
dramatic sloping roof, is a large cauldron
with smoking incense. The smoke is said to
bestow health and you'll see people wafting
it over their bodies. The current Hondō
was constructed in 1958, replacing the one
destroyed in WWII air raids. The style is
similar to the previous one, though the roof
tiles are now made of titanium.

The **Kannon image** (a tiny 6cm) is
cloistered away from view deep inside the
Main Hall (and admittedly may not exist
at all). Nonetheless, a steady stream of
worshippers visits the temple to cast coins,
pray and bow in a gesture of respect. Do
feel free to join in.

Off the courtyard stands a 53m-high
Five-Storey Pagoda, a 1973 reconstruction of a pagoda built by Tokugawa Iemitsu;
the current structure, renovated in 2017, is
the second-highest pagoda in Japan.

Omikuji

Don't miss getting your fortune told by an *omikuji* (paper fortune). Drop ¥100 into the slots by the wooden drawers at either side of the approach to the Main Hall, grab a silver canister and shake it. Extract a stick and note its number (in kanji). Replace the stick, find the matching drawer and withdraw a paper fortune (there's English on the back). If you pull out 大凶 (*dai-kyō*; great curse), never fear. Just tie the paper on the nearby rack, ask the gods for better luck, and try again!

Asakusa-jinja

On the east side of the temple complex is **Asakusa-jinja** (浅草神社; Map p66; ☑03-3844-1575; www.asakusajinja.jp; ⊗9am-4.30pm),

built in honour of the brothers who discovered the Kannon statue that inspired the construction of Sensō-ji. (Historically, Japan's two religions, Buddhism and Shintō, were intertwined and it was not uncommon for temples to include shrines and vice versa.) This section of Sensō-ji survived WWII and Asakusa-jinja's current structure dates to 1649. Painted a deep shade of red, it is a rare example of early Edo architecture.

Next to the shrine is the temple complex's eastern gate, **Niten-mon**, standing since 1618. Though it appears minor today, this gate was the point of entry for visitors arriving in Asakusa via boat – the main form of transport during the Edo period.

Sanja Matsuri festival

What's Nearby?

Edo-Tokyo Museum   Museum

(江戸東京博物館; ☎03-3626-9974; www.edo-tokyo-museum.or.jp; 1-4-1 Yokoami, Sumida-ku; adult/child ¥600/free; ☺9.30am-5.30pm, to 7.30pm Sat, closed Mon; ☒JR Sōbu line to Ryōgoku, west exit) Tokyo's history museum documents the city's transformation from tidal flatlands to feudal capital to modern metropolis via detailed scale re-creations of townscapes, villas and tenement homes, plus artefacts such as *ukiyo-e* and old maps. Reopened in March 2018 after a renovation, the museum also has interactive displays, multilingual touch-screen panels and audio guides. Still, the best way to tour the museum is with one of the gracious English-speaking volunteer guides, who can really bring the history to life.

Sumida Hokusai Museum   Museum

(すみだ北斎美術館; ☎03-5777-8600; http://hokusai-museum.jp; 2-7-2 Kamezawa, Sumida-ku; adult/child/student & senior ¥400/free/300; ☺9.30am-5.30pm Tue-Sun; ☒Oedo line to Ryōgoku, exit A4) The woodblock artist Hokusai Katsushika (1760–1849) was born and died close to the location of this museum, which opened in 2016 in a striking aluminium-clad building designed by Pritzker Prize–winning architect Sejima Kazuyo. The small permanent exhibition gives an overview of his life and work, mostly through replicas.

Tokyo Skytree   Tower

(東京スカイツリー; Map p66; ☎0570-55-0102; www.tokyo-skytree.jp; 1-1-2 Oshiage, Sumida-ku; 350m/450m observation decks ¥2060/3090; ☺8am-10pm; ☒Hanzōmon line to Oshiage, Tokyo Skytree exit) Tokyo Skytree opened in May 2012 as the world's tallest 'free-standing tower' at 634m. Its silvery exterior of steel mesh morphs from a triangle at the base to a circle at 300m. There are two observation decks, at 350m and 450m. You can see more of the city during daylight hours – at peak visibility you can see up to 100km away, all the way to Mt Fuji – but it is at night that Tokyo appears truly beautiful.

> ☑ **Don't Miss**
>
> Sensō-ji is home to many annual traditional festivals, the most famous of which is May's Sanja Matsuri. Ask for a list of events at a TIC.

STREETVJ / SHUTTERSTOCK ©

> ★ **Did You Know?**
>
> Tokyo Skytree employs an ancient construction technique used in pagodas: a *shimbashira* column, structurally separate from the exterior truss. It acts as a counterweight when the tower sways, cutting vibrations by 50%.

Shinjuku After Dark

Shinjuku is Tokyo's largest – and liveliest – nightlife district. There is truly something for everyone, from flashy cabarets to bohemian holes-in-the-wall.

Start Shinjuku Station (east exit)
Distance 1.5km
Duration one hour

Shokuan-dōri

Seibu Shinjuku

Ōme-kaidō

Kabukichō Ichiban-gai

2 Bask in Shinjuku's main drag, **Yasukuni-dōri**, where *izakaya* (Japanese pub-eateries) are stacked several stories high.

Shinjuku-nishiguchi
START

Yasukuni-dōri

Shinjuku

Shinjuku

NISHI-SHINJUKU

1 Start the evening with a round of *yakitori* at the historic cluster of stalls on **Omoide-yokochō** (p74).

3 Kabukichō, Tokyo's red-light district, is marked by an electric red *torii* (gate).

KABUKICHŌ

Ⓝ 0 ————— 200 m
0 ————— 0.1 miles

4 Don't miss the neighbourhood's newest landmark, **Shinjuku TOHO building**, with its enormous Godzilla statue.

7 Stroll **Golden Gai** (p78), a warren of tiny alleys and narrow buildings housing hundreds of small bars.

④

③

Central Rd

⑤

Kuyakusho-dōri

⑦

FINISH

GOLDEN
GAI

⑥

Yasukuni-dōri

SHINJUKU

Take a Break...
A late-night bowl of ramen at **Nagi** (p72).

Classic Photo Posing with the buxom robots outside the Robot Restaurant.

6 At **Don Quijote** (p67), an out-there, all-night emporium, get everything from wine to a nurse's costume.

5 Kabukichō cabaret **Robot Restaurant** (p80) glows bright enough to light all of Shinjuku.

◎ SIGHTS

◎ Ginza & Marunouchi

Tsukiji Market   Market

(場外市場, Jōgai Shijō; Map p58; www.tsukiji
.or.jp; 6-chōme Tsukiji, Chūō-ku; ⊘mostly
5am-2pm; Ⓢ Hibiya line to Tsukiji, exit 1) Tokyo's
main wholesale market may have moved to
Toyosu (豊洲市場, Toyosu Shijō; www.shijou.
metro.tokyo.jp; 6-chōme Toyosu, Kōtō-ku; ⊘5am-
5pm Mon-Sat, closed some Wed; ⓇYurikamome
line to Shijō-mae), but there are many reasons
to visit its old home. The tightly packed
rows of vendors (which once formed the
Outer Market) hawk market and culinary-
related goods, such as dried fish, seaweed,
kitchen knives, rubber boots and crockery.
It's also a fantastic place to eat, with great
street food and a huge concentration of
small restaurants and cafes, most specialising in seafood.

Imperial Palace   Palace

(皇居, Kōkyo; Map p58; ☑03-5223-8071; http://
sankan.kunaicho.go.jp; 1 Chiyoda, Chiyoda-
ku; ⊘tours usually 10am & 1.30pm Tue-Sat; Ⓢ Chiyoda line to Ōtemachi, exits C13b & C10) FREE The
Imperial Palace occupies the site of the
original Edo-jō, the Tokugawa shogunate's
castle. In its heyday this was the largest
fortress in the world, though little remains
today apart from the moat and stone walls.
Most of the 3.4-sq-km complex is off limits,
as this is the emperor's home, but join one
of the free tours organised by the Imperial
Household Agency to see a small part of
the inner compound.

Intermediatheque   Museum

(インターメディアテク; Map p58; ☑03-5777-
8600; www.intermediatheque.jp; 2nd & 3rd fl, JP
Tower, 2-7-2 Marunouchi, Chiyoda-ku; ⊘11am-
6pm, to 8pm Fri & Sat, usually closed Sun & Mon;
ⓇJR Yamanote line to Tokyo, Marunouchi exit)
FREE Dedicated to interdisciplinary experi-
mentation, Intermediatheque cherry-picks
from the vast collection of the University
of Tokyo (Tōdai) to craft a fascinating, contemporary museum experience. Go from
viewing the best ornithological taxidermy
collection in Japan to a giant pop-art print
or the beautifully encased skeleton of a
dinosaur. A handsome Tōdai lecture hall
is reconstituted as a forum for events,

Tsukiji Market

including playing 1920s' jazz recordings on a gramophone or old movie screenings.

Hama-rikyū Onshi-teien
Gardens

(浜離宮恩賜庭園, Detached Palace Garden; Map p58; ☎03-3541-0200; www.tokyo-park. or.jp/teien; 1-1 Hama-rikyū-teien, Chūō-ku; adult/child ¥300/free; ⊙9am-5pm; ⑤Ōedo line to Shiodome, exit A1) This beautiful garden, one of Tokyo's finest, is all that remains of a shogunate palace that was also an outer fort for Edo Castle. The main features are a large duck pond with an island that's home to a functioning tea pavilion, **Nakajima no Ochaya** (中島の御茶屋; tea ¥510 or ¥720; ⊙9am-4.30pm), as well as three other teahouses and wonderfully manicured trees (black pine, Japanese apricot, hydrangeas etc), some hundreds of years old.

◉ Roppongi & Akasaka

National Art Center Tokyo
Museum

(国立新美術館; Map p62; ☎03-5777-8600; www.nact.jp; 7-22-1 Roppongi, Minato-ku; admission varies; ⊙10am-6pm Wed, Thu & Sun-Mon, to 8pm Fri & Sat; ⑤Chiyoda line to Nogizaka, exit 6) Designed by Kurokawa Kishō, this architectural beauty has no permanent collection, but boasts the country's largest exhibition space for visiting shows, which have included Renoir and Modigliani. A visit here is recommended to admire the building's awesome undulating glass facade, its cafes atop giant inverted cones and the great gift shop, Souvenir from Tokyo (p65).

21_21 Design Sight
Museum

(21_21デザインサイト; Map p62; ☎03-3475-2121; www.2121designsight.jp; Tokyo Midtown, 9-7-6 Akasaka, Minato-ku; adult/child ¥1100/free; ⊙11am-7pm Wed-Mon; ⑤Ōedo line to Roppongi, exit 8) An exhibition and discussion space dedicated to all forms of design, the 21_21 Design Sight is a beacon for local art enthusiasts, whether they be designers or onlookers. The striking concrete and glass building, bursting out of the ground at sharp angles, was designed by Pritzker Prize–winning architect Ando Tadao.

Ghibli Museum, Mitaka

Master animator Miyazaki Hayao's Studio Ghibli (pronounced 'jiburi') is responsible for some of the best-loved films in Japan – and the world. Miyazaki designed the **Ghibli Museum, Mitaka** (ジブリ美術館; www.ghibli-museum.jp; 1-1-83 Shimo-Renjaku, Mitaka-shi; adult ¥1000, child ¥100-700; ⊙10am-6pm Wed-Mon; ☒JR Chūō-Sōbu line to Mitaka, south exit) and the end result is faithful to the dreamy, atmosphere that makes his animations so enticing. A must for anime lovers.

Looking like it was plucked from the pages of a fairy tale, the museum houses a whimsical workshop filled with books and artworks which inspired Miyazaki, oodles of original sketches and models, vintage animation tech, and of course, a hundreds-strong cast of your favourite characters and critters.

A highlight is a giant, plush replica of the cat bus from the classic *My Neighbor Totoro* (1988) that kids can climb on. There's also a small theatre where original animated shorts – only seen here! – are screened (you'll get a ticket when you enter). The film changes monthly to keep fans coming back.

Museum tickets are like gold and go quick, especially during holiday periods. With luck, there'll be a date and time slot that suits your plans: changes aren't possible and you can't just show up. Order up to four months in advance from select travel agencies, or up to a month ahead using Lawson Ticket; see the museum website for info.

Ghibli Museum, Mitaka

Ginza & Marunouchi

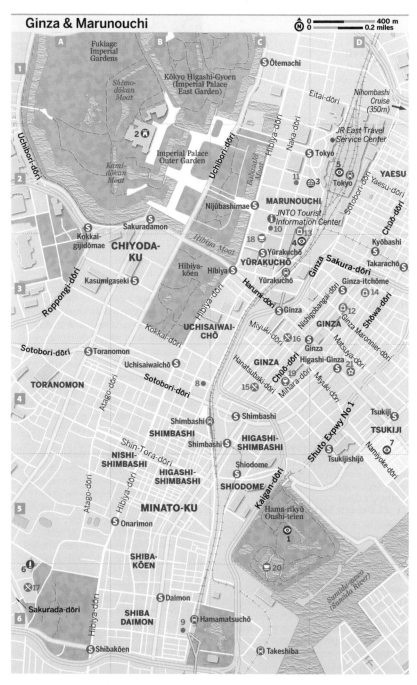

N
0 — 400 m
0 — 0.2 miles

Fukiage Imperial Gardens

Shimo-dōkan Moat

Kōkyo Higashi-Gyoen (Imperial Palace East Garden)

Kami-dōkan Moat

Imperial Palace Outer Garden

Uchibori-dōri

Uchibori-dōri

Ōtemachi

Eitai-dōri

Nihombashi Cruise (350m)

Naka-dōri

Hibiya-dōri

JR East Travel Service Center

Tokyo

Tokyo

YAESU

Yaesu-dōri

Sotobori-dōri

Chūo-dōri

11

3

Nijūbashimae

MARUNOUCHI

JNTO Tourist Information Center

10

13

Kyōbashi

Sakuradamon

Kokkai-gijidōmae

CHIYODA-KU

18

Yūrakuchō

Takarachō

Ginza Sakura-dōri

Hibiya-kōen

Hibiya

YŪRAKUCHŌ

Yūrakuchō

Ginza-itchōme

14

Kasumigaseki

Hibiya-dōri

Harumi-dōri

Ginza

Nishigobangai-dōri

12

Showa-dōri

Roppongi-dōri

Kokkai-dōri

Ginza

GINZA

Ginza Maronnier-dōri

UCHISAIWAI-CHŌ

Miyuki-dōri

16

Matsuya-dōri

Sotobori-dōri

Toranomon

Ginza

Higashi-Ginza

21

Uchisaiwaichō

Hanatsubaki-dōri

GINZA

Chūo-dōri

19

Atago-dōri

Sotobori-dōri

8

15

Minara-dōri

Miyuki-dōri

TORANOMON

Shuto Expwy No 1

Tsukiji

Shimbashi

Shimbashi

TSUKIJI

SHIMBASHI

HIGASHI-SHIMBASHI

Namiyoke-dōri

Shin-Tora-dōri

Shimbashi

7

NISHI-SHIMBASHI

Shiodome

Tsukijishijō

Atago-dōri

HIGASHI-SHIMBASHI

Hibiya-dōri

SHIODOME

Kaigan-dōri

MINATO-KU

Onarimon

Hama-rikyū Onshi-teien

1

SHIBA-KŌEN

6

20

17

Sakurada-dōri

Daimon

Sumida-gawa (Sumida River)

SHIBA DAIMON

9

Hamamatsuchō

Shibakōen

Takeshiba

Ginza & Marunouchi

Tokyo Tower   Tower

(東京タワー; Map p58; www.tokyotower.co.jp/
en.html; 4-2-8 Shiba-kōen, Minato-ku; adult/
child/student main deck ¥900/400/500, incl
special deck ¥2800/1200/1800; ⊙observation
deck 9am-10.30pm; ⑤Ōedo line to Akabanebashi,
Akabanebashi exit) Something of a shameless
tourist trap, this 1958-vintage tower –
painted bright orange and white in order to
comply with international aviation safety
regulations – remains a beloved symbol of
the city's post-WWII rebirth. At 333m it's
13m taller than the Eiffel Tower, which was
the inspiration for its design. Access the
main observation deck at 150m any time,
but to access the top deck (250m) a reservation for an allocated time slot is required.

◎ Shibuya & Harajuku

Shibuya Crossing   Street

(渋谷スクランブル交差点, Shibuya Scramble;
Map p62; ⑧JR Yamanote line to Shibuya, Hachikō
exit) Rumoured to be the busiest intersection in the world (and definitely in Japan),
Shibuya Crossing is like a giant beating
heart, sending people in all directions with
every pulsing light change. Nowhere else
says 'Welcome to Tokyo' better than this.
Hundreds of people – and at peak times
upwards of 3000 people – cross at a time,
coming from all directions at once, yet
to dodging each other with a practised,
nonchalant agility.

Yoyogi-kōen   Park

(代々木公園; Map p62; www.yoyogipark.info;
Yoyogi-kamizono-chō, Shibuya-ku; ⑧JR Yamanote
line to Harajuku, Omote-sandō exit) If it's a sunny
and warm weekend afternoon, you can
count on there being a crowd lazing around
the large grassy expanse that is Yoyogi-kōen.
You'll usually find revellers and noisemakers
of all stripes, from hula-hoopers to African
drum circles to retro greasers dancing
around a boom box. It's an excellent place
for a picnic and probably the only place in
the city where you can reasonably toss a
Frisbee without fear of hitting someone.

Ukiyo-e Ōta Memorial
Museum of Art   Museum

(浮世絵太田記念美術館; Map p62; ☎03-3403-
0880; www.ukiyoe-ota-muse.jp; 1-10-10 Jingūmae, Shibuya-ku; adult ¥700-1000, child free;
⊙10.30am-5.30pm Tue-Sun; ⑧JR Yamanote
line to Harajuku, Omote-sandō exit) This small
museum (where you swap your shoes for
slippers) is the best place in Tokyo to see
ukiyo-e. Each month it presents a seasonal,
thematic exhibition (with English curation
notes), drawing from the truly impressive
collection of Ōta Seizo, the former head
of the Toho Life Insurance Company. Most
exhibitions include a few works by masters
such as Hokusai and Hiroshige. The museum closes the last few days of the month
(between exhibitions).

From left: Shinjuku-gyoen; Bhudda statue, Nezu Museum; Tokyo Metropolitan Government Building

CLAIRE TAKACS / GETTY IMAGES ©

PICTUREPARTNERS / SHUTTERSTOCK ©

Nezu Museum Museum

(根津美術館; Map p62; www.nezu-muse.or.jp; 6-5-1 Minami-Aoyama, Minato-ku; adult/child ¥1100/free, special exhibitions extra ¥200; ⏱10am-5pm Tue-Sun; Ⓢ Ginza line to Omotesandō, exit A5) Nezu Museum offers a blend of old and new: a collection of Japanese, Chinese and Korean antiquities in a gallery space designed by architect Kuma Kengo. Select items from the extensive collection are displayed in seasonal exhibitions. The English explanations are usually pretty good. Behind the galleries is a woodsy strolling garden laced with stone paths and studded with teahouses and sculptures.

◎ Shinjuku

Tokyo Metropolitan Government Building Observatory

(東京都庁, Tokyo Tochō; www.metro.tokyo.jp; 2-8-1 Nishi-Shinjuku, Shinjuku-ku; ⏱observatories 9.30am-11pm; Ⓢ Ōedo line to Tochōmae, exit A4) **FREE** Tokyo's city hall – a landmark building designed by Kenzō Tange – has observatories (202m) atop both the south and north towers of Building 1 (the views are virtually the same). On a clear day

(morning is best), you may catch a glimpse of Mt Fuji beyond the urban sprawl to the west; after dark, it's illuminated buildings all the way to the horizon. Direct-access elevators are on the ground floor; last entry is at 10.30pm.

Yayoi Kusama Museum Museum

(草間弥生美術館; ☎03-5273-1778; www.yayoi kusamamuseum.jp; 07 Benten-chō, Shinjuku-ku; adult/child ¥1000/600; ⏱11am-5.30pm Thu-Sun; Ⓢ Tōzai line to Waseda, exit 1 or Tōei Ōedo line to Ushigome-yanagichō, east exit) Yayoi Kusama is one of Japan's most internationally famous contemporary artists, particularly known for her obsession with dots and pumpkins. She cut her teeth in New York City's 1950s avant-garde scene and remains prolific today, working from a studio near this new museum dedicated to her work. Kusama is in possession of most of her works, and shows them in rotating gallery exhibitions. Tickets for one of the limited 90-minute viewing slots must be purchased in advance online. They become available on the first of the month at 10am and tend to go fast.

SEAN PAVONE / SHUTTERSTOCK ©

Shinjuku-gyoen
Park

(新宿御苑; ☑03-3350-0151; www.env.go.jp/
garden/shinjukugyoen; 11 Naito-chō, Shinjuku-ku;
adult/child ¥200/50; ☺9am-4.30pm Tue-Sun;
⑤Marunouchi line to Shinjuku-gyoenmae, exit 1)
Shinjuku-gyoen was designed as an imperial retreat (completed 1906); since opening to the public in 1951, it has become a
favourite destination for Tokyoites seeking
a quick escape from the hurly-burly of
city life. The spacious manicured lawns
are perfect for picnicking. Don't miss the
greenhouse; the Taiwanese-style pavilion
(Goryō-tei) that overlooks the garden's
central pond; and the cherry blossoms in
spring.

Astro Boy Mural
Public Art

(アトムの壁画, Atom no hekiga; 2-14-26
Takadanobaba, Toshima-ku; ☒JR Yamanote line
to Takadanobaba) Japan's most celebrated
manga artist Tezuka Osamu lived most of
his life in Takadanobaba and the neighbourhood couldn't be prouder. In front of
the station is a mural with all the characters Tezuka created, including his most
famous, Astro Boy.

😊 ACTIVITIES

Spa LaQua
Onsen

(スパ ラクーア; ☑03-5800-9999; www.laqua.
jp; 5th-9th fl, Tokyo Dome City, 1-1-1 Kasuga,
Bunkyō-ku; weekday/weekend ¥2850/3174;
☺11am-9am; ⑤Marunouchi line to Kōrakuen, exit
2) One of Tokyo's few true onsen, this chic
spa complex, renovated in 2017, relies on
natural hot-spring water from 1700m below
ground. There are indoor and outdoor baths,
saunas and a bunch of add-on options,
such as *akasuri* (Korean-style whole-body
exfoliation). It's a fascinating introduction to
Japanese health and beauty rituals.

Jakotsu-yu
Bathhouse

(蛇骨湯; Map p66; ☑03-3841-8645; www.
jakotsuyu.co.jp; 1-11-11 Asakusa, Taitō-ku; adult/
child ¥460/180; ☺1pm-midnight Wed-Mon;
⑤Ginza line to Tawaramachi, exit 3) Unlike most
sentō (public baths), the tubs here are
filled with pure hot-spring water, naturally
the colour of weak tea. Another treat is the
lovely, lantern-lit, rock-framed *rotemburo*
(outdoor bath). Jakotsu-yu is a welcoming
place; it has English signage and doesn't
have a policy against tattoos.

Roppongi, Harajuku & Shibuya

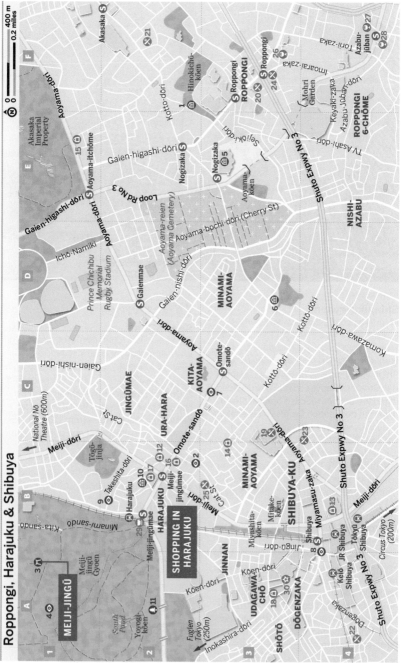

MEIJI-JINGŪ

Meiji-jingū Gyoen

South Pond

Yoyogi-kōen

National Nō Theatre (600m)

Tōgō-jinja

Meiji-dōri

Cat St

Gaien-nishi-dōri

JINGŪMAE

URA-HARA

Omote-sandō

Takeshita-dōri

HARAJUKU

Meiji-jingūmae

Kita-sandō

Minami-sandō

Meijijingūmae

SHOPPING IN HARAJUKU

Fuglen Tokyo (250m)

Inokashira-dōri

JINNAN

Kōen-dōri

UDAGAWA-CHŌ

SHŌTŌ

DŌGENZAKA

Dōgenzaka

Kōen-dōri

Miyashita-kōen

Jingū-dōri

Mitake-kōen

Miyamasu-zaka

SHIBUYA-KU

Shibuya

Keiō Shibuya

JR Shibuya

Tōkyū Shibuya

Circus Tokyo (200m)

Shuto Expwy No 3 Shibuya

Meiji-dōri

Shuto Expwy No 3

Aoyama-dōri

MINAMI-AOYAMA

Omote-sandō

KITA-AOYAMA

Aoyama-dōri

Gaien-nishi-dōri

Ichō-Namiki

Prince Chichibu Memorial Rugby Stadium

Galenmae

Gaien-higashi-dōri

Loop Rd No 3

Aoyama-reien (Aoyama Cemetery)

Aoyama-bochi-dōri (Cherry St)

MINAMI-AOYAMA

Kotto-dōri

Kotto-dōri

Komazawa-dōri

NISHI-AZABU

Shuto Expwy No 3

Akasaka Imperial Property

Aoyama-dōri

Aoyama-itchōme

Gaien-higashi-dōri

Nogizaka

Nogizaka

Aoyama-kōen

Kotto-dōri

Seijiki-dōri

Hinokichō-kōen

Roppongi

ROPPONGI

Roppongi

Mohri Garden

ROPPONGI 6-CHOME

TV Asahi-dōri

Keyaki-zaka

Azabu-jūban-dōri

Azabu-jūban

Imoarai-zaka

Torii-zaka

Akasaka

400 m
0.2 miles

Tokyo

1 · 2 · 3 · 4
A · B · C · D · E · F

Roppongi, Harajuku & Shibuya

🎓 COURSES

Wanariya — Traditional Craft

(和なり屋; Map p66; ☑03-5603-9169; www.wanariya.jp; 1-8-10 Senzoku, Taitō-ku; indigo dyeing/weaving from ¥1920/1980; ⏰10am-7pm irregular holidays; ⑤Hibiya line to Iriya, exit 1) A team of young and friendly Japanese runs this indigo-dyeing and traditional *hataori* (hand-loom-weaving) workshop. In under an hour you can learn to dye a T-shirt or a tote bag or weave a pair of coasters. It's a fantastic opportunity to make your own souvenirs. Book at least three days in advance.

Kitchen Kujo Tokyo — Cooking

(Map p66; ☑03-5832-9452; www.kujo.tokyo; 1-2-10 Yanaka, Taitō-ku; classes ¥6000-12,000; ⏰classes 10.30am or 1.30pm, bar 6-10.30pm Mon-Sat; ⑤Chiyoda line to Nezu, exit 2) The Kobayashi family and their translator and ramen chef Jun offer an interesting variety of cooking and culture classes at this handy studio devoted to cooking with organic products. Learn how to make tofu, miso, vegan ramen and curry rice with guest instructor Curryman (who dresses in a wacky costume). Also available are calligraphy, tea-ceremony and yoga classes.

Buddha Bellies — Cooking

(Map p66; ☑080-5001-9395; www.buddhabelliestokyo.jimdo.com; classes ¥5500-10,000; ⑤Chiyoda line to Yushima, exit 3) English-speaking sushi chef and sake sommelier Ayuko and her husband lead small hands-on classes in sushi, *bentō* (boxed lunch), udon and *wagashi* (Japanese sweets) making. Classes are held at Ayuko's home close to Yushima Station (she'll meet you at exit 3) and run usually from 11am, lasting 2½ hours. Try to book early.

🚌 TOURS

BUS TOURS

Bus tours are convenient for travellers who want to cover a lot of ground in one day (or want some respite from navigating).

Gray Line — Bus Tour

(Map p58; ☑03-5275-6525; www.jgl.co.jp/inbound; half-/full day ¥4900/9800) Offers half-day and full-day tours with stops covering key downtown sights, and day trips to Mt Fuji and Hakone. Pick-up from major hotels is available, otherwise most tours depart from the Dai-Ichi Hotel in Shimbashi (near Ginza).

teamLab Borderless

Digital-art collective teamLab has created 60 artworks for this new **museum** (☎03-6406-3949; https://borderless. teamlab.art; 1-3-8 Aomi, Kōtō-ku; adult/child ¥3200/1000; ⊙10am-7pm Mon-Thu & Sun, to 9pm Fri & Sat, closed 2nd & 4th Tue; ⑱; ⊠Yurikamome line to Aomi) that tests the border between art and the viewer: many are interactive. Not sure how? That's the point – go up to the artworks, move and touch them and see how they react. There is no suggested route; teamLab Borderless is all about exploration. Buy tickets in advance online.

teamLab Borderless
TEAMLAB BORDERLESS, ODAIBA, TOKYO ©

Hato Bus Tours Bus Tour
(Map p58; ☎03-3435-6081; www.hatobus. com; tours ¥1500-12,000; ⊠JR Yamanote line to Hamamatsuchō, south exit) This long-established bus-tour company offers hour-long, half-day and full-day bus tours. Shorter tours cruise by the sights in an open-air double-decker bus; longer ones make stops. Tours leave from Hato Bus terminals located in the annexe of the World Trade Centre in Hamamatsuchō, and Shinjuku and Tokyo train stations.

SkyBus Bus Tour
(Map p58; ☎03-3215-0008; www.skybus.jp; 2-5-2 Marunouchi, Chiyoda-ku; tours adult/child from ¥1600/700, Sky Hop Bus ¥3500/1700; ⊙ticket office 9am-6pm; ⊠JR Yamanote line to Tokyo, Marunouchi south exit) Open-top double-decker buses cruise through different neighbourhoods of the city for roughly

50 to 80 minutes. The Sky Hop Bus plan allows you to hop on and off buses across three routes. English-language guidance is provided via earphones on board.

WALKING TOURS

Walking tours offer insight into the history and culture of particular districts. Free tours led by English-speaking volunteer guides take place weekly around **Asakusa** (Map p66; ☎03-6280-6710; 2-18-9 Kaminari-mon, Taitō-ku; ⊙10.30am & 1.15pm Sat-Mon; ⑤Ginza line to Asakusa, exit 2), **Ueno** (Map p66; ☎03-6280-6710; www.tokyosgg.jp; 7-47 Ueno-kōen, Taitō-ku; ⊙10.30am & 1.30pm Wed, Fri & Sun; ⊠JR lines to Ueno, Ueno-kōen exit), **Yanaka** (Map p66; ☎03-6280-6710; www.tokyosgg.jp; 7-8-10 Yanaka, Taitō-ku; ⊙10.30am & 1.30pm Sun; ⊠Yamanote line to Nippori, north exit) and the **Imperial Palace East Garden** (Map p58; ☎03-6280-6710; JNTO Tourist Information Center, 3-3-1 Marunouchi, Chiyoda-ku; ⊙1pm Tue-Thu, Sat & Sun; ⑤Chiyoda line to Nijūbashimae, exit 1). No reservations needed.

🔒 SHOPPING

Ginza, home to high-end department stores and boutiques, has long been Tokyo's premier shopping district, though Harajuku – popular with younger shoppers – puts up a good fight for the title. Shibuya is another trendy district, while Asakusa is good for traditional crafts.

🔒 Ginza & Marunouchi

Itōya Arts & Crafts
(伊東屋; Map p58; ☎03-3561-8311; www.ito-ya.co .jp; 2-7-15 Ginza, Chūō-ku; ⊙10.30am-8pm Mon-Sat, to 7pm Sun; ⑤Ginza line to Ginza, exit A13) Explore the nine floors (plus several more in the nearby annexe) of stationery at this famed, century-old Ginza establishment. There are everyday items (such as notebooks and greeting cards) and luxuries (fountain pens and Italian leather agendas). You'll also find *washi* (handmade paper), *tenugui* (beautifully hand-dyed thin cotton towels) and *furoshiki* (wrapping cloths).

Okuno Building
Arts & Crafts

(奥野ビル; Map p58; 1-9-8 Ginza, Chūō-ku; ⏰most galleries noon-7pm; ⑤Yūrakuchō line to Ginza-itchōme, exit 10) This 1932 apartment block (cutting edge for its time) is a retro time capsule, its seven floors packed with some 40 tiny boutiques and gallery spaces. Climbing up and down the Escher-like staircases, or using the antique elevator, you'll come across mini-exhibitions that change weekly.

Ōedo
Antique Market
Antiques

(大江戸骨董市; Map p58; ☑03-6407-6011; www.antique-market.jp; 3-5-1 Marunouchi, Chiyoda-ku; ⏰9am-4pm 1st & 3rd Sun of month; ⓇJR Yamanote line to Yūrakuchō, Kokusai Forum exit) Held in the courtyard of **Tokyo International Forum** (東京国際フォーラム; Map p58; ☑03-5221-9000; www.t-i-forum.co.jp; ⏰7am-11.30pm) FREE, this is a brilliantly colourful event with hundreds of dealers in retro and antique Japanese goods, from old ceramics and kimono to kitsch plastic figurines and vintage movie posters. Check the website for exact dates.

ⓞ Roppongi & Akasaka

Japan Traditional Crafts
Aoyama Square
Arts & Crafts

(伝統工芸 青山スクエア; Map p62; ☑03-5785-1301; www.kougeihin.jp; 8-1-22 Akasaka, Minato-ku; ⏰11am-7pm; ⑤Ginza line to Aoyama-itchōme, exit 4) Supported by the Japanese Ministry of Economy, Trade and Industry, this is as much a showroom as a shop, exhibiting a broad range of crafts from around Japan, including lacquerwork boxes, woodwork, cut glass, textiles and pottery. There are some heirloom pieces here, but also beautiful items at reasonable prices.

Souvenir
from Tokyo
Gifts & Souvenirs

(スーベニアフロムトーキョー; Map p62; ☑03-6812 9933; www.souvenirfromtokyo.jp; basement, National Art Center Tokyo, 7-22-2 Roppongi, Minato-ku; ⏰10am-6pm Sat-Mon, Wed & Thu, to 8pm Fri; ⑤Chiyoda line to Nogizaka, exit 6) There's always an expertly curated, and ever-changing, selection of home-grown design bits and bobs that make for unique souvenirs at this shop.

Itōya

Ueno & Asakusa

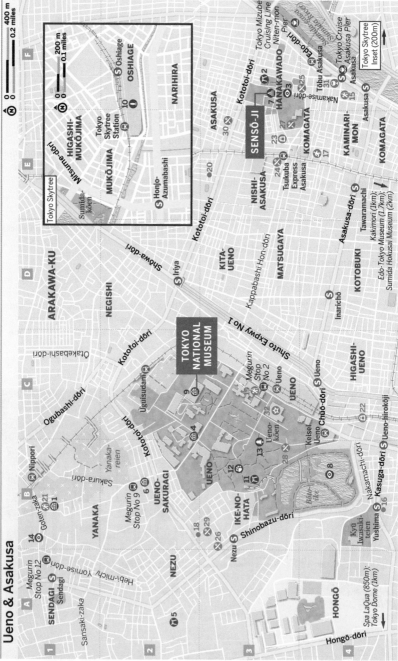

Ueno & Asakusa

◎ Shibuya & Harajuku

Tokyu Hands Department Store

(東急ハンズ; Map p62; http://shibuya.tokyu-hands.co.jp; 12-18 Udagawa-chō, Shibuya-ku; ◎10am-9pm; ◉JR Yamanote line to Shibuya, Hachikō exit) This DIY and *zakka* (miscellaneous things) store has eight fascinating floors of everything you didn't know you needed – reflexology slippers, bee-venom face masks and cartoon-character-shaped rice-ball moulds, for example. Most stuff is inexpensive, making it perfect for souvenir- and gift-hunting. Warning: you could lose hours in here.

d47 design travel store Design

(Map p62; ☎03-6427-2301; 8th fl, Shibuya Hikarie, 2-21-1 Shibuya, Shibuya-ku; ◎11am-8pm; ◉JR Yamanote line to Shibuya, east exit) The folks behind the D&D Department lifestyle brand and magazine are expert scavengers, searching Japan's nooks and crannies for outstanding examples of artisanship – be it ceramics from Ishikawa or linens from Fukui. An ever-changing selection of finds are on sale.

◎ Shinjuku

Beams Japan Fashion & Accessories

(ビームス・ジャパン; www.beams.co.jp; 3-32-6 Shinjuku, Shinjuku-ku; ◎11am-8pm; ◉JR Yamanote line to Shinjuku, east exit) Beams, a national chain of trendsetting boutiques, is a Japanese cultural institution and this multistorey Shinjuku branch has a particular audience in mind: you, the traveller. It's full of the latest Japanese streetwear labels, traditional fashions with cool modern twists, artisan crafts, pop art and more – all contenders for that perfect only-in-Tokyo souvenir. Set your budget before you enter.

Don Quijote Gifts & Souvenirs

(ドン・キホーテ; ☎03-5291-9211; www.donki.com; 1-16-5 Kabukichō, Shinjuku-ku; ◎24hr; ◉JR Yamanote line to Shinjuku, east exit) Fluorescent-lit bargain castle 'Donki' is filled to the brink with weird loot. Chaotic piles of electronic items and designer goods sit alongside sex toys, fetish costumes and packaged foods. It's a national chain but this Yasukuni-dōri branch is a local landmark.

Omote-sandō Architecture

The wide boulevard that runs through Harajuku, **Omote-sandō** (表参道; Map p62; S Ginza line to Omote-sandō, exits A3 & B4, R JR Yamanote line to Harajuku, Omote-sandō exit), is like a walk-through showroom of the who's who of contemporary architecture. Here you'll see buildings from several of Japan's Pritzker Prize winners. Highlights include the **Dior boutique** (2003), designed by SANAA with a filmy exterior that seems to hang like a dress; Itō Toyō's construction for **Tod's** (2004), with criss-crossing strips of concrete inspired by the zelkova trees below; and the convex glass fishbowl that is the **Prada Aoyama boutique** (2003), created by Herzog and de Meuron.

Prada Aoyama boutique
TUPUNGATO / SHUTTERSTOCK ©

🏛 Asakusa & Ryōgoku

Marugoto Nippon　　Food & Drinks

(まるごとにっぽん; Map p66; ☎03-3845-0510; www.marugotonippon.com; 2-6-7 Asakusa, Taitō-ku; ⊙10am-8pm; S Ginza line to Tawaramachi, exit 3) Think of this as a minimall, showcasing the best of Japan's speciality food and drink (ground floor) and arts and crafts (2nd floor). The 3rd floor showcases the products and attractions of different Japanese regions on a regularly changing basis.

Kakimori　　Stationery

(カキモリ; ☎050-1744-8546; www.kakimori.com; 1-6-2 Misuji, Taitō-ku; ⊙11am-7pm Tue-Sun; S Asakusa line to Kuramae, exit 3) Stationery

lovers flock from far and wide to this shop that allows you to custom build your own notebooks (from around ¥1000), choosing the paper, covers, binding and other bits and pieces to make a unique keepsake.

🍴 EATING

As visitors to Tokyo quickly discover, people here are absolutely obsessed with food. The city has a vibrant and cosmopolitan dining scene and a strong culture of eating out – popular restaurants are packed most nights of the week. Best of all, you can get superlative meals on any budget.

✴ Ginza & Marunouchi

Kyūbey　　Sushi ¥¥¥

(久兵衛; Map p58; ☎03-3571-6523; www.kyubey.jp; 8-7-6 Ginza, Chūō-ku; set meals lunch/dinner from ¥4400/11,000; ⊙11.30am-2pm & 5-10pm Mon-Sat; S Ginza line to Shimbashi, exit 3) Since 1935, Kyūbey's quality and presentation have won it a moneyed and celebrity clientele. Despite the cachet, this is a relaxed restaurant. The friendly owner, Imada-san, speaks excellent English as do some of his team of talented chefs, who will make and serve your sushi, piece by piece. The ¥8000 lunchtime *omakase* (chef's choice) is great value.

Tempura Kondō　　Tempura ¥¥¥

(てんぷら近藤; Map p58; ☎03-5568-0923; 9th fl, Sakaguchi Bldg, 5-5-13 Ginza, Chūō-ku; lunch/dinner course from ¥6500/11,000; ⊙noon-3pm & 5-10pm Mon-Sat; S Ginza line to Ginza, exit B5) Nobody in Tokyo does tempura vegetables like chef Kondō Fumio. The carrots are julienned to a fine floss; the corn is pert and juicy; and the sweet potato is comfort food at its finest. Courses include seafood, too. Lunch at noon or 1.30pm; last dinner booking at 8pm.
Reserve ahead.

✴ Roppongi & Akasaka

Kikunoi　　Kaiseki ¥¥¥

(菊乃井; Map p62; ☎03-3568-6055; www.kikunoi.jp; 6-13-8 Akasaka, Minato-ku; lunch/

dinner course from ¥11,900/16,000; noon-12.30pm Tue-Sat, 5-7.30pm Mon-Sat; ⑤ Chiyoda line to Akasaka, exit 7) Exquisitely prepared seasonal dishes are as beautiful as they are delicious at this Tokyo outpost of one of Kyoto's most acclaimed *kaiseki* (Japanese haute cuisine) restaurants. Kikunoi's third-generation chef, Murata Yoshihiro, has written a book on *kaiseki* (which has been translated into English) that the staff helpfully use to explain the dishes you are served.

Tofuya-Ukai
Kaiseki ¥¥¥

(とうふ屋うかい; Map p58; ☏03-3436-1028; www.ukai.co.jp; 4-4-13 Shiba-kōen, Minato-ku; set meals lunch/dinner from ¥5940/10,800; 11.45am-3pm & 5-7.30pm Mon-Fri, 11am-7.30pm Sat & Sun; ; ⑤ Ōedo line to Akabane-bashi, exit 8) One of Tokyo's most gracious restaurants is located in a former sake brewery (moved from northern Japan), with an exquisite traditional garden in the shadow of Tokyo Tower (p59). Seasonal preparations of tofu and accompanying dishes are served in the refined *kaiseki* style. Make reservations well in advance.

Vegetarians should advise staff when they book, and last orders for weekday lunch is 3pm, for dinner 7.30pm.

Honmura-An
Soba ¥

(本むら庵; Map p62; ☏03-5772-6657; www.honmuraantokyo.com; 7-14-18 Roppongi, Minato-ku; noodles from ¥900, set meals lunch/dinner ¥1600/7400; noon-2.30pm & 5.30-10pm Tue-Sun, closed 1st & 3rd Tue of month; ; ⑤ Hibiya line to Roppongi, exit 4) This fabled soba shop, once located in Manhattan, now serves its handmade buckwheat noodles at this rustically contemporary noodle shop on a Roppongi side street. The noodles' delicate flavour is best appreciated when served on a bamboo mat, with tempura or with dainty slices of *kamo* (duck).

Sougo
Japanese ¥

(宗胡; Map p62; ☏03-5414-1133; www.sougo.tokyo; 3rd fl, Roppongi Green Bldg, 6-1-8 Roppongi, Minato-ku; set meals lunch/dinner from ¥1500/6500; 11.30am-3pm & 6-11pm Mon-Sat; ; ⑤ Hibiya line to Roppongi, exit 3) Sit at the long counter beside the open kitchen or in booths and watch the expert chefs

Kaiseki at Kikunoi

prepare delicious and beautifully presented *shōjin-ryōri* (mainly vegetarian cuisine as served at Buddhist temples – some dishes use *dashi* stock, which contains fish). Lunch is a bargain. Reserve at least one day in advance for a vegan meal (lunch/dinner ¥7000/10,000).

⊗ Ebisu & Meguro

Tonki · Tonkatsu ¥
(とんき; ☎03-3491-9928; 1-2-1 Shimo-Meguro, Meguro-ku; meals ¥1800; ⊙4-10.45pm Wed-Mon, closed 3rd Mon of the month; 🚇JR Yamanote line to Meguro, west exit) Tonki is a Tokyo *tonkatsu* (crumbed pork cutlet) legend, deep-frying with an unchanged recipe for nearly 80 years. The seats at the counter – where you can watch the perfectly choreographed chefs – are the most coveted, though there is usually a queue. There are tables upstairs.

Yakiniku Champion · Barbecue ¥¥
(焼肉チャンピオン; ☎03-5768-6922; www.yakiniku-champion.com; 1-2-8 Ebisu, Shibuya-ku; dishes ¥780-3300, course from ¥5600; ⊙5pm-midnight; 🚇JR Yamanote line to Ebisu, west exit) Champion is one of Tokyo's best spots for *yakiniku* – literally 'grilled meat' and the Japanese term for Korean barbecue. The menu runs the gamut from sweetbreads to the choicest cuts of grade A5 *wagyū;* there's a diagram of the cuts as well as descriptions. It is a very popular restaurant so reservations are highly recommended.

⊗ Shibuya & Harajuku

Matsukiya · Hotpot ¥¥¥
(松木家; Map p62; ☎03-3461-2651; 6-8 Maruyama-chō, Shibuya-ku; meals from ¥5400; ⊙5-11pm Mon-Sat; 🚇JR Yamanote line to Shibuya, Hachikō exit) There are only two things on the menu at Matsukiya, established in 1890: *sukiyaki* (thinly sliced beef cooked in sake, soy and vinegar broth, and dipped in raw egg) and *shabu-shabu* (thin slices of beef or pork swished in hot broth and dipped in a citrusy soy or sesame sauce). The beef is top-grade *wagyū* from Ōmi. Meals include veggies and noodles cooked in the broths.

From left: *Tonkatsu* at Tonki; *gyōza*; *sukiyaki*

JUNICHI MIYAZAKI / LONELY PLANET ©

GOLEPHOTOGRAPHY / GETTY IMAGES ©

Narukiyo
Izakaya ¥¥¥

(なるきよ; Map p62; ☎03-5485-2223; 2-7-14 Shibuya, Shibuya-ku; dishes ¥700-4800; ☺6pm-12.30am; ☒JR Yamanote line to Shibuya, east exit) Cult favourite *izakaya*, Narukiyo serves seasonal Japanese cuisine with creative panache. The menu, which changes daily, is handwritten on a scroll and totally undecipherable; say the magic word, *omakase* (chef's choice; and set a price cap, say ¥5000 or ¥7000 per person), and trust that you're in good hands. Reservations are recommended.

Harajuku Gyōza-rō
Dumplings ¥

(原宿餃子楼; Map p62; 6-4-2 Jingūmae, Shibuya-ku; 6 gyōza ¥290; ☺11.30am-4.30am Mon-Sat, to 10pm Sun; ☒JR Yamanote line to Harajuku, Omote-sandō exit) *Gyōza* (dumplings) are the only thing on the menu here, but you won't hear any complaints from the regulars who queue up to get their fix. Have them *sui* (boiled) or *yaki* (pan-fried), with or without *niniku* (garlic) or *nira* (chives) – they're all delicious. Expect to wait on weekends or at lunchtime, but the line moves quickly.

Akihabara Electronics

From the 1970s to the 1990s, when the differences between NTSC and PAL actually mattered, and Japanese tech was years ahead of the rest, Akihabara was the global epicentre for consumer electronics and the place to get overseas models of the latest gear months before the rest of the world.

Akihabara survived globalisation and Amazon.com, reinventing itself as the centre of the *otaku* (geek) universe, catching J-pop culture fans in its gravitational pull. But you'll still find every Japanese electronics retailer and loads of duty-free and 'foreign-model' specialists here, hawking every kind of tech.

Both bargains and higher than expected prices coexist. Check back-home prices before buying and keep your passport handy for the consumption tax exemption if you spend more than ¥5000 in a single day in many shops. For a list of eligible shops, see www.akiba.or.jp.

HENKI / GETTY IMAGES ©

Udon noodles

World Breakfast
Allday   International ¥

(Map p62; ☑03-3406-7008; www.world-
breakfast-allday.com; 6-15-14 Jingūmae, Shibuya-
ku; meals ¥1080-1720; ☺7.30am-8pm; ✐; ⓡJR
Yamanote line to Harajuku, Takeshita exit) Each
month this restaurant focuses on a particular country's breakfast tradition, from
Indian *idli* (fermented rice and lentil cakes)
to Brazilian *pão de queijo* (cheese buns).
Classic English breakfasts and muesli are
served continuously. It's a cool concept
and also one of the few places in the city,
outside the hotels, where you can get a
decent hot breakfast.

⊗ Shinjuku

Kozue   Japanese ¥¥¥

(梢; ☑03-5323-3460; www.hyatt.com; 40th
fl, Park Hyatt Tokyo, 3-7-1-2 Nishi-Shinjuku,
Shinjuku-ku; lunch set menu ¥2480-10,800, dinner
set menu ¥14,040-24,850; ☺11.30am-2.30pm
& 5.30-9.30pm; ⓢŌedo line to Tochōmae, exit
A4) It's hard to beat Kozue's combination of
exquisite seasonal Japanese cuisine, artisan
crockery and distractingly good views over

Shinjuku. As the kimono-clad staff speak
English and the restaurant caters well to dietary restrictions and personal preferences,
this is a good spot for diners who don't want
to give up complete control. Reservations
essential for dinner and recommended for
lunch; 15% service charge.

Kanae   Izakaya ¥¥

(鼎; ☑050-3467-1376; basement fl, 3-12-12
Shinjuku, Shinjuku-ku; cover charge ¥540; dishes
¥660-1980; ☺5pm-midnight Mon-Sat, 4.30-
11pm Sun; ⓡJR Yamanote line to Shinjuku, east
exit) Kanae is a perfect example of one of
Shinjuku-sanchōme's excellent and all but
undiscoverable *izakaya:* delicious sashimi,
seasonal dishes and simple staples (the
potato salad is famous) in the basement of
an unremarkable building (there's a white
sign with a sake barrel out front). Seating
is at the counter or at a handful of tables;
reservations recommended.

Nagi   Ramen ¥

(凪; ☑03-3205-1925; www.n-nagi.com; 2nd fl,
Golden Gai G2, 1-1-10 Kabukichō, Shinjuku-ku;
ramen from ¥890; ☺24hr; ⓡJR Yamanote line to

Shinjuku, east exit) Nagi, once an edgy upstart in the ramen world, has done well and now has branches around the city. This tiny shop, one of the originals, up a stairway in Golden Gai, is still our favourite...we're clearly not alone as there's often a line. The house speciality is *niboshi* ramen (egg noodles in a broth flavoured with dried sardines).

Ueno & Yanesen

Hantei
Japanese ¥¥

(はん亭; Map p66; ☑03-3287-9000; www. hantei.co.jp; 2-12-15 Nezu, Bunkyō-ku; lunch/ dinner from ¥3200/3000; ☉noon-3pm & 5-10pm Tue-Sun; ⑤Chiyoda line to Nezu, exit 2) Housed in a beautifully maintained, century-old traditional wooden building, Hantei is a local landmark. Delectable skewers of seasonal *kushiage* (fried meat, fish and vegetables) are served with small, refreshing side dishes. Lunch includes eight or 12 sticks and dinner starts with six, after which you can order additional rounds (three/six skewers ¥800/1600).

Innsyoutei
Japanese ¥

(韻松亭; Map p66; ☑03-3821-8126; www.inn-syoutei.jp; 4-59 Ueno-kōen, Taitō-ku; lunch/dinner from ¥1680/5500; ☉restaurant 11am-3pm & 5-9.30pm, tearoom 3pm-5pm; ☒JR lines to Ueno, Ueno-kōen exit) In a gorgeous wooden building dating to 1875, Innsyoutei (pronounced 'inshotei' and meaning 'rhyme of the pine cottage') has long been a favourite spot for fancy *kaiseki*-style meals while visiting Ueno-kōen (p42). Without a booking (essential for dinner) you'll have a long wait but it's worth it. Lunchtime *bentō* (boxed meals) offer beautifully presented morsels and are great value.

Kamachiku
Udon ¥

(金竹; Map p66; ☑03-5815-4675; www.kamachi-ku.com; 2-14-18 Nezu, Bunkyō-ku; noodles from ¥850, small dishes ¥350-950; ☉11.30am-2pm Tue-Sun, 5.30-9pm Tue-Sat; ⑤Chiyoda line to Nezu, exit 1) Freshly made udon are the speciality at this popular restaurant, in a beautifully restored brick warehouse from 1910 that's incorporated into a building designed by Kuma Kengo. In addition to noodles, the

Tokyo Markets

Pretty much every weekend you'll find farmers markets and flea markets happening somewhere: larger ones take place at plazas in parks like Yoyogi-kōen and Shinjuku Chūō-kōen; many smaller ones are held on the grounds of Shintō shrines, such as Shinjuku's weekly **Hanazono-jinja Flea Market** (青空骨董市, Aozora Kottō-ichi; www.kottou-ichi.jp; Hanazono-jinja, 5-17 Shinjuku, Shinjuku-ku; ☉dawn-dusk Sun; ⑤Marunouchi line to Shinjuku-sanchōme, exits B10 & E2).

On the first weekend of the month, **Raw Tokyo** is a fusion flea and farmers market – the kind that has a DJ booth, live painting and food trucks. Every other weekend at the same spot, the **Farmer's Market @UNU** (Map p62; www.farmersmarkets.jp; 5-53-7 Jingūmae, Shibuya-ku; ☉10am-4pm Sat & Sun; ⑤Ginza line to Omote-sandō, exit B2) ✐ is Tokyo's best.

The long-running, twice-monthly **Ōedo Antique Market** (p65) draws hundreds of dealers selling all kinds of vintage items.

For an updated schedule of all the city's flea markets, see www.frma.jp (in Japanese). Though bargaining is permitted, it is considered bad form to drive too hard a bargain.

Ōedo Antique Market (p65)

menu includes a good selection of sake and lots of small dishes (such as grilled fish, veggies and a delicious Japanese-style omelette).

⧉ Food Alleys

Food alleys – often called *yokochō* – are a popular postwork gathering spot for Tokyoites. These narrow strips are lined with teeny-tiny bars and restaurants; some offer seating outside on stools or over-turned beer crates. Some favourites:

Ebisu-yokochō (恵比寿横町; www. ebisu-yokocho.com; 1-7-4 Ebisu, Shibuya-ku; dishes ¥500-1500; ⏰5pm-late; ☒JR Yamanote line to Ebisu, east exit) Locals love this retro arcade that is chock-a-block with everything from humble *yaki soba* (fried buckwheat noodles) to decadent *hotate-yaki* (grilled scallops). It's loud and lively pretty much every night; go early to get a table. Hours and prices vary by shop.

Omoide-yokochō (思い出横丁; Nishi-Shinjuku 1-chōme, Shinjuku-ku; skewers from ¥150; ⏰varies by shop; ☒JR Yamanote line to Shinjuku, west exit) Literally 'Memory Lane' (and less politely known as Shonben-yokochō, or 'Piss Alley'), Omoide-yokochō started as a postwar black market and somehow stuck around. Today, it's one of Tokyo's most recognisable sights. There are dozens of small restaurants, mostly serving *yakitori* (chicken, and other meats or vegetables, grilled on skewers), packed in; several have English menus.

Hoppy-dōri (ホッピー通り; Map p66; 2-5 Asakusa, Taitō-ku; dishes ¥500-700; ⏰noon until late, varies by shop; ☒Tsukuba Express to Asakusa, exit 4) Either side of the street popularly known as Hoppy-dōri – 'hoppy' is a cheap malt beverage – are rows of *izakaya* (Japanese pub-eateries) with outdoor seating on rickety stools and plastic tarps for awnings. Don't be put off – it's one of Asakusa's most atmospheric eating and drinking strips.

✪ Asakusa & Ryōgoku

Asakusa Imahan   Japanese ¥¥¥
(浅草今半; Map p66; ☎03-3841-1114; www. asakusaimahan.co.jp; 3-1-12 Nishi-Asakusa, Taitō-ku; lunch/dinner from ¥2000/8000; ⏰11.30am-9.30pm; ☒Tsukuba Express to Asakusa, exit 4) For a meal to remember, swing by this famous beef restaurant, in business since 1895. Choose between courses of sukiyaki and *shabu-shabu;* prices rise according to the grade of meat. For diners on a budget, Imahan sells 20 servings of a *gyūdon* (rice topped with sliced beef; ¥1500) per day.

Kappō Yoshiba   Japanese ¥¥
(割烹吉葉; ☎03-3623-4480; www.kapou-yoshiba.jp; 2-14-5 Yokoami, Sumida-ku; dishes ¥650-7800; ⏰11.30am-2pm & 5-10pm Mon-Sat; ⑤Ōedo line to Ryōgoku, exit 1) The former Miyagino sumo stable is the location for this one-of-a-kind restaurant that has preserved the *dōyō* (practice ring) as its centrepiece. Playing up to its sumo roots, you can order the protein-packed stew *chanko-nabe* (for two people from ¥5200), but Yoshiba's real strength is its sushi, freshly prepared in jumbo portions.

Onigiri Yadoroku   Japanese ¥
(おにぎり 浅草 宿六; Map p66; ☎03-3874-1615; www.onigiriyadoroku.com; 3-9-10 Asakusa, Taitō-ku; set lunch 2/3 onigiri from ¥690/930, onigiri ¥280-690; ⏰11.30am-5pm Mon-Sat, 6pm-2am Thu-Tue; ☒Tsukuba Express to Asakusa, exit 1) *Onigiri* (rice balls), wrapped in crispy sheets of *nori* (seaweed), are a great Japanese culinary invention. Try them freshly made at Tokyo's oldest *onigiri* shop, which feels more like a classy sushi counter. The set lunches are a great deal; at night there's a large range of flavours to choose from, along with alcohol.

🍸 DRINKING & NIGHTLIFE

Make like Lady Gaga in a karaoke box; sip sake with an increasingly rosy salaryman in a tiny postwar bar; or dance under the rays of the rising sun at an enormous bayside club: that's nightlife, Tokyo style. The city's drinking culture embraces everything from refined teahouses and indie coffee shops to craft-beer pubs and maid cafes.

Roppongi has the lion's share of foreigner-friendly bars, while Shinjuku offers the retro warren Golden Gai and the LGBT-friendly bar district Ni-chōme. Other top party districts include youthful Shibuya and Harajuku; Shimbashi and Yūrakuchō, which teem with white-collar workers; and Ebisu and nearby Daikanyama, both of which have some excellent bars.

🍵 Ginza & Marunouchi

Chashitsu Kaboku　　　Teahouse

(茶室 嘉木; Map p58; ☏03-6212-0202; www.ippodo-tea.co.jp; 3-1-1 Marunouchi, Chiyoda-ku; tea set ¥1080-2600; ⊙11am-7pm; 🚆JR Yamanote line to Yurakuchō, Tokyo International Forum exit) Run by famed Kyoto tea producer Ippōdō – which celebrated 300 years of business in 2017 – this teahouse is a fantastic place to experience the myriad pleasures of *ocha* (green tea). It's also one of the few places that serves *koicha* (thick tea), which is even thicker than ordinary matcha (powdered green tea). Sets are accompanied by a pretty, seasonal *wagashi*.

Ginza Lion　　　Beer Hall

(銀座ライオン; Map p58; ☏050-5269-7095; https://ginzalion.net; 7-9-20 Ginza, Chūō-ku; ⊙11.30am-11pm, until 10.30pm Sun; 🚇Ginza line to Ginza, exit A2) So what if Sapporo's beers are not among the best you can quaff in Tokyo? Dating to 1934, the gorgeous art deco design at Japan's oldest beer hall – including glass mosaic murals – is to die for. The oom-pah-pah atmosphere, with waiters ferrying frothy mugs and plates of Bavarian-style sausages to the tables, is also priceless.

🍸 Roppongi & Akasaka

Gen Yamamoto　　　Cocktail Bar

(ゲンヤモト; Map p62; ☏03-6434-0652; www.genyamamoto.jp; 1-6-4 Azabu-Jūban, Minato-ku; cover charge ¥1000, 4-/6-cocktail menu ¥4700/6700; ⊙3-11pm Tue-Sun; 🚇Namboku line to Azabu-jūban, exit 7) The delicious fruit-based drinks served here use local seasonal ingredients. Yamamoto's tasting

Onigiri at Onigiri Yadoroku

menus are designed to be savoured, not to get you sozzled (servings are small), and the bar's ambience – eight seats around a bar made from 500-year-old Japanese oak – is reminiscent of a traditional teahouse. We highly recommend the six-cocktail menu.

Brewdog
Craft Beer

(Map p62; ☎03-6447-4160; www.brewdogbar .jp; 5-3-2 Roppongi, Minato-ku; ☺5pm-midnight Mon-Fri, from 3pm Sat & Sun; 🛜; Ⓢ Hibiya line to Roppongi, exit 3) This Scottish craft brewery's Tokyo outpost is nestled off the main drag. Apart from its own brews, there's a great selection of other beers, including Japanese varieties on tap, mostly all served in small, regular or large (a full pint) portions. Tasty food plus computer and board games to while away the evening round out a class operation.

Ele Tokyo
Club

(Map p62; ☎03-5572-7535; www.eletokyo. com; Fukao Bldg, 1-4-5 Azabu-Jūban, Minato-ku; women free, men incl 1 drink Thu ¥2000, Fri & Sat ¥3000; ☺10pm-5am Thu-Sat; Ⓢ Ōedo line to Azabu-jūban, exit 7) Dress to impress to gain entry to this bling-tastic, two-level dance club that's one of the classier late-night joints around Roppongi. You must be over 20 years old and have photo ID.

🚇 Ebisu & Meguro

Gem by Moto
Bar

(ジェムバイモト; ☎03-6455-6998; 1-30-9 Ebisu, Shibuya-ku; ☺5pm-midnight Tue-Fri, 1-9pm Sat & Sun; 🚉 JR Yamanote line to Ebisu, east exit) Tiny Gem has a seriously good selection of interesting sakes from ambitious brewers. Start with one of the Gem originals (brewed in collaboration with the bar) – or let owner Chiba-san select one for you. Sake by the glass runs from ¥650 to ¥5000 (but most are on the more reasonable end). Cover charge ¥800; reservations recommended.

Bar Trench
Cocktail Bar

(バートレンチ; ☎03-3780-5291; www.small- axe.net; 1-5-8 Ebisu-nishi, Shibuya-ku; ☺7pm-2am Mon-Sat, 6pm-1am Sun; 🚉 JR Yamanote line to Ebisu, west exit) One of the pioneers of Tokyo's new cocktail scene, Trench (a suitable name for a bar hidden in a narrow

From left: Pouring a beer; strawberry cocktails; Fuglen Tokyo

alley) is a tiny place with an air of old-world bohemianism – but that might just be the absinthe talking. The always-changing original tipples are made with infusions, botanicals, herbs and spices. Drinks from ¥1500; cover ¥500.

Shibuya & Harajuku

Circus Tokyo   Club
(www.circus-tokyo.jp; 3-26-16 Shibuya, Shibuya-ku; ◈JR Yamanote line to Shibuya, new south exit) Circus, the Tokyo offshoot of an Osaka club, is aggressively underground: small, out of the way, in a basement (of course), with no decor to speak of and all attention laser-focused on the often experimental music. It's open most Fridays and Saturdays from 11pm, and sometimes other nights; check the schedule online. Cover ¥2000 to ¥3000 and drinks ¥600; ID required.

Fuglen Tokyo   Cafe
(www.fuglen.no; 1-16-11 Tomigaya, Shibuya-ku; ◷8am-10pm Mon & Tue, to 1am Wed & Thu, to 2am Fri, 9am-2am Sat, 9am-midnight Sun; ◈; ⓢChiyoda line to Yoyogi-kōen, exit 2) This

Shinjuku Station East

The east side of Shinjuku Station is home to Tokyo's largest nightlife district. In fact, it's so large that it contains multiple districts within it: **Shinjuku-nichōme** is Tokyo's LGBT enclave; **Shinjuku-sanchōme** is full of *izakaya* (Japanese pub-eateries) and bars popular with commuters stopping off on their way home; the tiny bars of Golden Gai (p78) are a draw for artists, musicians and, increasingly, travellers. Running through the middle of this is Yasukuni-dōri, the main artery, electrified with a thousand glowing signs and lined with karaoke parlours and wallet-friendly chain *izakaya*. Ikebukuro, too, has lots of bars and *izakaya* around the train station.

There are over 200 exits to the station, so don't be too overwhelmed trying to find somewhere: it can be difficult even for many Japanese. As a general rule, for fun and frivolity, head east.

Golden Gai

A Shinjuku institution for over half a century, **Golden Gai** (ゴールデン街; www.goldengai.jp; 1-1 Kabukichō, Shinjuku-ku; ℝJR Yamanote line to Shinjuku, east exit) is a collection of tiny bars, often no bigger than a closet and seating maybe a dozen. Each is as unique and eccentric as the 'master' or 'mama' who runs it. In a sense, Golden Gai – with the strong visual appeal of its low-slung wooden buildings – is their work of art. It's more than just a place to drink.

The best way to experience Golden Gai is to stroll the lanes and pick a place that suits your mood. Bars that expressly welcome tourists have English signs posted on their doors. Many have a cover charge (usually ¥500 to ¥1500), often posted on the door.

Note that while Golden Gai is highly photogenic it is also private property; do not take photos unless you have explicit permission.

Golden Gai
FOTOS593 / SHUTTERSTOCK ©

Tokyo outpost of a long-running Oslo coffee shop serves light-roast coffee during the day (from ¥360) and some of the city's most creative cocktails (from ¥1250) by night (Wednesday to Sunday). It's Tomigaya's principal gathering spot, with indoor and outdoor seating. Fuglen often hosts events with special food and drink or music; check the website for further information.

Shinjuku

Zoetrope   Bar
(ゾートロープ; ℐ03-3363-0162; 3rd fl, 7-10-14 Nishi-Shinjuku, Shinjuku-ku; ⊙5pm-midnight Mon-Sat; ℝJR Yamanote line to Shinjuku, west exit) A must-visit for whisky fans, Zoetrope has some 300 varieties of Japanese whisky behind its small counter – including hard-to-find bottles from small batch distilleries. It's a one-person show and the owner speaks English well. Cover charge ¥600; whisky by the glass from ¥400 to ¥19,000, though most are reasonably priced (around ¥800 to ¥1200), and there are some good-value tasting flights, too.

BenFiddich   Cocktail Bar
(ベンフィディック; ℐ03-6279-4223; 9th fl, 1-13-7 Nishi-Shinjuku, Shinjuku-ku; ⊙6pm-3am Mon-Sat; ℝJR Yamanote line to Shinjuku, west exit) BenFiddich is dark and tiny, with vials of infusions on the shelves and herbs hung to dry from the ceiling. The English-speaking barman, Kayama Hiroyasu, in a white suit, moves like a magician. There's no menu, so just tell him what you like and he'll concoct something delicious for you (we like the gimlet with herbs). Expect to pay around ¥2000 per drink.

New York Bar   Bar
(ニューヨークバー; ℐ03-5323-3458; www.restaurants.tokyo.park.hyatt.co.jp; 52nd fl, Park Hyatt Tokyo, 3-7-1-2 Nishi-Shinjuku, Shinjuku-ku; ⊙5pm-midnight Sun-Wed, to 1am Thu-Sat; ℝŌedo line to Tochōmae, exit A4) Head to the Park Hyatt's 52nd floor to swoon over the sweeping nightscape from the floor-to-ceiling windows at this bar of Lost in Translation fame. There's a cover charge of ¥2500 if you visit or stay past 8pm (7pm Sunday); go earlier and watch the sky fade to black. Cocktails start at ¥2160. Note: dress code enforced and 15% service charge levied.

Asakusa & Ryōgoku

Popeye   Pub
(ポパイ; ℐ03-3633-2120; www.lares.dti.ne.jp/~ppy; 2-18-7 Ryōgoku, Sumida-ku; sampler set of 3/10 beers ¥630/1750; ⊙5-11.30pm Mon-Fri,

Sumo tournament

from 3pm Sat; JR Sōbu line to Ryōgoku, west exit) Popeye boasts an astounding 100 beers on tap, including a huge selection of Japanese beers – from Echigo Weizen to Hitachino Nest Espresso Stout. The happy-hour deal (which runs from 5pm to 8pm, and from 3pm on Saturday) offers select brews with free plates of pizza, sausages and other munchables. It's extremely popular and fills up fast; get here early to grab a seat.

Kamiya Bar
Bar

(神谷バー; Map p66; 03-3841-5400; www.kamiya-bar.com; 1-1-1 Asakusa, Taitō-ku; 11.30am-10pm Wed-Mon; Ginza line to Asakusa, exit 3) One of Tokyo's oldest Western-style bars, Kamiya opened in 1880 and is still hugely popular. The house drink for over a century has been Denki Bran, a secret mix of brandy, gin, wine, curaçao and medicinal herbs. Order either 'blanc' (30 proof) or the 40 proof 'old' at the counter, then give your tickets to the server.

⭐ ENTERTAINMENT

Tokyo's range of entertainment is impressive. Take your pick from smoky jazz bars, grand theatres, rockin' live-music houses, comedy shows and major sports events. And don't be afraid to sample the traditional performing arts: the major venues will offer earphones or subtitles that have an English translation of the plots and dramatic dialogue.

Ryōgoku Kokugikan
Sumo

(両国国技館, Ryōgoku Sumo Stadium; 03-3623-5111; www.sumo.or.jp; 1-3-28 Yokoami, Sumida-ku; tickets ¥3800-11,700; JR Sōbu line to Ryōgoku, west exit) If you're in town when a tournament is on, don't miss the chance to catch the big boys of Japanese wrestling in action at the country's largest sumo stadium. The key spectacle is around 3.45pm when the *makuuchi* (top division) wrestlers in elaborately decorated aprons parade into the ring. Tickets can be bought online one month before the tournament opens.

Fun For Young & Old

In need of amusement-park thrills? The latest virtual-reality gaming? Brownie points with the kids?

Tokyo Joypolis (東京ジョイポリス; http://tokyo-joypolis.com; 3rd-5th fl, DECKS Tokyo Beach, 1-6-1 Daiba, Minato-ku; adult /child ¥800/500, all-rides passport ¥4300/ 3300, passport after 5pm ¥3300/2300; ◷10am-10pm; 🚇Yurikamome line to Odaiba Kaihin-kōen, north exit) An indoor amusement park stacked with virtual-reality attractions and thrill rides.

Sky Circus (スカイサーカス; ☎03-3989-3457; www.skycircus.jp; Sunshine 60, 3-1-1 Higashi-Ikebukuro, Toshima-ku; observatory ticket adult/child ¥1200/600, attractions extra; ◷10am-10pm; 🚇JR Yamanote line to Ikebukuro, east exit) A giddying exploration of VR-tech to send you bouncing, flying and zooming around the 'future' city.

Tokyo Disney Resort (東京ディズニーリゾート; ☎domestic calls 0570-00-8632, from overseas +81-45-330-5211; www. tokyodisneyresort.jp; 1-1 Maihama, Urayasu-shi, Chiba-ken; day ticket for 1 park adult/child ¥7400/4800, after 6pm ¥4200; ◷varies by season; 🚇JR Keiyō line to Maihama, south exit) One of the first Disney parks outside the US, and still a great day out.

Tokyo Joypolis
TK KURIKAWA / SHUTTERSTOCK ©

Tokyo Dome
Baseball

(東京ドーム; www.tokyo-dome.co.jp; 1-3 Kōraku, Bunkyō-ku; tickets ¥1700-6200; 🚇JR Chūō line to Suidōbashi, west exit) Tokyo Dome (aka

'Big Egg') is home to the Yomiuri Giants. Love 'em or hate 'em, they're the most consistently successful team in Japanese baseball. If you're looking to see the Giants in action, the baseball season runs from the end of March to the end of October. Tickets sell out in advance; get them early at www. giants.jp.

Kabukiza
Theatre

(歌舞伎座; Map p58; ☎03-3545-6800; www. kabukiweb.net; 4-12-15 Ginza, Chūō-ku; tickets ¥4000-20,000, single-act tickets ¥800-2000; 🚇Hibiya line to Higashi-Ginza, exit 3) The flamboyant facade of this venerable theatre is fitting for the extravagant dramatic flourishes that are integral to the traditional performing art of kabuki. Check the website for performance details and to book tickets; you'll also find an explanation about cheaper one-act, day seats.

National Nō Theatre
Theatre

(国立能楽堂, Kokuritsu Nō-gakudō; ☎03-3423-1331; www.ntj.jac.go.jp; 4-18-1 Senda-gaya, Shibuya-ku; adult ¥2700-4900, student ¥1900-2200; 🚇JR Sōbu line to Sendagaya) The traditional music, poetry and dances of nō, Japan's oldest continued mode of performing arts, unfold here on an elegant cypress stage. Each seat has a small screen displaying an English translation of the dialogue. Shows take place only a few times a month and can sell out quickly; purchase tickets online one month in advance.

Robot Restaurant
Cabaret

(ロボットレストラン; ☎03-3200-5500; www.shinjuku-robot.com; 1-7-1 Kabukichō, Shinjuku-ku; tickets ¥8000; ◷shows at 5.55pm, 7.50pm & 9.45pm, additional show at 4pm Fri-Sun; 🚇JR Yamanote line to Shinjuku, east exit) This Kabukichō spectacle has hit it big with its vision of 'wacky Japan': bikini-clad women ride around on giant robots against a backdrop of animated screens and enough LED lights to illuminate all of Shinjuku. You can book ahead online (at full price) or save up to ¥2000 per person by purchasing tickets at the venue if you have a discount flyer (these are available at Tourist Information Centers and Tokyo hotels).

WWW Live Music

(Map p62; ☎03-5458-7685; https://www. shibuya.jp; 13-17 Udagawa-chō, Shibuya-ku; tickets ¥3000-5000; ☒JR Yamanote line to Shibuya, Hachikō exit) In a former art-house cinema with the tell-tale tiered floor still intact, this is one of those rare venues where you could turn up just about any night and hear something good. The line-up varies from indie pop to hip-hop to electronica. Upstairs is WWW X, a bigger space.

Tokyo Bunka Kaikan Classical Music

(東京文化会館; Map p66; ☎03-3828-2111; www. t-bunka.jp; 5-45 Ueno-kōen, Taitō-ku; ☺library 1-8pm Tue-Sat, to 5pm Sun, closed irregularly; ☒JR lines to Ueno, Ueno-kōen exit) The Tokyo Metropolitan Symphony Orchestra and the Tokyo Ballet both make regular appearances at this concrete bunker of a building designed by Maekawa Kunio, an apprentice of Le Corbusier. Prices vary wildly; look out for monthly morning classical-music performances that cost only ¥500. The gorgeously decorated auditorium, with cloud-shaped acoustic panels on the wall, has superb acoustics.

ℹ INFORMATION

DANGERS & ANNOYANCES

The biggest threat to travellers in Tokyo is the city's general aura of safety; keep up the same level of caution and common sense that you would back home.

○ Drink-spiking continues to be a problem in Roppongi (resulting in robbery, extortion and, in extreme cases, physical assault). This is most often the case when touts are involved; never follow a tout into a bar, anywhere.

○ Men are likely to be solicited in Roppongi and neighbourhoods that are considered red-light districts, including Kabukichō (in Shinjuku) and Dōgenzaka (in Shibuya). Women – particularly solo women – are likely to be harassed in these districts.

Robot Restaurant

Tokyo Station

INTERNET ACCESS

Decent wi-fi is standard in Tokyo accommodations (though exceptions exist). The city has an increasing number of free hot spots, which can be found on subway platforms, on the streets of some districts and at many convenience stores, major attractions and shopping centres. Look for the sticker that says 'Japan Wi-Fi'.

TOURIST INFORMATION

At all JR East Travel Service Centers, located at both airports and at JR Tokyo, Shinjuku, Shibuya, Ikebukuro, Ueno and Hamamatsuchō Stations, you can book *shinkansen* (bullet-train) tickets, purchase rail passes or exchange rail-pass vouchers and get tourist information in English. The main branch, at **Tokyo Station** (JR 東日本トラベルサービスセンター; Map p58; ✆03-5221-8123; www.jreast.co.jp; 1-9-1 Marunouchi, Chiyoda-ku; ⊘7.30am-8.30pm; ☏; ☒JR Yamanote line to Tokyo, Marunouchi north exit), also offers currency exchange, same-day baggage storage (¥600), luggage forwarding, and booking services for ski and onsen getaways that are accessed via JR lines

(and with lodgings at partner hotels); bookings can also be made at the Shinjuku branch.

The **Tokyo Metropolitan Government Building Tourist Information Center** (✆03-5321-3077; info@tokyo-tourism.jp; 1st fl, Tokyo Metropolitan Government Bldg 1, 2-8-1 Nishi-Shinjuku, Shinjuku-ku; ⊘9.30am-6.30pm; ⑤Ōedo line to Tochōmae, exit A4) has English-speaking staff and a huge selection of pamphlets and brochures.

❶ GETTING THERE & AWAY

Flights, tours and cars can be booked online at lonelyplanet.com/bookings.

AIR

Tokyo has two international airports. **Narita Airport** (成田空港; NRT; ✆0476-34-8000; www.narita-airport.jp; ☏), in neighbouring Chiba Prefecture, is the primary gateway to Tokyo; most budget flights end up here. **Haneda Airport** (羽田空港; HND; ✆international terminal 03-6428-0888; www.haneda-airport.jp; ☏), on Tokyo Bay and closer to the city centre, is getting an increasing number of international flights; this is also where most domestic flights arrive. Flying into Haneda means quicker and cheaper access to central Tokyo. Both airports have smooth, hassle-free entry procedures, and are connected to the city centre by public transport.

BUS

The easiest port of entry for travellers coming by bus from other parts of Japan is the new **Shinjuku Bus Terminal** (バスタ新宿, Busuta Shinjuku; ☏03-6380-4794; www.shinjuku-busterminal. co.jp; 4th fl, 5-24-55 Sendagaya, Shibuya-ku; 🚆; ☖JR Yamanote line to Shinjuku, new south exit), part of the JR Shinjuku train station complex. There is a tourist information centre on the 3rd floor and direct access to JR rail lines on the 2nd floor. Another long-distance hub is the **JR Highway Bus Terminal** at Tokyo Station.

CAR & MOTORCYCLE

Driving in Tokyo, both on the *shutokō* (the convoluted expressway network) and the narrow lanes of neighbourhoods, can be challenging if you are not already used to driving such roads.

If your destination is a major hotel, arriving by rental car from other parts of Japan is a reasonable option; such hotels will have drop-off lanes and parking facilities (the latter at a cost).

Guesthouses and apartment rentals are often tucked deep in residential districts that are hard to navigate and will not have parking spaces – and may be located on roads so narrow that even brief (illegal) street parking would be tricky.

TRAIN

Tokyo Station (東京駅; Map p58; www.tokyo stationcity.com; 1-9 Marunouchi, Chiyoda-ku; ☖JR lines to Tokyo Station) is the terminus for all *shinkansen* that connect Tokyo to major cities all over Japan. From Tokyo Station you can transfer to the JR Chūō and JR Yamanote lines, as well as the Marunouchi subway line.

Shinkansen from points west (Kansai, western Honshū and Kyūshū) stop at Shinagawa (one stop before Tokyo Station for inbound trains), more useful for destinations in the city's west or south.

Meanwhile, *shinkansen* from points east (Tōhoku and Hokkaidō) will stop at Ueno (one stop before Tokyo Station for inbound trains),

Tokyo by Water

Tokyo is a bayside city bisected by the Sumida-gawa and criss-crossed by a lesser-known system of old canals and waterways. Getting on the water is a refreshing alternative to being stuck on the subway or a coach tour.

Pleasure boats

For a taste of local life, get on board a traditional *yakatabune* (flat-bottomed boat) and join a group of friends or workmates for a floating banquet, lubricated with plenty of beer and sake. Try **Funase** (船清; ☏for bookings 03-5770-5131; www.funasei.com; 1-16-8 Kita-Shinagawa, Shinagawa-ku; per person ¥10,800; ☖Keikyū line to Kita-Shinagawa) or **Tsukishima Monja Yakatabune** (月島もんじゃ屋形船; ☏in Japanese 03-6276-9963; www.4900yen.com; 2-6-3 Shin-Kiba, Kōtō-ku; day/evening from ¥5000/6500, child ¥2700; 🕐noon-10pm; Ⓢ Yūrakuchō line to Shin-Kiba, main exit).

Water Buses & Ferries

Tokyo Cruise (水上バス, Suijō Bus; ☏0120-977-311; www.suijobus.co.jp) and **Tokyo Mizube Cruising Line** (東京水辺ライン; ☏03-5608-8869; www.tokyo-park. or.jp/waterbus) water buses from Asakusa are the cheapest and most convenient way to try a river trip.

River Cruises

Offering a unique perspective of the city, **Nihombashi Cruise** (日本橋クルーズ; ☏03-5679-7311; www.ss3.jp/nihonbashi-cruise; 1 Nihombashi, Chūō-ku; 45/60/90min cruises ¥1500/2000/2500; Ⓢ Ginza line to Mitsukoshimae, exits B5 & B6) runs regular short cruises with commentary.

Kayaking

ZAC (☏03-6671-0201; www.zacsports.com; adult/child ¥5500/4500; Ⓢ Shinjuku line to Higashi-ōshima, Komatsugawa exit) can take you on a 90-minute guided paddle along the Kyunaka-gawa (actually a canal).

more useful for destinations on the city's east or north sides.

Both Shinagawa and Ueno are stops on the JR Yamanote line. From Shinagawa you can also get the Toei Asakusa subway line; from Ueno you can transfer to the Ginza and Hibiya subway lines.

❶ GETTING AROUND

TO/FROM NARITA AIRPORT

BUS

From Tokyo, there's a ticket counter inside the **Shinjuku Bus Terminal** (p83); you can also reserve online up to the day before departure.

Access Narita (www.accessnarita.jp; ¥1000) Discount buses depart roughly every 20 minutes (7.30am to 10.45pm) for Tokyo Station and Ginza (one to 1¼ hours). There's no ticket counter at the airport; go directly to bus stop 31 at Terminal 1, or stops 2 or 19 at Terminal 2, and pay on board. Luggage is restricted to one suitcase up to 20kg.

Friendly Airport Limousine (www.limousine bus.co.jp; adult/child ¥3100/1550) Coaches run to major hotels and train stations in central Tokyo. The journey takes 1½ to two hours depending on traffic. Travellers are allowed two bags up to 30kg each.

TRAIN

Catching a train is the fastest way to get into the city.

Both Japan Railways (JR) and the independent Keisei line run between central Tokyo and Narita Airport Terminals 1 and 2. For Terminal 3, take a train to Terminal 2 and then walk or take the free shuttle bus to Terminal 3 (budget an extra 15 minutes).

Tickets can be purchased upon arrival in the basement of either terminal, where the entrances to the train stations are located; you cannot buy tickets on the train. In general trains run slightly more frequently from the late morning to the late afternoon and less frequently earlier and later.

Seats on **Narita Express** (N'EX; www.jreast. co.jp) and **Keisei Skyliner** (www.keisei.co.jp) trains are all reserved; buy them at a ticket window or from the touch-screen machines.

It's also possible to catch local trains to the airport if you're looking to save cash, but it should be discouraged: it takes a long time, you may have to change trains with your heavy bags up to two or three times, and getting a seat, even outside the almost-all-day rush hours, is by no means guaranteed.

TAXI

Fixed-fare taxis run ¥20,000 to ¥22,000 for most destinations in central Tokyo, plus tolls (about ¥2000 to ¥2500). There's a 20% surcharge between 10pm and 5am. Credit cards accepted.

TO/FROM HANEDA AIRPORT

BUS

Purchase tickets at the kiosks at the arrivals hall. In Tokyo, there's a ticket counter inside the Shinjuku Bus Terminal.

Friendly Airport Limousine (www.limousinebus. co.jp) Coaches connect Haneda with major train stations and hotels in Shibuya (¥1030), Shinjuku (¥1230), Roppongi (¥1130), Ginza (¥930) and others, taking anywhere from 30 to 90 minutes depending on traffic. Buses for Shinjuku depart every 30 to 40 minutes (5am to 11.30pm) and at 12.20am, 1am, 1.40am and 2.20am; departures for other areas are less frequent. Fares double between midnight and 5am.

MONORAIL

Tokyo Monorail (www.tokyo-monorail.co.jp) Leaves approximately every 10 minutes (5am to midnight) for Hamamatsuchō Station (¥490, 15 minutes), which is a stop on the JR Yamanote line. Good for travellers staying near Ginza or Roppongi.

TRAIN

Keikyū Airport Express (www.haneda-tokyo-access.com) Trains depart several times an hour (5.30am to midnight) for Shinagawa (¥410, 12 minutes), where you can connect to the JR Yamanote line. From Shinagawa, some trains continue along the Asakusa subway line, which serves Higashi-Ginza, Nihombashi and Asakusa stations.

Note that the international and domestic terminals have their own stations; when travelling to the airport, the international terminal is the second-last stop.

TAXI

Fixed fares from designated airport taxi stands include Ginza (¥5900), Shibuya (¥6600), Shinjuku (¥7100), Ikebukuro (¥8900) and Asakusa (¥7200), plus highway tolls (around ¥800). There's a 20% surcharge between 10pm and 5am. Credit cards accepted.

BICYCLE

Tokyo is by no means a bicycle-friendly city. Bike lanes are almost nonexistent and you'll see no-parking signs for bicycles everywhere. (Ignore these at your peril: your bike could get impounded, requiring a half-day excursion to the pound and a ¥3000 fee.) Despite all this you'll see locals on bikes everywhere.

Cogi Cogi (www.cogicogi.jp; 24hr ¥2400) A bike-sharing system with ports around the city, including some hostels. There are instructions in English, but it's a little complicated to use. You'll need to download an app, register a credit card and have wi-fi on the go to sync with the ports.

TRAIN & SUBWAY

Tokyo's extensive rail network includes JR lines, a subway system and private commuter lines that depart in every direction for the suburbs, like spokes on a wheel. Journeys that require transfers between lines run by different operators cost more than journeys that use only one operator's lines. Major transit hubs include Tokyo, Shinagawa, Shibuya, Shinjuku, Ikebukuro and Ueno stations. Trains arrive and depart precisely on time and are generally clean and pleasant, though they get uncomfortably crowded during rush hours.

Tokyo has 13 subway lines, nine of which are operated by **Tokyo Metro** (www.tokyometro.jp) and four by **Toei** (www.kotsu.metro.tokyo.jp). The lines are colour-coded, making navigation fairly simple. Unfortunately a transfer ticket is required to change between the two; a Pasmo or Suica card makes this process seamless, but either way a journey involving more than one operator comes out costing slightly more. Rides on Tokyo Metro cost ¥170 to ¥240 (¥90 to ¥120 for children) and on Toei ¥180 to ¥320 (¥90 to ¥160 for children), depending on how far you travel.

Shinjuku

Metro station

DISCOUNT PASSES

If you're planning a packed day, you might consider getting an unlimited-ride ticket.

Tokyo Subway Ticket Good for unlimited rides on both Tokyo Metro and Toei subway lines for 24 (¥800), 48 (¥1200) or 72 (¥1500) hours; half-price for children. This pass is only available to foreign travellers on a tourist visa; for more information and sales points see www.tokyometro.jp.

Tokyo Metro One-Day Open Ticket (adult/child ¥600/300) Unlimited rides over a 24-hour period on Tokyo Metro subway lines only. Purchase at any Tokyo Metro station; no restrictions apply.

KEY ROUTES

Ginza subway line Shibuya to Asakusa, via Ginza and Ueno. Colour-coded orange.

Hibiya subway line Naka-Meguro to Ebisu, Roppongi, Ginza, Akihabara and Ueno. Colour-coded grey.

JR Yamanote line Loop line stopping at many sightseeing destinations, such as Shibuya, Harajuku, Shinjuku, Tokyo and Ueno. Colour-coded light green.

JR Chūō line Express between Tokyo Station and Shinjuku, and onwards to points west. Colour-coded reddish-orange.

JR Sōbu line Runs across the city centre connecting Shinjuku with Iidabashi, Ryōgoku and Akihabara. Colour-coded yellow.

Yurikamome line Elevated train running from Shimbashi to points around Tokyo Bay.

TAXI

Taxis only make economic sense for short distances or groups of four.

o Fares start at ¥410 for the first kilometre, then rise by ¥80 for every 237m you travel or for every 90 seconds spent in traffic.

o Surcharge of 20% between 10pm and 5am.

o Drivers rarely speak English, though most taxis have navigation systems. Have your destination written down in Japanese, or better yet, a business card with an address.

o Taxis take credit cards andrechargeable pay-in-advance IC cards.

Where to Stay

Tokyo is known for being expensive, but more budget and midrange options are popping up every year. As Tokyo is huge, it's smart to zero in on an area where you want to spend significant time.

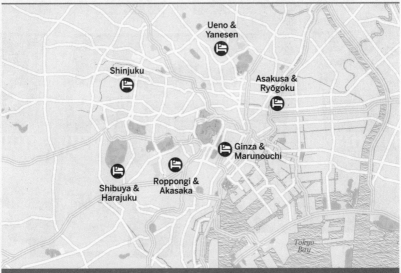

Neighbourhood	Atmosphere
Ginza & Marunouchi	Convenient for all sights and travel out of the city; a major business and commercial district with sky-high prices and relatively quiet weekends.
Roppongi & Akasaka	Nightlife district with lots of eating and drinking options, plus art museums; mix of midrange to high-end hotels; noisy and hectic at night with seedy pockets.
Shibuya & Harajuku	Convenient transport links and plenty of nightlife in Shibuya, with mostly midrange options. Can get extremely crowded.
Shinjuku	Superb transport links, food and nightlife options; very crowded around station areas; cheaper options around the red-light district.
Ueno & Yanesen	Ryokan (traditional Japanese inns) abound; lots of greenery, museums and easy airport access; good for families; the best ryokan tend to be isolated in residential neighbourhoods.
Asakusa & Ryōgoku	Atmospheric old city feel, great budget options and backpacker vibe; can feel quiet at night and far from more central areas.

Bronze *torii* and Yōmei-mon

BORIS-B / SHUTTERSTOCK ©

Nikkō

Ancient moss clinging to stone, perfectly aligned stone lanterns, vermilion gates and towering cedars: Nikkō (日光), a sanctuary holding the glories of the Edo period (1603–1868).

Great For...

☑ Don't Miss

While Tōshō-gū is the star attraction, Taiyūin-byō (p90), built two generations later, is considered more refined.

History

In the middle of the 8th century the Buddhist priest Shōdō Shōnin (735–817) established a hermitage at Nikkō. For centuries the mountains served as a training ground for Buddhist monks, though the area fell gradually into obscurity. Nikkō's enduring fame was sealed, however, when it was chosen as the site for the mausoleum of Tokugawa Ieyasu, the warlord who established the shogunate that ruled Japan for more than 250 years.

Ieyasu was laid to rest among Nikkō's towering cedars at a much less grand Tōshō-gū in 1617. Seventeen years later his grandson, Tokugawa Iemitsu, commenced work on the colossal shrine that can be seen today, using an army of some 15,000 artisans from across Japan who took two years to complete the project.

Gōjūnotō (Five Storey Pagoda)

LEONID ANDRONOV / SHUTTERSTOCK ©

ℹ️ Need to Know

Nikkō, 120km north of Tokyo, is best reached via the Tōbu Nikkō line from Asakusa.

✕ Take a Break

A local speciality is *yuba* (tofu skin) cut into strips; shops all over town sell it.

★ Top Tip

If the crowds get too much for you, seek refuge along the Kanman-ga-Fuchi Abyss (p91).

Tōshō-gū

Under extensive renovation until 2020, a Unesco World Heritage Site in an idyllic natural setting, **Tōshō-gū** (東照宮; www. toshogu.jp; 2301 Sannai; adult/child ¥1300/450; ⏰8am-4.30pm Apr-Oct, to 3.30pm Nov-Mar) is a lavishly ornate Shintō complex within which Tokugawa Ieyasu (1543–1616), the first shogun and founder of the Tokugawa Bakufu (Japan's last feudal military government) is enshrined. Among its standout structures is the dazzling Yōmei-mon; a five-storey pagoda; and the grand **Honji-dō** (本地堂) with its famous 'crying dragon'. Most of what you see was commissioned by Tokugawa's grandson in 1636.

The stone steps of **Omotesandō** lead past the towering stone *torii* (entrance gate), **Ishi-dorii**, and the **Gōjūnotō** (五重塔, Five Storey Pagoda; ¥300), an 1819 reconstruction of the original mid-17th-century pagoda, to **Omote-mon** (表門), Tōshō-gū's main gateway, protected on either side by Deva kings.

In the storehouses of the first courtyard, see if you can find the relief carvings of 'imaginary elephants' by an artist who had never seen the real thing. Then look for the monkey carvings demonstrating three principles of Tendai Buddhism, the allegorical 'hear no evil, see no evil, speak no evil'. There are a number of interesting buildings in the inner courtyards, including the **Yōmei-mon** (陽明門, Sunset Gate), which was reopened in 2017 after restoration of its brilliant gold-leaf decorations.

Within the **Honden** (本殿, Main Hall) and **Haiden** (拝殿, Hall of Worship) of the main courtyard are paintings of the 36 immortal poets of Kyoto, and at least a hundred painted dragons on the ceiling, dating to the Momoyama period.

Walk through the **Sakashita-mon** (坂下門) gate and follow the uphill path beneath

towering cedars to the appropriately sol-
emn **Okumiya** (奥宮), Ieyasu's tomb.

Rinnō-ji

The Tendai-sect temple **Rinnō-ji** (輪王
寺; ☑0288-54-0531; www.rinnoji.or.jp; 2300
Yamanouchi; adult/child ¥400/200; ◷8am-5pm
Apr-Oct, to 4pm Nov-Mar) was founded 1200
years ago by Shōdō Shōnin. The main hall
(Sanbutsu-dō) houses a trio of 8m gilded
wooden Buddha statues: Amida Nyorai
(a primal deity in the Mahayana Buddhist
canon) flanked by Senjū (deity of mercy
and compassion) and Batō (a horse-
headed Kannon).

Rinnō-ji's **Hōmotsu-den** (宝物殿, Treasure
Hall; ¥300) houses some 6000 treasures
associated with the temple; the separate
admission ticket includes entrance to the

Shōyō-en (逍遥園; in combination with
Hōmotsu-den ¥300) strolling garden.

You can buy a combination ticket that
covers entry to Rinnō-ji and Taiyūin-byō for
¥900.

Taiyūin-byō

Ieyasu's grandson Iemitsu (1604–51) is
buried at **Taiyūin-byō** (大猷院廟; adult/
child ¥550/250; ◷8am-4.30pm Apr-Oct, to
3.30pm Nov-Mar), and although the shrine
houses many of the same elements as
Tōshō-gū (drum tower, Chinese-style gates
etc), the more intimate scale, lighter tourist
footfall and gorgeous setting in a cryptomeria forest make it hugely appealing.

Look for dozens of lanterns donated by
daimyō (domain lords), and the gate **Niō-
mon**, whose guardian deities have a hand
up (to welcome those with pure hearts)

Nikkō railway station

and a hand down (to suppress those with impure hearts).

Kanman-ga-Fuchi Abyss

Escape the crowds along Kanman-ga-Fuchi Abyss (憾満ガ淵), a riverside path lined with a collection of Jizō statues, the small stone effigies of the Buddhist protector of travellers and children. It's said that if you try to count the statues there and again on the way back, you'll end up with a different number, hence the nickname 'Bake-jizō' (ghost Jizō). To find it, follow the Daiya-gawa west for about 1km from the Shin-kyo bridge, crossing another bridge near Jyoko-ji temple en route.

Getting There & Away

Nikkō is best reached from Tokyo via the Tōbu Nikkō line from Asakusa Station. You can usually get last-minute seats on the hourly reserved *tokkyū* (limited-express) trains (¥2800, 1¾ hours). *Kaisoku* (rapid) trains (¥1360, 2½ hours, hourly from 6.20am to 5.30pm) require no reservation, but you may have to change at Shimo-imaichi. Be sure to ride in the last two cars to reach Nikkō (some cars may separate at an intermediate stop).

JR Pass holders can take the Tōhoku *shinkansen* (bullet train) from Tokyo to Utsunomiya (¥4930, 50 minutes) and change there for an ordinary train to Nikkō (¥760, 45 minutes).

Station Design

Built in 1890, JR Nikkō station was designed by prolific American architect Frank Lloyd Wright (www.franklloyd wright.org).

ANOTAI V / SHUTTERSTOCK ©

★ Did You Know?

The much-photographed red footbridge **Shin-kyō** (神橋; adult/child ¥300/100; ☺8am-4.15pm) is where Shōdō Shōnin is said to have been carried across the Daiya-gawa on the backs of two giant serpents.

KYOTO

Kyoto at a Glance...

Kyoto is old Japan writ large: quiet temples, sublime gardens, colourful shrines and geisha scurrying to secret liaisons. With 17 Unesco World Heritage Sites, and more than 1000 Buddhist temples and 400 Shintō shrines, it is one of the world's most culturally rich cities. But Kyoto is not just about sightseeing. While the rest of Japan has adopted modernity with abandon, the old ways are still clinging on in Kyoto. Visit an old shōtengai (market street) and admire the ancient speciality shops: tofu sellers, washi (Japanese handmade paper) stores and tea merchants.

Two Days in Kyoto

Start your Kyoto experience in Southern Higashiyama, home to famous temples **Kiyomizu-dera** (p110) and **Chion-in** (p110). In the afternoon follow the **Path of Philosophy** (p114) to **Ginkaku-ji** (p113) in Northern Higashiyama. On the second day, visit stunning **Kinkaku-ji** (p102) and the **Ryōan-ji** (p103) Zen garden, then taxi to Arashiyama. End with an evening stroll through the historic geisha district, **Gion** (p99).

Four Days in Kyoto

With four days, we recommend doing the above in three days, to give yourself time to explore smaller sights en route and soak up the atmosphere. On the fourth day, stroll around downtown, hitting the excellent **Nishiki Market** (p106), craft shops and department stores and picnicking in **Kyoto Imperial Palace Park** (p107).

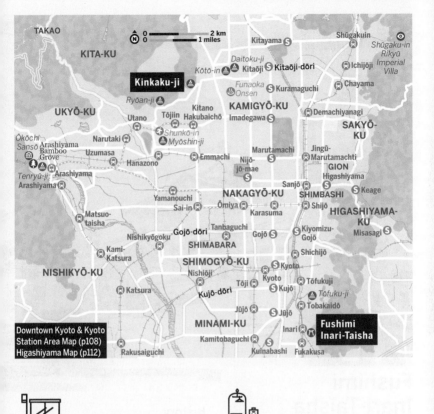

Downtown Kyoto & Kyoto
Station Area Map (p108)
Higashiyama Map (p112)

Arriving in Kyoto

The closest major airport is Kansai International Airport, about 75 minutes away from Kyoto by direct express train. Kyoto Station, in the south of the city, is served by the Tōkaidō *shinkansen* (bullet train), several JR main lines and a few private rail lines. The easiest way to get downtown from this station is to hop on the Karasuma subway line.

Where to Stay

From the cheapest dorms to the priciest ryokan (traditional Japanese inns), Kyoto has it all. You're limited only by budget and room availability. Good-value propositions can be found around the station, and the best ryokan are throughout Higashiyama and in the hills of Arashiyama. When Kyoto is jammed, nearby Osaka is a great Plan B.

For more information on best sleeping neighbourhoods, see p131.

TAKASHI IMAGES / SHUTTERSTOCK ©

Fushimi Inari-Taisha

With seemingly endless arcades of vermilion torii *(shrine gates) across a thickly wooded mountain, this vast complex is a world unto itself. One of the most impressive and memorable sights in Kyoto.*

Great For...

☑ Don't Miss

The classic photo op from inside the tunnel of *torii*.

History

Fushimi Inari-Taisha was dedicated to the gods of rice and sake by the Hata family in the 8th century. As the role of agriculture diminished, deities were enrolled to ensure prosperity in business. Nowadays the shrine is one of Japan's most popular, and is the head shrine for some 40,000 Inari shrines scattered the length and breadth of the country.

Messenger of Inari

As you explore the shrine, you will come across hundreds of stone foxes. The fox is considered the messenger of Inari, the god of cereals, and the stone foxes, too, are often referred to as 'Inari'. The key often seen

PATRYK KOSMIDER / SHUTTERSTOCK ©

❶ Need to Know

伏見稲荷大社; 68 Yabunouchi-chō, Fukaku-sa, Fushimi-ku; ☉dawn-dusk; ⓡJR Nara line to Inari or Keihan line to Fushimi-Inari; FREE

✗ Take a Break

Vermillion (バーミリオン; www.vermillion cafe.com; 85 Onmae-chō, Fukakusa-inari, Fushimi-ku; ☉9am-5pm; 🛜) has excellent coffee and cakes.

★ Top Tip

Don't be afraid to get lost – that's part of the fun at Fushimi.

in the fox's mouth is for the rice granary. On an incidental note, the Japanese tradition-ally see the fox as a sacred, somewhat mysterious figure capable of 'possessing' humans – the favoured point of entry is under the fingernails.

Hiking the Grounds

A pathway wanders 4km up the mountain and is lined with dozens of atmospheric subshrines. The walk around the upper pre-cincts is a pleasant day hike. It also makes for a very eerie stroll in the late afternoon and early evening, when the various grave-yards and miniature shrines along the path take on a mysterious air. It's best to go with a friend at this time.

What's Nearby?

Tōfuku-ji   Buddhist Temple

(東福寺; ☎075-561-0087; www.tofukuji.jp; 15-778 Honmahi, Higashiyama-ku; Hōjō garden ¥400, Tsūten-kyō bridge ¥400; ☉9am-4pm; ⓡKeihan line or JR Nara line to Tōfukuji) Home to a spec-tacular garden, several superb structures and beautiful precincts, Tōfuku-ji is one of the best temples in Kyoto. The present temple complex includes 24 subtemples. The huge **San-mon** is the oldest Zen main gate in Japan, the **Hōjō** (Abbot's Hall) was reconstructed in 1890, and the gardens were laid out in 1938.

The northern garden has moss and stonesthat are neatly arranged in a checkerboard pattern. From a viewing platform at the back of the gardens you can observe the **Tsūten-kyō** (Bridge to Heaven), which spans a valley filled with maple trees.

FILIPPOBACCI / GETTY IMAGES ©

Kyoto's Geisha Culture

Though dressed in the finest silks and often astonishingly beautiful, geisha are first and foremost accomplished musicians and dancers. These now-rare creatures – seemingly lifted from another world – still entertain in Kyoto today.

Great For...

☑ Don't Miss
A stroll through Gion at night.

Geiko & Maiko

The word geisha literally means 'arts person'; in Kyoto the term used is *geiko* – 'child of the arts'. It is the *maiko* (apprentice *geiko*) who are spotted on city streets in ornate dress, long trailing obi and towering wooden clogs, their faces painted with thick white make-up, leaving only a suggestive forked tongue of bare flesh on the nape of the neck. As geisha grow older their make-up becomes increasingly natural; by then their artistic accomplishments need no fine casing. At their peak in the 1920s, there were around 80,000 geisha in Japan. Today there are approximately 1000 (including apprentices), with nearly half working in Kyoto.

Maiko (apprentice *geiko*)

with a *danna* (patron) with whom the geisha would enter a contractual relationship not unlike a marriage (and one that could be terminated). A wealthy *danna* could help a woman fulfil her debt to the *okiya* or help her start her own. Other geisha married, which required them to leave the profession; some were adopted by the *okiya* and inherited the role of house mother; still others worked into old age.

Today's geisha begin their training no earlier than their teens – perhaps after being inspired by a school trip to Kyoto – while completing their compulsory education (in Japan, until age 15). Then they'll leave home for an *okiya* (they do still exist) and start work as an apprentice. While in the past a *maiko* would never be seen out and about in anything but finery, today's apprentices act much like ordinary teens in their downtime. For some, the magic is in the *maiko* stage and they never proceed to become geisha; those who do live largely normal lives, free to live where they choose, date as they like and change professions when they please.

Life of a Geisha Then & Now

Prior to the mid-20th century, a young girl might arrive at an *okiya* (geisha living quarters) to work as a maid. Should she show promise, the owner of the *okiya* would send her to begin training at the *kaburenjo* (school for geisha arts) at around age six. She would continue maid duty, waiting on the senior geisha of the house, while honing her skills and eventually specialising in one of the arts, such as playing the *shamisen* (three-stringed instrument resembling a lute or a banjo) or dance.

Geisha were often indebted to the *okiya* who covered their board and training. Given the lack of bargaining chips that have been afforded women in history, there is no doubt that many geisha of the past, at some point in their careers, engaged in compensated relationships; this would be

Hanamachi

Traditionally, the districts where geisha were licensed to entertain in *ochaya* (teahouses) were called *hanamachi*, which means 'flower town'. Of the five that remain in Kyoto, **Gion** (祇園周辺; Map p112; Higashiyama-ku; S Tōzai line to Sanjō, R Keihan line to Gion-Shijō), is the grandest. Many of

Kyoto's most upmarket restaurants and exclusive hostess bars are here.

On the other side of the river, **Ponto-chō** (先斗町; Map p108; Nakagyō-ku; ⑤Tōzai line to Sanjo-Keihan or Kyoto-Shiyakusho-mae, 🚊Keihan line to Sanjo, Hankyū line to Kawaramachi) has a very different feel, with very narrow lanes. Not much to look at by day, the street comes alive at night, with wonderful lanterns, traditional wooden exteriors, and elegant Kyotoites disappearing into the doorways of elite old restaurants and bars.

Experiencing Geisha Culture

Modern *maiko* and geisha entertain their clients in exclusive restaurants, banquet halls and traditional *ochaya* much like they did a century ago. This world is largely off limits to travellers, as a personal connection is required to get a foot in the door,

though some tour operators can act as mediator. Of course, these experiences can cost hundreds of dollars (if not more).

Ryokan Gion Hatanaka offers a rare chance to witness geisha perform and then interact with them. The inn's **Kyoto Cuisine & Maiko Evening** (ぎおん畑中; Map p112; ☑075-541-5315; www.kyoto-maiko.jp; 505 Gion-machi, Minami-gawa, Higashiyama-ku; per person ¥19,000; ☺6-8pm Mon, Wed, Fri & Sat; 🚌Kyoto City bus 206 to Gion or Chionin-mae, 🚊Keihan line to Gion-Shijō) is a regularly scheduled evening of elegant Kyoto *kaiseki* (haute cuisine) food and personal entertainment by both Kyoto *geiko* and *maiko*.

Geisha Dances

An excellent way to experience geisha culture is to see one of Kyoto's *odori* (annual public dance performances), a city tradi-

Geikos and *maikos* performing at Miyako Odori

tion for over a century. Get tickets as early as you can; your accommodation might be able to help.

Gion Odori (祇園をどり; Map p112; ☎075-561-0224; Gion, Higashiyama-ku; with/without tea ¥4500/4000; ☉shows 1.30pm & 4pm; ☒Kyoto City bus 206 to Gion) From 1 to 10 November, at the Gion Kaikan Theatre (祇園会館).

Kyō Odori (京おどり; Map p112; ☎075-561-1151; Miyagawachō Kaburenjo, 4-306 Miyagawasuji, Higashiyama-ku; with/without tea from ¥2800/2200; ☉shows 1pm, 2.45pm & 4.30pm; ☒Keihan line to Gion-Shijō) Put on by the

Photographing Geisha

A photo of a *maiko* is a much-coveted Kyoto souvenir; however bear in mind that these are young women – many of whom are minors – on their way to work. Be respectful and let them pass.

Miyagawa-chō geisha district, this wonderful geisha dance is among the most picturesque performances of the Kyoto year. It's held from the first to the third Sunday in April at the Miyagawa-chō Kaburen-jō Theatre (宮川町歌舞練場), east of the Kamo-gawa between Shijō-dōri and Gojō-dōri.

Miyako Odori (都をどり; Map p112; ☎075-541-3391; www.miyako-odori.jp; Gion Kōbu Kaburen-jō Theatre, 570-2 Gion-machi, Minami-gawa, Higashiyama-ku; tickets from ¥4000; ☉shows 12.30pm, 2.20pm & 4.10pm; ☒Kyoto City bus 206 to Gion, ☒Keihan line to Gion-Shijō) This 45-minute dance is a wonderful geisha performance. It's a real stunner and the colourful images are mesmerising. It's held throughout April, usually at Gion Kōbu Kaburen-jō Theatre. The building is under ongoing renovations until around 2021 and performances will be held at Minamiza (p128) in the meantime.

Kamogawa Odori (鴨川をどり; Map p108; ☎075-221-2025; Ponto-chō, Sanjō-sagaru, Nakagyō-ku; seat ¥2300, special seat with/without tea ¥4800/4200; ☉shows 12.30pm, 2.20pm & 4.10pm; ☒Tōzai line to Kyoto-Shiyakusho-mae) From 1 to 24 May at Ponto-chō Kaburen-jō Theatre.

Maiko Makeover

Ever wondered how you might look as a *maiko*? Give it a try at **Maika** (舞香; Map p112; ☎075-551-1661; www.maica.tv; 297 Miyagawa suji 4-chōme, Higashiyama-ku; maiko/geisha from ¥6500/8000; ☒Keihan line to Gion-Shijo or Kiyomizu-Gojo) in the Gion. Prices begin at ¥6500 for the basic treatment, which includes full make-up and formal kimono. If you don't mind spending some extra yen, it's possible to head out in costume for a stroll through Gion (and be stared at like never before!). The process takes about an hour. Call to reserve at least one day in advance.

BULE SKY STUDIO / SHUTTERSTOCK ©

Kinkaku-ji

Kyoto's famed 'Golden Pavilion', Kinkaku-ji is one of Japan's best-known sights. The main hall, covered in brilliant gold leaf, shining above its reflecting pond is truly spectacular.

Great For...

☑ Don't Miss

The mirror-like reflection of the temple in the Kyō-ko pond is extremely photogenic.

History

Originally built in 1397 as a retirement villa for shogun Ashikaga Yoshimitsu, Kinkaku-ji was converted to a Buddhist temple by his son in compliance with his wishes. In 1950 a young monk consummated his obsession with the temple by burning it to the ground. The monk's story is fictionalised in Mishima Yukio's 1956 novel *The Temple of the Golden Pavilion*. In 1955 a full reconstruction was completed, following the original design but extending the gold-foil covering to the lower floors.

The Pavilion & Grounds

The three-storey pavilion, covered in bright gold leaf with a bronze phoenix on top of the roof, is naturally the highlight. But there's more to this temple than its shiny main hall. Don't miss the Ryūmon-taki

Kinkaku-ji
🔺 *Ryōan-ji*

Utano Ryōanji Tōjiin Kitano
Narutaki Omura- Myōshinji Hakubaichō
Ninnaji *Myōshin-ji*

❶ Need to Know

金閣寺; 1 Kinkakuji-chō, Kita-ku; adult/child ¥400/300; ⊗9am-5pm; 🚌Kyoto City bus 205 from Kyoto Station to Kinkakuji-michi, 🚌Kyoto City bus 12 from Sanjō-Keihan to Kinkakuji-michi

✕ Take a Break

A small tea garden near the entrance serves *matcha* (powdered green tea) and sweets.

★ Top Tip

Avoid crowds by going early or late in the day, ideally on a weekday.

waterfall and Rigyo-seki stone, which looks like a carp attempting to swim up the falls. Nearby, there is a small gathering of stone Jizō figures onto which people throw coins and make wishes. The quaint teahouse Sekka-tei embodies the *wabi-sabi* (rustic simplicity) aesthetic of the Japanese tea ceremony.

What's Nearby?

Ryōan-ji   Buddhist Temple

(龍安寺; www.ryoanji.jp; 13 Goryōnoshitama-chi, Ryōan-ji, Ukyō-ku; adult/child ¥500/300; ⊗8am-5pm Mar-Nov, 8.30am-4.30pm Dec-Feb; 🚌Kyoto City bus 59 from Sanjō-Keihan to Ryoan-ji-mae) You've probably seen a picture of the rock garden here – it's one of the symbols of Kyoto and one of Japan's better-known sights. Ryōan-ji belongs to the Rinzai school of Zen Buddhism and was founded

in 1450. The garden, an oblong of sand with an austere collection of 15 carefully placed rocks, apparently adrift in a sea of sand, is enclosed by an earthen wall. The designer, who remains unknown to this day, provided no explanation.

An early-morning visit on a weekday is probably your best hope of seeing the garden free from the ever-present crowds.

Myōshin-ji   Buddhist Temple

(妙心寺; www.myoshinji.or.jp; 1 Myoshin-ji-chō, Hanazono, Ukyō-ku; main temple free, other areas of complex adult/child ¥500/100; ⊗9.10-11.40am & 1-4.40pm, to 3.40pm Nov-Feb; 🚌Kyoto City bus 10 from Sanjo-Keihan to Myōshin-ji Kita-mon-mae) Myōshin-ji is a separate world within Kyoto, a walled-off complex of temples and subtemples that invites lazy strolling. The subtemple of **Taizō-in** here contains one of the city's more-interesting gardens. Myōshin-ji dates to 1342 and belongs to the Rinzai school.

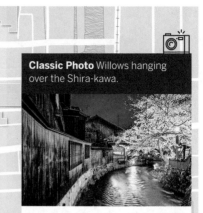

Classic Photo Willows hanging over the Shira-kawa.

Night Walk Through the Floating World

Gion is Kyoto's famous entertainment and geisha quarter. Take an evening stroll through the atmospheric streets, lined with 17th-century restaurants and teahouses lit up with lanterns.

Start Yasaka-jinja
Distance 3km
Duration 2 hours

4 At the fork in the road is the small Tatsumi shrine; take a left and walk west along the **Shira-kawa**.

7 End with a stroll through Kyoto's cosiest entertainment strip, **Ponto-chō** (p100).

SHIMBASHI

Nawate-dōri

Kiyamachi-dōri

Ponto-chō

Kamo-gawa

Shimbashi-dōri

4

GION

Shijō-dōri

7 FINISH

Kawaramachi

6

5

Gion-Shijo

5 Back on Shijō-dōri, you'll pass Kyoto's grand old kabuki theatre, **Minamiza** (p128).

6 Cross Kyoto's principle river, the **Kamo-gawa**, which runs through the heart of the city.

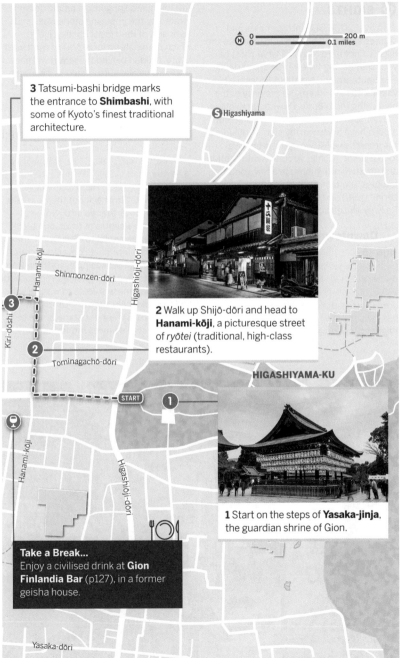

0 ——————— 200 m
0 ——————— 0.1 miles

Ⓢ Higashiyama

3 Tatsumi-bashi bridge marks the entrance to **Shimbashi**, with some of Kyoto's finest traditional architecture.

Shinmonzen-dōri

Hanami-kōji

Higashiōji-dōri

Kiri-dōshi

③

②

Tominagachō-dōri

2 Walk up Shijō-dōri and head to **Hanami-kōji**, a picturesque street of *ryōtei* (traditional, high-class restaurants).

HIGASHIYAMA-KU

START ①

Hanami-kōji

Higashiōji-dōri

1 Start on the steps of **Yasaka-jinja**, the guardian shrine of Gion.

Take a Break...
Enjoy a civilised drink at **Gion Finlandia Bar** (p127), in a former geisha house.

Yasaka-dōri

⊙ SIGHTS

With over 2000 Buddhist temples and shrines scattered over the city and into the hills, it's not hard to guess what most of your sightseeing time will be spent doing. The Southern and Northern Higashi-yama areas are where the majority of the big-hitting temples lie. Downtown Kyoto is the hot spot for shopping and dining, but it does have a few worthy sights, including the impressive Nijō-jō and the famous food market, Nishiki. Around Kyoto Station and south Kyoto, there are a few good temples, the famous Fushimi Inari-Taisha shrine (p96) and the excellent Kyoto Railway Museum.

⊙ Downtown Kyoto

Nijō-jō
Castle

(二条城; Map p108; 541 Nijōjō-chō, Nijō-dōri, Horikawa nishi-iru, Nakagyō-ku; adult/child ¥600/200; ⊙8.45am-5pm, last entry 4pm, closed Tue Dec, Jan, Jul & Aug; ⑤Tōzai line to Nijō-jō-mae, ⑤JR line to Nijō) The military might of Japan's great warlord generals,

the Tokugawa shoguns, is amply demonstrated by the imposing stone walls and ramparts of their great castle, Nijō-jō, which dominates a large part of northwest Kyoto. Hidden behind these you will find a superb palace surrounded by beautiful gardens. Avoid crowds by visiting the castle just after opening or shortly before closing.

Nishiki Market
Market

(錦市場; Map p108; Nishikikōji-dōri, btwn Teramachi & Takakura, Nakagyō-ku; ⊙9am-5pm; ⑤Karasuma line to Shijō, ⑤Hankyū line to Karasuma or Kawaramachi) Head to the covered Nishiki Market to check out the weird and wonderful foods that go into Kyoto cuisine. It's in the centre of town, one block north of (and parallel to) Shijō-dōri, running west off Teramachi covered arcade. Wander past stalls selling everything from barrels of *tsukemono* (pickled vegetables) and cute Japanese sweets to wasabi salt and fresh sashimi skewers. Drop into Aritsugu (p118) here for some of the best Japanese chef's knives money can buy.

Nishiki Market

Daitoku-ji
Buddhist Temple

(大徳寺; 53 Daitokuji-chō, Murasakino, Kita-ku;
🚌Kyoto City bus 205 or 206 to Daitokuji-mae,
🚇Karasuma line to Kitaōji) For anyone with
the slightest fondness for Japanese
gardens, don't miss this network of lanes
dotted with atmospheric Zen temples.
Daitoku-ji, the main temple here, serves
as headquarters for the Rinzai Daitoku-ji
school of Zen Buddhism. It's not usually
open to the public but there are several
subtemples with superb carefully raked
kare-sansui (dry landscape) gardens well
worth making the trip out for. Highlights
include **Daisen-in** (大仙院; 54-1 Daitokuji-chō;
adult/child ¥400/270; ⊙9am-5pm Mar-Nov, to
4.30pm Dec-Feb), Kōtō-in (p109), **Ryōgen-
in** (龍源院; ☎075-491-7635; 82-1 Daitokuji-chō;
adult/child ¥350/200; ⊙9am-4.30pm) and
Zuihō-in (瑞峯院; ☎075-491-1454; 81 Daitokuji-chō; adult/child ¥400/300; ⊙9am-5pm
Mar-Nov, to 4.30pm Dec-Feb).

Kyoto Imperial Palace
Historic Building

(京都御所, Kyoto Gosho; Map p108; ☎075-
211-1215; www.kunaicho.go.jp; Kyoto Gyōen,
Kamigyō-ku; ⊙9am-4.30pm Tue-Sun Mar-Sep,
to 4pm Oct-Feb, last entry 40min before closing;
🚇Karasuma line to Marutamachi or Imadegawa)
FREE The Kyoto Imperial Palace, known
as the 'Gosho' in Japanese, is a walled
complex situated in the middle of the
Kyoto Imperial Palace Park (京都御苑;
⊙dawn-dusk) **FREE**.

While this is no longer the official
residence of the Japanese emperor, it's
still a grand edifice, though it doesn't rate
highly in comparison with other attractions in Kyoto. Visitors can wander around
the marked route in the grounds where
English-language signs explain the history
of the buildings. Entrance is via the main
Seishomon Gate of the palace, where you
will be given a map.

Sentō Imperial Palace
Historic Building

(仙洞御所, Sentō Gosho; Map p108; ☎075-
211-1215; www.kunaicho.go.jp; Kyoto Gyōen,
Kamigyō-ku; ⊙tours 9.30am, 11am, 1.30pm,

Kyoto's Machiya

One of the city's most notable architectural features are its *machiya,* long and
narrow wooden row houses that func-
tioned as both homes and workplaces.
The shop area was located in the front of
the house, while the rooms lined up behind it formed the family's private living
quarters. Although well suited to Kyoto's
humid, mildew-prone summers, a
wooden *machiya* has a limited lifespan of
about 50 years. In modern times, they've
also been up against the increasing costs
of traditional materials and workmanship
and the siren call of low-maintenance
concrete. Many owners have replaced
their *machiya* with seven-storey apartment buildings; occupying the ground
floor, they can live off the rent of their
tenants. The result is that Kyoto's urban
landscape – once a harmonious sea of
clay-tiled two-storey wooden townhous-
es – is now a jumble of ferro-concrete
offices and apartment buildings.

However, *machiya* are making
a comeback. After their numbers
drastically declined, the old townhous-
es began to acquire an almost exotic
appeal. Astute developers began to
convert them into restaurants, clothing
boutiques and even hair salons. Today
such shops are a major draw for the
city's tourist trade, and not only foreign
visitors – the Japanese themselves
(especially Tokyoites) – love their
old-fashioned charm.

Machiya, Gion
EVERGREENPLANET / SHUTTERSTOCK ©

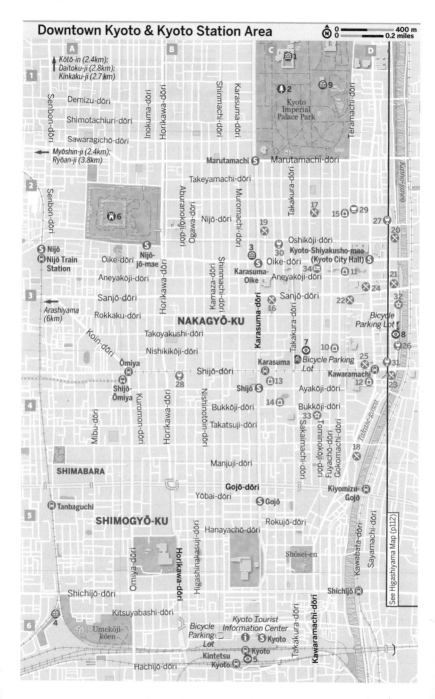

Downtown Kyoto & Kyoto Station Area

Kōtō-in (2.4km);
Daitoku-ji (2.8km);
Kinkaku-ji (2.7 km)

Senbon-dōri

Demizu-dōri

Shimotachiuri-dōri

Sawaragichō-dōri

Myōshin-ji (2.4km);
Ryōan-ji (3.8km)

Inokuma-dōri

Horikawa-dōri

Shinmachi-dōri

Karasuma-dōri

Kyoto
Imperial
Palace Park

Teramachi-dōri

Kamo-gawa

Marutamachi ⑤ Marutamachi-dōri

Senbon-dōri

Takeyamachi-dōri

Aburanokōji-dōri

Ōmeya-dōri

Muromachi-dōri

Nijō-dōri

⑥ 6

Takakura-dōri

17 ⑧   15 ⑭ ⑨ 29

⑤ Nijō
⑭ Nijō Train
Station

Arashiyama
(6km)

Oike-dōri

Shinmachi-dōri

Nijō-
jō-mae ⑤

19 ⑧

27 ⑭

20 ⑧

Oshikōji-dōri

3 ⑧ 30 Kyoto-Shiyakusho-mae
⑤ Oike-dōri (Kyoto City Hall) ⑤

Aneyakōji-dōri

Karasuma-
Oike

Aneyakōji-dōri

34 ⑨

⑩ 11

21 ⑧

Kōin-dōri

Sanjō-dōri

Rokkaku-dōri

Takoyakushi-dōri

Nishikikōji-dōri

Horikawa-dōri

Karasuma-dōri

Shinmachi-dōri

NAKAGYŌ-KU

16 ⑧

Sanjō-dōri

Takakura-dōri

22 ⑧

Bicycle
Parking Lot ⑧

32 ⑧

⑧ 8

7 ⑧
⑧ 10 ⑨

⑨ 26

Ōmiya ⑮

Karasuma ⑤ Bicycle Parking
Lot

25 ⑧

31 ⑭

Shijō-dōri

Kuromon-dōri

Shijō-
Ōmiya

Mibu-dōri

Horikawa-dōri

Nishinotōin-dōri

28 ⑮

Shijō ⑤

⑩ 13

Shijō ⑤

14 ⑨

Ayakōji-dōri

Kawaramachi

12 ⑨

23 ⑧

Bukkōji-dōri

Takatsuji-dōri

Bukkōji-dōri

33 ☆

Sakaimachi-dōri

Tominokōji-dōri

Fuyachō-dōri

Gokomachi-dōri

18 ⑧

Manjuji-dōri

SHIMABARA

Gojō-dōri

Yōbai-dōri

⑤ Gojō

Kiyomizu-
Gojō ⑭

⑭ Tanbaguchi

SHIMOGYŌ-KU

Hanayachō-dōri

Higashinakasuji-dōri

Rokujō-dōri

Sayamachi-dōri

Kawabata-dōri

Shōsei-en

See Higashiyama Map (p112)

Omiya-dōri

Horikawa-dōri

Shichijō-dōri

Shichijō ⑭

Kitsuyabashi-dōri

⑭ 4

Umekōji-
kōen

Bicycle
Parking
Lot

Kyoto Tourist
Information Center
ⓘ ⑤ Kyoto

Takakura-dōri

Kawaramachi-dōri

Kintetsu
Kyoto ⑤

Kyoto ⑤ 5

Hachijō-dōri

Downtown Kyoto & Kyoto Station Area

2.30pm & 3.30pm Tue-Sun; **S**Karasuma line to Marutamachi or Imadegawa) **FREE** The Sentō Gosho is the second imperial property that is located within the Kyoto Imperial Palace Park (the other one is the Imperial Palace itself). The structures are not particularly grand, but the gardens, which were laid out in 1630 by renowned landscape designer Kobori Enshū, are excellent. Admission is by one-hour tour only (in Japanese; English audio guides are free). You must be over 18 years old and bring your passport. Your ticket can be printed or shown on a smartphone.

Kōtō-in   Buddhist Temple
(高桐院; 73-1 Daitokuji-chō, Murasakino, Kita-ku; ¥400; ◷9am-4.30pm; ⒜Kyoto City bus 205 or 206 to Daitokuji-mae, **S**Karasuma line to Kitaōji) On the far western edge of the Daitoku-ji complex (p107), the sublime garden of this subtemple is one of the best in Kyoto and worth a special trip. It's located within a fine bamboo grove that you traverse via a moss-lined path. Once inside there is a small stroll garden that leads to the cen-

trepiece: a rectangle of moss and maple trees, backed by bamboo. Take some time to relax on the verandah here to soak it all up.

Kyoto International
Manga Museum   Museum
(京都国際マンガミュージアム; Map p108; www.kyotomm.jp; Karasuma-dōri, Oike-agaru, Nakagyō-ku; adult/child ¥800/100; ◷10am-6pm Tue-Thu; ⊞; **S**Karasuma or Tōzai lines to Karasuma-Oike) Located in an old elementary school building, this museum is the perfect introduction to the art of manga (Japanese comics). It has 300,000 manga in its collection, 50,000 of which are on display in the *Wall of Manga* exhibit. While most of the manga and displays are in Japanese, the collection of translated works is growing. In addition to the galleries that show both the historical development of manga and original artwork done in manga style, there are beginners' workshops and portrait drawings on weekends.

Visitors with children will appreciate the children's library and the occasional

Kyoto's Top Temples

Nanzen-ji (p113)

Ginkaku-ji (p113)

Kinkaku-ji (p102)

Kiyomizu-dera (p110)

Shōren-in (p110)

From left: Nanzen-ji (p113); Ginkaku-ji (p113); Kiyomizu-dera

performances of *kami-shibai* (humorous traditional Japanese sliding-picture shows), not to mention the artificial lawn where the kids can run free. The museum hosts six-month-long special exhibits yearly: check the website for details.

Southern Higashiyama

Kiyomizu-dera   Buddhist Temple

(清水寺; Map p112; ☎075-551-1234; www.kiyomizudera.or.jp; 1-294 Kiyomizu, Higashiyama-ku; adult/child ¥400/200; ☺6am-6pm, closing times vary seasonally; ☒Kyoto City bus 206 to Kiyomizu-michi or Gojō-zaka, ☒Keihan line to Kiyomizu-Gojō) A buzzing hive of activity perched on a hill overlooking the basin of Kyoto, Kiyomizu-dera is one of Kyoto's most popular and most enjoyable temples. It may not be a tranquil refuge, but it represents the favoured expression of faith in Japan. The excellent website is a great first port of call for information on the temple, plus a how-to guide to praying here. Note that the Main Hall is undergoing renovations and may be covered, but is still accessible.

Shōren-in   Buddhist Temple

(青蓮院; Map p112; 69-1 Sanjōbō-chō, Awata-guchi, Higashiyama-ku; adult/child ¥500/free; ☺9am-5pm; ☒Tōzai line to Higashiyama) This temple is hard to miss, with its giant camphor trees growing just outside the walls. Fortunately, most tourists march right on past, heading to the area's more famous temples. That's their loss, because this intimate little sanctuary contains a superb landscape garden, which you can enjoy while drinking a cup of green tea (¥500; ask at the reception office, not available in summer).

Chion-in   Buddhist Temple

(知恩院; Map p112; www.chion-in.or.jp; 400 Rinka-chō, Higashiyama-ku; adult/child ¥500/250, grounds free; ☺9am-4.30pm, last entry 3.50pm; ☒Tōzai line to Higashiyama) A collection of soaring buildings, spacious courtyards and gardens, Chion-in serves as the headquarters of the Jōdo sect, the largest school of Buddhism in Japan. It's the most popular pilgrimage temple in Kyoto and it's always a hive of activity. For visitors with a taste for the grand, this temple is sure to satisfy.

EVERYTHING / SHUTTERSTOCK ©

Kōdai-ji — Buddhist Temple

(高台寺; Map p112; ☎075-561-9966; www.
kodaiji.com; 526 Shimokawara-chō, Kōdai-ji,
Higashiyama-ku; adult/child ¥600/250; ⊙9am-
5.30pm; ☐Kyoto City bus 206 to Yasui, ⑤Tōzai
line to Higashiyama) This exquisite temple
was founded in 1605 by Kita-no-Mandokoro
in memory of her late husband, Toyotomi
Hideyoshi. The extensive grounds include
gardens designed by the famed landscape
architect Kobori Enshū, and teahouses
designed by the renowned master of the
tea ceremony, Sen no Rikyū. The ticket
also allows entry to the small Sho museum
across the road from the entrance to
Kōdai-ji.

Kyoto National Museum — Museum

(京都国立博物館; Map p112; www.kyohaku.
go.jp; 527 Chaya-machi, Higashiyama-ku;
admission varies; ⊙9.30am-5pm Fri &
Sat, closed Mon; ☐Kyoto City bus 206 or 208 to
Sanjūsangen-dō-mae, ☐Keihan line to Shichijō)
The Kyoto National Museum is the city's
premier art museum and plays host to the
highest-level exhibitions in the city. It was
founded in 1895 as an imperial repository

for art and treasures from local temples
and shrines. The **Heisei Chishinkan**,
designed by Taniguchi Yoshio and opened
in 2014, is a brilliant modern counterpoint
to the original red-brick **main hall** building,
which was closed and undergoing structur-
al work at the time of research. Check the
Kyoto Visitor's Guide to see what's on while
you're in town.

Kawai Kanjirō Memorial Hall — Museum

(河井寛治郎記念館; Map p112; ☎075-561-
3585; 569 Kanei-chō, Gojō-zaka, Higashiyama-ku;
adult/child ¥900/300; ⊙10am-5pm Tue-Sun;
☐Kyoto City bus 206 or 207 to Umamachi) This
small memorial hall is one of Kyoto's most
commonly overlooked little gems. The
hall was the home and workshop of one
of Japan's most famous potters, Kawai
Kanjirō (1890–1966). The 1937 house is
built in rural style and contains examples of
Kanjirō's work, his collection of folk art and
ceramics, his workshop and a fascinating
nobori-gama (stepped kiln). The museum
is near the intersection of Gojō-dōri and
Higashiōji-dōri.

Higashiyama

N 0 ━━━━━ 400 m
   0 ━━━━━ 0.2 miles

Kyoto University

Shūgaku-in Rikyū Imperial Villa (4km)

Shirakawa-dōri

🅰3

11 ◉

Kaguraoka-dōri

Shirakawa-dōri

Konoe-dōri

Yoshidahigashi-dōri

SAKYŌ-KU

Tetsugaku-no-Michi (Path of Philosophy)

Higashiōji-dōri

Jingū-Marutamachi

🅡

26 Higashitakeyachō-dōri

Reisen-dōri

Marutamachi-dōri

Nijō-dōri

🟊33 Okazaki-kōen

Nijō-dōri

Shira-kawa

🅰2

10 🅰

Higashiōji-dōri

Biwa-ko Sosui Canal

Shirakawa-dōri

Sanjō Keihan

🆂

Sanjō 🅡

Sanjō-dōri 🆂

23 🅡 Higashiyama

Keage 🆂

🅡25

Hanami-kōji

17 🅡

🅰12

🅰1

SHIMBASHI

19 🆇 28🟊🅰15

20 🆇

Shijō-dōri

13 🅰

Higashiyama Driveway

Biwa-ko Sosui Canal

Gion-Shijō 🆂

24 🅡 31

🟊30

18 🅡

GION

🟊32

HIGASHIYAMA-KU

Hanami-kōji

16 🅡

🅰6

8 🅰 🆇21

🅿

4 ◉

29 🅡

Yasaka-dōri

22 🆇

🟊14

Higashiōji-dōri

Kiyomizu-michi

Sanjō-dōri

See Downtown Kyoto & Kyoto Station Area Map (p108)

Higashiyama Driveway

Chawan-zaka

🅰7

5 🏛

Shibutani-dōri

Gojō-dōri

9 🏛

Shichijō-dōri

27 🅡

↓ Tōfuku-ji (1.8km);
↓ Fushimi Inari-Taisha (2.5km)

Higashiyama

Kennin-ji   Buddhist Temple
(建仁寺; Map p112; www.kenninji.jp; 584 Komatsu-chō, Yamatoōji-dōri, Shijo-sagaru, Higashiyama-ku; ¥500; ☺10am-5pm Mar-Oct, to 4.30pm Nov-Feb; 🚉Keihan line to Gion-Shijō) Founded in 1202 by the monk Eisai, Kennin-ji is the oldest Zen temple in Kyoto. It is an island of peace and calm on the border of the boisterous Gion nightlife district and it makes a fine counterpoint to the worldly pleasures of that area. The highlight at Kennin-ji is the fine and expansive *kare-sansui* garden. The painting of the twin dragons on the roof of the **Hōdō** hall is also fantastic.

◎ Northern Higashiyama

Ginkaku-ji   Buddhist Temple
(銀閣寺; Map p112; 2 Ginkaku-ji-chō, Sakyō-ku; adult/child ¥500/300; ☺8.30am-5pm Mar-Nov, 9am-4.30pm Dec-Feb; 🚌Kyoto City bus 5 to Ginkakuji-michi stop) Home to a sumptuous garden and elegant structures, Ginkaku-ji is one of Kyoto's premier sites. The temple started its life in 1482 as a retirement villa for shogun Ashikaga Yoshimasa, who desired a place to retreat from the turmoil of a civil war. While the name Ginkaku-ji literally translates as 'Silver Pavilion', the shogun's ambition to cover the building with silver was never realised. After Ashikaga's death, the villa was converted into a temple.

Nanzen-ji   Buddhist Temple
(南禅寺; Map p112; www.nanzenji.com; 86 Fukuchi-chō, Nanzen-ji, Sakyō-ku; adult/child from ¥300/150, grounds free; ☺8.40am-5pm Mar-Nov, to 4.30pm Dec-Feb; 🚌Kyoto City bus 5 to Eikandō-michi, Ⓢ Tōzai line to Keage) This is one of the most rewarding temples in Kyoto, with its expansive grounds and numerous subtemples. At its entrance stands the massive **San-mon**. Steps lead up to the 2nd storey, which has a great view over the city. Beyond the gate is the main hall of the temple, above which you will find the **Hōjō**, where the Leaping Tiger Garden is a classic Zen garden well worth a look.

Eikan-dō   Buddhist Temple
(永観堂; Map p112; ☏075-761-0007; www.eikando.or.jp; 48 Eikandō-chō, Sakyō-ku; adult/child ¥600/400; ☺9am-5pm; 🚌Kyoto City bus 5 to Eikandō-michi, Ⓢ Tōzai line to Keage) Perhaps Kyoto's most famous (and most crowded) autumn-foliage destination, Eikan-dō is a superb temple just a short walk south of

Hozu-gawa River Trip

The **Hozu-gawa river trip** (☎0771-22-5846; www.hozugawakudari.jp; Hozu-chō, Kameoka-shi; adult/child 4-12yr ¥4100/2700) is a great way to enjoy the beauty of Kyoto's western mountains without any strain on the legs. With long bamboo poles, boatmen steer flat-bottom boats down the Hozu-gawa from Kameoka, 30km west of Kyoto Station, through steep, forested mountain canyons, before arriving at Arashiyama.

Between 10 March and 30 November there are seven trips daily leaving on the hour from 9am to 2pm, with the last trip at 3.30pm. During winter the number of trips is reduced to four per day (10am, 11.30am, 1pm and 2.30pm) and the boats are heated.

The ride lasts two hours and covers 16km through occasional sections of choppy water – a scenic jaunt with minimal danger. The scenery is especially breathtaking during cherry-blossom season in April and maple-foliage season in autumn.

The boats depart from a dock that is eight minutes' walk from Kameoka Station. Kameoka is accessible by rail from Kyoto Station or Nijō Station on the JR Sagano (San-in) line.

Boating on Hozu-gawa
PURIPAT LERTPUNYAROJ / SHUTTERSTOCK ©

the famous Path of Philosophy. Eikan-dō is made interesting by its varied architecture, its gardens and its works of art. It was founded as Zenrin-ji in 855 by the priest Shinshō, but the name was changed to Eikan-dō in the 11th century to honour the philanthropic priest Eikan.

Path of Philosophy (Tetsugaku-no-Michi)   Area

(哲学の道; Map p112; Sakyō-ku; 🚌Kyoto City bus 5 to Eikandō-michi or Ginkakuji-michi, Ⓢ Tōzai line to Keage) The Tetsugaku-no-Michi is one of the most pleasant walks in Kyoto. Lined with a great variety of flowering plants, bushes and trees, it is a corridor of colour throughout most of the year. Follow the traffic-free route along a canal lined with cherry trees that come into spectacular bloom in early April. It only takes 30 minutes to do the walk, which starts at Nyakuōji-bashi, above Eikan-dō, and leads to Ginkaku-ji.

Shūgaku-in Rikyū Imperial Villa   Notable Building

(修学院離宮; ☎075-211-1215; www.kunaicho.go.jp; Shūgaku-in, Yabusoe, Sakyō-ku; ⊙tours 9am, 10am, 11am, 1.30pm & 3pm Tue-Sun; 🚌Kyoto City bus 5 from Kyoto Station to Shūgakuinrikyū-michi) FREE One of the highlights of northeast Kyoto, this superb imperial villa was designed as a lavish summer retreat for the imperial family. Its gardens, with their views down over the city, are worth the trouble it takes to visit. The one-hour tours are held in Japanese, with English audio guides free of charge. You must be over 18 years to enter and bring your passport.

◎ Arashiyama

Arashiyama Bamboo Grove   Park

(嵐山竹林; Ogurayama, Saga, Ukyō-ku; ⊙dawn-dusk; 🚌Kyoto City bus 28 from Kyoto Station to Arashiyama-Tenryuji-mae, 🚆JR Sagano/San-in line to Saga-Arashiyama or Hankyū line to Arashiyama, change at Katsura) FREE The thick green bamboo stalks seem to continue endlessly in every direction and there's a strange quality to the light at this famous bamboo grove. It's most atmospheric on the approach to Ōkōchi Sansō villa and you'll be unable to resist trying to take a few photos, but you might be disappointed

Arashiyama Bamboo Grove

with the results: photos just can't capture the magic of the place. The grove runs from outside the north gate of Tenryū-ji to just below Ōkōchi Sansō.

Ōkōchi Sansō
Historic Building

(大河内山荘; 8 Tabuchiyama-chō, Sagaoguray-ama, Ukyō-ku; adult/child ¥1000/500; ⏱9am-5pm; ⛟Kyoto City bus 28 from Kyoto Station to Arashiyama-Tenryuji-mae, ⛟JR Sagano/San-in line to Saga-Arashiyama or Hankyū line to Arashiyama, change at Katsura) This is the lavish estate of Ōkōchi Denjirō, an actor famous for his samurai films. The sprawling gardens may well be the most lovely in all of Kyoto, particularly when you consider the brilliant views eastwards across the city. The house and teahouse are also sublime. Be sure to follow all the trails around the gardens. Hold onto the tea ticket you were given upon entry to claim the *matcha* and sweet that's included with admission.

Tenryū-ji
Buddhist Temple

(天龍寺; ☎075-881-1235; www.tenryuji.com; 68 Susukinobaba-chō, Saga-Tenryū-ji, Ukyō-ku; adult/child ¥800/600, garden only ¥500/300; ⏱8.30am-5pm; ⛟Kyoto City bus 28 from Kyoto Station to Arashiyama-Tenryuji-mae, ⛟JR Sagano/San-in line to Saga-Arashiyama or Hankyū line to Arashiyama, change at Katsura) A major temple of the Rinzai school, Tenryū-ji has one of the most attractive gardens in Kyoto, particularly during the spring cherry-blossom and autumn-foliage seasons. The main 14th-century Zen garden, with its backdrop of the Arashiyama mountains, is a good example of *shakkei* (borrowed scenery). Unfortunately, it's no secret that the garden here is world class, so it pays to visit early in the morning or on a weekday.

◉ Kyoto Station Area

Kyoto Station
Notable Building

(京都駅; Map p108; www.kyoto-station-building.co.jp; Karasuma-dōri, Higashishiokōji-chō, Shiokōji-sagaru, Shimogyō-ku; ⛟Kyoto Station) The Kyoto Station building is a striking steel-and-glass structure – a kind of futuristic cathedral for the transport age – with a tremendous space that arches above you as you enter the main concourse. Be sure to take the escalator from the 7th floor on the east side of the building up to the 11th-floor glass corridor, Skyway (open 10am to 10pm), that runs high above the main concourse of the station, and catch some views from the 15th-floor Sky Garden terrace.

Kyoto Railway Museum
Museum

(梅小路蒸気機関車館; Map p108; www.kyoto-railwaymuseum.jp; Kankiji-chō, Shimogyō-ku; adult ¥1200, child ¥200-500; ⏰10am-5.30pm, closed Wed; 🚼; 🚌Kyoto City bus 103, 104 or 110 from Kyoto Station to Umekōji-kōen/Kyoto Railway Museum-mae) This superb museum is spread over three floors that showcase 53 trains, ranging from vintage steam locomotives in the outside Roundhouse Shed to commuter trains and the first *shinkansen* from 1964. Kids will love the interactive displays and impressive railroad diorama with miniature trains zipping through the intricate landscape. You can also take a 10-minute ride on one of the smoke-spewing choo-choos (adult/child ¥300/100).

🏃 ACTIVITIES

Whether you want to get back to nature on a hike or a scenic boat ride, learn the art of the tea ceremony, soak your weary sightseeing bones in a local onsen (hot spring) or learn how to perfect Kyoto cuisine at a cooking class, this city has got you covered.

Camellia Tea Experience
Tea Ceremony

(茶道体験カメリア; Map p112; 📞075-525-3238; www.tea-kyoto.com; 349 Masuya-chō, Higashiyama-ku; per person ¥2000; 🚌Kyoto City bus 206 to Yasui) Camellia is a superb place to try a simple Japanese tea ceremony. It's located in a beautiful old Japanese house just off Ninen-zaka. The host speaks fluent English and explains the ritual simply and clearly to the group, while managing to perform an elegant ceremony. The price includes a bowl of *matcha* and a sweet.

En
Tea Ceremony

(えん; Map p112; 📞080-3782-2706; www.teaceremonyen.com; 272 Matsubara-chō, Higashiyama-ku; per person ¥2500; 🚌Kyoto

SEAN PAVONE / SHUTTERSTOCK ©

City bus 206 to Gion or Chionin-mae) A small teahouse located near Gion where you can experience a Japanese tea ceremony with a minimum of fuss or expense. Check the website for times. English explanations are provided, and reservations recommended. It's a bit tricky to find: it's down a little alley off Higashiōji-dōri – look for the sign south of Tenkaippin Rāmen. Cash only is accepted.

Funaoka Onsen   Onsen

(船岡温泉; 82-1 Minami-Funaoka-chō-Murasakino, Kita-ku; ¥430; ⏰3pm-1am Mon-Sat, from 8am Sun; 🚃Kyoto City bus 206 to Senbon Kuramaguchi) This old *sentō* (public bath) situated on Kuramaguchi-dōri is Kyoto's best. It boasts an outdoor bath, a sauna, a cypress-wood tub, an electric bath, a herbal bath and a few more for good measure. To get here, head west about 400m on Kuramaguchi-dōri from the Kuramaguchi and Horiikawa intersection. It's on the left, not far past the Lawson convenience store. Look for the large rocks.

🍴 COURSES

Uzuki   Cooking

(www.kyotouzuki.com; 2hr class per person from ¥5000) Learn how to cook some of the delightful foods you've tried in Kyoto with this highly recommended cooking class for groups of two to three people, conducted in a Japanese home. You will learn how to cook a variety of dishes (vegan courses are offered) and then sit down and enjoy the fruits of your labour.

Shunkō-in   Meditation

(春光院; 📞075-462-5488; www.shunkoin. com; Myōshin-ji, 42 Myoshin-ji-chō, Hanazono, Ukyō-ku; classes ¥3500; 🚃JR Sagano/San-in line to Hanazono) A subtemple of Myōshin-ji (p103), Shunkō-in is run by a monk who has studied abroad and made it his mission to introduce foreigners to his temple and Zen Buddhism. Regular introductory meditation classes are held in English; check the website for the schedule. You can also stay overnight in the **accommodation** (春光院; s ¥8800, d/tr per person ¥7500/6000; 🅿@🛜) here.

Kyoto's Best Gardens

Ryōan-ji (p103)

Tōfuku-ji (p97)

Sentō Imperial Palace (p107)

Ōkōchi Sansō (p115)

From left: Ryōan-ji (p103); Tōfuku-ji (p97); Ōkōchi Sansō (p115)

The Tea Ceremony

Chanoyu (literally 'water for tea') is usually translated as 'tea ceremony', but it's more like performance art, with each element – from the gestures of the host to the feel of the tea bowl in your hand – carefully designed to articulate an aesthetic experience. It's had a profound and lasting influence on the arts in Japan; whether you take part in a ceremony or simply pause to admire a teahouse, *sado* (the way of tea) will colour your Kyoto experience.

The careful design of space and selection of utensils, good company and, of course, good tea – all comes together in the tea ceremony. A formal tea ceremony might last hours and include several courses of food and drink, like a dinner party. The actual preparation and drinking of the tea follows a highly ritualised sequence: the utensils are carefully washed and presented; the tea bowl is held just so. It's an insistence on correctness that infuses much of the arts in Japan.

For a small taste of the experience, several establishments offer short versions that are geared towards travellers. Try En (p116) or Camellia Tea Experience (p116).

Preparation for tea ceremony
GREG ELMS / LONELY PLANET ©

Tea ceremony (¥5500, 90 minutes) and Japanese calligraphy (¥3500, 90 minutes) courses are also on offer; check the website for schedules.

🔖 SHOPPING

Kyoto has a fantastic variety of both traditional and modern shops. Most are located in the Downtown Kyoto area, making the city a very convenient place to shop. Whether you're looking for fans, kimono and tea, or the latest electronics, hip fashion and ingenuous gadgets, Kyoto has plenty to offer.

Aritsugu   Homewares

(有次; Map p108; ☑075-221-1091; 219 Kajiya-chō, Nishikikōji-dōri, Gokomachi nishi-iru, Nakagyō-ku; ⊘9am-5.30pm; ℝHankyū line to Kawaramachi) While you're in Nishiki Market (p106), have a look at this store – it has some of the best kitchen knives in the world. Choose your knife – all-rounder, sushi, vegetable – and the staff will show you how to care for it before sharpening and boxing it up. You can also have your name engraved in English or Japanese. Knives start at around ¥10,000.

Ippōdō Tea   Tea

(一保堂茶舗; Map p108; ☑075-211-3421; www.ippodo-tea.co.jp; Teramachi-dōri, Nijō-agaru, Nakagyō-ku; ⊘9am-6pm; ⑤Tōzai line to Kyoto-Shiyakusho-mae) This old-style tea shop sells some of the best Japanese tea in Kyoto, and you'll be given an English leaflet with prices and descriptions of each one. Its *matcha* makes an excellent and lightweight souvenir. Ippōdō is north of the city hall, on Teramachi-dōri. It has an adjoining teahouse, Kaboku Tearoom (p126); last order 5.30pm.

Wagami no Mise   Arts & Crafts

(倭紙の店; Map p108; ☑075-341-1419; 1st fl, Kajinoha Bldg, 298 Ōgisakaya-chō, Higashinotōin-dōri, Bukkōji-agaru, Shimogyō-ku; ⊘9.30am-5.30pm Mon-Fri, to 4.30pm Sat; ⑤Karasuma line to Shijō) This place sells a fabulous variety of *washi* for reasonable prices and is a great spot to pick up a gift or souvenir. Look for the Morita Japanese Paper Company sign on the wall out the front.

Kyūkyo-dō
Arts & Crafts

(鳩居堂; Map p108; ☎075-231-0510; www.
kyukyodo.co.jp; 520 Shimohonnōjimae-chō,
Teramachi-dōri, Aneyakōji-agaru, Nakagyō-ku;
⏰10am-6pm Mon-Sat; Ⓢ Tōzai line to Kyoto-
Shiyakusho-mae) This old shop that is located in the Teramachi covered arcade sells
a good selection of incense, *shodō* (calligraphy) goods, tea-ceremony supplies and
washi. Prices are on the high side but the
quality is good. Overall, this is your best
one-stop shop for distinctively Japanese
souvenirs.

Takashimaya
Department Store

(高島屋; Map p108; ☎075-221-8811; Shijō-
Kawaramachi Kado, Shimogyō-ku; ⏰10am-8pm;
Ⓡ Hankyū line to Kawaramachi) The *grande
dame* of Kyoto department stores, Takashimaya is almost a tourist attraction in its
own right, from the mind-boggling riches of
the basement food floor to the wonderful
selection of lacquerware and ceramics on
the 6th. Check out the kimono display on
the 5th floor.

Tokyu Hands
Department Store

(東急ハンズ京都店; Map p108; ☎075-254-
3109; http://kyoto.tokyu-hands.co.jp; Shijō-dōri,
Karasuma higashi-iru, Shimogyō-ku; ⏰10am-
8.30pm; Ⓢ Karasuma line to Shijō) While the
Kyoto branch of Tokyu Hands doesn't have
the selection of bigger branches in places
like Tokyo, it's still well worth a browse for
fans of gadgets and unique homewares.
It's a good place for an interesting gift or
souvenir, from Hario coffee equipment and
lacquerware *bentō* boxes to stationery and
cosmetics.

Zōhiko
Arts & Crafts

(象彦; Map p108; ☎075-229-6625; www.zohiko.
co.jp; 719-1 Yohojimae-chō, Teramachi-dōri,
Nijō-agaru, Nakagyō-ku; ⏰10am-6pm; Ⓢ Tōzai
line to Kyoto-Shiyakusho-mae) Zōhiko is the
best place in Kyoto to buy one of Japan's
most beguiling art-and-craft forms:
lacquerware. If you aren't familiar with just
how beautiful these products can be, you
owe it to yourself to make the pilgrimage to
Zōhiko. You'll find a great selection of cups,
bowls, trays and various kinds of boxes.

Takashimaya

Ichizawa Shinzaburo
Hanpu
Fashion & Accessories

(一澤信三郎帆布; Map p112; ☏075-541-0436;
www.ichizawa.co.jp; 602 Takabatake-chō,
Higashiyama-ku; ⊙9am-6pm, closed Tue; Ⓢ Tōzai
line to Higashiyama) This company has been
making its canvas bags for over 110 years
and the store is often crammed with those
in the know picking up a skillfully crafted
Kyoto product. Originally designed as 'tool'
bags for workers to carry sake bottles, milk
and ice blocks, the current designs still
reflect this idea. Choose from a range of
styles and colours.

✖ EATING

Kyoto is one of the world's great food cities.
In fact, when you consider atmosphere,
service and quality, it's hard to think of a
city where you get more bang for your dining buck. You can pretty much find a great
dining option in any neighbourhood but
the majority of the best spots are clustered
downtown.

✖ Downtown Kyoto
Roan Kikunoi
Kaiseki ¥¥¥

(露庵菊乃井; Map p108; ☏075-361-5580;
www.kikunoi.jp; 118 Saito-chō, Kiyamachi-dōri,
Shijō-sagaru, Shimogyō-ku; lunch/dinner from
¥7000/13,000; ⊙11.30am-1.30pm & 5-8.30pm
Thu-Tue; ℝHankyū line to Kawaramachi or Keihan
line to Gion-Shijō) Roan Kikunoi is a fantastic
place to experience the wonders of *kaiseki*.
It's a lovely intimate space located right
downtown. The chef takes an experimental
and creative approach and the results are
a wonder for the eyes and palate. Highly
recommended. Reserve through your hotel
or ryokan or at least a few days in advance.

Café Bibliotec Hello!
Cafe ¥

(カフェビブリオティックハロー！; Map
p108; ☏075-231-8625; 650 Seimei-chō, Nijō-dōri,
Yanaginobanba higashi-iru, Nakagyō-ku; meals
from ¥850; ⊙11.30am-midnight; ☏; Ⓢ Tōzai line
to Kyoto-Shiyakusho-mae) As the name suggests, books line the walls of this cool cafe
located in a converted *machiya* attracting a
mix of locals and tourists. It's a great place
to relax with a book or to tap away at your

Soba at Honke Owariya

JUNICHI MIYAZAKI / LONELY PLANET ©

laptop over a coffee (¥450) or light lunch. Look for the huge banana plants out the front.

Giro Giro Hitoshina   Kaiseki ¥¥
(Map p108; ☏075-343-7070; 420-7 Nanba-chō, Nishi-kiyamachi-dōri, Matsubara-sagaru, Shimogyō-ku; kaiseki ¥4100; ☺5.30pm-midnight; ☒Hankyū line to Kawaramachi or Keihan line to Kiyomizu-Gojō) Giro Giro takes traditional *kaiseki* and strips any formality so you're left with great food but in a boisterous atmosphere and with thousands more yen in your pocket. In a quiet lane near Kiyamachi-dōri, things liven up inside with patrons sitting at the counter around the open kitchen chatting with chefs preparing inventive dishes.

Honke Owariya   Noodles ¥
(本家尾張屋; Map p108; ☏075-231-3446; www.honke-owariya.co.jp; 322 Kurumaya-chō, Nijō, Nakagyō-ku; dishes from ¥810; ☺11am-7pm; ☒Karasuma or Tōzai lines to Karasuma-Oike) Set in an old sweets shop in a traditional Japanese building on a quiet downtown street, this is where locals come for excellent soba (buckwheat-noodle) dishes. The highly recommended house speciality, *hourai soba* (¥2160), comes with a stack of five small plates of soba with a selection of toppings, including shiitake mushrooms, shrimp tempura, thin slices of omelette and sesame seeds.

Yoshikawa   Tempura ¥¥¥
(吉川; Map p108; ☏075-221-5544; www.kyoto-yoshikawa.co.jp; 135 Matsushita-chō, Tominokōji, Oike-sagaru, Nakagyō-ku; lunch ¥3000-25,000, dinner ¥8000-25,000; ☺11am-1.45pm & 5-8pm; ☒Tōzai line to Karasuma-Oike or Kyoto-Shiyakusho-mae) This is the place to go for delectable tempura with a daily changing menu. Attached to the Yoshikawa ryokan, it offers table seating, but it's much more interesting to sit and eat around the small intimate counter and observe the chefs at work. Reservation is required for the private tatami room, and counter bar for dinner. Note: counter bar is closed Sunday.

¡◎¡ Kaiseki Cuisine

In a city blessed with excellent dining options, one not to be missed is the refined and elegant experience of *kaiseki* (Japanese haute cuisine). *Kaiseki* consists of a number of small courses, largely vegetarian, served on exquisite dinnerware where the preparation and service is as outstanding as the food itself. Diners are usually served in private rooms at speciality restaurants, such as the highly regarded Kikunoi (p123) and Kitcho Arashiyama (p124), and many ryokan serve *kaiseki* for guests. Prices are elevated for this fine-dining experience, but you don't need to spend a week's travel budget on dinner to get a taste of *kaiseki*.

Reservations are recommended and smart casual is the way to go at **Kiyamachi Sakuragawa** (木屋町 櫻川; Map p108; ☏075-255-4477; Kiyamachi-dōri, Nijō-sagaru, Nakagyō-ku; lunch/dinner sets from ¥7000/16,000; ☺noon-2pm & 6-10pm Mon-Sat; ☒Tōzai line to Kyoto-Shiyakus-ho-mae), an excellent place for your first *kaiseki* dinner. Otherwise, you might wish to consider a cheaper *kaiseki* lunch at **Tagoto Honten** (田ごと本店; Map p108; ☏075-221-1811; www.kyoto-tagoto.co.jp; 34 Otabi-chō, Shijō-dōri, Kawaramachi nishi-iru, Nakagyō-ku; lunch/dinner from ¥1850/6000; ☺11.30am-3pm & 4.30-9pm; ☒Keihan line to Shijō or Hankyū line to Kawaramachi).

Kaiseki meal

From left: udon noodles; *kaiseki* at Kikunoi; sukiyaki at Mishima-tei

Menami
Japanese ¥¥

(めなみ; Map p108; ☎075-231-1095; www. menami.jp; Kiyamachi-dōri, Sanjō-agaru, Nakagyō-ku; dishes ¥400-1600; ⏱5-11pm Mon-Sat; ⒮Tōzai line to Kyoto-Shiyakusho-mae, ⓇKeihan line to Sanjō) This welcoming neighbourhood favourite specialises in *obanzai-ryōri cuisine* – a type of home-style cooking that uses seasonal ingredients – done creatively and served as tapas-size plates. Don't miss the delicious spring rolls that are wrapped with *yuba* (生ゆば春巻, tofu skin). Try to book a counter seat where you can eye off bowls filled with dishes to choose from while watching the chefs in action.

Mishima-tei
Japanese ¥¥¥

(三嶋亭; Map p108; ☎075-221-0003; 405 Sakurano-chō, Teramachi-dōri, Sanjō-sagaru, Nakagyō-ku; sukiyaki lunch/dinner from ¥7720/14,850; ⏱11.30am-10.30pm Thu-Tue; ⒮Tōzai line to Kyoto-Shiyakusho-mae) Mishima-tei, around since 1873, is a good place to sample sukiyaki (thin slices of beef cooked in sake, soy and vinegar broth, and dipped in raw egg) as the quality of the meat is

very high, which is hardly surprising when there is a butcher downstairs. It's at the intersection of the Sanjō and Teramachi covered arcades.

Biotei
Vegetarian ¥

(びお亭; Map p108; ☎075-255-0086; 2nd fl, M&I Bldg, 28 Umetada-chō, Sanjō-dōri, Higashinotōin nishi-iru, Nakagyō-ku; lunch/dinner sets from ¥890/1385; ⏱11.30am-2pm & 5-8.30pm Tue, 11.30am-2pm Wed & Fri, Thu, 5-8.30pm Sat; ✍; ⒮Tōzai or Karasuma lines to Karasuma-Oike) Located diagonally across from Nakagyō post office, this is a favourite of Kyoto vegetarians, serving à la carte and daily sets with dishes such as deep-fried crumbed tofu and black seaweed salad with rice, miso and pickles. The seating is rather cramped but the food is excellent, beautifully presented and carefully made from quality ingredients.

Sushi no Musashi
Sushi ¥

(寿しのむさし; Map p108; ☎075-222-0634; www.sushinomusashi.com; Kawaramachi-dōri, Sanjō-agaru, Nakagyō-ku; plates from ¥146; ⏱11am-10pm; ⒮Tōzai line to Kyoto-Shiyakusho-

JUNICHI MIYAZAKI / LONELY PLANET ©

mae, ⊠Keihan line to Sanjō) If you've never tried a *kaiten-sushi* (conveyor-belt sushi restaurant), don't miss this place – most dishes are a mere ¥146. Not the best sushi in the world, but it's cheap, reliable and fun. It's also easy to eat here: you just grab what you want off the conveyor belt. If you don't see what you want, there's an English menu to order from.

✖ Southern Higashiyama

Kikunoi
Kaiseki ¥¥¥

(菊乃井; Map p112; ✆075-561-0015; www.kiku-noi.jp; 459 Shimokawara-chō, Yasakatoriimae-sagaru, Shimokawara-dōri, Higashiyama-ku; lunch/dinner from ¥10,000/16,000; ⌚noon-1pm & 5-8pm; ⊠Keihan line to Gion-Shijō) Michelin-starred chef Mutara serves some of the finest *kaiseki* in the city. Located in a hidden nook near Maruyama-kōen, this restaurant has everything necessary for the full over-the-top *kaiseki* experience, from setting to service to exquisitely executed cuisine, often with a creative twist. Reserve through your hotel at least a month in advance.

Kagizen Yoshifusa
Teahouse ¥

(鍵善良房; Map p112; ✆075-561-1818; www.kagizen.co.jp; 264 Gion machi, Kita-gawa, Higashiyama-ku; kuzukiri ¥1080, tea & sweet ¥880; ⌚9.30am-6pm, closed Mon; ⊠Hankyū line to Kawaramachi, Keihan line to Gion-Shijō) This Gion institution is one of Kyoto's oldest and best-known *okashi-ya* (sweet shops). It sells a variety of traditional sweets and has a lovely tearoom out the back where you can sample cold *kuzukiri* (transparent arrowroot noodles) served with a *kuro-mitsu* (sweet black sugar) dipping sauce, or just a nice cup of *matcha* tea and a sweet.

Omen Kodai-ji
Noodles ¥

(おめん 高台寺店; Map p112; ✆075-541-5007; 362 Masuya-chō, Kōdaiji-dōri, Shimokawara higashi-iru, Higashiyama-ku; noodles from ¥1150; ⌚11am-9pm; ⊠Kyoto City bus 206 to Higashiyama-Yasui) Housed in a remodelled Japanese building with a light, airy feeling, this branch of Kyoto's famed Omen noodle chain is the best place to stop while exploring the Southern Higashiyama district. Upstairs has fine views over the area.

The signature udon (thick, white wheat noodles) served in broth with a selection of fresh vegetables is delicious.

Chidoritei — Sushi ¥

(千登利亭; Map p112; ☑075-561-1907; 203 Rokken-cho, Donguri-dori, Yamato-oji Nishi-iru, Higashiyama-ku; sushi sets ¥600-2200; ☺11am-8pm, closed Thu; ☒Keihan line to Gion-Shijō) Family-owned Chidoritei is a snug little sushi restaurant that is tucked away in the backstreets of Gion, far away from the bustle. It's a great place to try delicious traditional Kyoto *saba-zushi* – mackerel hand pressed into lightly vinegared rice and wrapped in *konbu* (a type of seaweed). In summer, the speciality here is conger-eel sushi.

Gion Yuki — Izakaya ¥

(遊亀祇園店; Map p112; ☑075-525-2666; 111-1 Tominaga-chō, Higashiyama-ku; dishes ¥380-800; ☺5-10pm Mon-Fri, to midnight Sat; ☒Keihan line to Gion-Shijō) Squeeze in at the counter for front-row seats to watch the chefs do their thing at this lively *izakaya* (Japanese pub-eatery). Seafood is big on the menu, from sashimi plates and grilled fish to tasty tempura, and sake is the drink of choice – no surprise considering the owner is a sake brewer. Look for the short hanging red curtains.

⊗ Arashiyama

Kitcho Arashiyama — Kaiseki ¥¥¥

(吉兆嵐山本店; ☑075-881-1101; www.kyoto-kitcho.com; 58 Susukinobaba-chō, Saga-Tenryū-ji, Ukyō-ku; lunch/dinner from ¥51,840/64,800; ☺11.30am-3pm & 5-9pm Thu-Tue; ☒; ☒Kyoto City bus 28 from Kyoto Station to Arashiyama-Tenryuji-mae, ☒JR Sagano/San-in line to Saga-Arashiyama or Hankyū line to Arashiyama, change at Katsura) Considered to be one of the best *kaiseki* restaurants in Kyoto (and Japan, for that matter), Kitcho Arashiyama is the place to sample the full *kaiseki* experience. Meals are served in private rooms that are overlooking beautiful gardens. The food, service, staff explanations and restaurant atmosphere are all first rate. Make bookings online via its website well in advance.

Shōjin-ryōri (Buddhist vegetarian cuisine)

KO FUJIMURA / GETTY IMAGES ©

Shigetsu
Vegetarian, Japanese ¥¥

(篩月; ☏075-882-9725; 68 Susukinobaba-chō, Saga-Tenryū-ji, Ukyō-ku; lunch sets ¥3500, ¥5500 & ¥7500; ⏰11am-2pm; ☏; ☐Kyoto City bus 28 from Kyoto Station to Arashiyama-Tenryuji-mae, ☐JR Sagano/San-in line to Saga-Arashiyama or Hankyū line to Arashiyama, change at Katsura) To sample *shōjin-ryōri* (Buddhist vegetarian cuisine), try Shigetsu in the precincts of Tenryū-ji (p115). This healthy fare has been sustaining monks for more than a thousand years in Japan, so it will probably get you through an afternoon of sightseeing, although carnivores may be left craving something more. Shigetsu has beautiful garden views. Prices include temple admission.

Arashiyama Yoshimura
Noodles ¥

(嵐山よしむら; ☏075-863-5700; Togetsu-kyō kita, Saga-Tenryū-ji, Ukyō-ku; soba from ¥1000, sets from ¥1280; ⏰11am-5pm; ☐Kyoto City bus 28 from Kyoto Station to Arashiyama-Tenryuji-mae, ☐JR Sagano/San-in line to Saga-Arashiyama or Hankyū line to Arashiyama, change at Katsura) For a tasty bowl of soba noodles and a million-dollar view looking over to the Arashiyama mountains and the Togetsu-kyō bridge, head to this extremely popular eatery (prepare to queue during peak times) just north of the famous bridge, overlooking the Katsura-gawa. There's an English menu but no English sign; look for the big glass windows and the stone wall.

🍸 DRINKING & NIGHTLIFE

Kyoto is a city with endless options for drinking, whether it's an expertly crafted single-origin coffee served in a hipster cafe, a rich *matcha* prepared at a traditional tearoom, carefully crafted cocktails and single malts in a sophisticated six-seater bar, or Japanese craft beer in a brewery. Check ahead in *Kansai Scene* to see what's going on.

🔵 Downtown Kyoto

Bungalow
Craft Beer

(バンガロー; Map p108; ☏075-256-8205; www.bungalow.jp; 15 Kashiwaya-chō, Shijō-dōri, Shimogyō-ku; ⏰3pm-2am Mon-Sat; ☐Hankyū line to Ōmiya) Spread over two floors with an open-air downstairs bar, Bungalow serves a great range of Japanese craft beer along with natural wines in a cool industrial space. The regularly changing menu features 10 beers on tap from all over Japan and it also serves excellent food.

Sake Bar Yoramu
Bar

(酒バー よらむ; Map p108; ☏075-213-1512; www.sakebar-yoramu.com; 35-1 Matsuya-chō, Nijō-dōri, Higashinotoin higashi-iru, Nakagyō-ku; ⏰6pm-midnight Wed-Sat; ⑤Karasuma or Tōzai lines to Karasuma-Oike) Named for Yoramu, the Israeli sake expert who runs Sake Bar Yoramu, this place is highly recommended for anyone after an education in sake. It's very small and can only accommodate a handful of people. If you're not sure what you like, go for a sake tasting set of three (¥1700). By day, it's a soba restaurant called Toru Soba.

Bar K6
Bar

(バーK6; Map p108; ☏075-255-5009; 2nd fl, Le Valls Bldg, Nijō-dōri, Kiyamachi higashi-iru, Nakagyō-ku; ⏰6pm-3am, to 5am Fri & Sat; ⑤Tōzai line to Kyoto-Shiyakusho-mae, ☐Keihan line to Jingu-Marutamachi) Overlooking one of the prettiest stretches of Kiyamachi-dōri, this upscale modern Japanese bar has a great selection of single maltwhiskies and some of the best cocktails in town. It's popular with well-heeled locals and travellers staying at some of the top-flight hotels nearby.

World
Club

(ワールド; Map p108; ☏075-213-4119; www.world-kyoto.com; Basement, Imagium Bldg, 97 Shin-chō, Nishikiyamachi, Shijō-agaru, Shimogyō-ku; cover ¥2000-3000; ⏰8pm-late; ☐Hankyū line to Kawaramachi) World is Kyoto's largest club and it naturally hosts some of the biggest events. It has two floors, a dance floor and lockers where you can leave your stuff while you dance the night away. Events include everything from deep soul to reggae and techno to salsa.

Atlantis Bar

(アトランティス; Map p108; ☑075-241-1621; 161 Matsumoto-chō, Ponto-chō-Shijō-agaru, Nakagyō-ku; cocktails from ¥900; ⏰6pm-2am, to 1am Sun; ☒Hankyū line to Kawaramachi) This is a slick Ponto-chō bar that welcomes foreigners and draws a fair smattering of Kyoto's beautiful people, and wannabe beautiful people. In summer you can sit outside on a platform looking over the Kamo-gawa (terrace closes at 11pm). It's often crowded so you may have to wait a bit to get in, especially if you want to sit outside.

Kaboku Tearoom Teahouse

(喫茶室嘉木; Map p108; Teramachi-dōri, Nijō-agaru, Nakagyō-ku; ⏰10am-6pm; ⑤Tōzai line to Kyoto-Shiyakusho-mae) A casual tea-room attached to the Ippōdō Tea (p118) store, Kaboku serves a range of teas and provides a great break while exploring the

shops in the area. Try the *matcha* and grab a counter seat to watch it being prepared.

🍵 Southern Higashiyama

Beer Komachi Craft Beer

(ビア小町; Map p112; ☑075-746-6152; www.beerkomachi.com; 444 Hachiken-chō, Higashiyama-ku; ⏰5-11pm, from 3pm Sat & Sun, closed Tue; ☜; ⑤Tōzai line to Higashiyama) Located in the Furokawa-chō covered shopping arcade close to Higashiyama Station, this tiny casual bar is dedicated to promoting Japanese craft beer. There are usually seven Japanese beers on tap, which rotate on an almost daily basis. There's a great bar-food menu and a list of sake if you're not much of a beer drinker.

Tōzan Bar Bar

(Map p112; ☑075-541-3201; www.kyoto.regency.hyatt.com; Hyatt Regency Kyoto, 644-2 Sanjūsangendō-mawari, Higashiyama-ku; ⏰5pm-midnight; ☒Keihan line to Shichijō) Even if you're not spending the night at the Hyatt Regency, drop by the cool and cosy underground bar for a tipple or two. Kitted out by renowned design firm Super Potato, the

From left: Geisha performing at Miyako Odori (p101); tea ceremony; Minamiza kabuki theatre (p128)

dimly lit atmospheric space features interesting touches, such as old locks, wooden beams, an antique-book library space and a wall feature made from traditional wooden sweet moulds.

Gion Finlandia Bar   Bar

(ぎをん フィンランディアバー; Map p112; ☑075-541-3482; www.finlandiabar.com; 570-123 Gion-machi, Minamigawa, Higashiyama-ku; cover ¥500; ☺6pm-3am; ℝKeihan line to Gion-Shijō) This stylish, minimalist Gion bar in an old geisha house is a great place for a quiet civilised drink. There's no menu, so just prop up at the bar and let the bow-tied bartender know what you like, whether it's an expertly crafted cocktail or a high-end Japanese single malt. Friday and Saturday nights can get busy, so you may have to queue.

🅞 Northern Higashiyama

Kick Up   Bar

(キックアップ; Map p112; ☑075-761-5604; 331 Higashikomonoza-chō, Higashiyama-ku; ☺7pm-midnight, closed Wed; Ⓢ Tōzai line to Keage) Located just across the street from the Westin Miyako Kyoto, this wonderful bar attracts a regular crowd of Kyoto expats, local Japanese and guests from the Westin. It's subdued, relaxing and friendly.

Metro   Club

(メトロ; Map p112; ☑075-752-4765; www. metro.ne.jp; BF Ebisu Bldg, Kawabata-dōri, Marutamachi-sagaru, Sakyō-ku; ☺8pm-3am; ℝKeihan line to Jingū-Marutamachi) Metro is part disco, part live house and it even hosts the occasional art exhibition. It attracts an eclectic mix of creative types and has a different theme nightly. Metro is inside exit 2 of the Jingū-Marutamachi Station on the Keihan line.

⭐ ENTERTAINMENT

If you've never seen the otherworldly spectacle of kabuki (stylised Japanese theatre) or the colourful extravagance of a geisha dance (p100), you've come to the right place: Kyoto is the best city in Japan to enjoy traditional Japanese performing arts. In addition, you'll find a lively music scene,

plenty of cinemas and modern performances of all sorts.

Minamiza
Theatre

(南座; Map p112; www.kabukiweb.net; Shijō-Ōhashi, Higashiyama-ku; ꊮKeihan line to Gion-Shijō) This theatre in Gion is the oldest kabuki theatre in Japan. The major event of the year is the **Kaomise festival** in December, which features Japan's finest kabuki actors.

Taku-Taku
Live Music

(磔磔; Map p108; ☎075-351-1321; Tominokō-ji-dōri-Bukkōji, Shimogyō-ku; tickets ¥1500-4000; ꊮHankyū line to Kawaramachi) One of Kyoto's most atmospheric live-music venues, with a long history of hosting some great local and international acts. Check the *Kyoto Visitor's Guide* and flyers in local coffee shops and record stores for details on upcoming events. It can be hard to spot: look for the wooden sign with black kanji on it and go through the gate.

ROHM Theatre Kyoto
Theatre

(京都観世会館; Map p112; ☎075-771-6051; www.rohmtheatrekyoto.jp; 44 Okazaki Enshō-ji-chō, Sakyō-ku; tickets from ¥3000; ⊘box office 10am-7pm; ꊯTōzai line to Higashiyama) Housed in a striking modernist building, ROHM Theatre hosts everything from international ballet and opera performances to comedy shows, classical music concerts and *nō* (stylised dance-drama performed on a bare stage).

❶ INFORMATION

INTERNET ACCESS

It's getting much easier for travellers to get online in Kyoto, with almost all hotels and hostels offering free wi-fi for their guests and some now offering smartphones with wi-fi in hotel rooms. If you want constant access to wi-fi when you're out and about, your best bet is either renting a portable device or buying a data-only SIM for an unlocked smartphone.

TOURIST INFORMATION

Kyoto Tourist Information Center (京都総合観光案内所, TIC; Map p108; ☎075-343-0548; 2F Kyoto Station Bldg, Shimogyō-ku; ⊘8.30am-7pm; ꊮKyoto Station) Stocks bus and city maps, has plenty of transport info and English speakers are available to answer your questions.

❶ GETTING THERE & AWAY

Travel between Kyoto and other parts of Japan is a breeze. Kansai is served by the Tōkaidō and San-yō *shinkansen* lines, several JR main lines and a few private rail lines. It is also possible to travel to/from Kyoto and other parts of Honshū, Shikoku and Kyūshū by long-distance highway buses. Kyoto is served by two airports (Kansai International Airport and Osaka International Airport), and is relatively close to Nagoya, in case you can only get a flight to Centrair airport.

Flights, cars and tours can be booked online at lonelyplanet.com/bookings.

❶ GETTING AROUND

TO/FROM THE AIRPORT

The fastest and most convenient way to move between Kansai International Airport (KIX) and Kyoto is the special JR Haruka airport express (reserved/unreserved ¥3370/2850, 1¼ hours). It's actually cheaper to buy a JR West Kansai Area Pass as this is valid for unreserved seats on the JR Haruka express to KIX and costs ¥2300. Buy tickets at the JR ticket office inside the north entrance of Kyoto Station, to the left of the platform ticket gates (you'll need to show your passport).

If you have time to spare, save money by taking the *kankū kaisoku* (Kansai airport express) between the airport and Osaka Station, and then taking a regular *shinkaisoku* (special rapid train) to Kyoto. The total journey by this route takes about 95 minutes with good connections and costs around ¥1750.

Geishas performing Kyō Odori (p101)

MK Taxi Sky Gate Shuttle limousine van service (☎075-778-5489; www.mktaxi-japan. com; one-way to Kansai airport ¥4200, to Itami airport ¥2900) is a door-to-door service that will drop you off at most places in Kyoto – simply go to the staff counter at the south end of the KIX arrivals hall and they will do the rest. From Kyoto to the airport it is necessary to make reservations two days in advance to arrange pick-up from your hotel in Kyoto.

BICYCLE

Kyoto is a great city to explore on a bicycle. With the exception of the outlying areas, it is mostly flat and there is a useful bike path running the length of the Kamo-gawa.

Many guesthouses hire or lend bicycles to their guests and there are also hire shops around Kyoto Station, in Arashiyama and in Downtown Kyoto. With a decent bicycle and a good map, you can easily make your way all around the city. Dedicated bicycle tours are also available.

Bicycle helmets are only required to be worn by law by children 12 years and under.

Note that cycling on the following streets is prohibited:

- Kawaramachi-dōri, between Oike-dōri and Bukkoji-dōri
- Shijo-dōri, between Higashioji-dōri and Karasuma-dōri
- Sanjo-dōri, between Kiyamachi-dōri and Kawaramachi-dōri

For more information, visit Cycle Kyoto (www. cyclekyoto.com).

BUS

Kyoto has an intricate network of bus routes providing an efficient way of getting around at moderate cost. Most of the routes used by visitors have announcements and bus-stop information displays in English. Most buses run between 7am and 10pm, though a few run earlier or later.

Bus entry is accessed through the back door and exit is via the front door. Inner-city buses charge a flat fare (¥230 for adults, ¥120 for children ages six to 12, free for those younger), which you drop into the clear plastic receptacle

🚌 Discount Passes

One-day unlimited travel passes

There's a one-day card valid for unlimited travel on Kyoto City buses and some of the Kyoto buses (these are different companies) that costs ¥600 and a one-day subway pass that also costs ¥600. A one-day unlimited bus and subway pass costs ¥900.

Kyoto Sightseeing Pass Allows unlimited use of the Kyoto City buses, subway and some of the Kyoto bus routes for one day ¥900 or two days ¥1700.

Kansai Thru Pass This pass is a real bonus to travellers who plan to do a fair bit of exploration in the Kansai area. It enables you to ride on city subways, private railways and city buses in Kyoto, Nara, Osaka, Kōbe, Kōya-san, Shiga and Wakayama. It also entitles you to discounts at many attractions in the Kansai area. A two-day pass costs ¥4000 and a three-day pass costs ¥5200. For more information, visit www.surutto.com.

Kyoto City Subway Pass (adult/child ¥600/300) Allows unlimited travel on the city's subway for one day, plus discounts on some sights. You can buy it from the Kyoto Tourist Information Center (p128) or any subway ticket office.

on top of the machine next to the driver on your way out. A separate machine gives change for ¥100 and ¥500 coins or ¥1000 notes.

On buses serving the outer areas, take a *seiri-ken* (numbered ticket) on boarding. When alighting, an electronic board above the driver displays the fare corresponding to your ticket number (drop the *seiri-ken* into the ticket box with your fare).

TAXI

Taxis are a convenient, but expensive, way of getting from place to place about town. A taxi can usually be flagged down in most parts of the city at any time. There are also a large number of *takushī noriba* (taxi stands) in town, outside most train/subway stations, department stores etc.

There is no need to touch the back doors of the cars at all – the opening/closing mechanism is controlled by the driver.

TRAIN & SUBWAY

The main train station in Kyoto is Kyoto Station, which is in the south of the city, just below Shichijō-dōri and is actually two stations under one roof: JR Kyoto Station and Kintetsu Kyoto Station.

In addition to the private Kintetsu line that operates from Kyoto Station, there are two other private train lines in Kyoto: the Hankyū line that operates from Downtown Kyoto along Shijō-dōri and the Keihan line that operates from stops along the Kamo-gawa.

Where to Stay

Kyoto has many lodgings (in all price ranges) in beautiful old buildings – though be mindful that this will mean stairs and possibly thin walls. For modern convenience, there are plenty of hotels.

Neighbourhood	Atmosphere
Kyoto Station Area	Lots of choices in all price ranges; convenient for travel in and out of the city; plenty of easy dining options. Far from most sightseeing districts; not particularly attractive area.
Downtown Kyoto	In the heart of everything – shops, restaurants and nightlife. Though it can feel rather hectic, with crowded pavements and fairly high ambient noise on street level. Good transit links.
Southern Higashiyama	The city's main sightseeing district, with beautiful walks in every direction. Fewer dining options than downtown; crowded in the cherry-blossom season.
Northern Higashiyama	Lots of sights nearby; peaceful and green; nice day and evening strolls. Just not many places to stay or eat out this way.
Arashiyama & Sagano	One of the main sightseeing districts with some truly beautiful ryokan (traditional Japanese inns); magical at night. Inconvenient for other parts of the city; quiet at night and lacking budget options.

NARA

Nara at a Glance...

Japan's first permanent capital, Nara (奈良) is one of the country's most rewarding destinations. With eight Unesco World Heritage Sites, it's second only to Kyoto as a repository of Japan's cultural legacy. The centrepiece is the Daibutsu (Great Buddha), one of the world's largest bronze figures and rival to Mt Fuji and Kyoto's Golden Pavilion (Kinkaku-ji) as Japan's single most impressive sight. The Great Buddha is housed in Tōdai-ji, a soaring temple that presides over Nara-kōen, a park that is home to about 1200 deer. In pre-Buddhist times the deer were considered messengers of the gods and today they enjoy the status of National Treasure.

One Day in Nara

Nara is compact: it's quite possible to pack the highlights – the temples, shrines and museums of Nara-kōen – into one full day. Many travellers visit Nara as a side trip from Kyoto.

Two Days in Nara

Overnighting in Nara gives you time to take it slower, and also to get a head start in the morning – before the day trippers arrive. You'll be able to take more time in the museums, visit less-famous (and less-crowded) temples and explore other quarters like the historic Nara-machi district. There are also excellent lodgings and restaurants here.

Kyoto
(40km)
**KYOTO
PREFECTURE**

0 — 1 km
0 — 0.5 miles

Yamato-
Saidaiji

Tōdai-ji

Nigatsu-dō

Kintetsu
Nara

Tōdai-ji
Nandai-mon

Nara-
kōen

Osaka
(30km)

Nara

Nishinokyō

Kintetsu
Kōriyama

Kōriyama

Nara Map (p143)

Arriving in Nara

Nara is most often visited as part of
a journey to the Kansai region that
includes Kyoto (40km to the north) and
Osaka (30km to the west). Given the
excellent train links between the three
cities, it's better to use public transport
than to drive (parking and traffic in
Nara can be a challenge). For travellers
coming from elsewhere via *shinkansen*
(bullet train), travel via Kyoto.

Where to Stay

There are several budget guesthouses
and easy-access hotels within the
vicinity of Nara's train stations. Though
not as convenient to the sights, the
guesthouses and ryokan (traditional
Japanese inns) in Naramachi, south of
the town centre, are an attractive alternative. Many are in heritage structures.

Daibutsu

Tōdai-ji

Nara's star attraction is the famous Daibutsu (Great Buddha), centrepiece of this grand temple on the Unesco World Heritage List, with origins going back to AD 728. The Daibutsu-den (大仏殿; Great Buddha Hall) is among the largest wooden buildings in the world.

Great For...

☑ **Don't Miss**

Standing in awe at the 15m-tall gilt-bronze Daibutsu, first created in the 8th century.

Except for the Daibutsu-den, which houses the Daibutsu, most of Tōdai-ji's grounds can be visited free of charge.

Daibutsu

The Daibutsu is an image of Dainichi Nyorai (also known as Vairocana Buddha), the cosmic Buddha believed to give rise to all worlds and their respective Buddhas. Historians believe that Emperor Shōmu ordered the building of the Buddha as a charm against smallpox, which had ravaged Japan in preceding years. Originally cast in 746, the present statue was recast in the Edo period. It stands 15m high and consists of 437 tonnes of bronze and 130kg of gold. Over the centuries the statue took quite a beating from earthquakes and fires, losing its head a couple of times (note the slight

Statue of Komokuten

DMSTUDIO HOUSE / SHUTTERSTOCK ©

Tōdai-ji Daibutsu-den

Nigatsu-dō & Sangatsu-dō

Kintetsu Nara

Tōdai-ji Nandai-mon

Nara

Nara-kōen

ⓘ Need to Know

東大寺; www.todaiji.or.jp; 406-1 Zōshi-chō; Daibutsu-den adult/child ¥600/300; ⊙Daibutsu-den 7.30am-5.30pm Apr-Oct, 8am-5pm Nov-Mar

✕ Take a Break

Go for tea at Mizuya-chaya (p145) near Nigatsu-dō.

★ Top Tip

Everyone makes a beeline for the Daibutsu-den; budget time to visit some subtemples.

difference in colour between the head and the body).

As you circle the statue towards the back, you'll see a wooden column with a hole through its base. Popular belief maintains that those who can squeeze through the hole, exactly the same size as one of the Great Buddha's nostrils, are guaranteed enlightenment. There's usually a line of children waiting to give it a try and parents waiting to snap their pictures. A hint for bigger 'kids': try going through with one or both arms above your head – someone on either end to push and pull helps, too.

Nandai-mon

The great Nandai-mon (東大寺南大門; South Gate) contains two fierce-looking Niō guardians. These recently restored wooden

images, carved in the 13th century by the famed sculptor Unkei, are some of the finest wooden statues in all of Japan, if not the world. They are truly dramatic works of art and seem ready to spring to life at any moment. The gate is about 200m south of the Tōdai-ji temple enclosure.

Nigatsu-dō & Sangatsu-dō

Two subtemples of Tōdai-ji uphill from the Daibutsu-den, **Nigatsu-dō & Sangatsu-dō** (二月堂; ⊙24hr), are far less clamorous. Nigatsu-dō, a National Treasure from 1669 (originally built c 750), has a verandah with sweeping views across town. Sangatsu-dō is the oldest building in the Tōdai-ji complex and home to a small collection of fine Nara-period statues.

Tōdai-ji

VISIT THE GREAT BUDDHA

The Daibutsu (Great Buddha) at Nara's Tōdai-ji is one of the most arresting sights in Japan. The awe-inspiring physical presence of the vast image is striking. It's one of the largest bronze Buddha images in the world and it's contained in an equally huge building, the Daibutsu-den hall, which is among the largest wooden buildings on earth.

Tōdai-ji was built by order of Emperor Shōmu during the Nara period (710–784) and the complex was finally completed in 798, after the capital had been moved from Nara to Kyoto. Most historians agree the temple was built to consolidate the country and serve as its spiritual focus. Legend has it that over two million labourers worked on the temple, but this is probably apocryphal. What's certain is that its construction brought the country to the brink of bankruptcy.

The original Daibutsu was cast in bronze in eight castings over a period of three years. It has been recast several times over the centuries. The original Daibutsu was covered in gold leaf and one can only imagine its impact on visitors during the eighth century AD.

The temple belongs to the Kegon school of Buddhism, one of the six schools of Buddhism popular in Japan during the Nara period. Kegon Buddhism, which comes from the Chinese Huayan Buddhist sect, is based on the Flower Garland Sutra. This sutra expresses the idea of worlds within worlds, all manifested by the Cosmic Buddha (Vairocana or Dainichi Nyorai). The Great Buddha and the figures that surround him in the Daibutsu-den Hall are the perfect physical symbol of this cosmological map.

Kokuzo Bosatsu
Seated to the left of the Daibutsu is Kokuzo Bosatsu, the bodhisattva of memory and wisdom, to whom students pray for help in their studies and the faithful pray for help on the path to enlightenment.

The Daibutsu (Great Buddha)
Known in Sanskrit as 'Vairocana' and in Japanese as the 'Daibutsu', this is the Cosmic Buddha that gives rise to all other Buddhas, according to Kegon doctrine. The Buddha's hands send the messages 'fear not' (right) and 'welcome' (left).

FACT FILE

THE DAIBUTSU

Height 14.98m

Weight 500 tonnes

Nostril width 50cm

THE DAIBUTSU-DEN HALL

Height 48.74m

Length 57m

Number of roof tiles 112,589

Komokuten

Standing to the left of the Daibutsu is Komokuten (Lord of Limitless Vision), who serves as a guardian of the Buddha. He stands upon a *jaki* (demon), which symbolises ignorance, and wields a brush and scroll, which symbolises wisdom.

Buddhas around Dainichi

Sixteen smaller Buddhas are arranged in a halo around the Daibutsu's head, each of which symbolises one of the Daibutsu's different manifestations. They are graduated in size to appear the same size when viewed from the ground.

Tamonten

To the right of the Daibutsu stands Tamonten (Lord Who Hears All), another of the Buddha's guardians. He holds a pagoda, which is said to represent a divine storehouse of wisdom.

Hole in Pillar

Behind the Daibutsu you will find a pillar with a 50cm hole through its base (the size of one of the Daibutsu's nostrils). It's said that if you can crawl through this, you are assured of enlightenment.

Nyoirin Kannon

Seated to the right of the Daibutsu is Nyoirin Kannon, one of the esoteric forms of Kannon Bodhisattva. This is one of the bodhisattvas that preside over the six different realms of karmic rebirth.

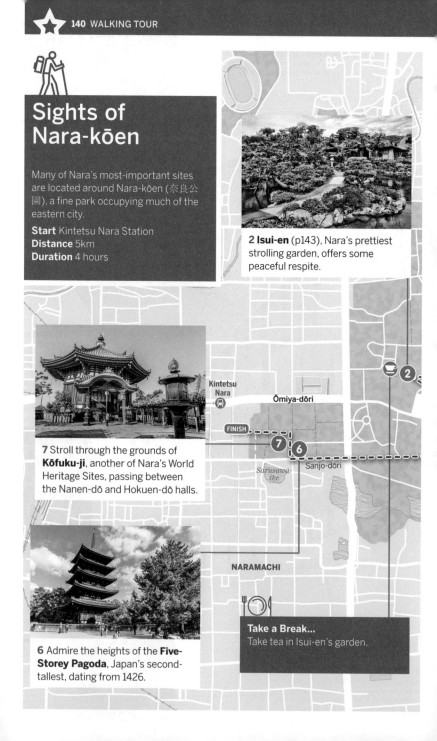

Sights of Nara-kōen

Many of Nara's most-important sites are located around Nara-kōen (奈良公園), a fine park occupying much of the eastern city.

Start Kintetsu Nara Station
Distance 5km
Duration 4 hours

2 Isui-en (p143), Nara's prettiest strolling garden, offers some peaceful respite.

Kintetsu Nara

Ōmiya-dōri

FINISH

7 Stroll through the grounds of **Kōfuku-ji**, another of Nara's World Heritage Sites, passing between the Nanen-dō and Hokuen-dō halls.

Sarusawa-ike

Sanjo-dōri

NARAMACHI

Take a Break...
Take tea in Isui-en's garden.

6 Admire the heights of the **Five-Storey Pagoda**, Japan's second-tallest, dating from 1426.

3 Admire the Niō guardians at the massively impressive southern gate of **Tōdai-ji Nandai-mon** (p137) before exploring Tōdai-ji.

4 Climb the steps to **Nigatsu-dō & Sangatsu-dō** (p137), viewing the graceful curves of the Daibutsu-den and the Nara plain.

Classic Photo A close-up of one of Nara-kōen's famously tame deer.

1 On entering the park you'll be greeted by Nara-kōen's **deer** hoping for *shika-sembei* (deer biscuits; ¥150), sold by vendors.

5 Explore **Kasuga Taisha** (p142), Nara's grandest Shintō shrine, with many smaller subshrines within.

⊙ SIGHTS

Hōryū-ji · Buddhist Temple

(法隆寺; www.horyuji.or.jp; adult/child ¥1500/750; ⊙8am-5pm Mar-Oct, to 4.30pm Nov-Apr) Hōryū-ji was founded in 607 by Prince Shōtoku, considered by many to be the patron saint of Japanese Buddhism. It's renowned not only as one of the oldest temples in Japan but also as a repository for some of the country's rarest and most-outstanding examples of early Buddhist sculpture. There's an entire gallery of Hōryū-ji treasures at the Tokyo National Museum (p40). Some of the temple's buildings are considered to be the world's oldest existing wooden structures.

Kasuga Taisha · Shinto Shrine

(春日大社; www.kasugataisha.or.jp; 160 Kasugano-chō; ⊙6am-6pm Apr-Sep, 6.30am-5pm Oct-Mar) FREE Founded in the 8th century, this sprawling shrine at the foot of Mikasa-yama was created to protect the new capital, Nara. It was ritually rebuilt every 20 years, according to Shintō tradition, until the late 19th century and is still kept in pristine condition. Many of its buildings are painted vermilion, in bold contrast to the cedar roofs and surrounding greenery. The corridors are lined with hundreds of lanterns, which are illuminated during the twice-yearly **Mantōrō** (Lantern Festival; ¥500; ⊙5.30-8.30pm 3 Feb, 7-9.30pm 14 & 15 Aug).

Nara National Museum · Museum

(奈良国立博物館, Nara Kokuritsu Hakubutsukan; ☑050-5542-8600; www.narahaku.go.jp; 50 Noboriōji-chō; ¥520, special exhibitions ¥1100-1420; ⊙9.30am-5pm Tue-Sun) This world-class museum of Buddhist art is divided into two sections. Built in 1894 and strikingly renovated in 2016, the Nara Buddhist Sculpture Hall & Ritual Bronzes Gallery displays a rotating selection of about 100 butsu-zō (statues of Buddhas and bodhisattvas) at any one time, about half of which are National Treasures or Important Cultural Properties. Chinese bronzes in the Ritual Bronzes Gallery date as far back as the 15th century BC. Each image has detailed English explanations.

Hōryū-ji

JOSHUA HAWLEY / SHUTTERSTOCK ©

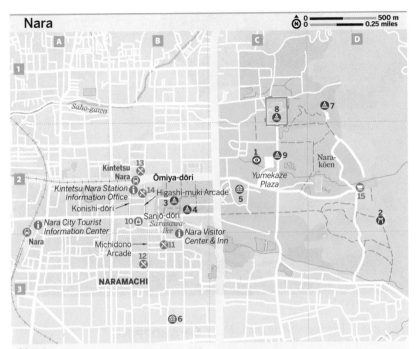

Nara

⊙ Sights
1 Isui-en & Neiraku Art Museum	C2
2 Kasuga Taisha	D2
3 Kōfuku-ji	B2
4 Kōfuku-ji Five-Storey Pagoda	B2
5 Nara National Museum	C2
6 Naramachi Kōshi-no-Ie	B3
7 Nigatsu-dō	D1
8 Tōdai-ji	C1
9 Tōdai-ji Nandai-mon	C2

ⓐ Shopping
10 Nipponichi	B2

⊗ Eating
11 Hirasō	B3
12 Kura	B3
13 Sakura Burger	B2
14 Washokuya Happoh	B2

⊙ Drinking & Nightlife
15 Mizuya-chaya	D2

Isui-en & Neiraku Art Museum
Gardens

(依水園・寧楽美術館; 74 Suimon-chō; museum & garden adult/child ¥900/300; ⊙9.30am-4.30pm Wed-Mon Dec-Mar & Jun-Sep, daily Apr, May, Oct & Nov) Isui-en is an elegant garden in two parts: one created in the 17th century, in the style of an Edo-period (1603–1868) strolling garden, and another added in the early 20th century. Both make fantastic use of the technique of *shakkei* (borrowed scenery), incorporating the mountains behind Kasuga Taisha into the design. For ¥850 you can have *matcha* (powdered green tea) and a Japanese sweet in the teahouse. Admission covers the adjoining Neiraku Art Museum, displaying Chinese and Korean ceramics and bronzes.

Naramachi Kōshi-no-Ie
Historic Building

(ならまち格子の家; ☑0742-23-4820; 44 Gangōji-chō; ⊙9am-5pm Tue-Sun) **FREE** This well-preserved merchant's house that

Kakinoha-zushi (pressed sushi wrapped in persimmon leaf)

is situated in Naramachi, with its lattice front, beamed ceilings, old kitchen, *tansu* (chest of drawers) stairs and inner garden, is an excellent place to explore the finer details of traditional Japanese architecture. An English-language leaflet is available.

🎯 TOURS

Nara Walk   Tours

(奈良ウォーク; ☑090-9708-0036; www.nara walk.com; ⊙Mar-Nov or by appointment) Nara Walk does a popular three-hour morning walking tour that is led by English-speaking guides who take groups around the highlights of Nara-kōen (Tōdai-ji), Kasuga Taisha etc; adult/child ¥3000/1000).

Meet at 10am in front of JR Nara Station (no bookings are required). It also offers a two-hour afternoon stroll around Nara-machi (adult/child ¥2000/free; bookings are required), and custom tours upon request.

🛍 SHOPPING

Nipponichi   Arts & Crafts

(日本市; ☑0742-23-5650; 1-1 Tsunofuri-shinyamachi; ⊙10am-7pm) Good-quality tea towels, homewares and totes with cute Nara motifs (lots of deer) from a centuries-old local linen producer.

🍴 EATING & DRINKING

Hirasō   Japanese ¥¥

(平宗; ☑0742-22-0866; www.hiraso.jp; 30-1 Imamikado-chō; sushi dishes ¥970-1450, lunch sets ¥1350-2300, dinner sets ¥2650-4200; ⊙10am-8pm Tue-Sun) A good place to sample local Nara specialities like *kakinoha-zushi* (pressed sushi wrapped in persimmon leaf – don't eat the leaf!) and *chagayu* (rice porridge made with roasted green tea). Look for the lattice-wood front.

Kura   Izakaya ¥

(蔵; ☑0742-22-8771; 16 Kōmyōin-chō; dishes ¥100-1000; ⊙5-10pm) This popular spot in Naramachi is styled like an old storehouse and has just 16 seats around a counter amid dark-wood panels and an old beer sign. Indulge in *mini-katsu* (mini pork cutlets), *yakitori* (grilled chicken skewers) and *oden* (fish cake and veggie hotpot). Reservations recommended; it's often full.

Washokuya Happoh
Japanese ¥¥

(和食屋八寶; ☑0742-26-4834; www.happoh. com; 22 Higashimuki-nakamachi; lunch set meals ¥950-1380, dinner set meals from ¥3000, à la carte dishes ¥380-2800; ⏰11.30am-10.30pm Mon-Sat, to 10pm Sun) A reliable choice offering a variety of dishes, from sashimi to tempura to noodles to *wagyū* (Japanese beef). Try its speciality: dishes marinated in sake lees. The place is big enough for you to be able to get a table (and lunch is, generously, served until 4pm); ingredients are listed on the menu to help diners with allergies or dietary restrictions.

Sakura Burger
Burgers ¥

(さくらバーガー; ☑0742-31-3813; http:// sakuraburger.com; 6 Higashi-muki Kita-machi; burgers ¥960-1330; ⏰11am-4pm & 5-9pm Fri-Tue; 🐕) This popular burger joint serves juicy patties on toasted buns loaded with your choice of toppings. It also does hot dogs (from ¥540) and sandwiches (from ¥820). There are only a few tables, though, so the queue moves slowly.

Mizuya-chaya
Teahouse

(水谷茶屋; ☑0742-22-0627; www.mizuyachaya. com; 30 Kasugano-chō; ⏰10am-4pm Thu-Tue) In a small, wooded, brookside clearing between Nigatsu-dō and Kasuga Taisha, this quaint thatched-roof teahouse is one of Nara's most atmospheric spots. Stop by for a cup of *matcha* (¥700 including a sweet), *onigiri* (rice balls; ¥350 to ¥400) or a bowl of udon (¥580 to ¥850).

ℹ INFORMATION

Nara has several TICs with English-speaking staff, maps and more.

Kintetsu Nara Station Information Office
(☑0742-24-4858; ⏰9am-9pm; 🕿) In front of Kintetsu Nara Station (near the top of the stairs above exit 3 from the station).

Nara City Tourist Information Center (奈良市 観光センター; ☑0742-22-3900; ⏰9am-9pm) Located in the old Nara Station building just outside the east exit of JR Nara Station. This is the city's main tourist information centre. You can store luggage here (¥600 per piece per day; counter open 9am to 7pm).

Nara Visitor Center & Inn (奈良県猿沢イン; Nara-ken Sarusawa Inn; ☑0742-81-7461; www. sarusawa.nara.jp; 3 Ikeno-chō; ⏰8am-9pm) On the southern side of Sarusawa-ike, with lots of useful info and free luggage storage. It also offers cultural experiences, including free origami lessons and, on Wednesday, a 45-minute tea ceremony (¥2000 per person).

ℹ GETTING THERE & AWAY

TO/FROM KYOTO

The Kintetsu Nara line is the fastest and most-convenient connection between Kyoto (Kintetsu Kyoto Station, in Kyoto Station) and central Nara (Kintetsu Nara Station). Comfortable, all-reserved *tokkyū* (limited-express) trains (¥1130, 35 minutes) run directly; *kyūkō* (express) trains (¥620, 50 minutes) usually require a change at Yamato-Saidaiji. For JR Pass holders, *kaisoku* (rapid) trains on the JR Nara line connect JR Kyoto Station with JR Nara Station (¥710, 45 minutes, several departures per hour).

TO/FROM OSAKA

The Kintetsu Nara line connects Osaka (Namba Station) with Nara (Kintetsu Nara Station; ¥560, 45 minutes). All-reserved *tokkyū* trains take five minutes less but cost almost double.

For JR Pass holders, the JR Yamatoji line links JR Nara Station with Osaka via *kaisoku* trains (Namba Station ¥560, 45 minutes; Tennō-ji Station ¥470, 30 minutes).

ℹ GETTING AROUND

To skip the 15-minute walk between JR Nara Station and the temple and shrine districts (about five minutes from Kintetsu Nara Station), take the bus (¥210 per ride). Two circular bus routes cover the Nara-kōen area: bus 1 (anticlockwise) and bus 2 (clockwise).

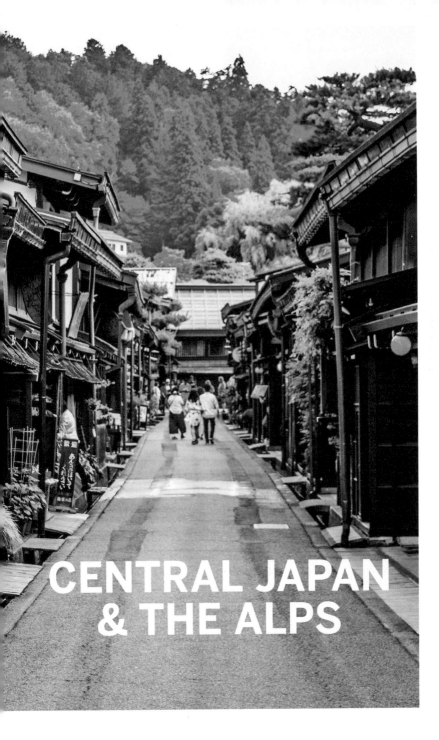

CENTRAL JAPAN
& THE ALPS

Central Japan & the Alps at a Glance...

The awesome Japan Alps rise sharply near the border of Gifu and Nagano Prefectures before rolling north to the dramatic Sea of Japan coast. All but one (Mt Fuji) of Japan's 30 highest peaks are here. There are opportunities for challenging treks and gentle ones, like the Kiso Valley trail between well-preserved Magome and Tsumago. North of the Kiso Mountains, the Hida Mountains are home to the World Heritage–listed villages of Ogimachi and Ainokura, famed for their thatch-roofed gasshō-zukuri architecture, and centrepiece Takayama, one of Japan's most likeable cities. Further east, Matsumoto has a magnificent castle and alpine scenery.

Two Days in Central Japan & the Alps

From Nagoya, take the train to the village of Magome in the morning and spend the afternoon hiking the old Nakasendō postal road to Tsumago, another historic village, where you can spend the night in a ryokan. The next day, continue by train to the castle town of Matsumoto.

Four Days in Central Japan & the Alps

On the morning of your third day, pick up a rental car in Matsumoto and drive over to Shiragawa-gō (about a three-hour drive) to explore the historic architecture for which the region is famed. End up in charming Takayama, where you can reconnect with the train network.

Previous page: Takayama Old Town (p156)

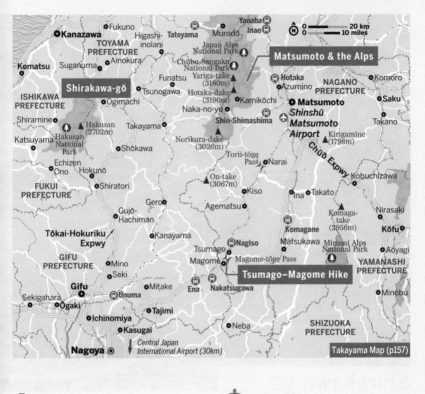

Takayama Map (p157)

Arriving in Central Japan & the Alps

Nagoya is a convenient hub on the Tokaidō Shinkansen line between Tokyo (¥10,360, 1¾ hours) and Kansai (Kyoto ¥5070, 35 minutes; Shin-Osaka ¥5830, 50 minutes), from where you can transfer for trains to the Alps or pick up a car (the easiest way to get around). Convenient local airports include Central Japan International Airport (in Nagoya) and Shinshū Matsumoto Airport.

Where to Stay

While you'll find hotels in larger cities, the Alps are an excellent place to sample more traditional accommodation. Villages in the Kiso Valley have beautiful ryokan (traditional Japanese inns); in Shirakawa-gō you can stay in a (minimally modernised) old farmhouse. Onsen (hot-spring) resorts are scattered around Takayama and Matsumoto.

PAKPOOM PHUMMEE / SHUTTERSTOCK ©

Shirakawa-gō

The remote, mountainous districts of Shirakawa-gō (白川郷) are best known for farmhouses in the thatched gasshō-zukuri style. They're rustic and lovely whether set against the vibrant colours of spring, draped with the gentle mists of autumn, or peeking through a carpet of snow.

Great For...

☑ **Don't Miss**

Sleeping in a thatch-roofed house in Ainokura, a World Heritage–listed village.

Passionate debate continues around the impact tour buses have upon these unique communities, and how best to mitigate disruption to daily life. To avoid the crowds, steer clear of weekends, holidays, and cherry-blossom and autumn-foliage seasons.

Ogimachi

Ogimachi (荻町), the Shirakawa-gō region's central and most-accessible settlement, has some 600 residents and the largest concentration of *gasshō-zukuri* buildings – more than 110. There are a few houses in town, including Shirakawa-gō's largest *gasshō* house (a designated National Treasure), **Wada-ke** (和田家; ☎05769-6-1058; adult/child ¥300/100; ⊙9am-5pm). It once belonged to a wealthy silk-trading family and dates back to the mid-Edo period. Upstairs

you'll find silk-harvesting equipment and a valuable lacquerware collection.

Gasshō-zukuri Folk Village

Over two dozen *gasshō-zukuri* buildings have been relocated to the **Gasshō-zukuri Folk Village** (合掌造り民家園, Gasshō-zukuri Minka-en; ☑05769-6-1231; www.shirakawago-minkaen.jp; 2499 Ogimachi; adult/child ¥600/400; ⊗8.40am-5pm Apr-Nov, 9am-6pm Fri-Wed Dec-Mar) in Ogimachi. While great for getting to see a variety of structures, the arrangement can feel contrived. Several houses are used for demonstrating regional crafts such as woodwork, straw handicrafts and ceramics (in Japanese only, reservations required). Pick up free multilingual maps at the **Tourist Information Center** (白川郷観光協会; ☑05769-6-1013; 2495-3 Ogimachi; ⊗9am-5pm) by the main bus stop in front.

❶ Need to Know

You need a car to reach most of Shirakawa-gō's sights, located in Ogimachi.

✕ Take a Break

The Gasshō-zukuri Folk Village is a nice place for a picnic.

★ Top Tip

For Ogimachi views, climb the path (five minutes) to **Shiroyama Tenbōdai** (Observation Point) from the intersection of Rtes 156 and 360.

Ainokura & Suganuma

Stroll through Ainokura to **Ainokura Minzoku-kan** (相倉民族館; ☑0763-66-2732; 352 Ainokura; ¥210; ⊗8.30am-5pm), a folklore museum with displays of local crafts and paper. It's divided into two buildings, the former Ozaki and Nakaya residences (prominent local families).

Between Suganuma and Ainokura, in the hamlet of Kaminashi, you'll find **Murakami-ke** (村上家; ☑0763-66-2711; www.murakamike.jp; 742 Kaminashi; adult/child ¥300/150; ⊗8.30am-5pm Wed-Mon Apr-Nov, 9am-4pm Wed-Mon Dec-Mar), one of the oldest *gasshō* houses in the region (dating to 1578). It's now a small museum; the proud owner delights in showing visitors around and might sing you some local folk songs. Close by, the main hall of Hakusan-gū shrine dates to 1502.

Tsumago–Magome Hike

This rewarding hike, along a twisty, craggy old post road, connects two of the most attractive towns along the Nakasendō (中仙道), one of five highways originally connecting Edo (now Tokyo) with Kyoto.

Great For...

☑ Don't Miss

Staying overnight in a *minshuku* or ryokan here; there are lovely, inexpensive options.

From Magome (elevation 600m), the 7.8km hike to Tsumago (elevation 420m) follows a steep, largely paved road until it reaches its peak at the top of Magome-tōge (pass) – elevation 801m. After the pass, the trail meanders by waterfalls, forest and farmland. The route is easiest in this direction and is clearly signposted in English; allow three to six hours to enjoy it.

Magome-juku

Pretty Magome-juku (馬篭) is the furthest south of the Kiso Valley post villages. Its buildings line a steep, cobblestone pedestrian road; the rustic shopfronts and mountain views will keep your finger on the shutter. Magome's **Tourist Information Center** (観光案内館; ☑0264-59-2336; www. kiso-magome.com; 4300-1 Magome; ⊘9am-5pm) is located up the hill, to the right.

Tsumago

/GETTY IMAGES ©

Tsumago–Magome Hike **⑦**

Nagiso ⑧ ● Nagiso
Tadachi ⑧ ● Tsumago
Magome-tōge Pass
🚍 ● Magome
Nakatsugawa 🚍 ● Ochiaigawa
🚉 ● Nakatsugawa

❶ Need to Know

Magome and Tsumago are in the Kiso Valley, northeast of transit hub Nagoya.

✗ Take a Break

Both towns have lunch spots and snack vendors but are quiet after dark.

★ Top Tip

Use luggage forwarding between the towns' Tourist Information Centers. Deposit bags between 8.30am and 11.30am, for 1pm delivery.

www.tumago.jp/english; 2159-2 Azuma; ⊙8.30am-5pm) is in the town centre. Some English is spoken and there's English-language literature.

Tsumago

Tsumago (妻籠) feels like an open-air museum, about 15 minutes' walk from end to end. It was designated by the government as a protected area for the preservation of traditional buildings: modern developments like telephone poles aren't allowed to mar the scene. The dark-wood glory of its lattice-fronted buildings is particularly beautiful at dawn and dusk. Among the most impressive structures is the restored **waki-honjin** (脇本陣 (奥谷)・歴史資料館, Rekishi Shiryōkan; 2159-2 Azuma; adult/child ¥600/300; ⊙9am-5pm), a former rest stop for the retainers of the *daimyō* (domain lords'). The adjacent Local History Museum houses elegant exhibitions about Kiso and the Nakasendō, with some English signage.

Tsumago's **Tourist Information Center** (観光案内館; ☑0264-57-3123;

Getting There & Away

Catch a *tokkyū* (limited-express) Shinano train on the JR Chūō line from Nagoya to Nakatsugawa (for Magome ¥2500, 55 minutes) or Nagiso (for Tsumago ¥2840, one hour); getting to Nagiso may require a transfer in Nakatsugawa.

Buses run approximately once an hour between Nakatsugawa Station and Magome-juku (¥540, 30 minutes) and between Nagiso Station and Tsumago (¥270, 10 minutes, eight daily). There's infrequent bus service between Magome and Tsumago (¥600, 25 minutes), via Magome-tōge.

Kappabashi, Kamikōchi

PIUS LEE / SHUTTERSTOCK ©

Matsumoto & the Alps

Delightful Matsumoto, in the centre of sprawling Nagano Prefecture and easily accessible from Tokyo and Nagoya, is the gateway city for the Northern Japan Alps and a fascinating destination in its own right.

Great For...

☑ Don't Miss

Climbing Matsumoto castle for a palpable sense of history and breathtaking mountain vistas.

Matsumoto-jo

Japan's oldest wooden **castle** (松本城; www. matsumoto-castle.jp; 4-1 Marunōchi; adult/child ¥610/300; ⏰8.30am-5pm early Sep–mid-Jul, to 6pm mid-Jul–early Sep) is one of four castles designated National Treasures. The striking black-and-white three-turreted *donjon* (main keep) was completed around 1595, earning the nickname Karasu-jō (Crow Castle). You can climb steep steps all the way to the top, with impressive views.

Kamikōchi

Mention Kamikōchi to Japanese outdoors enthusiasts and their eyes will light up. They'll tell you that this is where it's at and where you should be. In the late 19th century, foreigners 'discovered' this remote valley and mountainous region and coined the term 'Japan Alps'. Open from 23 April to

Matsumoto-jo

SKYEARTH / SHUTTERSTOCK ©

❶ Need to Know

Matsumoto connects with Tokyo's Shinjuku Station (*tokkyū* ¥6900, 2¾ hours, hourly), Nagoya (*tokkyū* ¥6030, two hours) and Nagano (Shinano *tokkyū* ¥2840, 50 minutes; Chūō *futsū* ¥1140, 1¼ hours).

✖ Take a Break

Eat *tai-yaki* (carp-shaped filled waffles) on castle-side benches on **Nawate-dōri**.

★ Top Tip

Enquire at the **Tourist Information Center** (☎0263-32-2814; www.visit matsumoto.com; 1-1-1 Fukashi; ☺9am-5.45pm) for free bicycles.

15 November, it's feasible to visit in a day from Matsumoto, but you may be surprised by the number of day trippers. Staying overnight in the handful of lodges is expensive, but affords you the quiet beauty of the walking trails once the tour buses have departed. For detailed information on how to get here, see www.kamikochi.org.

Utsukushi-ga-hara-kogen Plateau

Atop this Alpine plateau (2000m) you'll find an **open-air museum** (美ヶ原美術館, Utsukushi-ga-hara Bijutsukan; www.utsukushi-oam.jp; adult/child/student ¥1000/700/800; ☺9am-5pm late Apr-early Nov), walking trails among more than 200 varieties of summer flora and the rare opportunity (in Japan) to see cows in pasture. Visit the area as a day trip from Matsumoto. There are infrequent buses, but your best bet is to rent a car and

drive along mountain roads. The area is only open from late April to early November.

Nakabusa Onsen

Lovers of rustic, remote hot springs should consider an overnight stay at this **onsen ryokan** (中房温泉; ☎0263-77-1488; www.nakabusa.com; 7226 Nakabusa; r per person incl 2 meals from ¥10,000; ☺Apr-Nov; [P][✳][🛜]) high in the Alps. Come for the isolation and the many wonderful baths, not for luxury. Day trippers can use one of the smaller *rotemburo* (outdoor baths; ¥700) between 9.30am and 4pm. The closest town is Azumino, 13km from Matsumoto. Ask the **Tourist Information Center** (☎0263-82-9363; www.azumino-e-tabi.net/en; 5952-3 Hotaka; ☺9am-5pm Apr-Nov, 10am-4pm Dec-Mar) about the limited buses (¥1700, one hour) from Azumino, or rent a car in Matsumoto.

Takayama

Takayama (officially known as Hida Taka-yama; 飛騨高山) has one of Japan's most atmospheric townscapes, with Meiji-era inns, hillside shrines and a pretty riverside setting. Most sights are clearly signposted in English and are within walking distance of the train station. The scenic Miya-gawa river bisects the town. Once across, you're in the infinitely photogenic Sanmachi-suji district, with its sake breweries, cafes, retailers and immaculately preserved *furui machinami* (古い町並み; private houses).

◎ SIGHTS

Karakuri Museum   Museum
(飛騨高山獅子会館・からくりミュージアム; ☑0577-32-0881; www.takayamakarakuri.jp; 53-1 Sakura-machi; adult/child ¥600/400; ☺9am-4.30pm) On display here are over 300 *shishi* (lion) masks, instruments and drums related to festival dances. The main draw is the twice-hourly puppet show where you can see the mechanical *karakuri ningyō* (marionettes) in action.

Kusakabe
Folk Museum   Historic Building
(日下部民藝館, Kusakabe Mingeikan; ☑0577-32-0072; 1-52 Ōjin-machi; adult/child ¥500/300; ☺9am-4.30pm Mar-Nov, to 4pm Wed-Mon Dec-Feb) This merchant and moneychanger's house, dating from the 1890s, showcases the striking craftsmanship of traditional Takayama carpenters. Inside is a collection of folk art. Rumour has it that a Rockefeller tried to buy the property after WWII; his offer was politely declined.

Takayama Shōwa-kan   Museum
(高山昭和館; ☑0577-33-7836; www.takayama-showakan.com; 6 Shimoichino-machi; adult/child ¥800/500; ☺9am-6pm) This nostalgia bonanza from the Shōwa period (1926–89) focuses on 1955 to 1965, a time of great optimism between Japan's postwar mal-aise and the 1980s economic boom. Lose yourself in the delightful mishmash, from movie posters to cars and everything in between, lovingly presented in a series of themed rooms.

Yoshijima
Heritage House   Historic Building
(吉島家, Yoshijima-ke; ☑0577-32-0038; 1-51 Ōjin-machi; adult/child ¥500/300; ☺9am-5pm Mar-Nov, to 4.30pm Wed-Sun Dec-Feb) Design buffs shouldn't miss Yoshijima-ke, well documented in architectural publications. Lack of ornamentation allows you to focus on the spare lines, soaring roof and skylight.

🔒 SHOPPING

Miya-gawa Asa-ichi   Market
(宮川朝市; www.asaichi.net; ☺7am-noon) Stalls here are primarily produce-centric, with seasonal fruit (don't miss the apples in autumn), vegetables and traditional snacks. Permanent storefronts offer handicrafts and souvenirs.

🍴 EATING

Heianraku   Chinese ¥
(平安楽; ☑0577-32-3078; 6-7-2 Tenman-machi; dishes from ¥740; ☺11.30am-1pm & 5-8pm Wed-Mon; 🖉) Atmospheric, inexpensive, welcoming and delicious are all words that spring to mind when describing this won-derful second-generation eatery serving up Chinese delights, including transcendent *gyōza* (dumplings), in a traditional Japa-nese shopfront on Kokubunji-dōri. Special diets catered to and English spoken.

Kyōya   Shokudo ¥¥
(京や; ☑0577-34-7660; www.kyoya-hida.jp; 1-77 Ōjin-machi; mains ¥800-5200; ☺11am-10pm Wed-Mon) This Takayama institution specialises in regional dishes such as *hoba-miso* (sweet miso paste grilled on a magnolia leaf) and *Hida-gyū* (beef) soba. Sit on tatami mats around long charcoal grills, under a dark-timber cathedral ceiling. It's situated on a corner, by a bridge over the canal. Look for sacks of rice over the doorway.

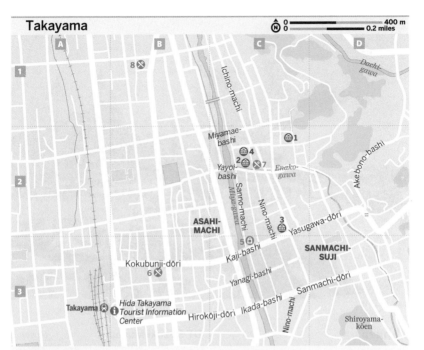

Takayama

Sakurajaya Fusion ¥¥
(さくら茶屋; ☏0577-57-7565; 3-8-14
Sowa-machi; dinner courses from ¥3000;
⏱11.30am-2pm & 6-10pm Thu-Tue; 🚲)
Sakurajaya happens when you take a
Japanese man to Germany, introduce him
to European culinary arts, hone his craft,
then return him to the quiet back lanes of
Takayama. His artisanal creations draw
from both German and Japanese lines.

ℹ INFORMATION

Hida Takayama Tourist Information Center (
飛騨高山観光案内所; ☏0577-32-5328; www.
hida.jp; ⏱8.30am-5pm Nov-Mar, to 6.30pm

Apr-Oct) Directly in front of JR Takayama Station,
knowledgeable English-speaking staff dispense
maps in many languages, and a wealth of useful
pamphlets. Staff are unable to assist with
accommodation reservations.

ℹ GETTING THERE & AROUND

From Tokyo or cities to the south (Kyoto, Osaka,
Hiroshima, Fukuoka), Takayama can be reached
by catching a frequent *shinkansen* (bullet train)
service to Nagoya, then connecting with the JR
Takayama line (*tokkyū* ¥5510, 2½ hours).

Most sights in Takayama can be covered easily
on foot.

Kenroku-en

Kanazawa

The array of cultural attractions in Kanazawa (金沢) make the city the drawcard of the Hokuriku region and a rival to Kyoto as the historical jewel of mainland Japan. Best known for Kenroku-en, a castle garden from the 17th century, it also boasts beautifully preserved samurai and geisha districts, attractive temples, a wealth of museums and a wonderful market.

◎ SIGHTS

21st Century Museum of Contemporary Art   Museum

(金沢21世紀美術館; ☏076-220-2800; www.kanazawa21.jp; 1-2-1 Hirosaka; ☺10am-6pm Tue-Thu & Sun, to 8pm Fri & Sat) **FREE** A low-slung glass cylinder, 113m in diameter, forms the perimeter of this contemporary gallery, which celebrated its 10th birthday in 2014. Museum entry is free, but admission fees are charged for special exhibitions. Inside, galleries are arranged like boxes on a tray. Check the website for event info and fees.

DT Suzuki Museum   Museum

(鈴木大拙館; ☏076-221-8011; www.kanazawa-museum.jp; 3-4-20 Honda-machi; adult/child/senior ¥300/free/200; ☺9.30am-4.30pm Tue-Sun) This spiritual museum is a tribute to Daisetsu Teitaro Suzuki, one of the foremost Buddhist philosophers of our time. Published in Japanese and English, Suzuki is largely credited with introducing Zen to the West. This stunning concrete complex embodies the heart of Zen.

Kenroku-en   Gardens

(兼六園; ☏076-234-3800; www.pref.ishikawa.jp/siro-niwa/kenrokuen; 1-1 Marunouchi; adult/child/senior ¥310/100/free; ☺7am-6pm Mar–mid-Oct, 8am-4.30pm mid-Oct–Feb) This Edo-period garden draws its name (*kenroku* means 'combined six') from a renowned Sung-dynasty garden in China that dictated six attributes for perfection: seclusion, spaciousness, artificiality, antiquity, abundant water and broad views. Kenroku-en has them all. Arrive before the crowds.

Myōryū-ji
Buddhist Temple

(妙立寺; Ninja-dera; ☎076-241-0888; www.myouryuji.or.jpl; 1-2-12 Nomachi; adult/child ¥1000/700; ⏰by reservation only 9am-4pm Mon-Fri, to 4.30pm Sat & Sun) Completed in 1643 in Teramachi, the temple was designed to protect its lord from attack. It contains hidden stairways, escape routes, secret chambers, concealed tunnels and trick doors. Contrary to popular belief, it has nothing to do with ninja. Admission is by tour only (in Japanese with an English guidebook). Phone for reservations with English-speaking staff.

⊗ EATING

Kaiseki Tsuruko
Japanese ¥¥¥

(懐石 つる幸; ☎076-264-2375; www.turukou.com; 6-5 Takaoka-machi; lunch/dinner from ¥10,000/15,000; ⏰noon-3pm & 6-10pm) *Kaiseki* (Japanese haute cuisine) dining is a holistic experience of hospitality, art and originality. This outstanding restaurant is a true gourmand's delight, offering an experience beyond what you might enjoy in a ryokan. Dress to impress. A ¥5000 lunch course is available for groups of two or more.

Sentō
Chinese ¥¥

(仙桃; ☎076-234-0669; 2F Ōmichō Ichiba, 88 Aokusa-machi; dishes from ¥650, set menus from ¥980; ⏰11am-3pm & 5-10.30pm Wed-Mon) Upstairs in **Ōmi-chō Market** (近江町市場; 35 Ōmi-chō; ⏰9am-5pm), chefs from Hong Kong prepare authentic Szechuan- and Hong Kong–style dishes (including dim

sum) from scratch. Delicious lunch and dinner set menus are excellent value. The spicy, salted squid is exquisite, and the *tan-tanmen* (sesame and chilli ramen) will have you coming back for a second bowl.

Janome-sushi Honten
Sushi ¥¥

(蛇之目寿司本店; ☎076-231-0093; 1-1-12 Kōrinbō; set menu ¥3000, Kaga ryōri sets from ¥4400; ⏰noon-2pm & 5.30-10.30pm Thu-Tue) Kanazawa institution Janome-sushi Honten has been known for sashimi and Kaga cuisine since 1931. Dinner *omakase* (chef's choice) menus start at ¥3000.

ⓘ INFORMATION

Kanazawa Tourist Information Center (石川県金沢観光情報センター; ☎076-232-6200, KGGN 076-232-3933; www.kggn.sakura.ne.jp; 1 Hirooka-machi; ⏰9am-7pm) This excellent office inside Kanazawa Station has incredibly helpful staff and a plethora of well-made English-language maps and publications, including *Eye on Kanazawa*. Goodwill Guide Network (KGGN) can also assist with hotel recommendations and free guiding in English – give two weeks' notice.

ⓘ GETTING THERE & AROUND

The direct *shinkansen* trip between Kanazawa and Tokyo (¥14,120) takes 2½ hours.

The Kanazawa Loop Bus (ride/day pass ¥200/500, every 15 minutes from 8.30am to 6pm) circles major tourist attractions in 45 minutes.

FUJI FIVE LAKES

Fuji Five Lakes at a Glance...

Japan's highest and most-famous peak is the big draw of the Fuji Five Lakes (富士五湖) region, but even if you don't intend to climb Fuji-san, it's still worth coming here to enjoy the great outdoors around the volcano's northern foothills, and to admire the mountain photogenically reflected in the lakes. Yamanaka-ko is the easternmost lake, followed by Kawaguchi-ko, Sai-ko, Shōji-ko and Motosu-ko. Particularly during the kōyō (autumn foliage season), the lakes make a good overnight trip out of Tokyo for leisurely strolling, lake activities and hiking in the nearby mountains.

One Day in Fuji Five Lakes

Travellers who have 'climbing Fuji' on their bucket list but have little time tend to take the bus in from Tokyo, climb through the night, and take the bus back in the morning. Outside the climbing season, you can also visit as a day trip from Tokyo, either to visit the Fifth Station or to enjoy views from Kawaguchi-ko.

Two Days in Fuji Five Lakes

Climbing over two days (and overnighting in a mountain hut) allows for a more leisurely pace, and is also a strategy for beating the crowds. If you're not climbing, spending the night in one of the lake towns gives you more opportunities to hunt for Fuji views, often best first thing in the morning.

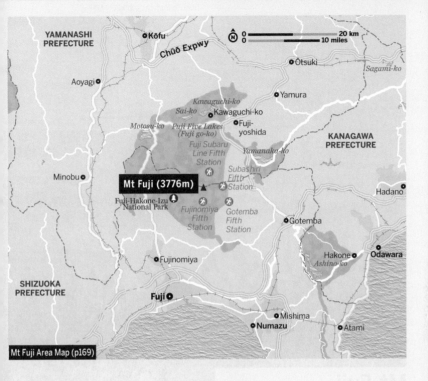

Mt Fuji Area Map (p169)

Arriving in Fuji Five Lakes

The Fuji Five Lakes area is most easily reached from Tokyo by bus or train, with Fuji-Yoshida and Kawaguchi-ko the principal gateways. It's also possible to bus in from Tokyo straight to the Fuji Subaru Line Fifth Station (alternatively known as Kawaguchi-ko Fifth Station or Yoshidaguchi Fifth Station) on the mountain during the official climbing season.

Where to Stay

If you're not overnighting in a mountain hut, Fuji-Yoshida and Kawaguchi-ko make good bases. Upscale options in Kawaguchi-ko have onsen, often with Fuji views. Hostels are good for meeting other hikers and picking up climbing info. Campgrounds and small inns dot the perimeters of the other lakes.

Sunrise from the summit of Mt Fuji

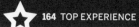

Mt Fuji

Catching a glimpse of Mt Fuji (富士山; 3776m) will take your breath away. Climbing it and watching the sunrise from the summit is one of Japan's superlative experiences.

Great For...

☑ Don't Miss

Watching the sunrise from the summit is a profound, once-in-a-lifetime experience.

Climbing Mt Fuji

The mountain is divided into 10 'stations' from base (First Station) to summit (Tenth). The original pilgrim trail runs from the base station, but these days most climbers start from the halfway point at one of the four active Fifth Stations, all of which can be accessed via bus or car. The vast majority of climbers hike the **Kawaguchi-ko Trail** from the Fuji Subuaru Line Fifth Station, also referred to as the Kawaguchi-ko Fifth Station. The less trodden, but more scenic, forested **Subashiri Trail** is a good alternative; it merges with the Yoshida Trail at the Eighth Station. Other Fifth Stations are **Fujinomiya**, which is best for climbers coming from the west (Nagoya, Kyoto and beyond) and the seldom-used and neglected **Gotemba Trail**, a tough 7½-hour climb to the summit.

Fuji Subaru
Line Fifth
Station
Taishikan
Fujisan
Mt Fuji Hotel
Fuji-Hakone-Izu
National Park
Subashiri
Fifth Station
Gotemba
Fifth Station
Fujinomiya
Fifth Station
Hōei-san
(2693m)

ℹ Need to Know

The official climbing season runs from 1 July to 31 August.

✕ Take a Break

Rest in a mountain hut; it's polite to order something small.

★ Top Tip

Check summit weather conditions before climbing: www.fujimountainguides. com/mt-fuji-weather-forecast.html.

The intersection of trails is not well marked and it's easy to get lost, especially on the way down; climbing with experienced guides is strongly recommended.

Fuji Subaru Line Fifth Station

The road from Kawaguchi-ko to the Fuji Subaru Line Fifth Station stays open as long as the weather permits (from roughly mid-April to early December). Even when summiting is off-limits, it's still possible to take the bus here just to stand in awesome proximity to the snowcapped peak. From roughly mid-May to late October, you can hike the flat **Ochūdō Trail** (御中道) that hugs the mountain at the tree line; it stretches 4km to Okuniwa (奥庭), where you'll have to double back. At either end of the climbing season, check conditions

before setting out. Buses run from both Kawaguchi-ko and Fujisan Stations to the starting point at Fuji Subaru Line Fifth Station in season.

Know Before You Go

Make no mistake: Mt Fuji is a serious mountain, high enough for altitude sickness, and on the summit it can go from sunny and warm to wet, windy and cold remarkably quickly. Even if conditions are fine, you can count on it being close to freezing in the morning, even in summer. Also be aware that visibility can rapidly disappear with a blanket of mist rolling in suddenly. To avoid altitude sickness, be sure to take it slowly and take regular breaks. If you're suffering severe symptoms, you'll need to make an immediate descent. At a minimum, bring clothing for cold and wet weather, including a hat and gloves, plus at least 2L of water (you can buy more on the mountain during the climbing season), a map and snacks. If you're climbing at night, bring a torch (flashlight) or headlamp with spare batteries. Don't forget plenty of cash for buying snacks, other necessities and souvenirs from the mountain huts and to use their toilets (¥200).

When to Climb

To time your arrival for dawn you can either start up in the afternoon, stay overnight in a mountain hut and continue early in the morning, or climb the whole way at night. You don't want to arrive on the top too long before dawn, as it will be very cold and windy, even at the height of summer. Authorities strongly caution against climbing outside the regular season, when the weather is highly unpredictable and first-aid stations on the mountain are closed. Despite this, many people do climb out of season, as it's the best time to avoid the crowds. During this time, climbers generally head off at dawn, and return early afternoon – however, mountain huts on the Yoshida Trail stay open later into September when weather conditions may still be good; a few open the last week of June, when snow still blankets the upper stations.

Mountain Huts

Conditions in mountain huts are spartan (a blanket on the floor sandwiched between other climbers), but reservations are recommended and are essential on weekends. It's also important to let huts know if you cancel at the last minute; be prepared to cover the cost of your no-show. Camping on the mountain is only permitted at the designated campsite near Fuji Subaru Line Fifth Station. These huts at the Eighth Station usually have English-speaking staff:

Taishikan (太子館; ☏0555-22-1947; www.mfi. or.jp/w3/home0/taisikan; per person incl 2 meals from ¥8500)

Fuji Subaru Line Fifth Station (p165)

Fujisan Hotel (富士山ホテル; ☑late Jun–mid-Sep 0555-24-6512, reservations 0555-22-0237; www.fujisanhotel.com; per person with/without 2 meals from ¥8350/5950; ⊜)

Fuji-Spotting

Mt Fuji has many different personalities depending on the season. Winter and spring months are your best bet for seeing it in all its clichéd glory; however, even during these times the snowcapped peak may be visible only in the morning before it retreats behind its cloud curtain. Its elusiveness, however, is part of the appeal, making sightings all the more special. Here are some of our top spots for viewing, both in the immediate and greater area:

Kawaguchi-ko On the north side of the lake, where Fuji looms large over its shimmering reflection.

Motosu-ko The famous view depicted on the ¥1000 bill can be seen from the northwest side of the lake.

Panorama-dai The end of this hiking trail (p171) rewards you with a magnificent front-on view of the mountain.

Kōyō-dai Mt Fuji can be seen from this lookout (adult/child ¥200/150), particularly stunning in the autumn colours.

Resources

The official website for climbing Mt Fuji is www.fujisan-climb.jp. Get the *Climbing Mt Fuji* brochure from the Fuji-Yoshida (p171) or Kawaguchi-ko (p170) TICs.

Tours

There are several reliable companies based in the Fuji Five Lakes region and at Fuji Subaru Line Fifth Station, offering private tours with English-speaking guides.

Fuji Mountain Guides (☑042-445-0798; www.fujimountainguides.com; 2-day Mt Fuji tours per person ¥48,600)

Discover Japan Tours (www.discover-japan-tours.com; tours per person from ¥10,000)

Sightseeing Bus

The **Fuji Lakes Sightseeing Bus** (2-day passes adult/child ¥1500/750) has three looping routes that start and finish at Kawaguchi-ko Station, with numbered stops for all the sightseeing spots around the western lakes. It's a hop-on,-hop-off service with buses every 15 to 30 minutes (seasonal). Pick up the excellent map and timetable from Kawaguchi-ko Station, where patient English-speaking staff can answer all sightseeing bus-related queries. The red line follows Kawaguchi-ko's northern shore and western area, the green line goes around Sai-ko and Aokigahara, and the blue line travels around Shōji-ko to the eastern end of Motosu-ko.

Kawaguchi-ko

⊙ SIGHTS

Fujisan World Heritage Center — Museum

(富士ビジターセンター; ☑0555-72-5502; www.fujisan-whc.jp; 6663-1 Funatsu; adult/child ¥420/free; ⊗8.30am-5pm, to 6pm or 7pm in peak season, closed 4th Tue of month) The flashy South Hall of this visitor centre has imaginative, interactive displays detailing the spiritual and geological history of the mountain, as well as a dramatic video installation projected onto a fabric Mt Fuji suspended across the exhibition hall. The blue-line bus stops here. An observation deck at the North Hall (free) affords great views of Mt Fuji.

Ide Sake Brewery — Brewery

(井出醸造; ☑0555-72-0006; www.kainokaiun.jp; 8 Funatsu; tours ¥500) This small-scale brewery has been producing sake using Mt Fuji spring water for 21 generations. Tours (9.30am and 3pm; 40 minutes) provide a fascinating insight into the production process and include tastings and a souvenir glass. Reservations essential for English tours.

Kubota Itchiku Art Museum — Museum

(久保田一竹美術館; ☑0555-76-8811; www.itchiku-museum.com; 2255 Kawaguchi; adult/child ¥1300/400; ⊗9.30am-5.30pm Wed-Mon Apr-Nov, 10am-4.30pm Wed-Mon Dec-Mar) In a Gaudí-influenced building above the lake, this charming museum displays the kimono art of Kubota Itchiku (1917–2003). You might see Mt Fuji in the wintertime, or the cherry blossoms of spring spread across oversized kimonos that have been painstakingly dyed, embroidered and hand-painted. The red-line bus stops here.

✖ EATING & DRINKING

Sanrokuen — Japanese ¥¥

(山麓園; ☑0555-73-1000; 3370-1 Funatsu; set meals ¥2160-4320; ⊗11am-7.30pm Fri-Wed) In this beautiful old thatched building, diners sit on the floor around traditional *irori* charcoal pits grilling their own meals –

Hōtō

Mt Fuji Area

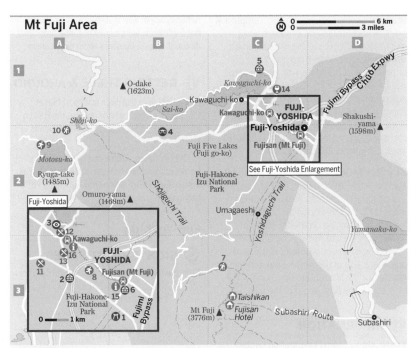

Mt Fuji Area

skewers of fish, meat, tofu and veggies. From Kawaguchi-ko Station, go west, then bear left (south) after the 7-Eleven; after 600m you'll spot the thatched roof on the west side of the road. Reservations strongly recommended.

Hōtō Fudō
Noodles ¥¥

(ほうとう不動; ☎0555-72-8511; www. houtou-fudou.jp; 707 Kawaguchi; hōtō ¥1080;

⊙11am-7pm) *Hōtō* are Kawaguchi-ko's local noodles, hand-cut and served in a thick miso stew with pumpkin, sweet potato and other vegetables. It's a hearty meal best sampled at this chain with five branches around town. This is the most architecturally interesting one, an igloo-like building in which you can also sample *basashi* – horsemeat sashimi (¥1080).

Idaten
Tempura ¥

(いだ天; ☎0555-73-9218; 3486-4 Funatsu;
meals from ¥800; ◷11am-10pm) Load up on
some delicious, deep-fried goodness pre-
or post-hike at the Idaten counter, where
you can watch the chefs prepare your tempura to order. Aside from Instagrammable
Fuji-san-themed sets (tempura arranged
like a mountain) you can also order à la
carte (various vegetables are ¥90 to ¥180
apiece; a jumbo shrimp is ¥1000).

Sky Bar Moon Dance
Rooftop Bar

(☎0555-72-1234; www.mzn.co.jp; 187 Azagawa;
◷4-10.30pm Apr-Sep; ☞) When conditions
are just right at this open-air rooftop
bar, lights twinkling on the far shore of
Kawaguchi-ko and mighty Fuji-san swathed
in evening mist, you wouldn't want to be
anywhere else in the world. Find it in the
Mizno, a stylish boutique hotel on the hillside above the east shore of the lake.

ℹ INFORMATION

Kawaguchi-ko Tourist Information Center
(☎0555-72-6700; ◷8.30am-5.30pm) To the
right as you exit Kawaguchi-ko Station, the TIC
has English speakers as well as maps, brochures,
discount coupons and info about public onsen.

ℹ GETTING THERE & AROUND

Kawaguchi-ko is the main transport hub of
the region, served by highway bus, the Fujikyu
Railway and the Fuji-Tōzan bus, which heads to
Mt Fuji.

The Fuji Lakes sightseeing buses (p167) start
from Kawaguchi-ko Station, as do buses to Fuji
Subaru Line Fifth Station (Kawaguchi-ko Fifth
Station).

Fuji-Yoshida

◎ SIGHTS & ACTIVITIES

Fuji Sengen-jinja
Shinto Shrine

(冨士浅間神社; ☎0555-22-0221; www.sengen
jinja.jp; 5558 Kami-Yoshida; ◷grounds 24hr,
staffed 9am-5pm) FREE A necessary prelim-
inary to the Mt Fuji ascent is a visit to this
atmospheric shrine (8th century, rebuilt
1800s) dedicated to Sakuya-hime, the

Fuji-Q Highland

TAKASHI IMAGES / SHUTTERSTOCK ©

goddess of the mountain. An avenue of towering cedars leads to the main gate, which is rebuilt every 60 years (slightly larger each time), and its two 1-tonne *mikoshi* (portable shrines), used in the annual Yoshida no Himatsuri festival. From Fujisan Station it's a 20-minute uphill walk, or take a bus to Sengen-jinja-mae (¥150, five minutes).

Togawa-ke Oshi-no-ie Restored Pilgrim's Inn   Historic Building

(御師旧外川家住宅; 3-14-8 Kami-Yoshida; adult/child ¥100/50; ⊙9.30am-4.30pm Wed-Mon) Fuji-Yoshida's *oshi-no-ie* (pilgrims' inns) have served visitors to the mountain since the days when climbing Mt Fuji was a pilgrimage rather than a tourist event. Very few still function as inns but Togawa-ke Oshi-no-ie, dating to 1768 and wonderfully preserved, evokes the fascinating Edo-era practice of Mt Fuji worship, back when up to 100 pilgrims at a time would have shared the tatami floors here en route to the mountain. The audio guide is recommended.

Fuji-Q Highland   Amusement Park

(www.fujiq.jp; 5-6-1 Shin-Nishihara; day passes adult/child ¥5700/4300; ⊙9am-5pm Mon-Fri, to 8pm Sat & Sun) The extreme roller coasters at this amusement park are not for the faint of heart – though they are a memorable way to bag Fuji views. Thomas Land, based on Thomas the Tank Engine, slows it down for the little ones, and there's also a resort hotel, onsen and shops. Fun for all the family, one stop west of Fujisan Station.

🍴 EATING & DRINKING

Fuji-Yoshida is known for its *te-uchi udon* (handmade wheat-flour noodles). The Fuji-Yoshida Tourist Information Center has a map and a list of restaurants.

ℹ️ INFORMATION

Fuji-Yoshida Tourist Information Center

(☑0555-22-7000; ⊙9am-5pm) Next to Fujisan (Mt Fuji) train station; the clued-up staff can provide info on climbing, as well as brochures and maps of the area.

ℹ️ GETTING THERE & AROUND

As one of the main gateways to the Fuji Five Lakes area, Fujisan Station is served by hourly direct buses from Tokyo Station (¥1800, two hours), and trains from Shinjuku Station on the JR Chūō line (¥2340, two hours), changing at Otsuki Station.

If you're heading straight to one of the hostels, the closest stop is Gekkō-ji. Fujikyu Highland Station serves Fuji-Q Highland.

A sightseeing bus pass covering Fuji-Yoshida and Yamanaka-ko areas (two days ¥1340) can be purchased at Fujisan Station.

Motosu-ko

⊙ ACTIVITIES

Kōan Motosu   Water Sports

(浩庵キャンプ場; ☑0556-38-0117; www.kouan-motosuko.com; 2926 Nakanokura; paddleboarding per hour/day ¥1500/4000, kayaking per hour for 2 people per hour/per day ¥2000/5000; ⊙8am-4pm) Kōan Motosu offers paddleboarding and kayaking, and sells (but doesn't rent) scuba gear.

Panorama-dai   Hiking

(パノラマ台) This trail ends in a spectacular head-on view of Mt Fuji and panoramic views of the surrounding lakes and mountains. Midway through, stop at the signed viewpoint to spot Fuji-san between the trees. It's a one-hour hike through the woods from the trailhead, which starts at the Panorama-dai-shita bus stop. Take a blue-line bus (38 minutes from Kawaguchi-ko).

ℹ️ GETTING THERE & AWAY

Blue-line buses from Kawaguchi-ko Station only go as far as the east shore of Motosu-ko before looping back to the station. It's a further 5km to reach the north shore and the famous Fuji view. At the time of research, there was just one daily bus (10.18am, 50 minutes) from Kawaguchi-ko Station (bay 4), returning at 1.47pm.

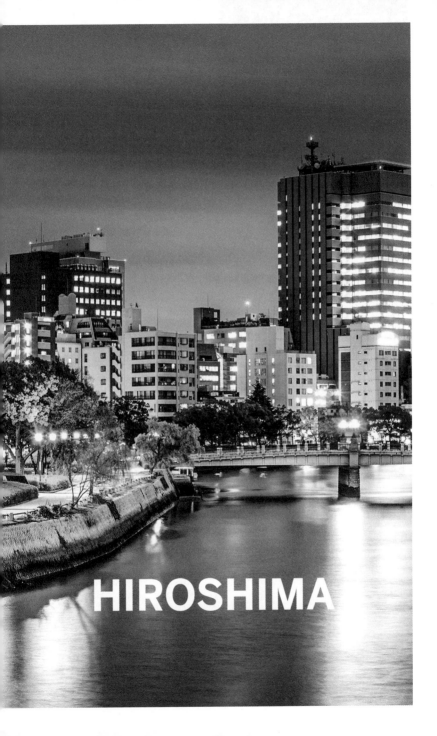

HIROSHIMA

In This Chapter

Hiroshima at a Glance...

To most people, Hiroshima (広島) means just one thing: the city's name will forever evoke 6 August 1945, when Hiroshima was targeted in the world's first atomic-bomb attack. Peace Memorial Park is a constant reminder of that day, attracting visitors from all over the world with its powerful message of peace. Present-day Hiroshima, meanwhile, is far from depressing. With its wide, tree-lined boulevards, laid-back friendliness and vibrant eating and drinking scene, the city is an attractive destination in its own right. It's also the jumping-off point for visits to Miyajima, an island in Hiroshima Bay with a captivating seaside shrine.

One Day in Hiroshima

It is possible to explore Hiroshima in a day. Spend the morning at the Peace Memorial Park sights and then, after lunch, make your way to Miyajima – sunset is a pretty time to be here. Keep in mind though, that the Peace Memorial Museum will be upsetting to many; you may not want to rush off to the next attraction.

Two Days in Hiroshima

With two days, you can give a full day each to Hiroshima and Miyajima. In Hiroshima, be sure to spend time sampling the city's local specialities, which include *Hiroshima-yaki* (a kind of savoury pancake) and sake. With a whole day for Miyajima you can explore the island's shrine and ascend Misen for views over Hiroshima Bay.

Kake

N 0 ___ 10 km
0 ___ 5 miles

HIROSHIMA
PREFECTURE

*Hiroshima
Airport*

Higashihiroshima

Peace Memorial Park

JR Hiroshima

Mazda
Museum

Hiroshima

Hatsukaichi

Takehara

*Floating
Torii*

*Itsukushima-
jinja*

*Daishō-
in*

Misen & Ropeway

Miyajima

Kure

Eta-jima

*Sea of
Aki*

Hiroshima Map (p181)

Arriving in Hiroshima

Hiroshima is in western Honshū, on the coast of the Seto Inland Sea. Most travellers arrive via *shinkansen* (bullet train), as part of the classic itinerary that runs westward from Tokyo via Kyoto and Osaka. Hiroshima's *shinkansen* station is conveniently located near downtown. You can also fly from major cities around Japan to Hiroshima Airport, 40km east of the city.

Where to Stay

Hiroshima's accommodation is clustered around the station, near Peace Memorial Park, and along the main thoroughfares of Aioi-dōri and Heiwa-Ōdōri – lots of bars and restaurants are here. The city is compact enough that wherever you base yourself you're only a short walk or tram ride away from the main sights. For an atmospheric alternative, sleep in a ryokan (traditional Japanese inn) on Miyajima.

Cenotaph (foreground) and the Atomic Bomb Dome (p178)

Peace Memorial Park

Hugged by rivers on both sides, Peace Memorial Park is a large, leafy space criss-crossed by walkways and dotted with memorials to the victims of the 1945 atomic bomb.

Great For...

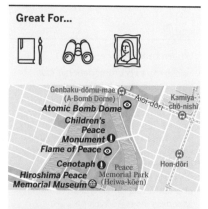

Genbaku-dōmu-mae ⓐ
(A-Bomb Dome) ⊙ *Aioi-dōri*   Kamiya-chō-nishi ⓐ
Atomic Bomb Dome ⊙
Children's Peace Monument ❶
Flame of Peace ⊙
                                    Hon-dōri ⓐ
Cenotaph ❶   Peace
Hiroshima Peace   Memorial Park
Memorial Museum 🏛   (Heiwa-kōen)

❶ Need to Know

平和記念公園; Heiwa-kinen-kōen;
🚉Genbaku-dōmu-mae

★ **Top Tip**

The Atomic Dome is particularly evocative at night, when the propped-up ruins are floodlit.

The Bombing of Hiroshima

At 8.15am on 6 August 1945, the US B-29 bomber *Enola Gay* released the 'Little Boy' atomic bomb over Hiroshima. The 2000°C (3630°F) blast obliterated 90% of the city and instantly killed 80,000 people. The bomb exploded over the town centre, filled with wooden homes and shops. This created intense firestorms that raced through the city for three days and destroyed 92% of buildings, fuelled by broken gas pipes and electrical lines. Toxic black rain fell 30 minutes after the blast, carrying 200 different types of radioactive isotopes, contaminating the thirsty wounded who drank it.

Around 350,000 people were present that day. In the following months, 130,000 died of radiation exposure and other secondary effects, including intensive burns. Most casualties were civilians, including

firefighters and 90% of the city's doctors who came to help; 20,000 forced Korean labourers; and 6,000 junior-high-school students who had been clearing fire breaks in anticipation of a regular attack.

The Japanese government says around 187,000 atomic-bomb survivors were still alive in 2015, many living through the mental trauma, cancers, and other effects of radiation. No residual radiation remains today.

Atomic Bomb Dome

The starkest reminder of the destruction visited upon Hiroshima in WWII is the **Atomic Bomb Dome** (原爆ドーム, Genbaku Dome; 1-10 Otemachi; ⊙24hr) **FREE**. Built by a Czech architect in 1915, it was the Industrial Promotion Hall until the bomb exploded almost directly above it. Everyone inside was

Hiroshima Peace Memorial Museum

killed, but the building was one of very few left standing near the epicentre. A decision was taken after the war to preserve the shell as a memorial.

Hiroshima Peace Memorial Museum

The main building, **Hiroshima Peace Memorial Museum** (広島平和記念資料館; www.pcf.city.hiroshima.jp; 1-2 Nakajima-chō, Naka-ku; adult/child ¥200/free; ⊘8.30am-7pm Aug, to 6pm Mar-Jul & Sep-Nov, to 5pm Dec-Feb), houses a collection of items salvaged from the bomb's aftermath. The displays are confronting and personal – ragged clothes,

> ☑ **Don't Miss**
>
> The pond's **Flame of Peace** (平和の灯) will only be extinguished when every nuclear weapon has been destroyed.

ALEXANDER VOW / SHUTTERSTOCK ©

a child's melted lunch box, a watch stopped at 8.15am – and there are some grim photographs. The east building presents a history of Hiroshima and of the development and destructive power of nuclear weapons. At the exit, don't miss the first-person video accounts and guestbook of world-leader visitors – including the first visit by a sitting US president, Barack Obama in 2016, who gifted origami cranes.

Memorial Hall for the Atomic Bomb Victims

A softly lit internal walkway leads down into this deeply moving **memorial space** (国立広島原爆死没者追悼平和祈念館; www.hiro-tsuitokinenkan.go.jp; 1-6 Nakajima-chō, Naka-ku; ⊘8.30am-7pm Aug, to 6pm Mar-Jul & Sep-Nov, to 5pm Dec-Feb) `FREE` whose walls show a panorama of Hiroshima at the time of the bomb. A fountain at the centre represents the moment the bomb was dropped, while the water offers relief to the victims. An adjoining room shows the names and photographs of those who perished.

Children's Peace Monument

The Children's Peace Monument (原爆の子の像) was inspired by Sasaki Sadako, just two years old at the time in 1945. At age 11 she developed leukaemia, and decided to fold 1000 paper cranes. In Japan, the crane is a symbol of longevity and happiness, and Sadako believed if she folded 1000 she would recover. Sadly she died before reaching her goal, but her classmates folded the rest. Surrounding the monument are strings of thousands of colourful paper cranes sent by school children from around the country and the world.

Cenotaph

The curved concrete cenotaph (原爆死没者慰霊碑) houses a list of the names of all the known victims of the atomic bomb. It stands at one end of the pond at the centre of the park, framing the Flame of Peace.

⊙ SIGHTS & ACTIVITIES

Hiroshima City
Manga Library
Library

(広島市まんが図書館; ☎082-261-0330; www.
library.city.hiroshima.jp/manga; 1-4 Hijiyama-
kōen; ⊙10am-5pm Tue-Sun; ☒Hijiyama-
shita) An obvious pit stop for all manga
(Japanese comics) enthusiasts, the
Hiroshima City Manga Library has a small
section of foreign-language manga as well
as a collection of vintage and rare manga.
Grab the English-language pamphlet from
the front desk and head up to the 2nd floor
of the library.

Mazda
Car Museum
Museum

(マツダミュージアム; ☎082-252-5050; www.
mazda.com/about/museum; ⊙by reservation
Mon-Fri; ☒Mukainada) **FREE** Mazda is popular for the chance to see the impressive
7km automotive industry assembly line.
English-language tours (90 minutes) are
available at 10am weekdays, but it's best
to check the website or with the tourist
office for the current times. Reservations
are required and can be made online or by
phone.

Hiroshima-jō
Castle

(広島城, Hiroshima Castle; www.rijo-castle.
jp; 21-1 Moto-machi; tower ¥370; ⊙9am-6pm
Mar-Nov, to 5pm Dec-Feb; ☒Kamiya-chō)
Also known as Carp Castle (鯉城; Rijō),
Hiroshima-jō was originally constructed
in 1589, but much of it was dismantled
following the Meiji Restoration. What re-
mained was totally destroyed by the bomb
and rebuilt in 1958. In the north end there's
a small five-level museum with historical
items, but most visitors go for the tower
with views over the impressive moat. The
surrounding park is a pleasant (and free)
place for a stroll. Enter from the east or
south.

Hiroshima Sightseeing
Loop Bus
Bus

(www.chugoku-jrbus.co.jp; single/day pass
¥200/400) The *meipurū-pu* (sightseeing
loop bus) has two overlapping bus routes
– orange and green – taking in the main
sights and museums of the city, including

Hiroshima-jō

COWARDLION / SHUTTERSTOCK ©

Hiroshima

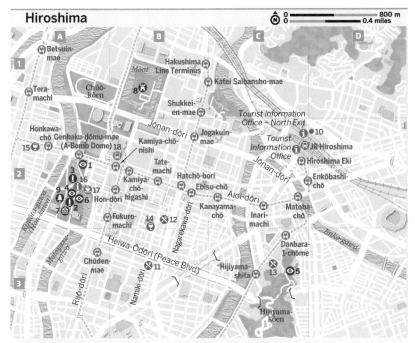

Hiroshima

the Peace Memorial Park and the Atomic Bomb Dome.

Both sightseeing bus routes begin and end on the *shinkansen* entrance (north) side of Hiroshima Station, running from about 9am to 6pm (the green route runs later during summer).

⊗ EATING & DRINKING

Hiroshima has an excellent range of Japanese and international eating options for all budgets, especially west of Peace Memorial Park and south of the Hon-dōri covered arcade. Many restaurants offer good-value set-lunch menus, and mall basements are budget-friendly. Hiroshima is famous

Worth a Trip: Sandan-kyō

Sandan-kyō (三段峡; Sandan Gorge) is an 11km ravine that is located about 50km northwest of Hiroshima, within the Nishi-Chūgoku-Sanchi Quasi-National Park (西中国山地国定公園). A trail follows the flow of the Shibaki-gawa through the gorge, providing visitors with access to waterfalls, swimming holes, forests and fresh air. The hike is very popular in autumn, when the leaves change colour. The Hiroshima tourist office (p184) has a hiking map in English.

A dozen buses a day run from the **Hiroshima Bus Centre** (広島バスセンター; www.h-buscenter.com; 3rd fl, 6-27 Motomachi; ⓢKamiya-chō-nishi) to Sandan-kyō – it's best to catch the one express service (¥1440, 80 minutes, 8am) which returns at 3pm. The bus terminates at the southern end of the gorge.

for oysters and *Hiroshima-yaki* (noodle- and meat-layered *okonomiyaki*; savoury pancakes). Breakfast options are limited to bakeries.

Okonomi-mura   Okonomiyaki ¥

(お好み村; www.okonomimura.jp; 2nd-4th fl, 5-13 Shintenchi; dishes ¥800-1300; ⓢ11am-2am; ⓢEbisu-chō) This Hiroshima institution is a touristy but fun place to get acquainted with *okonomiyaki* and chat with the cooks over a hot griddle. There are 25 stalls spread over three floors, each serving up hearty variations of the local speciality. Pick a floor and find an empty stool at whichever counter takes your fancy. Look for the entrance stairs off Chūō-dōri, on the opposite side of the square to the white Parco shopping centre.

Hassei   Okonomiyaki ¥

(八誠; ☏082-242-8123; 4-17 Fujimi-chō; dishes ¥600-1300; ⓢ11.30am-2pm & 5.30-11pm Tue-Sat, 5.30-11pm Sun; ⓢChūden-mae) The walls of this popular *okonomiyaki* specialist are covered with the signatures and messages of famous and not-so-famous satisfied

From left: *Okonomiyaki*; Okonomi-mura; Sandan-kyō

customers. The tasty, generous layers of cabbage, noodles and other ingredients are indeed satisfying – a half-order of *okonomiyaki* is probably more than enough at lunchtime.

The Hassei *okonomiyaki* shop is located on a side street one block south of Heiwa-Ōdōri.

Tōshō
Tofu ¥¥

(豆匠; ☑082-506-1028; www.toufu-tosho.jp; 6-24 Hijiyama-chō; set meals ¥2000-5000; ☺11am-3pm & 5-10pm Mon-Sat, to 9pm Sun; ☑; ☐Danbara-1-chōme) In a traditional wooden building overlooking a large garden with a pond and waterfall, Tōshō specialises in homemade tofu, served in a variety of tasty and beautifully presented forms by kimono-clad staff. Even the sweets are tofu based. There is a range of set courses, with some pictures and basic English on the menu.

Organza
Bar

(ヲルガン座; ☑082-295-1553; www.organ-za.com; 2nd fl, Morimoto Bldg, 1-4-32 Tōkaichi-machi; ☺5.30pm-2am Tue-Fri, 11.30am-2am Sat, 11.30am-midnight Sun; ☐Honkawa-chō)

📖 Hiroshima Reads

● *Hiroshima* (1946) by John Hersey – article by Pulitzer Prize–winning writer (available on www.newyorker.com).

● *Hiroshima: Three Witnesses* (1990); edited by Richard H Minear – translation of three first-hand accounts.

● *Black Rain* (1965) by Ibuse Masuji – novel depicting the lives of survivors.

● *Sadako and the Thousand Paper Cranes* (1977) by Eleanor Coerr – aimed at younger readers, based on the true story of Sasaki Sadako.

Origami cranes
KOHARUIKEHATA / GETTY IMAGES ©

HIROSE PHOTO OFFICE / SEBUN PHOTO / GETTY IMAGES ©

🧘 Day Trip to Miyajima

The small island of Miyajima (宮島) has good hikes, temples and a much-photographed *torii* (shrine gate) that seems to float on the water at high tide. Unfortunately, the *torii* is closed for repairs for two to three years from June 2019, but **Itsukushima-jinja** (厳島神社; 1-1 Miyajima-chō; ¥300; ☉6.30am-5.30pm Jan-Nov, to 5pm Dec), which traces its origins back as far as the late 6th century, is open throughout. The shrine's unique pier-like construction is a result of the island's sacred status: commoners were not allowed to set foot on the island and had to approach by boat through the *torii*.

Beyond the shrine, sacred Misen is Miyajima's highest mountain (530m), and the island's finest walk. You can avoid most of the uphill climb by taking the two-stage **ropeway** (弥山; www.miyajima-ropeway.info; one way/return adult ¥1000/1800, child ¥500/900; ☉9am-5pm) with its giddying sea views, which leaves you with a 30-minute walk to the top, where there is an excellent observatory.

The cheeky deer will eat the map right out of your pocket if you're not careful.

The **Aqua Net** (www.aqua-net-h.co.jp; one-way/return ¥2000/3600, 45 minutes, 10-15 daily) ferry runs direct to Miyajima from Peace Memorial Park.

Ferries (¥180, 10 minutes) regularly shuttle across to the island from the mainland ferry terminal near Miyajima-guchi Station on the JR San-yō line.

Itsukushima-jinja

Bookshelves, old-fashioned furniture, a piano and a stuffed deer head all add to the busy surrounds at this smoky lounge-bar. Organza hosts an eclectic schedule of live events (from acoustic guitar to cabaret), some with a cover charge, and food is also served. Lunch is available here on weekends only.

Koba   Bar

(コバ; ☎082-249-6556; 3rd fl, Rego Bldg, 1-4 Naka-machi; ☉6pm-2am Thu-Tue; 🚊Ebisu-chō) It's bound to be a good night if you drop into this laid-back place, where the friendly metal-loving musician owner 'Bom-san' can be found serving drinks and cooking up small tasty meals. There is occasional live music.

ℹ️ INFORMATION

In addition to the tourist offices, check out **Hiroshima Navigator** (www.hiroshimacvb.jp) for tourism and practical information, as well as downloadable audio guides to the sights. *Get Hiroshima* (www.gethiroshima.com), an expat-run website and magazine, has an events calendar, restaurant and bar reviews, and regular feature articles.

Hiroshima Rest House (広島市平和記念公園レストハウス; ☎082-247-6738; www.mk-kousan.co.jp/rest-house; 1-1 Nakajima-machi; ☉8.30am-7pm Aug, to 6pm Mar-Jul & Sep-Nov, to 5pm Dec-Feb; 🚊Genbaku-dōmu-mae) Situated in Peace Memorial Park next to Motoyasu-bashi bridge, this air-conditioned tourist office has comprehensive information, English-speaking staff and a small shop selling souvenirs.

Tourist Information Office (観光案内所; ☎082-261-1877; ☉9am-5.30pm; 📶) This tourist information office is located inside the Hiroshima train station near the southern exit – you will find English-speaking staff here. There is another tourist information branch that is situated at the **north (shinkansen) exit** (☎082-263-6822; ☉9am-5.30pm) of the Hiroshima train station.

Traditional Hiroshima tram

ℹ GETTING THERE & AWAY

Hiroshima Station is on the JR San-yō line, which passes westwards to Shimonoseki. It's also a major stop on the Tokyo–Osaka–Hakata *shinkansen* line. Note that if you're travelling from Tokyo or Kyoto, you may need to change trains at Osaka or Okayama en route.

ℹ GETTING AROUND

Most sights in Hiroshima are accessible either on foot or with a short tram (streetcar) ride.

Hiroshima's trams (www.hiroden.co.jp) will get you almost anywhere you want to go for a flat fare of ¥180. You pay by dropping the fare into the machine by the driver as you get off the tram. If you have to change trams to get to your destination, you should ask for a *norikae-ken* (transfer ticket).

OSAKA

Osaka at a Glance...

If Kyoto was the city of the courtly nobility and Tokyo the city of the samurai, then Osaka (大阪) was the city of the merchant class. Japan's third-largest city is a place where things have always moved a bit faster, where people are a bit brasher and interactions are peppered with playful jabs – and locals take pride in this. Osaka is not a pretty city in the conventional sense – though it does have a lovely river cutting through the centre – but it packs more colour than most. The acres of concrete are cloaked in dazzling neon; shopfronts are vivid, unabashed cries for attention.

Two Days in Osaka

Start your first morning with a visit to **Osaka-jō** (p194) then spend the afternoon exploring Osaka's **Minami** (p196) shopping-and-dining district. Come dusk, join the nightly throngs in neon-lit **Dōtombori** (p194). On day two, take a day trip to the castle, **Himeji-jō** (p206), capped off by a visit to the **Umeda Sky Building** (p198) for views over the city.

Four Days in Osaka

On day three, take a cycling tour of the city with **Cycle Osaka** (p199; we love the food route). In the late afternoon, rest your weary legs at **Spa World** (p198) then go for *kushikatsu* (deep-fried skewers; p193) in **Shin-Sekai**. Spend your last morning at the **National Museum of Ethnology** (p194) or at the bay-front **Osaka Aquarium Kaiyūkan** (p197), then catch a **bunraku** (puppet-theatre) performance (p198).

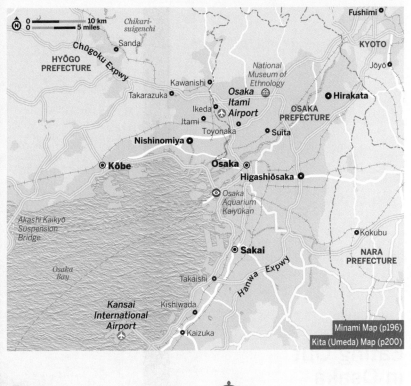

Arriving in Osaka

International and some domestic flights go to Kansai International Airport (KIX), 50km south of Osaka. KIX is well connected to the city with direct train lines and buses. Shin-Osaka Station is served by the Tōkaidō-Sanyō *shinkansen* (bullet train; running between Tokyo and Hakata in Fukuoka) and the eastern terminus of the Kyūshū *shinkansen* to Kagoshima. Departures are frequent.

Where to Stay

Osaka has plenty of accommodation in all budgets, including some stylish new hostels and guesthouses; at the midrange your best bet is a chain hotel. Base yourself in Minami for access to a larger selection of bars, restaurants and shops, or in Kita for fast access to long-distance transport.

Kaiten-sushi (p193)

Eating Out in Osaka

Above all, Osaka is a city that loves to eat: its unofficial slogan is kuidaore *('eat until you drop'). It really shines in the evening, when it seems that everyone is out for a good meal – and a good time. It's most famous for its comfort food – dishes that are deep-fried or grilled and stuffed with delicacies like octopus and squid.*

Great For...

ℹ️ **Need to Know**

The Minami district is the centre of Osaka's eating and drinking scene.

★ **Top Tip**
Surprisingly good restaurants can be found in mall and train-station food courts.

Okonomiyaki

Thick, savoury pancakes filled with shredded cabbage and your choice of meat, seafood, vegetables and more (the name means 'cook as you like'). Often prepared on a *teppan* (steel plate) set into your table, the cooked pancake is brushed with a savoury Worcestershire-style sauce, decoratively striped with mayonnaise and topped with dried bonito flakes, which seem to dance in the rising steam. Slice off a wedge using a tiny *kote* (trowel), and – warning – allow it to cool a bit before taking that first bite.

Chibō (千房; Map p196; ☎06-6212-2211; www.chibo.com; 1-5-5 Dōtombori, Chūō-ku; mains ¥885-1675; ⊙11am-1am Mon-Sat, to midnight Sun; ⓢMidō-suji line to Namba, exit 14) is one of Osaka's most famous *okonomiyaki* restaurants. It almost always has a line, but it moves fast because there is seating on multiple floors (though you might want to hold out for the coveted tables overlooking the canal, Dōtombori-gawa).

Tako-yaki

These doughy dumplings stuffed with octopus (*tako* in Japanese) are grilled in specially made moulds. They're often sold as street food, served with pickled ginger, topped with savoury sauce, powdered *aonori* (seaweed), mayonnaise and bonito flakes and eaten with toothpicks. Nibble carefully first as the centre can be molten hot!

Try them at **Wanaka Honten** (わなか本店; Map p196; ☎06-6631-0127; www.takoyaki-wanaka.com; 11-19 Sennichi-mae, Chūō-ku; tako-yaki per 8 from ¥450; ⊙10am-11pm Mon-Fri, from 8.30am Sat & Sun; ⓢMidō-suji line to

Okonomiyaki

Namba, exit 4), which uses custom copper hotplates (instead of cast iron) to make dumplings that are crisper on the outside than usual (but still runny inside).

Kushikatsu

Yakitori refers to skewers of grilled meat, seafood and/or vegetables; *kushikatsu* is the same ingredients crumbed, deep fried and served with a savoury dipping sauce (double-dipping is a serious no-no). For many Japanese, a pilgrimage to **Ganso Kushikatsu Daruma Honten** (元祖串か つ だるま本店; Map p196; 🕽06-6645-7056; www.kushikatu-daruma.com; 2-3-9 Ebisu-Higashi, Naniwa-ku; skewers ¥120-240; 🕙11am-10.30pm; Ⓢ Midōsuji line to Dōbutsuen-mae, exit 5) is a necessary part of any visit to Osaka. Opened in 1929, it's said to be the birthplace of *kushikatsu*.

Kaiten-sushi

This Osaka invention (from the 1950s) goes by many names in English: conveyor-belt sushi, sushi-go-round or sushi train. It's all the same – plates of sushi that run past you along a belt built into the counter (you can also order off the menu). **Kaiten Sushi Ganko** (回転寿司がんこ; Map p200; 🕽06-4799-6811; Eki Maré, Osaka Station City, Kita-ku; plates ¥130-735; 🕙11am-11pm; 🚃 JR Osaka, Sakurabashi exit), inside JR Osaka's Eki Marché food court, is a popular choice – meaning the two whirring tracks of plates are continuously restocked with fresh options.

Kappō-ryōri

Osaka's take on Japanese haute cuisine is casual: the dishes are similar to what you might find at a Kyoto *ryōtei* (formal restaurant with tatami seating) – incorporating intensely seasonal ingredients and elaborate presentation – but at *kappō* restaurants, diners sit at the counter, chatting with the chef who hands over the dishes as they're finished. Despite the laid-back vibe these restaurants can be frightfully expensive.

Shoubentango-tei (正弁丹吾亭; Map p196; 🕽06-6211-3208; 1-7-12 Dōtombori, Chūō-ku; dinner course ¥3780-10,800; 🕙5-10pm; Ⓢ Midō-suji line to Namba, exit 14) isn't, despite its pedigree: established over 100 years ago, it was a literati hang-out in the early 20th century. Even the cheapest course, which includes five dishes decided that day by the chef, tastes – and looks! – like a luxurious treat; reservations are necessary for all but the cheapest course.

> ☑ **Don't Miss**
>
> Dōtombori is Osaka's biggest street-food destination; it gets awfully crowded in the evening.

PRIMAGEFACTORY / GETTY IMAGES ©

> ✖ **Take a Break**
>
> Many street-food counters have tables and chairs out the back.

⊙ SIGHTS

Dōtombori
Area

(道頓堀; Map p196; www.dotonbori.or.jp; ⑤Midō-suji line to Namba, exit 14) Highly photogenic Dōtombori is the city's liveliest night spot and the centre of the southern part of town. Its name comes from the 400-year-old canal, Dōtombori-gawa, now lined with pedestrian walkways and with a riot of illuminated billboards glittering off its waters. Don't miss the famous **Glico running man** sign. South of the canal is a pedestrianised street that has dozens of restaurants vying for attention with the flashiest of signage.

National Museum of Ethnology
Museum

(国立民族学博物館; ☎06-6876-2151; www.minpaku.ac.jp; 10-1 Senri Expo Park, Suita; adult/child ¥420/free; ⊙10am-5pm, closed Wed; ☐Osaka Monorail to Banpaku-kinen-kōen) This ambitious museum showcases the world's cultures, presenting them as the continuous (and tangled) strings that they are. There are plenty of traditional masks, textiles and pottery, but also Ghanaian barbershop signboards, Bollywood movie posters and even a Filipino jeepney. Don't miss the music room, where you can summon global street performances via a touch panel. There are also exhibits on Okinawan history and Japan's indigenous Ainu culture. There's English signage, but the audio guide gives more detail.

Osaka-jō
Castle

(大阪城, Osaka Castle; Map p200; www.osakacastle.net; 1-1 Osaka-jō, Chūō-ku; grounds/castle keep free/¥600, combined with Osaka Museum of History ¥900; ⊙9am-5pm, open later at certain times in spring & summer; ⑤Chūō line to Tanimachi 4-chōme, exit 9, ☒JR Loop line to Osaka-jō-kōen) After unifying Japan in the late 16th century, General Toyotomi Hideyoshi built this castle (1583) as a display of power, using, it's said, the labour of 100,000 workers. Although the present structure is a 1931 concrete reconstruction (refurbished in 1997), it's nonetheless quite a sight, looming dramatically over the surrounding park and moat. Inside is an excellent collection of art, armour, and day-to-day implements related to the castle, Hideyoshi and Osaka.

From left: Folklore exhibit at National Museum of Ethnology; Abeno Harukas; Osako-jō

An 8th-floor observation deck has 360-degree views.

Hideyoshi's original granite structure was said to be impregnable, yet it was destroyed in 1614 by the armies of Tokugawa Ieyasu (the founder of the Tokugawa shogunate). Ieyasu had the castle rebuilt – using the latest advancements to create terrifically imposing walls of enormous stones. The largest stones are estimated to weigh over 100 tonnes; some are engraved with the crests of feudal lords.

Thirteen structures, including several turrets, remain from this 17th-century reconstruction. Osaka citizens raised money themselves to rebuild the main keep; in 1931 the new tower was revealed, with glittering gold-leaf tigers stalking the eaves.

At night the castle is lit with floodlights (and looks like a ghostly structure hovering above ground). Visit the lawns on a warm weekend and you might catch local musicians staging casual shows. The castle and park are at their colourful best (and most crowded) in the cherry-blossom and autumn-foliage seasons.

Navigating Osaka

Osaka is roughly divided into Kita (Japanese for 'north'), also known as Umeda, the strait-laced business district encircling Osaka Station, and Minami ('south'), which contains the bustling shopping and nightlife zones of Namba, Shinsaibashi, Amerika-mura and Dōtombori near Namba Station.

Fair warning: Osaka's larger stations can be disorienting, particularly Osaka Station. Exits are often confusingly labelled, even for Japanese. Adding to the confusion, *shinkansen* (bullet trains) stop at Shin-Osaka Station, three subway stops (about five minutes) north of Umeda and JR Osaka Station on the Midō-suji line.

Abeno Harukas   Notable Building

(あべのハルカス; Map p196; www.abeno harukas-300.jp; 1-1-43 Abeno-suji, Abeno-ku; observation deck: adult ¥1500; child ¥500-700, under 4yr free; ⊘observation deck 9am-10pm;

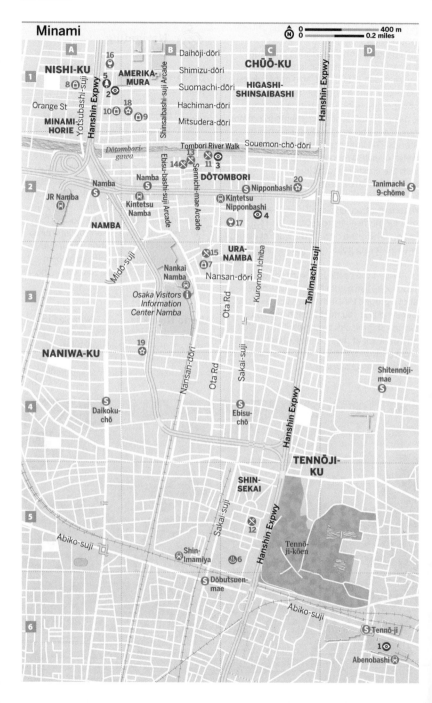

Minami

N 0 ——— 400 m
0 ——— 0.2 miles

A

NISHI-KU

16

AMERIKA-MURA

8

5

2

18

10

9

Orange St

MINAMI-HORIE

Yotsubashi-suji

Hanshin Expwy

B

Shinsaibashi-suji Arcade

Daihōji-dōri

Shimizu-dōri

Suomachi-dōri

Hachiman-dōri

Mitsudera-dōri

C

CHŪŌ-KU

HIGASHI-SHINSAIBASHI

Hanshin Expwy

D

Dōtombori-gawa

Ebisu-bashi-suji Arcade

Tombori River Walk

Souemon-chō-dōri

13

14

11 3

Sennichi-mae Arcade

DŌTOMBORI

20

Namba

JR Namba

Namba

Kintetsu Namba

NAMBA

Nipponbashi

Kintetsu Nipponbashi

4

17

Tanimachi 9-chōme

Midō-suji

Nankai Namba

Osaka Visitors Information Center Namba

URA-NAMBA

15

7

Nansan-dōri

Kuromon Ichiba

Tanimachi-suji

NANIWA-KU

19

Nansan-dōri

Ota Rd

Ota Rd

Sakai-suji

Shitennōji-mae

Daikoku-chō

Ebisu-chō

Hanshin Expwy

TENNŌJI-KU

SHIN-SEKAI

12

Abiko-suji

Sakai-suji

Hanshin Expwy

Tennō-ji-kōen

Shin-Imamiya

6

Dōbutsuen-mae

Abiko-suji

Tennō-ji

1

Abenobashi

Minami

Ⓢ Midō-suji to Tennōji, ⓇJR Loop line to Tennōji)
This César Pelli–designed tower, which
opened in March 2014, is Japan's tallest
building (300m, 60 storeys). The observatory on the 16th floor is free, but admission
is required for the highly recommended
top-level **Harukas 300 observation deck**,
which has incredible 360-degree views of
the whole Kansai region through windows
that run several storeys high. There's also
an open-air atrium. It houses Japan's
largest department store (Kintetsu, floors
B2–14), the **Abeno Harukas Art Museum**
(あべのハルカス美術館; ☑06-4399-9050;
www.aham.jp; admission varies by exhibition;
☺10am-8pm Tue-Fri, to 6pm Sat & Sun) on the
16th floor, a hotel, offices and restaurants.

Amerika-Mura   Area
(アメリカ村, America Village, Ame-Mura; Map
p196; www.americamura.jp; Nishi-Shinsaibashi,
Chūō-ku; Ⓢ Midō-suji line to Shinsaibashi, exit 7)
West of Midō-suji, Amerika-Mura is a
compact enclave of hip, youth-focused
and offbeat shops, plus cafes, bars, tattoo
and piercing parlours, nightclubs, hair
salons and a few discreet love hotels. In
the middle is **Triangle Park** (三角公園,
Sankaku-kōen), an all-concrete 'park' with
benches for sitting and watching the fashion parade. Come nighttime, it's a popular
gathering spot.

Osaka Aquarium
Kaiyūkan   Aquarium
(海遊館; ☑06-6576-5501; www.kaiyukan.com;
1-1-10 Kaigan-dōri, Minato-ku; adult ¥2300,
child ¥600-1200; ☺10am-8pm, last entry 7pm;
Ⓢ Chuō line to Osaka-kō, exit 1) Kaiyūkan
is among Japan's best aquariums. An
800m-plus walkway winds past displays of
sea life from around the Pacific 'ring of fire':
Antarctic penguins, coral-reef butterflyfish,
unreasonably cute Arctic otters, Monterey
Bay seals and unearthly jellyfish. Most
impressive is the ginormous central tank,
housing a whale shark, manta rays and
thousands of other fish. Note there are also
captive dolphins here, which some visitors
may not appreciate; there is growing evidence that keeping cetaceans in captivity is
harmful for the animals.

Kuromon Ichiba   Market
(黒門市場, Kuromon Market; Map p196; www.
kuromon.com; Nipponbashi, Chūō-ku; ☺most
shops 9am-6pm; Ⓢ Sakai-suji line to Nipponbashi, exit 10) An Osaka landmark for over a
century, this 600m-long market is in equal
parts a functioning market and a tourist
attraction. Vendors selling fresh fish, meat,
produce and pickles attract chefs and local
home cooks; shops offering takeaway sushi
or with grills set up (to cook the steaks,
oysters, giant prawns etc that they sell)
cater to visitors – making the market excellent for grazing and photo ops.

Bunraku Theatre

Bunraku is traditional Japanese puppet theatre. Almost-life-sized puppets are manipulated by black-clad, on-stage puppeteers, to evoke dramatic tales of love, duty and politics. The art form may not have originated in Osaka but it became popular here. Bunraku's most famous playwright, Chikamatsu Monzaemon (1653–1724), wrote plays about Osaka's merchants and the denizens of the pleasure quarters, the social classes otherwise generally ignored in the Japanese arts at the time. Not surprisingly, the art form found a wide audience among them, and a theatre was established to stage Chikamatsu's plays in Dōtombori. Bunraku has been recognised on the Unesco World Intangible Cultural Heritage list, and the **National Bunraku Theatre** (国立文楽劇場; Map p196; ☑06-6212-2531, ticket centre 0570-07-9900; www.ntj.jac.go.jp; 1-12-10 Nipponbashi, Chūō-ku; full performance ¥2400-6000, single act ¥500-1500; ⊙opening months vary, check the website; ⑤Sakai-suji line to Nipponbashi, exit 7) works to keep the tradition alive, with performances and an exhibition in the lobby about the history of bunraku and its puppeteers and main characters. Learn more at the Japan Arts Council's website: www2.ntj.jac.go.jp/unesco/bunraku/en.

Bunraku show
COWARD_LION / GETTY IMAGES ©

Umeda Sky Building   Notable Building
(梅田スカイビル; Map p200; ☑06-6440-3855; www.kuchu-teien.com; 1-1-88 Ōyodonaka, Kita-ku; adult/child ¥1500/700; ⊙observation decks 9.30am-10.30pm, last entry 10pm; ®JR Osaka, north central exit) Osaka's landmark Sky Building (1993) resembles a 40-storey, space-age Arc de Triomphe. Twin towers are connected at the top by a 'floating garden' (really a garden-free observation deck), which was constructed on the ground and then hoisted up. The 360-degree city views from here are breathtaking day or night. Getting there is half the fun – an escalator in a see-through tube takes you up the last five storeys (not for vertigo sufferers). The architect, Hara Hiroshi, also designed Kyoto Station (p115).

🏃 ACTIVITIES

Spa World   Onsen
(スパワールド; Map p196; ☑06-6631-0001; www.spaworld.co.jp; 3-4-24 Ebisu-higashi, Naniwa-ku; day pass ¥1300; ⊙10am-8.45am the next day; ⑤Midō-suji line to Dōbutsu-en-mae, exit 5, ®JR Loop line to Shin-Imamiya) This huge, seven-storey onsen (hot-spring) complex contains dozens of options from saunas to salt baths, styled after a mini-UN's worth of nations. Gender-separated 'Asian' and 'European' bathing zones (bathe in the buff, towels provided) switch monthly. Swimsuits (rental ¥600, or BYO) are worn in swimming pools and *ganbanyoku* (stone baths; additional ¥800 Monday to Friday, ¥1000 Saturday and Sunday).

Universal Studios Japan   Amusement Park
(ユニバーサルスタジオジャパン, Universal City; ☑0570-200-606; www.usj.co.jp; 2-1-33 Sakura-jima, Konohana-ku; 1-day pass adult/child ¥7400/5100, 2-day pass ¥13,400/9000; ⊙varies seasonally; ®JR Yumesaki line to Universal City) Modelled after sister parks in the US, 'USJ' bursts with Hollywood-movie-related rides, shows, shops and restaurants. Top billing goes to the ¥45 billion (!) **Wizarding World**

Umeda Sky Building

of Harry Potter, a painstakingly re-created Hogsmeade Village (shop for magic wands, Gryffindor capes and butterbeer) plus the 'Harry Potter and the Forbidden Journey' thrill ride through Hogwart's School.

Ofune Camome   Cruise

(御舟かもめ; Map p200; ☑050-3736-6333; www.ofune-camome.net; cruises ¥2100-4500, child half-price; Ⓢ Tanimachi line to Temmabashi, exit 18) This small wooden boat, with a few beanbags on the prow, cruises up and down the Yodo-gawa alongside Naka-no-shima; its small size means that, unless the tide is really high, it can go places that larger boats can't. The captain speaks some English and explains the significance of the buildings and bridges. Book at least three days in advance.

🄶 TOURS

Cycle Osaka   Cycling

(Map p200; ☑080-5325-8975; www.cycleo-saka.com; 2-12-1 Sagisu, Fukushima-ku; half-/full-day tours ¥5000/10,000; 🄡 JR Loop line to

Fukushima) English-speaking guides lead well-organised tours to sights both well known and less well known, along the river banks and through the markets. The food route (¥8000) is particularly recommend-ed. Fees include bicycle and helmet rental, water and food. It also rents out bikes (¥1500 per day).

🄰 SHOPPING

Osaka is the biggest shopping destination in western Japan, with an overwhelming number of malls, department stores, shopping arcades, electronics dealers, bou-tiques and secondhand shops. More and more places are offering to waive the sales tax on purchases over ¥10,000. Look for signs in the window; passport is required. Flea markets take place every month at shrines and temples.

Dōguya-suji Arcade   Market

(道具屋筋; Map p196; www.doguyasuji.or.jp; Sen-nichi-mae, Chūō-ku; ⊙10am-6pm; Ⓢ Midō-suji line to Namba, exit 4) This long arcade sells

Kita (Umeda)

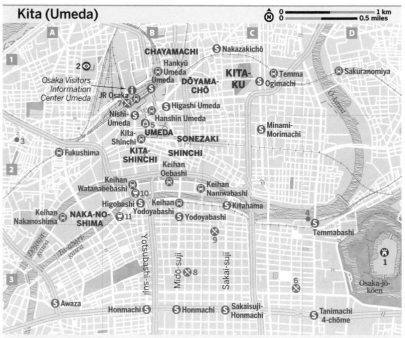

Kita (Umeda)

just about anything related to the preparation, consumption and selling of Osaka's principal passion: food. There's everything from bamboo steamers and lacquer miso soup bowls to shopfront lanterns, plastic food models and, of course, moulded hotplates for making *tako-yaki* (octopus dumplings). Hours vary by store.

Standard Books   Books

(スタンダードブックストア; Map p196; ☑06-6484-2239; www.standardbookstore.com; 2-2-12 Nishi-Shinsaibashi, Chūō-ku; ◷11am-10.30pm; Ⓢ Midō-suji line to Shinsaibashi, exit 7) This

cult-fave Osaka bookstore prides itself on not stocking any bestsellers. Instead, it's stocked with small-press finds, art books, indie comics and the like, plus CDs, quirky fashion items and accessories.

Time Bomb Records   Music

(Map p196; ☑06-6213-5079; www.timebomb.co.jp; B1, 9-28 Nishi-Shinsaibashi, Chūō-ku; ◷noon-9pm; Ⓢ Midō-suji line to Shinsaibashi, exit 7) One of the best record stores in the city, Time Bomb stocks an excellent collection of vinyl and CDs from '60s pop and '70s punk to alternative, soul and psychedelic. Find out about gigs around town here, too.

EATING

Osaka has a rich food culture that ranks as the number one reason to visit. You'll find great food at street counters, in train station basements and along shopping arcades, behind both graceful traditional facades and loud, over-the-top shopfronts.

Yoshino Sushi   Sushi ¥¥

(吉野鮨; Map p200; ☑06-6231-7181; www.yoshi-no-sushi.co.jp; 3-4-14 Awaji-machi, Chūō-ku; lunch from ¥2700; ☺11am-1.30pm Mon-Fri; ⓢMidō-suji line to Honmachi, exit 1) In business since 1841, Yoshino specialises in Osaka-style sushi, which is *hako-sushi* ('pressed sushi'). This older version of the dish (compared to the newer, hand-pressed Tokyo-style *nigiri-sushi*) is formed by a wooden mould, resulting in Mondrian-esque cubes of spongy omelette, soy-braised shiitake mushrooms, smokey eel and vinegar-marinated fish on rice. Reservations recommended.

Yotaro Honten   Tempura ¥¥

(与太呂本店; Map p200; ☑06-6231-5561; 2-3-14 Kōraibashi, Chūō-ku; tempura set ¥2500, sea bream rice ¥4300; ☺11am-1pm & 5-7pm, closed Thu; ⓢSakaisuji line to Kitahama) This two-Michelin-starred restaurant specialises in exceptionally light and delectable tempura served at the counter, where you can watch the chefs, or in private rooms. The tasty sea bream dish serves two to three people and the filling tempura sets are fantastic value. Look for the black-and-white sign and black slatted bars across the windows. Reserve in advance through your hotel.

Imai Honten   Udon ¥¥

(今井本店; Map p196; ☑06-6211-0319; www.d-imai.com; 1-7-22 Dōtombori, Chūō-ku; dishes from ¥800; ☺11am-10pm, closed Wed; ⓢMidō-suji line to Namba, exit 14) Step into an oasis of calm amid Dōtombori's chaos to be welcomed by staff at one of the area's oldest and most-revered udon specialists. Try *kitsune udon* – noodles topped with soup-soaked slices of fried tofu. Look for the traditional exterior and the willow tree outside.

Dōguya-suji Arcade (p199)

From left: Amerika-Mura (p197); Osaka Aquarium Kaiyūkan (p197), designed by Peter Chermayeff; Kuromon Ichiba (p197)

Gout
Bakery ¥

(グウ; Map p200; ☎06-6585-0833; 1-1-10 Honmachi, Chūō-ku; bread from ¥200; ◷7.30am-8pm, closed Thu; ⑤Tanimachi line to Tanimachi 4-chōme, exit 4) One of Osaka's best bakeries, Gout (pronounced 'goo', as in French) sells baguettes, pastries, croissants, sandwiches and coffee to take away or eat in. It's perfect for picking up picnic supplies before heading to nearby Osaka-jō.

🍷 DRINKING & NIGHTLIFE

Osakans love to let loose: the city is teeming with *izakaya* (Japanese pub-eateries), bars and nightclubs. Craft beer and coffee scenes are on the rise, too; see the *Osaka Craft Beer Map* (www.facebook.com/osakacraftbeermap). In the summertime, rooftop beer gardens open atop department stores. Check *Kansai Scene* (www.kansaiscene.com) for nightclub information; hostel staff and English-speaking bartenders at pubs popular with expats are another good information source.

Misono Building
Bar

(味園ビル; Map p196; 2nd fl, Misono Bldg, 2-3-9 Sennichi-mae, Chūō-ku; ◷6pm-late; ⑤Sakai-suji line to Nipponbashi, exit 5) With a waterfall and a grand, spiralling staircase out front, the Misono Building (built c 1956) was once a symbol of the high life. It's now fallen into a kind of decadent decay, making the building a lure for underground culture types, who have turned the 2nd floor into a strip of tiny, eccentric bars.

Beer Belly
Craft Beer

(Map p200; ☎06-6441-0717; www.beerbelly.jp/tosabori; 1-1-31 Tosabori, Nishi-ku; ◷5pm-2am Mon-Fri, 3-11pm Sat, 3-9pm Sun; ⑤Yotsubashi line to Higobashi, exit 3) Beer Belly is run by Osaka's best microbrewery, Minoh Beer, and features Minoh's award-winning classics and seasonal offerings (pints from ¥930). Pick up a copy of Osaka's *Craft Beer Map* here to further your local beer adventures. From the subway exit, double back and take the road that curves behind the APA Hotel.

Circus
Club

(Map p196; ☎06-6241-3822; www.circus-osaka
.com; 2nd fl, 1-8-16 Nishi-Shinsaibashi, Chūō-ku;
entry ¥1000-2500; ⓢMidō-suji line to Shinsaibashi, exit 7) This small club is the heart of
Osaka's underground electronic scene. The
dance floor is nonsmoking. It's open on
Friday and Saturday nights and sometimes
during the week. Look up for the small sign
in English and bring photo ID.

40 Sky Bar & Lounge
Cocktail Bar

(Map p200; ☎06-6222-0111; www.conrad
hotels3.hilton.com; 3-2-4 Nakanoshima, Kita-ku,
Conrad Osaka; cover after 8.30pm ¥1400;
🕙10am-midnight; ⓢYotsubashi line to Higobashi,
exit 2) If heights aren't your thing, you'll
need a stiff drink once you've peered down
over the city from the 40th floor at this
ultrasuave hotel bar. Service is impeccable
and there's a good range of food and bar
snacks to go with well-made cocktails.

⊕ ENTERTAINMENT

Tourist-information centres have details of
major productions and traditional cultural
performances. *Kansai Scene* (www.kansai
scene.com) is also a useful resource for
what's on. For live music and more underground happenings, ask around at record
stores such as Time Bomb (p200), **King
Kong** (キングコング本店; Map p200; ☎06-
6348-2260; B1, Maru Bldg, 1-9-20 Umeda, Kita-ku;
🕙11am-8pm; ⓢYotsubashi line to Nishi-Umeda,
exit 6, ⓡJR Osaka, south central exit) and **Flake**
(Map p196; ☎06-6534-7411; www.flakerecords.
com; No 201, 2nd fl, Sono Yotsubashi Bldg, 1-11-9
Minami-Horie, Nishi-ku; 🕙noon-9pm; ⓢYotsub-
ashi line to Yotsubashi, exit 6).

Namba Bears
Live Music

(難波ベアーズ; Map p196; ☎06-6649-5564;
http://namba-bears.main.jp; 3-14-5 Namba-naka,
Naniwa-ku; 🕙hours vary; ⓢMidō-suji line to
Namba, exit 4) For going on three decades
this has been the place to hear underground music live in Osaka. It's a small,
bare-concrete, smokey space – well suited
to the punk, rock and indie bands that play
here. In keeping with the alternative spirit,
you can bring in your own beer. Most shows
start at 7pm; tickets usually cost ¥2000 to
¥2500.

Discount Passes

Enjoy Eco Card (エンジョイエコカード; weekday/weekend ¥800/600, child ¥300) One-day unlimited travel on subways, city buses and Nankō Port Town line, plus admission discounts. At subway ticket machines, push 'English', insert cash, select 'one-day pass' or 'one-day pass weekend'.

ICOCA Card Re-chargeable, prepaid transport pass with an IC-chip, which you wave over the reader at ticket gates. Works on most trains, subways and buses in the Kansai area. Purchase it (¥2000, including ¥500 deposit) at any ticket machine. If you're arriving at Kansai International Airport (KIX), get a discounted **ICOCA & Haruka** combo ticket that includes travel from the airport to Shin-Osaka Station (¥3300) or Tennōji (¥3100) on the JR Haruka Kansai-Airport Express train and an ICOCA card preloaded with ¥1500 (and the ¥500 deposit). Return the card to any station window to get the deposit and any credit back.

Osaka Amazing Pass (大阪周遊パス; www.osp.osaka-info.jp) Foreign visitors to Japan can purchase one-day passes (¥2500)for unlimited travel on city subways, buses and trains and admission to around 35 sights (including Osaka-jō and the Umeda Sky Building); or two-day passes (¥3300) that cover the same sights but only travel on city subways and buses. Passes are sold at tourist information centres and city subway stations.

Yokoso Osaka Ticket (www.howto-osaka.com; ¥1500) Includes one-way fare on the Nankai Express Rapit from KIX to Nankai Namba Station and one-day travel on city subway and Nankō Port Town lines, plus admission discounts. Buy online in advance.

Hokage Live Music

(火影; Map p196; ☎06-6211-2855; www.music barhokage.net; Basement fl, 2-9-36 Nishi-Shinsaibashi, Chūō-ku; tickets around ¥1500; ⏰hours vary; Ⓢ Midō-suji line to Shinsaibashi, exit 7) Looking like an office with the inner walls ripped out (which is entirely likely), Hokage seems to be made for its rock, punk and noise bands. It's a small space, where the band might take up half the room, and a good place to discover local bands.

ℹ INFORMATION

DANGERS & ANNOYANCES

Osaka has a rough image in Japan, with the highest number of reported crimes per capita of any city in the country – though it remains significantly safer than most cities of comparable size. Still, it's wise to employ the same common sense here that you would back home.

○ Purse snatchings are not uncommon, so be mindful.

○ Nishinari-ku (also called Airin-chiku), south of Shinimamiya Station (just below Shin-Sekai), has a sizeable homeless population and an organised-crime presence. There are a number of budget accommodations here targeting foreign travellers; while it's unlikely you'd encounter any real danger, female travellers, particularly solo female travellers, do risk drawing unwanted attention, especially at night.

INTERNET ACCESS

Most accommodations have wi-fi or internet access, as do an increasing number of cafes, and Osaka has been expanding free wi-fi in public areas around town (details at www. ofw-oer.com).

TOURIST INFORMATION

Osaka Visitors Information Center Umeda
(大阪市ビジターズインフォメーションセンター・梅田; Map p200; ☎06-6345-2189; www.osaka-info.jp; JR Osaka Station; ⏰7am-11pm; ⓇJR Osaka, north central exit) The main tourist office, with English information, pamphlets and maps, is on the 1st floor of the central

north concourse of JR Osaka Station. There are also branches on the 1st floor of **Nankai Namba Station** (大阪市ビジターズインフォメーションセンター・なんば; Map p196; 06-6631-9100; 9am-8pm; Midō-suji line to Namba, exit 4, Nankai Namba) and at Kansai International Airport. Tourist offices can help book accommodation if you visit in person. The tourist information website (www.osaka-info.jp) is a good resource, too.

GETTING THERE & AWAY

AIR

Two airports serve Osaka: **Kansai International Airport** (関西空港; KIX; www.kansai-airport.or.jp) for all international and some domestic flights; and the domestic **Itami Airport** (伊丹空港; ITM; 06-6856-6781; www.osaka-airport.co.jp; 3-555 Hotaru-ga-ike, Nishi-machi, Toyonaka), also confusingly called Osaka International Airport. KIX is about 50km southwest of the city, on an artificial island in the bay. Itami is located 12km northwest of Osaka.

TRAIN

Shin-Osaka Station is on the Tōkaidō-Sanyō *shinkansen* line (between Tokyo and Hakata in Fukuoka) and the eastern terminus of the Kyūshū *shinkansen* to Kagoshima. Departures are frequent.

Destinations include Tokyo (¥14,450, 2½ hours), Hiroshima (¥10,440, 1½ hours), Hakata (¥15,000, three hours) and Kagoshima (¥21,900, 4¾ hours).

GETTING AROUND

TO/FROM KIX

Nankai Express Rapit (¥1430, 40 minutes) All-reserved twice-hourly service (7am to 11pm) between Nankai Kansai-Airport Station (in Terminal 1) and Nankai Namba Station; Nankai Airport Express trains take about 10 minutes longer and cost ¥920. To reach Nankai Kansai-Airport Station from Terminal 2, you will need to take a shuttle bus to Terminal 1.

JR Haruka Kansai-Airport Express Twice-hourly service (6.30am to 10pm) between KIX and Tennōji Station (unreserved seat ¥1710, 30 minutes) and Shin-Osaka Station (¥2330, 50 minutes). More frequent JR Kansai Airport rapid trains also run between KIX, Tennōji (¥1060, 50 minutes) and Osaka Station (¥1190, 68 minutes); the last train departs at 11.30pm. All these stations connect to the Midō-suji subway line. It departs from Terminal 1; you need to take a free shuttle bus if you arrive at Terminal 2.

TO/FROM ITAMI AIRPORT

Osaka Monorail Connects the airport to Hotarugaike (¥200, three minutes) and Senri-Chūō (¥330, 12 minutes), from where you can transfer, respectively, to the Hankyū Takarazaka line or Hankyū Senri line for Osaka Station.

Osaka Airport Limousine (www.okkbus.co.jp) Frequent buses connect the airport with Osaka Station (¥640, 25 minutes), Osaka City Air Terminal (OCAT; ¥640, 35 minutes) in Namba and Shin-Osaka Station (¥500, 25 minutes). At Itami, buy your tickets from the machine outside the arrivals hall.

TRAIN & SUBWAY

Trains and subways should get you everywhere you need to go (unless you stay out past midnight, when they stop running).

The JR Kanjō-sen – the Osaka loop line – makes a circuit south of JR Osaka Station, though most sights fall in the middle of it.

There are eight subway lines, but the one that short-term visitors will find most useful is the Midō-suji (red) line, running north–south and stopping at Shin-Osaka, Umeda (next to Osaka Station), Shinsaibashi, Namba and Tennōji stations. Single rides cost ¥180 to ¥370 (half-price for children).

The Metro Osaka Subway app (available from the iTunes store) is very handy to have as some subway stations in Osaka don't have a route/fare map in English. You can search for fares using the app and plan your journey.

SEAN PAVONE / SHUTTERSTOCK ©

Himeji-jō

Japan's most magnificent castle, Himeji-jō, is a Unesco World Heritage Site, a National Treasure and one of only a handful of original castles remaining.

Great For...

☑ **Don't Miss**

See Himeji-jō in the James Bond flick *You Only Live Twice* (1967) or Kurosawa Akira's *Ran* (1985).

History

Although there have been fortifications in Himeji since 1333, today's castle was built in 1580 by Hideyoshi Toyotomi and was enlarged some 30 years later by Terumasa Ikeda. Terumasa was awarded the castle by Tokugawa Ieyasu when the latter's forces defeated the Hideyoshi armies. In the following centuries it was home to 48 successive lords. The castle reopened in 2015 after an extensive five-year renovation.

Himeji-jō

Himeji-jō is nicknamed Shirasagi-jō ('White Egret Castle') for its lustrous white-plaster exterior and stately form on a hill rising from the plain. There's a five-storey main *tenshū* (keep) and three smaller keeps, all surrounded by moats and defensive walls

punctuated with rectangular, circular and triangular openings for firing guns and shooting arrows. The main keep's walls also feature *ishiotoshi* – narrow openings that allowed defenders to pour boiling water or oil onto anyone trying to scale the walls after making it past the other defences.

It takes about 1½ hours to follow the arrow-marked route around the castle and inside the keep. (Note that the keep is inaccessible to wheelchairs and strollers.) Last entry is an hour before closing.

Kōkō-en

Across Himeji Castle's western moat is **Kōkō-en** (好古園; adult/child ¥300/150, combination ticket with Himeji-jō ¥1040/360; ⏰9am-6pm May-Aug, to 5pm Sep-Apr), a stunning reconstruction of the former samurai quarters. Nine Edo period–style homes

boast gardens with various combinations of waterfalls, koi ponds, intricately pruned trees, bamboo, flowering shrubs and a wisteria-covered arbour. If it feels like you're on a movie set amid the stone and plaster walls lining the paths, you would be right; many Japanese historical dramas have been shot here. The teahouse serves *matcha* (powdered green tea; ¥500); the restaurant **Kassui-ken** (活水軒) serves a *bentō* (boxed meal) of *anago* (conger eel, a local speciality; ¥2080).

Getting There & Away

The castle is a 15-minute walk from Himeji Station. The **Himeji Tourist Information Office** (姫路市観光案内所; ☎079-287-0003; Ground fl, Himeji Station; ⏰9am-7pm) has English maps and bicycles to lend – first come, first served.

The San-yō *shinkansen* (bullet train) connects Shin-Osaka and Himeji (¥3240, 35 minutes), in neighbouring Hyōgo Prefecture.

NAOSHIMA

Naoshima at a Glance...

Naoshima (直島) is one of Japan's great success stories: a rural island on the verge of becoming a ghost town, now a world-class centre for contemporary art. The Benesse project started in the early 1990s, when the Benesse Corporation chose Naoshima as the setting for its growing collection of modern art. Many of Japan's most lauded architects have contributed structures, including museums, a boutique hotel and even a bathhouse – all designed to enhance the island's natural beauty and complement its existing settlements. It has also inspired some Japanese to pursue a slower life outside the big cities, relocating to Naoshima to open cafes and inns.

Two Days in Naoshima

If you're short on time, it is possible to do Naoshima as a day trip, but considering the time and effort it takes to get here it's worth spending at least one night on the island. In two days you can make your way through the highlights of the Benesse Art Site.

Four Days in Naoshima

With more time, you can explore all the nooks and crannies of Naoshima, getting a feel for the rhythms of island life. You'll also have time to make day trips to some of the less-visited islands that have their own attractive museums and art sites.

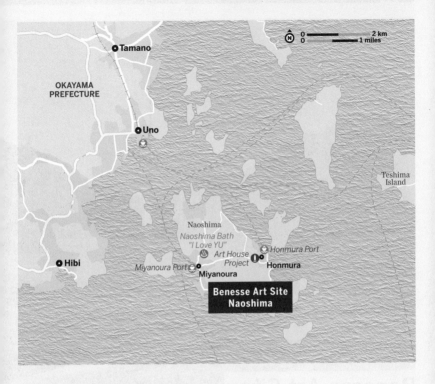

Tamano

OKAYAMA
PREFECTURE

Uno

Hibi

Teshima
Island

Naoshima
*Naoshima Bath
"I Love YU"*
Art House
Project
Miyanoura Port
Miyanoura

Honmura Port

Honmura

**Benesse Art Site
Naoshima**

0   2 km
0   1 miles

Arriving in Naoshima

Naoshima is an island in the Seto Inland
Sea off the coast of western Honshū.
The nearest major city on the mainland is Okayama, a stop on the San-yō
shinkansen (bullet train) between Osaka
and Hiroshima. Ferries depart from near
Uno Station, an hour from Okayama
on the JR Uno line. Ferry route maps
and the latest timetables can be found
on the Benesse Art Site website (www.
benesse-artsite.jp/en/access) or at the
tourist offices in Okayama.

Where to Stay

There's only one hotel on the island, Benesse House, part of Benesse Art Site.
Otherwise there are several privately
run *minshuku* (guesthouses); not a
lot of English is spoken, but locals are
becoming increasingly used to foreign
guests. There's also the beachfront
campsite Tsutsuji-sō (www.tsutsujiso.
com) with Mongolian-style *pao* tents.
Budget travellers might consider staying in Okayama and visiting Naoshima
as a day trip.

Lee Ufan Museum

TADASU YAMAMOTO ©

Benesse Art Site Naoshima

This is a captivating blend of avant-garde art and rural Japan, a collection of world-class museums and creative installations in a gorgeous natural setting on the Seto Inland Sea.

Great For...

☑ Don't Miss

The yellow *Pumpkin* sculpture by Yayoi Kusama, which has become a symbol of Naoshima.

Art House Project

Naoshima's **Art House Project** (家プロジェクト; www.benesse-artsite.jp; Honmura; single/combined ticket ¥410/1030; ⊙10am-4.30pm Tue-Sun) 🍃, which began in 1998, has turned over half-a-dozen traditional buildings to contemporary artists. Highlights include Ōtake Shinrō's shack-like **Haisha**, its Statue of Liberty sculpture rising up through the levels of the house; James Turrell's experiment with light in **Minami-dera**, where you enter in total darkness... and wait; and Sugimoto Hiroshi's play on the traditional **Go'o Shrine**, with a glass staircase and narrow underground 'Stone Chamber'.

Buy a ticket at the Marine Station Tourist Information Center (p214), Honmura Lounge & Archive (p214), or the Ueda Tobacco Shop near the Nōkyō-mae bus

Kan Yasuda's *The Secret of the Sky*

TADASU YAMAMOTO ©

❶ Need to Know

Museums are in the island's south; the Art House Project is in Honmura.

✕ Take a Break

Find cafes near the port at Miyanoura and near the Art House Project.

★ Top Tip

Buy timed entry tickets online to avoid queuing when you arrive.

Chichū Art Museum

About a 20-minute walk away from Benesse House is another Ando Tadao creation, **Chichū Art Museum** (地中美術館; www.benesse-artsite.jp; adult/child ¥2060/free; ⊙10am-6pm Tue-Sun Mar-Sep, to 5pm Oct-Feb). A work of art itself, the museum consists of a series of cool concrete-walled spaces sitting snugly underground. Lit by natural light, it provides a remarkable setting for several Monet water-lily paintings, some monumental sculptures by Walter De Maria and installations by James Turrell. Outside is the Chichū garden, created in the spirit of Monet's garden in Giverny.

Lee Ufan Museum

The **Lee Ufan Museum** (李禹煥美術館; www.benesse-artsite.jp; adult/child ¥1030/free; ⊙10am-6pm Tue-Sun Mar-Sep, to 5pm Oct-Feb) houses works by renowned Korean-born artist (and philosopher) Lee Ufan, who was a leading figure in the Mono-ha movement of the 1960s and '70s.

stop (the nearest stop for Art House Project), TVC Rental and Benesse House.

Benesse House Museum

The **Benesse House Museum** (ベネッセ ハウスミュージアム; www.benesse-artsite.jp/ en; adult/child ¥1030/free; ⊙8am-9pm) was the first art space to open on Naoshima, in 1992. Award-winning architect Ando Tadao designed the stunning structure situated on the south coast of the island.

Among the artworks here are pieces by Andy Warhol, David Hockney and Japanese artists such as Ōtake Shinrō. Art installations are dotted across the adjacent shoreline and forest, blending architecture into nature.

Setouchi Triennale

This **festival** (瀬戸内国際芸術祭; Setouchi International Art Festival; http://setouchi-art fest.jp) of art, music, drama and dance comes around every three years and has a packed calendar of events occurring on multiple Inland Sea islands, many on Naoshima and Teshima. Previous schedules have been spread across three seasons (spring, summer and autumn).

Check the excellent website for the lowdown on events and ferry passes. The recommended three-season festival 'passport' ticket (¥3800 if bought in advance, or ¥4800 on-site), which covers entry to most sites, offers significant savings for those visiting a number of sites and museums. Book your accommodation well ahead if you plan on staying on Naoshima or even in Takamatsu during the festival.

Recycled art by Yoichiza, Setouchi Triennale
AFLO CO. LTD. / ALAMY STOCK PHOTO ©

ACTIVITIES

Naoshima Bath "I Love YU"
Bathhouse

(直島銭湯; www.benesse-artsite.jp; 2252-2 Higashicho; adult/child ¥650/300; ⊗1-9pm Tue-Sun) For a unique bathing experience, take a soak at this colourful fusion of Japanese bathing tradition and contemporary art, designed by Ōtake Shinrō, where there really is an elephant in the room. It's a couple of minutes' walk inland from Miyanoura Port. Look for the building with the palm trees out front. The name is a play on words – *yū* refers to hot water in Japanese.

EATING

Cafe Salon Naka-Oku
Cafe ¥

(カフェサロン中奥; ☑087-892-3887; www. naka-oku.com; Honmura; set lunch ¥650-800, dishes ¥480-980; ⊗11.30am-3pm & 5.30-9pm Wed-Mon;) Up on a small hill at the rear of a farming plot, Naka-Oku is a good option in the Honmura area, and one of only a couple of places open in the evenings here. It's all wood-beamed warmth and cosiness, with homey specialities such as *omuraisu* (omelette filled with fried rice) at lunchtime and small dishes with drinks in the evening.

This is one of the few restaurants in the area open on Mondays.

Museum Restaurant Issen
Kaiseki ¥¥¥

(ミュージアムレストラン日本料理一扇; ☑087-892-3223; www.benesse-artsite.jp/en/ stay; breakfast ¥2615, lunch sets ¥2000-2900, dinner sets ¥7720-9500; ⊗7.30-9.30am, 11.30am-2.30pm & 6-9.45pm) The artfully displayed *kaiseki* (Japanese haute cuisine) dinners at this contrastingly austere restaurant in Benesse House Museum's basement (though with Andy Warhol works on the wall) are almost too pretty to eat. Courses feature Setouchi seafood, but there is a veg-dominated option (request a couple of days ahead) and the menu changes with the seasons. Breakfast and lunch are also served. Reservations are highly recommended.

INFORMATION

Honmura Lounge & Archive (☑087-840-8273; ⊗10am-4.30pm Tue-Sun) Tourist information next to Honmura Port, with a rest area and left-luggage service. Tickets for the Art House Project can be purchased here.

Marine Station Tourist Information Centre (☑087-892-2299; www.naoshima.net; ⊗8.30am-6pm) At Miyanoura Port. Has a comprehensive bilingual map of the island (also downloadable from the website), a walking map and a full list of accommodation options. Note that staff don't make accommodation reservations. Tickets for the Art House Project can also be purchased here.

OSAMU WATANABE ©

Naoshima Bath "I Love YU" designed by Shinro Ohtake

ⓘ GETTING THERE & AWAY

Naoshima can be visited on a day trip from Okayama or Takamatsu and it makes a good stopover if you're travelling between Honshū and Shikoku. Extra-large lockers or left-luggage services are available at the ports.

From Okayama, take the JR Uno line to Uno (¥580, one hour); this usually involves a quick change of trains at Chayamachi, crossing the same platform. Ferries go to Naoshima's main Miyanoura Port from the port near Uno Station (¥290, 15 to 20 minutes, hourly). There are also ferries from Uno to the island's Honmura Port (¥290, 20 minutes, five daily). Heading back to Okayama at night, you may find trains from Uno have finished or are two hours away, in which case it can be better to take a bus to Okayama Station (¥650, one hour, one to two hourly) from outside Uno Station at bus stop 1.

ⓘ GETTING AROUND

Naoshima is great for cycling and there are a few rental places around Miyanoura Port. **Cafe Ougiya Rent-a-Cycle** (☑090-3189-0471; www. ougiya-naoshima.jp; bike per day ¥300-2000; ☺9am-6pm) is inside the Marine Station at the port. A few electric bikes (¥1000 per day) and scooters (¥1500 per day) are also available. Prices are similar at the other rental shops nearby.

Naoshima 'town bus' minibuses run between Miyanoura, Honmura and the Benesse Art Site area (Tsutsuji-sō campground stop) in the south once or twice an hour – expect queues during the Setouchi Triennale festival. It costs ¥100 per ride (no change given). From Tsutsuji-sō, there's a free Benesse shuttle, stopping at all the Benesse Art Site museums. In busy seasons buses can fill up quickly, especially towards the end of the day, when people are returning to the port to catch ferries. Be sure to check the timetables and allow enough buffer time.

HOKKAIDŌ

Hokkaidō at a Glance...

Hokkaidō (北海道) is the Japan of wide-open spaces, with 20% of the country's land area but only 5% of its population. There are large swathes of wilderness here, with primeval forests, tropical-blue caldera lakes, fields of alpine wildflowers and bubbling, in-the-rough hot springs. In the summer, all this (plus the cooler, drier weather) draws hikers, cyclists and strollers. Winter is a different beast entirely: copious dumps of dry, powdery snow turn Hokkaidō's mountains into peaks of meringue. In recent decades, Niseko has emerged as Asia's top ski resort and a global destination, backed up by a thriving, cosmopolitan après-ski scene.

Two Days in Hokkaidō

It would be hard to do Hokkaidō justice in two days. In winter, you could base yourself in Sapporo, skiing at Teine during the day and basking in the nightlife of Susukino after dark. Year-round you could pack in a visit to Sapporo, Noboribetsu Onsen and Tōya-ko, the latter two are part of Shikotsu-Tōya National Park (and easily accessible by train).

Four Days in Hokkaidō

If you're here for the snow, this is a nice amount of time to hole up in one of Hokkaidō's top-rate ski resorts, like Niseko or Furano. In the green season, rent a car and head to Shikotsu-Tōya National Park for hiking, hot springs and beautiful vistas. Either way, allow at least an evening for Sapporo.

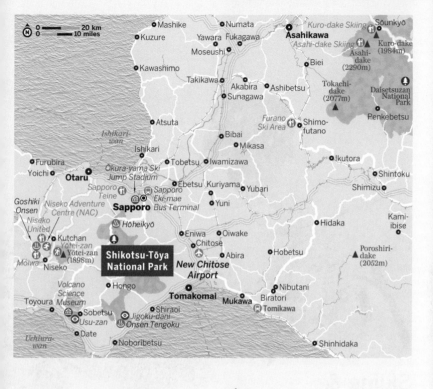

Arriving in Hokkaidō

New Chitose Airport is located 45km southeast of Sapporo, in Chitose. With flights to more than 25 cities in Japan and many cities in Asia, this is where most travellers will arrive. Sapporo is the largest city and the principal hub for trains and buses. Unless you're spending time in Sapporo, it's most convenient to pick up a rental car at the airport.

Where to Stay

Of all of Hokkaidō's ski resorts, Niseko has the best spread of accommodation, as well as the best après-ski scene (centred in Hirafu Village). Furano is quieter, with most guests holed up in one of the two Prince Hotels at the base. The Susukino district in Sapporo makes for a good base, with its high concentration of dining and nightlife options.

Furano Ski Area

Skiing & Snowsports

Cold fronts from Siberia bring huge dumps of light, powdery snow, which has earned Hokkaidō a reputation as a paradise for skiers and snowboarders. You'll find both international-level resorts and remote back-country opportunities.

Great For...

☑ Don't Miss

Carving first tracks into Hokkaidō's famous powder.

Niseko

As far as most foreign skiers are concerned, Niseko is how you say 'powder' in Japanese. It gets a whopping 15m of snow every year! **Niseko United** (ニセコユナイテッド; www.niseko.ne.jp; adult/child ¥7400/4500; ◷8.30am-8.30pm Nov-Apr) covers the four resorts on Niseko Annupuri (1308m): Annupuri, Niseko Village, Grand Hirafu and Hanazono. While you can buy individual passes for each, part of what makes Niseko so great (in addition to that famous powder) is that you can buy a single all-mountain pass, an electronic tag that gives you access to 60 runs and 18 lifts and gondolas. The all-mountain pass also gets you free rides on the hourly shuttle that runs between the resorts. Eight-hour and multiday passes are available, too.

Snowboarding at Niseko

GRAFFITI MAIDORG / SHUTTERSTOCK ©

All the resorts have terrain for all levels, though quieter Hanazono is considered best for families. There are plenty of English-speaking instructors and back-country guides; rental shops (of which there are many) also typically have a few foreign staff on hand. Niseko takes a pretty hard stance against rope-ducking (sneaking into off-piste areas). Avalanches do happen; when conditions are deemed safe, gates to select off-piste areas are opened.

Moiwa (モイワ; ☑0136-59-2511; www. niseko-moiwa.jp; 448 Niseko, Niseko-chō; lift ticket ¥4300; ⏰8am-4pm) is Niseko's 'fifth Beatle', right next to Annupuri but not part of Niseko United. It's a small resort that's quietly built up a loyal following for its deep powder and back-country opportunities. Moiwa follows Niseko's policy of no

Need to Know

Ski season runs December to April, with the best snow and biggest crowds in February.

Take a Break

The village of Hirafu is the centre of Niseko's lively après-ski scene.

★ Top Tip

Book early; accommodation in popular resorts like Niseko fill up months in advance.

rope-ducking – it just doesn't have any ropes. Experienced skiers can ski from Moiwa over to Annupuri if the gate is open. As always, check the daily avalanche report (http://niseko.nadare.info).

For information on getting to and around Niseko, see p231.

Furano

More or less in the centre of Hokkaidō, Furano shot to world fame after hosting FIS Ski and Snowboard World Cup events. Relatively undiscovered in comparison to Niseko, Furano rewards savvy powder fiends with polished runs through pristine birch forests. **Furano Ski Area** (富良野スキー一場; ☑0167-22-1111; www.princehotels.com; lift ticket full day/night ¥5500/1800; ⏰day 8.30am-7.30pm, night 4.30-7.30pm Dec–early May; 🚗) has predominantly beginner and intermediate slopes, though there are some steep advanced runs. If you're travelling as a family, a major bonus here is that children aged 12 and under get a free lift pass. Eleven lifts, including the fastest gondola in Japan, help to keep the crowds in check.

If you're not staying at one of the Prince Resorts, try lodging in the Kitanomine area, near the slopes and with a decent spread of restaurants and bars.

Furano is 125km from New Chitose Airport and 142km to Sapporo. Be extremely careful in the winter months as roads in this area can be icy and treacherous. Ten buses daily run between Sapporo and Furano (¥2260, 2½ hours), stopping at Kitanomine Iriguchi, for the Kitanomine district, before the terminus at JR Furano Station.

Sapporo Teine

You can't beat **Teine** (サッポロテイネ; ☑011-223-5830, bus pack reservations 011-223-5901; www.sapporo-teine.com; day pass adult/child ¥5200/2600; ⊗9am-5pm Nov-May, to 9pm Dec-Mar; 🐦) for convenience, as the slopes lie quite literally on the edge of Sapporo – so close that buses run directly from downtown hotels. You can swish down slopes used in the Sapporo 1972 Winter Olympics by day and enjoy the raucous restaurants, bars and clubs of Susukino by night.

Teine has two zones: the lower, more beginner- and family-oriented Olympia Zone; and the higher, more-challenging Highland Zone. There are 15 runs and nine lifts. A variety of packages, many including return bus transfer from Sapporo to the slopes, bring the price down. Note that Teine can get very crowded, particularly on weekends and school holidays.

Back Country

Some excellent options for back-country skiing exist in Hokkaidō, though this is a relatively new sphere of adventure tourism. Daisetsuzan National Park – Daisetsuzan literally means 'Big Snow Mountain' – is a top destination. On the northeastern side of the park, **Kuro-dake** (☑0165-85-3031; www.rinyu.co.jp/kurodake; pass ¥3800) has one ropeway and lift and is becoming

Teine

popular with those who like vertical and challenging terrain. Hokkaidō's highest mountain, **Asahi-dake** (www.asahidake. hokkaido.jp; day pass ¥4500; ☺1 Dec–6 May), offers an extreme experience on a smoking volcano (not for beginners); there's one ropeway (500 vertical metres), dry powder and scenic views here. Some ski and snowboard operators in Furano run back-country tours to Asahi-dake and Kuro-dake. If you come on your own, it's advisable to hire a local guide; your accommodation should be able to help with that (ask well in advance).

★ Top Tips
An excellent website for checking out Japan's ski scene is www.snowjapan.com (in English).

LEONARDO CERRONI / GETTY IMAGES ©

Extreme skiing is possible on Rishiri-zan, a classic volcanic cone on its own remote island off the coast of northern Hokkaidō. This is true back-country stuff (no lifts) with plenty of hiking up, followed by steep descents down the volcano – which sees few skiers or boarders – all the while taking in the breathtaking ocean views. You'll need a guide from **Rishiri Nature Guide Service** (利尻自然ガイドサービス; ☎0163-82-2295; www.maruzen.com/tic/guide). Book early!

For back-country tours around Niseko, **NAC** (ニセコアドベンチャーセンター; ☎0136-23-2093; www.nacadventures.jp; 179-53 Yamada, Kutchan-chō; ☺8am–9pm) has experienced English-speaking guides and instructors.

Hokkaidō Ski Basics

What to Bring Almost everything you'll need is available in Japan. If you have large feet (longer than 30cm), bring your own boots. If you're on the big side, bring your own clothing and gloves, too.

Costs Japan is a surprisingly reasonable place to go skiing or snowboarding; Niseko is the priciest of Japan's resorts. Lift tickets and accommodation are competitively priced as the number of domestic skiers has been in decline for years.

Food The slopes have plenty of pizza, ramen and other snacks. Given its international clientele, Niseko's resort villages have numerous restaurants serving Western food.

☑ Don't Miss
Niseko's Hirafu Village has Japan's best après-ski scene.

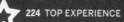

SEAN PAVONE / SHUTTERSTOCK ©

Shikotsu-Tōya National Park

Shikotsu-Tōya National Park (支笏洞爺国立公園) contains pockets of wilderness – with caldera lakes, mountains and hot-spring resorts – carved out of a large area within easy striking distance from Sapporo.

Great For...

☑ Don't Miss

Hōheikyō in Jōzankei, often voted Hokkaidō's best onsen (hot spring).

Jōzankei

Jōzankei (定山渓) sits along the Toyohira-gawa, deep in a gorge. It's the closest major onsen town to Sapporo – only an hour away – and an easy escape for those after some R&R. The resort is especially pretty (and popular) in autumn, when the leaves change colour – a sight that can be viewed from many an outdoor bath.

There are several resort-style hotels here with baths, but none hold a candle to **Hōheikyō** (豊平峡; ☏011-598-2410; www.hoheikyo.co.jp; 608 Jōzankei; adult/child ¥1000/500; ☺10am-10.30pm). Set above town on the gorge's forested slope, Hōheikyō can boast of having Hokkaidō's largest outdoor bath. The whole rambling structure is shack-like, which just adds to the appeal of having stumbled upon something great. The door curtains indicating

Jōzankei

Yōtei-・⚡️ ▲ Yōtei-zan (1898m)　▲● Eniwa-dake
-zan　　　　○　　　　Eniwa-dake Tozan-guchi
Makkari ○ Kimobetsu　　(1320m)　⚡️ Seventh
　　　　　　　　　　　　　　　　　Station
　　　　　Otaki ○ Shikotsu-Tōya
Volcano　　　　National Park　Poroto
Science　　　　　　　　　○ Kotan
Museum ○ Sōbetsu　　　　○ Shiraoi
Abuta ○ 🏛️　　　　◎ **Jigoku-**
Usu-zan　　**Onsen** ♨️ **dani**
　　Date ○ **Tengoku**

❶ Need to Know

A car is best for exploring Shikotsu-Tōya National Park (993 sq km).

✕ Take a Break

All the resort towns have a few restaurants; many open only for lunch.

★ Top Tip

Hokkaidō is bear country. Carry a bear bell into the mountains and check recent sightings at visitor centres.

which baths are for men and which women are swapped daily.

Five buses run between Sapporo Ekimae Bus Terminal and Jōzankei daily (¥770, one hour), continuing on to Hōheikyō (¥840, 1¼ hours), the final stop.

Yōtei-zan

The perfect conical volcano **Yōtei-zan** (羊蹄山) is also known as Ezo-Fuji because of its striking resemblance to Fuji-san. One of Japan's 100 Famous Mountains, it sits in its own little pocket of Shikotsu-Tōya National Park, just 10km from Niseko. It's a stunning backdrop: you can only miss it if it's hidden in cloud.

Be prepared for a big climb if you want to tackle Yōtei-zan. The most popular of four trailheads is Yōtei-zan tozan-guchi (羊蹄山登山口) at 350m, which means a more

than 1500m vertical climb to the summit at 1898m. Most people climb and descend in a day – get an early start and allow six to nine hours return, depending on how fit you are. Be mentally and physically prepared – the weather can change quickly on this exposed volcano, especially above the 1600m tree line. Make sure you have enough food and drink. There is an emergency hut at 1800m.

The upper reaches of Yōtei-zan are covered in alpine flowers during the summer. From the peak, the Sea of Japan, the Pacific Ocean and Tōya-ko are all visible – unless, of course, you are inside a cloud!

Yōtei-zan is best accessed from Niseko. If you want to attempt this by public transport, catch the 6.40am bus (¥300, 11 minutes, Monday to Saturday) from JR Kutchan Station; the last return is at 8.07pm. Hiking season is mid-June through mid-October.

Noboribetsu Onsen

Noboribetsu Onsen (登別温泉) is a serious onsen: you can smell the sulphur from miles away. While the town is small, there are countless springs here, sending up mineral-rich waters. The source of the waters is **Jigoku-dani** (地獄谷) `FREE`, a hissing, steaming volcanic pit above town. A wooden boardwalk leads out to a boiling geyser. According to legend, this hellish landscape is home to the *oni* (demon) Yukujin. Don't worry: he's kind and bestows luck. You'll find his statues around town.

Onsen Tengoku (温泉天国; ☎0143-84-2111; www.takimotokan.co.jp; Dai-ichi Takimoto-kan, 55 Noboribetsu Onsen-chō; ¥2000, after 4pm ¥1500; ⊗9am-6pm), the bathhouse attached to the Dai-ichi Takimoto-kan hotel, deserves singling out because it is truly spectacular, an 'onsen heaven' (*tengoku* means 'heaven'). The sprawling complex, awash in pastel tiles, fountains and mirrors, has more variety than any others here, with seven different springs and several outdoor baths.

JR Muroran train line runs from Sapporo to Noboribetsu (¥4480, 1¼ hours). Frequent buses (¥340, 15 minutes) connect the train station with Noboribetsu Onsen bus terminal, at the southern end of town; a taxi between the train station and town should cost ¥2000. Direct highway buses run between Noboribetsu Onsen bus terminal and Sapporo (¥1950, 100 minutes), as well as New Chitose Airport (¥1370, one hour).

Tōya-ko

At the southwestern side of Shikotsu-Tōya National Park, Tōya-ko (洞爺湖) is an almost classically round caldera lake with a large island (Naka-jima) sitting in the middle. Tōya-ko Onsen (洞爺湖温泉), the small resort on the lake's southern shore, has free hand baths and foot baths throughout town (an onsen treasure hunt!). There's a fireworks display on the lake every night

Oyunuma Naural Footbath, Noboribetsu

at 8.45pm from April until October, and paddle steamers running lake cruises. The 50km circumference of the lake can be rounded by car or bicycle.

But what sets Tōya-ko apart is its truly active volcano, **Usu-zan** (有珠山; ☎0142-74-2401; www.wakasaresort.com; 184-5 Shōwa Shin-zan, Sōbetsu-chō; ropeway adult/child return ¥1600/800; ◎9am-4pm), which has erupted four times since 1910, most recently in 2000. The eruptions at Usu-zan (729m) were among the first to be recorded by modern means (and work here significantly advanced science in early detection). At the **Volcano Science Museum** (火山科学館;

> **★ Top Tip**
> Ask at the local TIC for a list of places offering *higaeri-onsen* (day bathing; ¥500 to ¥2000).

☑0142-75-2555; www.toyako-vc.jp; 142-5 Tōya-ko Onsen; adult/child ¥600/300; ◎9am-5pm; P) you can see video footage of eruptions in action, and before and after photos that clearly show new land masses forming.

Shōwa Shin-zan (昭和新山; 398m) – whose name means 'the new mountain of the Shōwa period' – arose from a wheat field following the 1943 eruption of Usu-zan. A ropeway runs up to a viewing platform for Shōwa Shin-zan, with Tōya-ko behind it. From the observation deck a trail heads out on a 90-minute circuit (open May to October) around the outer rim of Usu-zan.

The JR Muroran line runs from Sapporo to Tōya (¥5920, two hours). From the train station, it's a 15-minute bus (¥330, twice hourly) or taxi ride (¥1800) to the bus terminal in Tōya-ko Onsen. Buses (one way/round trip ¥340/620, 10.10am, 12.45pm, 1.40pm and 3.50pm) run from the Tōya-ko Onsen bus terminal to the ropeway. A taxi should cost ¥1800; all the way from JR Tōya-ko Station, ¥3000.

Shikotsu-ko

Shikotsu-ko (支笏湖) is the second-deepest lake in Japan and renowned for its clear water. While it is 250m above sea level, its deepest spot is 363m, 113m below sea level. Shikotsu-ko Onsen (支笏湖温泉), on the eastern side of the lake, is the only town. This compact little resort village has some nice short walks, including a nature trail for birdwatchers. Sightseeing boats head out onto the lake and there are rental bicycles, boats and canoes. There is no public transport to Shikotsu-ko.

Sapporo

◎ SIGHTS

Sapporo Beer Museum   Museum
(サッポロビール博物館; ☎011-748-1876; www.
sapporoholdings.jp/english/guide/sapporo; N7E9
Higashi-ku; ☺10.30am-6.30pm; [P]; ☒88 to Sapporo Biiru-en, [S]Tōhō line to Higashi-Kuyakusho-
mae, exit 4) FREE This legendary Sapporo
attraction is in the original Sapporo Beer
brewery, a pretty, ivy-covered building.
There's no need to sign up for the tour;
there are English explanations throughout
about Japan's oldest beer (the brewery
was founded in 1876). At the end there's a
tasting salon (beers ¥200 to ¥300) where
you can compare Sapporo's signature
Black Label with Sapporo Classic (found
only in Hokkaidō) and Kaitakushi Pilsner,
a re-creation of the original recipe (found
only here).

Ōkura-yama
Ski Jump Stadium   Museum
(大倉山ジャンプ競技場; ☎011-641-8585;
www.sapporowintersportsmuseum.com; 1274

Miyano-mori, Chūō-ku; combined lift & museum
ticket ¥1000, museum only ¥600; ☺9am-6pm
late Apr-early Nov, 9.30am-5pm early Nov-late
Apr; [P]) This ski-jump slope was built on
the side of Ōkura-yama for the Sapporo
1972 Winter Games. At 133.6m it's just
slightly shorter than Sapporo TV Tower,
with a 33-degree incline. What would it feel
like to whiz down that? You can hazard a
guess after taking the rickety old lift up to
the top and staring down the slope. Keep
that image in mind when you try the highly
amusing computerised simulator in the
museum below.

Ōdōri-kōen   Park
(大通公園; www.sapporo-park.or.jp/odori;
[S]Tōzai, Tōhō & Namboku lines to Ōdōri) This ha-
ven in the heart of the city is fully 13 blocks
(1.5km) long, with the **TV Tower** (さっぽ
ろテレビ塔; Sapporo Terebi-tō; www.tv-tower.
co.jp; Ōdōri-nishi 1-chōme; adult/child ¥720/300;
☺9am-10pm; [S]Tōzai, Tōhō & Namboku lines to
Ōdōri, exits 2 & 7) at its eastern end. Among
the green lawns and flower gardens are
benches, fountains and sculptures; don't
miss Noguchi Isamu's elegant **Black Slide**

Ōdōri-kōen

Mantra (ブラックスライドマントラ) This is also where many of the city's major events and festivals take place.

✖ EATING & DRINKING

Menya Saimi   Ramen ¥

(麺屋彩未; ☏011-820-6511; Misono 10-jō Toyohira-ku; ramen from ¥750; ⊘11am-3.15pm & 5-7.30pm Tue-Sun; Ⓟ; ⑤Tōhō line to Misono, exit 1) Sapporo takes its ramen very seriously and Saimi is oft-voted the best ramen shop in the city (and sometimes the country) – and it's not overrated. You will have to queue, which is annoying, but you will be rewarded with a mind-blowing meal for the same price as a convenience store *bentō*.

Daruma   Barbecue ¥¥

(だるま; ☏011-552-6013; www.best.miru-kuru. com/daruma; S5W4; plates from ¥750; ⊘5pm-3am; ⑤Namboku line to Susukino, exit 5) This is where Sapporoites take friends visiting from out of town for the local speciality, *jingisukan* (all-you-can-eat lamb dish). There's nothing fancy here, just quality meat and a warm homely vibe. Daruma, in business for more than 60 years, is popular and has a few branches around town (see the website), which is good because the main shop draws long lines. Come early or late to beat the crowds.

Sapporo Biergarten   Brewery

(サッポロビール園; ☏reservation hotline 0120-150-550; www.sapporo-bier-garten.jp; N7E9 Higashi-ku; ⊘11.30am-10pm; ☐88 to Sapporo Biiru-en, ⑤Tōhō line to Higashi-Kuyakusho-mae, exit 4) This complex next to the Sapporo Beer Museum has no fewer than five beer halls, the best of which is Kessel Hall, where you can tuck into *jingisukan* washed down with all-you-can-drink draught beer direct from the factory (¥3900 per person). Reservations highly recommended. From the subway it's a 10-minute walk; the bus stops right out front.

Niseko Green Season

Niseko is making a big push to become a year-round destination. The buzz isn't quite there yet, but the infrastructure is building, with operators offering rafting, kayaking and mountain-biking tours. The combination of mountains and farmlands means Niseko is excellent for hiking and cycling, too. There are also 25 onsen in the area, from luxurious hotel baths to mountain hideaways.

AZUKI25 / GETTY IMAGES ©

ℹ INFORMATION

There is a tourist help desk in the basement of the arrivals hall at New Chitose Airport.

Hokkaidō-Sapporo Food & Tourist Information Centre (北海道さっぽろ「食と観光」情報館; ☏011-213-5088; www.sapporo.travel; JR Sapporo Station; ⊘8.30am-8pm; ⓡJR Sapporo, west exit) This huge info centre has maps, timetables, brochures and pamphlets in English for Sapporo and all of Hokkaidō. Staff speak English and are helpful. It's located on the ground floor of Sapporo Stellar Pl, inside the station's north concourse.

ℹ GETTING THERE & AROUND

New Chitose Airport (新千歳空港; CTS; ☏0123-23-0111; www.new-chitose-airport.jp) is located 45km southeast of Sapporo, in Chitose. With flights to more than 25 cities in Japan and many cities in Asia, this is where most travellers will arrive.

Sapporo Beer Museum (p228)

Rapid Airport trains (¥1070, 36 minutes) depart every 15 minutes for JR Sapporo Station. Frequent buses (¥1030, 70 minutes) also make the trip, stopping not just at JR Sapporo Station but also at major hotels. For a taxi to central Sapporo, budget about ¥14,000.

Sapporo has three useful subway lines that run from 6am to midnight: the east–west Tōzai line; the north–south Namboku line; and the curving Tōhō line. Fares start at ¥200. One-day passes cost ¥830 and only ¥520 on weekends (half-price for children).

Sapporo Eki-mae Bus Terminal (札幌駅前 バスターミナル; 🚇JR Sapporo) is the city's main bus depot. It's located beneath the Esta building on the south side of JR Sapporo Station.

Niseko

🎯 ACTIVITIES

Goshiki Onsen Onsen
(五色温泉; 📞0136-58-2707; 510 Niseko, Niseko-chō; ¥700; ⏰8am-8pm May-Oct, 10am-7pm Nov-Apr) At the base (750m) of active volcano Iwaonupuri, Goshiki Onsen has soaring views from the outdoor baths and sulphur-rich, highly acidic (pH 2.6!) waters. It's attached to a deeply rustic ryokan, but most visitors just come for the baths. You need a car to get here; some lodgings do excursions to the baths.

🍴 EATING & DRINKING

The slopes have plenty of pizza, ramen and other snacks. After hours, Hirafu has an international spread of restaurants and buzzes during ski season (many places shut in the low season). Year-round, Kutchan town has lots of *izakaya* (Japanese pub-eateries), especially on Miyako-dōri; there's a supermarket next to JR Kutchan Station.

Musu Bar + Bistro Bistro ¥¥
(Mūsu バー+ビストロ; 📞0136-21-7002; www. musuniseko.com; 190-13 Yamada; mains ¥1000-1600; ⏰7.30am-10pm) Musu offers great food, sweet service, and a lovely airy dining experience, plus easily the best cocktail menu in Niseko, with treats like the Yuzu Negroni (¥1400) or the Climber's Club

(¥1400), the latter using a shiitake-mushroom-infused brandy. Breakfasts, whether a flaky croissant with homemade jelly or a yoghurt and fruit plate, hit the spot.

Niseko Loft Club — Barbecue ¥¥

(ニセコロフト倶楽部; ☑0136-44-2883; www.loftclub1989.com; 397-5 Sōga, Niseko-chō; per 300g ¥1900; ☺5-11pm; P) Down the road from the Annupuri slopes, Loft Club glitters with fairy lights and the warm, glowing promise of a filling meal washed down with beer and lively conversation. The speciality here is *yakiniku* (grill-it-yourself meat), but rather than just the usual beef and pork, there's lamb and venison on the menu, too. Dishes are to share.

Graubunden — Cafe ¥

(グラウビュンデン; ☑0136-23-3371; www.graubunden.jp; 132-26 Yamada, Kutchan-chō; breakfast mains ¥600-1000, lunch mains ¥1000-1200; ☺8am-7pm Fri-Wed; P 🖥 🍴) This is Niseko's original hang-out spot in Hirafu East Village, a standby with season regulars and long-time expats for its sandwiches, omelettes and cakes. Service could be friendlier, especially at busy times, but the food is tasty enough to keep people coming back for more.

Sprout — Cafe

(スプラウト; ☑0136-55-5161; www.sprout-project.com; N1W3-10, Kutchan-chō; coffee from ¥400; ☺8am-8pm; 🖥) This popular hang-out run by a former outdoor guide serves Niseko's best coffee. It's 100m up the road from JR Kutchan Station, decked out like a very cool campsite. There's a huge library of outdoor books and magazines (in Japanese) here, too.

ℹ INFORMATION

Hirafu Welcome Centre (ひらふウエルカムセンター; ☑0136-22-0109; www.grand-hirafu.jp; 204 Yamada, Kutchan-chō; ☺8.30am-9pm) Near the Hirafu gondola (and where direct buses

to/from New Chitose Airport originate and terminate), with English-language information. Open only during the snow season.

Niseko Tourist Information (ニセコ観光案内所; ☑0136-21-2551; www.niseko-ta.jp; 41-5 Aza Kabayama; ☺8am-5pm; 🖥) At JR Niseko Station, with pamphlets, maps, bus timetables; can help with bookings. It also has a centre at the View Plaza Michi-no-Eki on Rte 66 heading into town.

ℹ GETTING THERE & AWAY

During the ski season, **Chūō Bus** (中央バス; ☑Sapporo terminal 011-231-0600; www.chuo-bus.co.jp) coaches run from Sapporo Eki-mae Bus Terminal (one-way/return ¥2240/4000, three hours) and New Chitose Airport (one-way/return ¥2600/4500, 3¾ hours) to Niseko; travel times are dependent on weather conditions. Drop-off points include the Welcome Centre in Hirafu, the Hilton and Annupuri. Reservations are necessary, and it's recommended that you book well ahead of your departure date.

The JR Hakodate line runs from Sapporo to Kutchan (¥1840, 2½ hours), Hirafu (¥1840, 3½ hours) and Niseko (¥2160, three hours) stations. You will need to transfer in Otaru, where you can also get trains directly to New Chitose Airport.

Note that JR Hirafu Station is actually inconvenient for central Hirafu, unless you've arranged for pick-up.

ℹ GETTING AROUND

Buses (¥300, 15 minutes) run irregularly (and infrequently in summer) between JR Kutchan Station and the ski villages; it's better to arrange pick-up.

During snow season, **Niseko United Shuttle** (www.niseko.ne.jp) runs a service (roughly hourly 8am to 11pm) between Hirafu, Niseko Village and Annupuri (free for all-mountain pass holders). From 5pm to 11pm, the shuttle route extends to JR Kutchan Station, giving you more dining options. Pick up a schedule from any of the tourist information centres.

KAGOSHIMA

Kagoshima at a Glance...

Sunny Kagoshima (鹿児島), at the southern tip of Kyūshū, has a personality to match its climate: the prefectural capital, also Kagoshima, has been voted Japan's friendliest city nationwide. Its backdrop/deity is Sakurajima, a very active volcano just across the bay. Locals raise their umbrellas against the mountain's recurrent eruptions, when fine ash coats the landscape like snow and obscures the sun like fog – mystical and captivating. The city is also the jumping-off point for trips to Yakushima, a Unesco World Heritage Site renowned for its virgin forests, and Ibusuki, where the big attraction is the beachside baths where steam rises through sand.

Two Days in Kagoshima

For a short trip, head straight to Yaku-shima. A night there will give you time to do a short hike and hit a seaside onsen (hot spring). Take the ferry back to Kagoshima in the afternoon, and spend the evening sampling the food and drink for which the southern city is famous.

Four Days in Kagoshima

More time gives you an opportunity for longer hikes deep into the interior of Yakushima, and also a buffer if bad weather hits. Budget an extra day in Kagoshima, to rent a car and drive to Kirishima-jingu and volcano Sakurajima or head south to the hot-sand baths at Ibusuki.

Arriving in Kagoshima

It is possible to get here by *shinkansen* (bullet train) from Honshū destinations such as Hiroshima, Osaka, Kyoto and even Tokyo, though it's a long ride. If you're short on time, fly one or both ways to Kagoshima Airport, which has both international connections to Shanghai, Hong Kong, Taipei and Seoul, and convenient domestic flights, including to Tokyo, Osaka and Okinawa (Naha).

Where to Stay

Kagoshima has plenty of good-value places to sleep. The station area is a bit quiet; to take advantage of the city's dining and drinking options, stay in or around Tenmonkan. On Yakushima, the most convenient place to be based is Miyanoura. In July and August and the spring Golden Week holiday, it's best to try and reserve ahead since places fill up early.

Yakushima forest

Hiking on Yakushima

Yakushima is covered in primeval forest – some of the last virgin forest left in Japan; hiking into the interior is the best way to experience the island's beauty.

Great For...

☑ **Don't Miss**

The island's famous *yakusugi* (屋久杉; *Cryptomeria japonica*) – ancient cedar trees.

Jōmon-sugi

This enormous *yakusugi* tree is estimated to be between 3000 and 7000 years old, and though no longer living, it remains a majestic sight. Most hikers reach the tree via the 19.5km, eight-to-10-hour round trip from **Arakawa-tozanguchi** (Arakawa trailhead; 荒川登山口). From March through November, to limit traffic congestion and environmental impact, all hikers must transfer to an Arakawa Mountain Bus (round trip ¥1740) from the Yakusugi Museum parking lot to get to Arakawa-tozanguchi; you must buy a ticket at least a day in advance.

Shiratani-unsuikyō

Shorter than the Jōmon-sugi hike – about three to four hours return – and arguably more beautiful, this hike passes waterfalls, moss-lined rocks and towering *yakusugi* to

Hiking in Shiratani-unsuikyō

IPPEI NAOI / GETTY IMAGES ©

ⓘ Need to Know

Trails are crowded mid-July to mid-September; shoulder season is better (except for Golden Week).

✕ Take a Break

Buy provisions at supermarket **Yakuden** (ヤクデン; ☑997-42-1501; 1197-1 Miyanoura; ⊗9am-10pm), just north of the pier entrance.

★ Top Tip

If you're hiking, ask your lodging to prepare a *bentō* (boxed meal) the night before.

the overlook at Taiko-iwa. The **trailhead** (白谷雲水峡登山口; ¥300) at 622m is served by up to 10 daily buses to and from Miyanoura (¥550, 40 minutes, March to November).

Yakusugi Land

A great way to see *yakusugi* without a long trek into the forest, **Yakusugi Land** (ヤクスギランド; ☑0997-42-3508; www.y-rekumori .com; 1593 Miyanoura; ¥300; ⊗9am-5pm) offers shorter hiking courses over wooden boardwalks, and longer hikes deep into the ancient cedar forest. There are four buses a day to and from Anbō (¥740, 40 minutes).

Know Before You Go

Keep in mind that Yakushima is a place of extremes: the interior of the island is one of the wettest places in Japan. In the winter the peaks may be covered in snow, while

the coast is still relatively balmy. Don't set off on a hike without a good map and the proper gear. **Nakagawa Sports** (ナカガワスポーツ; ☑0997-42-0341; www.yakushima-sp.com; 421-6 Miyanoura; ⊗9am-7pm, closed every other Wed) rents out everything from raingear and waterproof hiking boots (also in large sizes) to tents and baby carriers.

The Yakumonkey guide (www.yakumonkey.com), available for purchase online, has detailed descriptions of hikes and trails. Also helpful is the detailed Japanese-language trail map **Yama-to-Kougen-no-Chizu-Yakushima** (山と高原の地図屋久島; ¥1080), available at major bookshops in Japan. Even though trails can be very crowded during holidays, be sure to alert someone at your accommodation of your intended route and fill in a *tōzan todokede* (route plan) at the trailhead.

Kagoshima

◎ SIGHTS

Museum of the Meiji Restoration
Museum

(維新ふるさと館; ☎099-239-7700; 23-1 Kaijiya-chō; ¥300; ⏱9am-5pm; ☒JR Kagoshima-Chūō) This museum offers insights into the unique social system of education, samurai loyalty and sword techniques that made Satsuma one of Japan's leading provinces. There's a good smartphone app in English. Hourly audiovisual presentations – told by animatronic Meiji-era reformers, including Saigō Takamori and Sakamoto Ryōma – detail the Satsuma Rebellion and the ground-breaking visits of Satsuma students to the West.

Sengan-en
Gardens

(仙巌園·磯庭園, Iso-teien; ☎099-247-1551; 9700-1 Yoshinochō; with/without villa entry ¥1300/1000; ⏱8.30am-5.30pm, Goten 9am-5pm; ☑) In 1658, the 19th Shimazu lord laid out his pleasure garden on this hilly, rambling bayside property of groves, hillside trails and one of Japan's most impressive pieces of 'borrowed scenery': the fuming peak of Sakurajima.

Allow 45 minutes for a leisurely stroll through the garden, and 30 minutes more for a self-guided tour of the 25-room **Goten** ('the house' on signage), the Shimazu clan's former villa. As sprawling as it is, the villa is now only one-third of its original size!

◎ EATING & DRINKING

Kumasotei
Japanese ¥¥

(熊襲亭; ☎099-222-6356; 6-10 Higashi-Sengoku-chō; set meals lunch/dinner from ¥1500/3000; ⏱11am-2pm & 5-10pm; ☒Tenmonkan-dōri) This atmospheric multistorey restaurant near central Tenmonkan covers all your *Satsuma-ryōri* needs: *Satsuma-age* (deep-fried fish cake), *tonkatsu* (pork ribs), *kurobuta shabu-shabu* (black-pork hotpot), and lots of fresh fish and seafood. Look for the vertical sign with red lettering and large wooden kanji above the entryway.

From left: *Tonkatsu*; display in the Museum of the Meiji Restoration display; Sengan-en

KAN_KHAMPANYA / SHUTTERSTOCK ©

KEREN SU / GETTY IMAGES ©

Kurokatsutei
Tonkatsu ¥

(黒かつ亭; ☎099-213-9600; www.kurokatutei.
net; 2-2 Yamashita-chō; sets lunch ¥770-1080,
dinner ¥960-1740, donburi ¥880-970; ⏲11am-
3.30pm & 5-11.20pm; 🚈Asahi-dōri) If your
favourite way to enjoy *kurobuta*
(Kagoshima-style black pork) is deep-
fried, this institution does it in prodigiously
crunchy crust, as *tonkatsu* (cutlets) or
donburi (rice bowls). Reasonably priced
teishoku (set meals) come with generous
sides of cabbage rice and delicate, pork-
broth-based miso soup. The Kurokatsutei
set lunch features two of the best-selling
pork cuts: fillet and loin.

Kagomma Furusato Yatai-mura
Japanese ¥

(かごっまふるさと屋台村; ☎099-255-1588;
6-4 Chūō-chō; prices vary; ⏲lunch & dinner, stall
hours vary; 🚈Takami-bashi, 🚈Kagoshima-
Chūō) *Yatai-mura* means 'food-stall
village', and some two dozen stalls near
Kagoshima-Chūō Station offer a taste of
Kagoshima of old. Follow your nose to your
favourites, such as *sumibi-yaki* (coal-fired
chicken), sashimi, *teppan-yaki* beef and fish
dishes. Booth 16 serves delicious Kagoshima *kurobuta* (wild boar) *shabu-shabu* style
(¥1280).

Honkaku Shōchū Bar Ishizue
Bar

(本格焼酎Bar 礎; ☎099-227-0125; www.
honkakushochu-bar-ishizue.com; 4th fl, Flower
Bldg, 6-1 Sengoku-chō; ¥2000; ⏲8pm-3am;
🚈Tenmonkan-dōri) This chic, amber-and-
wood *shōchū* (alcohol distilled from
potatoes, wheat, rice or barley) bar has
everything going for it, and it's one of the
finest places to drink Kagoshima's prefectural liquor. There are more than 1500
choices from around the prefecture, each
with its own story, and English-speaking
staff to explain. Reserve ahead, especially
Friday and Saturday nights.

ℹ️ INFORMATION

Tourist Information Center (鹿児島中央駅総
合観光案内所; ☎099-253-2500; JR Kagoshima-
Chūō Station; ⏲8am-8pm)Located at JR
Kagoshima-Chuo station.

JAPAN IMAGE / SHUTTERSTOCK ©

Nagata Inaka-hama

Tourism Exchange Centre (観光交流センタ
ー; ☎099-298-5111; 1-1 Uenosono-chō; ⊙9am-
7pm; 🚉Takamibashi) Located near the Museum
of the Meiji Restoration and has superfriendly
staff that can help with maps and pamphlets and
make hotel reservations.

ℹ️ GETTING THERE & AROUND

JR Kagoshima-Chūō Station is the terminus of
the Kyūshū *shinkansen,* which has stops including Kumamoto (¥6420, 52 minutes), Hakata
(¥9930, 90 minutes), Hiroshima (¥17,150, 2½
hours) and Shin-Osaka (¥21,380, 3¾ hours).

Also stopping at Kagoshima Station, the JR
Nippō line travels to Miyazaki (*tokkyū* ¥3710, two
hours) and Beppu (¥9090, five hours).

Trams are the easiest way to get around
town. Rte 1 starts from Kagoshima Station and
goes through the centre into the suburbs. Rte
2 diverges at Takami-baba (高見馬場) to JR
Kagoshima-Chūō Station and terminates at
Kōrimoto.

Yakushima

◉ SIGHTS

Yakusugi Museum   Museum
(屋久杉自然館; ☎0997-46-3113; www.yakusugi-
museum.com; 273 9343 Anbō; adult/child
¥600/400; ⊙9am-5pm, closed 1st Tue of the
month) In a forested spot with sea views, the
Yakusugi Museum has informative, beautifully designed exhibits about *yakusugi* and
the history of the islanders' relationship to
these magnificent trees. The museum has
an excellent audio guide in English. It's conveniently located on the road leading up to
Yakusugi Land (p237). Two daily buses run
to and from Miyanoura (¥960, 80 minutes,
March to November).

Nagata Inaka-hama   Beach
(永田いなか浜) On the island's northwest
coast, Nagata Inaka-hama is a beautiful
beach for sunsets, and it's where sea
turtles lay their eggs from May to July. It's
beside the Inaka-hama bus stop, served by
Nagata-bound buses from Miyanoura.

🛬 ACTIVITIES

Yudomari Onsen
Onsen

(湯泊温泉; 1714-28 Yudomari; ¥100; ⊙24hr)
This blissfully serene onsen at the ocean's
edge can be entered at any tide. Get off at
the Yudomari bus stop and take the road
opposite the post office in the direction of
the sea. Once you enter the village, the way
is marked. It's a 300m walk and you pass a
great banyan tree en route.

Hirauchi Kaichū Onsen
Onsen

(平内海中温泉; ☑0997-43-5900; Hirauchi,
Kumage; ¥100; ⊙24hr) Onsen lovers will be in
heaven here. The outdoor baths are in the
rocks by the sea and can only be entered
at or close to low tide. You can walk to the
baths from the Kaichū Onsen bus stop, but
the next stop, Nishikaikon, is actually closer. From Nishikaikon, walk downhill towards
the sea for about 200m and take a right at
the bottom of the hill.

🍴 EATING

Shiosai
Seafood ¥¥

(潮騒; ☑0997-42-2721; 305-3 Miyanoura; dishes
¥450-1100; ⊙11.30am-2pm & 5.30-9.30pm
Fri-Wed) Find a full range of Japanese standards such as *sashimi teishoku* (sashimi set;
¥1700) or *ebi-furai teishoku* (fried shrimp
set; ¥1400). Look for the blue and whitish
building with automatic glass doors along
the main road through Miyanoura.

ℹ️ INFORMATION

Miyanoura Tourist Information Centre (宮之
浦観光案内所; ☑0997-42-1019; www.yakukan.
jp; 823-1 Miyanoura; ⊙9am-5pm) A helpful office
on the road leading away from the port; you can't
miss its dramatic architecture. Staff here can
help you find lodgings and answer all questions
about the island.

Anbō Tourist Office (安房観光案内所;
☑0997-46-2333; www.yakukan.jp; 410-155 Anbō;
⊙9am-4pm) Just north of the river, this is full of
helpful information.

🏔️ Visiting Sakurajima

Kagoshima's iconic symbol Sakurajima
has been spewing an almost continuous
stream of smoke and ash since 1955,
and it's not uncommon for it to have
more than 1000, mostly small, 'burps'
per year. In 1914 more than 3 billion
tonnes of lava swallowed numerous
island villages – 1000-plus homes – and
joined Sakurajima to the mainland to
the southeast.

Despite its volatility, Sakurajima is
currently friendly enough for visitors to
get fairly close. Of the volcano's three
peaks, only Minami-dake (South Peak;
1040m) is active. Climbing the mountain is prohibited, but there are several
lookout points.

One of the best reasons for making
the trek across the bay is the gorgeous
trip itself. Frequent passenger and car
ferries shuttle around the clock between
Kagoshima and Sakurajima (¥160, 15
minutes).

If you have time, grab a car at **Sakurajima Rentacar** (☑099-293-2162; 2hr/day
from ¥4800/11,000) and drive the loop;
stopping at the **Buried Torii** (黒神埋没鳥
居) and the **Arimura Lava Observatory**
(有村溶岩展望所; ☑099-298-5111; 952
Arimura; ⊙24hr) **FREE**. The drive takes one
or two hours and you could spend a night
on the volcano at the delightfully fading
Rainbow Sakurajima Hotel (レインボー
桜島; ☑099-293-2323; www.rainbow-sakura-
jima.com; 1722-16 Yokoyama-chō; r per person
incl 2 meals from ¥9700; P⭐❄️📶).

View of Sakurajima from Arimura Lava Observatory
WINDYBOY / SHUTTERSTOCK ©

(¥9000, one hour 50 minutes for direct sailings, two hours 40 minutes with a stop in Tanegashima). There are also two hydrofoils per day between Kagoshima and Anbō Port (2½ hours) on Yakushima. Booking ahead is wise.

The regular ferry **Yakushima 2** (屋久島２フェリー; ☏099-266-0731;www.ferryyakusima2.com) sails from Kagoshima's Minamifutō pier for Yakushima's Miyanoura port (one way/return ¥4900/8900). It leaves at 8.30am and takes four hours.

The **Hibiscus** (フェリーはいびすかす; ☏099-261-7000; www.yakushimaferry.com) also sails between Kagoshima and Yakushima, leaving at 6pm, stopping overnight in Tanegashima, and arriving at Miyanoura at 7am the following day. Fares vary by routing. Reservations aren't generally necessary for this ferry, which usually departs from Kagoshima's Taniyama pier.

Local buses travel the coastal road part way around Yakushima roughly every hour or two, though only a few head up into the interior. Your best bet is to rent a car from the port.

🛕 Kirishima Jingū

In the city of Kirishima, 60km north-east of Kagoshima city, picturesque, tangerine Kirishima-jingū is dedicated to Ninigi-no-mikoto, who, according to Kojiki (a book compiled in 712), led the gods from the heavens to the Takachiho-no-mine summit. Though the original dates from the 6th century, the present shrine was built in 1715 and is regarded by most Japanese as a 'power spot': it certainly has presence.

Surrounded by forests and hot-spring villages, the shrine is a quick and easy drive from Kagoshima in a rental car. Otherwise, it's a pleasant hour-long train ride from JR Kagoshima station to JR Kirishima-jingū station. From there buses (¥240, 15 minutes) run to the shrine, at the foot of which is a little village with a handful of inns and restaurants. Connection times between the infrequent buses and trains aren't great: allow at least half a day to visit the shrine in this manner.

Temple guard statue at Kirishima Jingū
LARS IN ASIA / SHUTTERSTOCK ©

🅘 GETTING THERE & AROUND

Hydrofoil services operate between Kagoshima and Yakushima, some of which stop at Tanegashima en route. **Tane Yaku Jetfoil** (☏in Kagoshima 099-226-0128, in Miyanoura 0997-42-2003; www.tykousoku.jp; ⏱8.30am-5.30pm Mon-Fri, to 7pm Sat & Sun) runs six Toppy and Rocket hydrofoils per day between Kagoshima (leaving from the high-speed ferry terminal just to the south of Minamifutō pier) and Miyanoura

Ibusuki

In southeastern Satsuma Peninsula, around 50km from Kagoshima, the palmy hot-spring resort of Ibusuki (指宿) is known for its 'sand baths', in which attendants bury guests up to their necks in beach sand heated by underground onsen.

🅞 ACTIVITIES

Tamatebako Onsen　　　　　Onsen
(たまて箱温泉; ☏0993-35-3577; 3292 Fukumo-to Yamakawa; bath/bath & sand bath ¥510/1130; ⏱9.30am-7.30pm Fri-Wed) Consistently topping lists of the world's best onsen, Tamatebako is in two parts: conventional, ocean-view baths on a cliffside and a suna-mushi (sand bath). Gender-separated baths are Japanese (more popular) or Western style and switch daily; on odd-numbered days men get the Japanese bath, with a view of Kaimondake. Sand-bath admission includes yukata (cotton bathrobes); towels can be rented.

Ibusuki Sunamushi Kaikan Saraku

Ibusuki Sunamushi
Kaikan Saraku Onsen

(いぶすき砂むし会館 砂楽; ☑0993-23-3900;
www./sa-raku.sakura.ne.jp; 5-25-18 Yunohama;
bath/bath & sand bath ¥610/1080; ☺8.30am-
9pm, closed noon-1pm Mon-Fri) Pay at the
entrance, change into a *yukata* and wander
down to the beach where, under a canopy
of bamboo-slat blinds, women with shovels
bury you in hot volcanic sand. Reactions
range from panic to euphoria. It's said that
10 minutes will get rid of impurities, but
many people stay longer. Afterwards, soak
in the onsen.

❶ GETTING THERE & AROUND

Ibusuki Station is about 1½ hours from Kagoshima by bus (¥950) or 51 minutes by train
from Kagoshima-chūō (*tokkyū* ¥2130). Train
geeks and sightseers will love the one-of-a-kind
wood-panelled Ibutama *tokkyū* with specially
angled seats for breathtaking bay views.

The Nottari-Oritari My Plan Bus (¥1100 per
day) offers unlimited hop-on, hop-off service
around Ibusuki highlights. Rent bikes (¥500 for
two hours) from the station. Car-rental offices
are steps away.

OLLIO815 / GETTY IMAGES ©

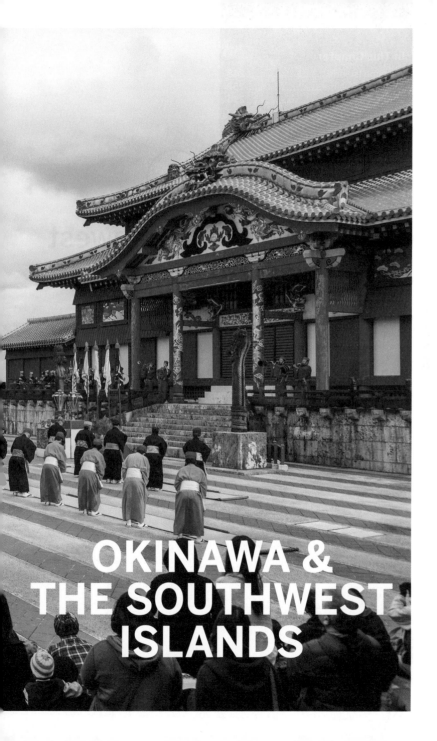

OKINAWA &
THE SOUTHWEST
ISLANDS

In This Chapter

Okinawa & the Southwest Islands at a Glance...

Known as the Southwest Islands, the Nansei-shotō (南西諸島) comprises several chains of semitropical, coral-fringed isles far removed from the concerns of mainland life. The slow pace and unique cultural heritage of the former Ryūkyū kingdom endures, a vibrant contrast to Japan's obsession with modernity, technology and homogeneity. At the southern reaches of the archipelago are the gorgeous Yaeyama Islands, which include the main islands of Ishigaki-jima and Iriomote-jima plus a spread of 17 isles. Okinawa's bustling capital Naha is the region's largest hub, attracting steady streams of shopping, sun-seeking and honeymooning tourists from Japan and neighbouring Asian nations.

Two Days in Okinawa

For a short trip, zero in on the cultural (and culinary) attractions of Naha, with its castle, museum, markets and lively *izakaya* (Japanese pub-eateries). From here it's a short ride ride to the pretty, laid-back Kerama Islands, where you can log some beach time.

Four Days in Okinawa

With more time you can embark on an island-hopping adventure around the truly remote Yaeyama Islands. Each offers a completely different experience: after getting your feet wet on main island Ishigaki-jima, take your pick from the old-world charm of Taketomi-jima; the wilds of Iriomote-jima; or the epic diving in Yonaguni-jima.

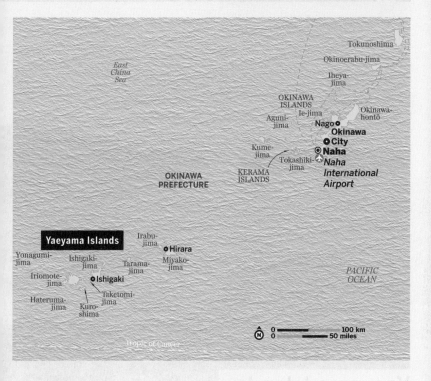

Arriving in Okinawa

Naha International Airport (OKA) has connections with Seoul, Taipei, Hong Kong and Shanghai and major cities across Japan. From Naha you can fly to other islands further south, or connect to closer ones by jetfoil.

Where to Stay

Most visitors in Naha tend to stay on or around Kokusai-dōri, the main tourist strip; you can have your pick from budget guesthouses to reputable chain hotels. If visiting the Yaeyamas and seeking resort-style accommodation, plan to stay on Ishigaki-jima; Taketomi-jima has some nice boutique hotels and guesthouses in traditional structures. The most common form of accommodation out here, however, is the family-run *minshuku* (guesthouse).

Yaeyama Islands

At the far southwestern end of the Southwest Islands are the gorgeous Yaeyama Islands (八重山諸島; Yaeyama-shotō). Near the Tropic of Cancer, they are renowned for their lovely beaches, superb diving and lush landscapes.

Great For...

☑ Don't Miss

Taketomi-jima and Iriomote-jima's *hoshi-suna* ('star sand'), actually the dried skeletons of marine protozoa.

Perhaps the best feature of the Yaeyamas is the ease with which you can travel between them; you can easily explore three or four islands in one trip.

Ishigaki-jima

Blessed with excellent beaches and brilliant dive sites, Ishigaki-jima (石垣島) also possesses an attractive, low-lying geography that invites long drives and day hikes. A series of roads branch out from Ishigaki city and head along the coastline and into the interior. At the north end of the island, on the west coast, is **Sunset Beach** (サンセットビーチ; www.i-sb.jp), a long strip of sand with a bit of offshore reef. As the name implies, this is one of the island's best spots to watch the sun set into the East China Sea. Shower and toilet facilities are also located here. **Kabira-wan** (川平湾)

Kabira-wan

Yonaguni-jima
(80 km)

Manta
Scramble

Sunset
Beach

Kabira-
wan

Hoshisuna-
no-hama

Ishigaki-
jima

Shirahama Port

Taketomi-
jima

● Shiraho

Iriomote-
jima

Ida-no-
hama

Ōhara

Kaiji-
hama

Ishigaki-jima Rittō
Ferry Terminal

ℹ Need to Know

Ishigaki-jima is the Yaeyama transit hub, with flights from Tokyo, Osaka and Naha.

✕ Take a Break

Cafe Taniwha (カフェたにふぁ; ☑0980-88-6352; http://youkoso.cafe-taniwha.com; 188 Ōkawa; ☺11am-11pm Tue-Sat) on Ishigaki-jima is a great spot to hang out.

★ Top Tip

Renting a car is best for Ishigaki-jima and Iriomote-jima. Without one, explore car-free Taketomi-jima.

is a sheltered bay with white-sand shores and a couple of interesting clump-like islets offshore. Swimming is not allowed in the bay as pearls are cultivated here, but there's no shortage of glass-bottomed boats offering up a look at the reef life below.

The most popular dive spot on Ishigaki-jima is **Manta Scramble**, off the coast of Kabira Ishizaki. Although you'll likely be sharing with a fair number of dive boats, you're almost guaranteed to see a manta (or four) in season. At Kabira-based **Diving School Umicoza** (海講座; ☑0980-88-2434; www.umicoza.com; 1287-97 Kabira; 1/2 dives with equipment rental ¥9450/12,600; ☺8am-6pm), all the dive guides speak English and the shop itself has a long-running reputation for professionalism and reliability.

Taketomi-jima

A mere 15-minute boat ride from Ishigaki-jima, the tiny island of Taketomi-jima (竹富島) is a living museum of Ryūkyū culture. Centred on a flower-decorated village of traditional houses complete with red *kawara* (tiled) roofs, coral walls and *shiisā* (lion-dog roof guardians) statues, Taketomi is a breath of fresh air if you're suffering from an overdose of modern Japan.

In order to preserve the island's historical ambience, residents have joined together to ban some signs of modernism. The island is criss-crossed by crushed-coral roads bedecked with bougainvillea and is free of chain convenience stores.

While Taketomi is besieged by Japanese day trippers in the busy summer months, the island remains blissfully quiet at night. This is true even in summer, as the island offers little in the way of after-dark entertainment. Taketomi truly weaves its spell after the sun dips below the horizon.

Yonaguni-jima

About 125km west of Ishigaki and 110km east of Taiwan, Yonaguni-jima (与那国島) is Japan's westernmost inhabited island. Its known for its strong sake, small horses, marlin fishing and the jumbo-sized Yonaguni atlas moth, the largest moth in the world; however, most visitors come to see what lies beneath the waves.

In 1985 a local diver discovered what appeared to be human-made 'ruins' off the south coast of the island, which came to be known as the Kaitei Iseki, (Yonaguni Monument). Some claim the ruins, which look like the steps of a sunken pyramid, are the remains of a Pacific Atlantis, though science suggests they're the result of natural geological processes. Adding to the underwater allure are the large schools of hammerhead sharks that frequent the waters in winter off the west coast, making Yonaguni perhaps the most-famous single diving destination in Japan.

Diving Service MARLIN (ダイビングサービスMARLIN; ☏0980-87-3365; www.yonagunidiving.com/iseki; 309 Yonaguni; 1/2 dives from ¥6500/11,000) and **Yonaguni Diving Service** (与那国ダイビングサービス; ☏0980-87-2658; www.yonaguniyds.com; 3984-3 Yonaguni; 2-dive boat trips ¥12,500, equipment rental ¥4600) can get you down there.

Iriomote-jima

Although only 20km west of Ishigaki-jima, Iriomote-jima (西表島) could easily qualify as Japan's last frontier. Dense jungles and mangrove swamp blanket more than 90% of the island, and it's fringed by some of

Iriomote-jima

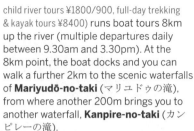

the most beautiful coral reefs in Japan. If you're super-lucky, you may spot one of the island's rare *yamaneko,* a nocturnal and rarely seen wildcat (they're most often seen crossing the road at night, so drive carefully).

Several rivers penetrate far into the lush interior of the island and these can be explored by riverboat or kayak. Add to the mix beautiful sun-drenched beaches and spectacular diving and snorkelling, and it's easy to see why Iriomote-jima is one of the best destinations in Japan for grassroots nature lovers.

That said, if you're not an avid explorer of the great outdoors, Iriomote's lack of infrastructure means you'll be better suited to visiting other islands.

Urauchi-gawa Kankō (浦内川観光; ☑0980-85-6154; www.urauchigawa.com; adult/child river tours ¥1800/900, full-day trekking & kayak tours ¥8400) runs boat tours 8km up the river (multiple departures daily between 9.30am and 3.30pm). At the 8km point, the boat docks and you can walk a further 2km to the scenic waterfalls of **Mariyudō-no-taki** (マリユドゥの滝), from where another 200m brings you to another waterfall, **Kanpire-no-taki** (カンピレーの滝).

Island Hopping

Ferries depart from Ishigaki city's Ishigaki-jima Rittō Ferry Terminal (p258) for Taketomi-jima (¥600, 10 minutes, up to 45 daily) and Iriomote-jima (Uehara/Ōhara ¥2060/1570, one hour, up to 20 daily). Uehara port is the more convenient of Iriomote's two ports.

Yonaguni is harder to get to: **Ryūkyū Air Commuter** flies once daily between Yonaguni and Naha, and operates three flights a day between Yonaguni and Ishigaki-jima. **Fukuyama Kaiun** (福山海運; ☑in Ishigaki 0980-82-4962, in Yonaguni 0980-87-2555) operates two ferries a week between Ishigaki-jima and Kubura Port on Yonaguni (¥3550, four hours). Be warned: these are not for the faint of stomach.

Gōyā champurū

K321 / SHUTTERSTOCK ©

Okinawan Cuisine

Okinawa's food culture is recognisably distinct from that of mainland Japan. Eating your way through the islands – sampling the signature local ingredients, from both land and sea – is literally a treat.

Okinawan cuisine originated in the splendour of the Ryūkyū court and the humble lives of the impoverished islanders. Healthy eating is considered extremely important; indeed, islanders have long held that medicine and food are essentially the same. (We note that Okinawans are among the world's longest-living people.)

Local Specialities

One of the island's staple foods is pork, acidic and rich in protein. Every part of the pig is eaten. *Mimigā* (ミミガー) is thinly sliced pig's ears marinated in vinegar, perfect with local Orion beer. *Rafutē* (ラフテー) is pork stewed with ginger, brown sugar, rice wine and soy sauce until it falls apart. If you need stamina, try *ikasumi-jiru* (イカスミ汁), which is stewed pork in black squid ink.

Great For...

☑ Don't Miss

Gōyā (bitter melon), the local ingredient most often associated with Okinawa.

Okinawan cuisine

MIKA / GETTY IMAGES ©

Awamori

Okinawa has its own signature distilled spirit called *awamori* (泡盛), made of long-grain rice. It has 30% to 60% alcohol, and although it's usually served *mizu-wari* (水割; watered down), it has a good kick.

Local Ingredients

Gōyā (ごーやー; bitter melon) Gnarly gourd that appears in all kinds of dishes and juice, possibly responsible for Okinawans' longevity.

Kokutō (黒糖) Dark brown, mineral-rich unrefined sugar; used for snacking and in dishes sweet and savoury.

Shīkuwāsā (シークワーサー) Very sour citrus native to Okinawa and Taiwan, used as a garnish or in cocktails and soft drinks.

Tōfuyō (豆腐瘍) Type of *shima-dōfu* with a strong flavour from fermentation in *awamori*.

Umi-budō (海ぶどう) Literally 'sea grapes' – teeny-tiny bunches of spherical algae, usually eaten raw.

While stewing is common, Okinawans prefer stir-frying and refer to the technique as *champurū* (チャンプルー). Best-known is *gōyā champurū* (ゴーヤーチャンプルー), a mix of pork, bitter melon and the island's uniquely sturdy tofu, *shima-dōfu* (島豆腐).

Okinawa-soba (沖縄そば) is udon served in pork broth. Most common are *sōki-soba* (ソーキそば), topped with pork spare ribs; and *Yaeyama-soba* (八重山そば) with tiny pieces of tender pork, bean sprouts and scallions.

Other local specialities bear the imprint of the post-war American Occupation, including *tako raisu* (タコライス), taco fillings served on sticky rice, and Blue Seal (ブルーシール) ice cream.

Naha

◉ SIGHTS

Okinawa Prefectural Museum & Art Museum   Museum

(沖縄県立博物館・美術館; ☏098-941-8200; www.museums.pref.okinawa.jp; Omoromachi 3-1-1; prefectural/art museum ¥410/310; ⊙9am-6pm Tue-Thu & Sun, to 8pm Fri & Sat) Opened in 2007, this museum of Okinawa's history, culture and natural history is easily one of the best museums in Japan. Displays are well laid out, attractively presented and easy to understand, with excellent bilingual interpretive signage. The art-museum section holds interesting special exhibits (admission prices vary) with an emphasis on local artists. It's about 15 minutes' walk northwest of the Omoromachi monorail station.

Shuri-jō   Castle

(首里城; ☏098-886-2020; www.oki-park.jp/shurijo; 1-2 Kinjō-chō, Shuri; ¥820, with 1- or 2-day monorail pass discounted to ¥660; ⊙8.30am-7pm Apr-Jun & Oct-Nov, to 8pm Jul-Sep, to 6pm Dec-Mar, closed 1st Wed & Thu Jul) This

reconstructed castle was originally built in the 14th century and served as the administrative centre and royal residence of the Ryūkyū kingdom until the 19th century. Enter through the **Kankai-mon** (歓会門) and go up to the **Hōshin-mon** (奉神門), which forms the entryway to the inner sanctum of the castle. Visitors can enter the impressive **Seiden** (正殿), which has exhibits on the castle and the Okinawan royals.

Okinawa Prefectural Peace Memorial Museum   Museum

(沖縄県平和祈念資料館; ☏098-997-3844; www.peace-museum.pref.okinawa.jp; 614-1 Aza Mabuni, Itoman; ¥300; ⊙9am-5pm) The centrepiece of the Peace Memorial Park focuses on the suffering of the Okinawan people during the island's invasion and under the subsequent American Occupation. While some material may stir debate, the museum's mission is to serve as a reminder of the horrors of war, so that such suffering is not repeated. There is a free English-language audio guide available, providing great detail on the 2nd-floor exhibit.

From left:Okinawa Prefectural Museum; Daichi Makishi Kōsetsu Ichiba; Kokusai-dōri at night

Daichi Makishi
Kōsetsu Ichiba Market

(第一牧志公設市場; 2-10-1 Matsuo; ⊗8am-8pm, restaurants 10am-7pm) In Naha, a great place to sample everyday Okinawan eats is at one of the 2nd-floor eateries in this covered food market just off Ichibahon-dōri, about 200m south of Kokusai-dōri. The colourful variety of fish and produce on offer here is amazing. Don't miss the wonderful local restaurants upstairs.

✴ EATING

Ryūkyū Ryōri
Nuchigafū Okinawan ¥¥

(琉球料理ぬちがふぅ; ☑098-861-2952; www.ja-jp.facebook.com/ryukyucuisine.nuchigafu; 1-28-3 Tsuboya; set dinner from ¥3000; ⊗11.30am-5pm & 5.30-10pm Wed-Mon) For a memorable, elegant meal in Naha, don't pass up dinner at the hilltop Nuchigafū, off the southern end of **Tsuboya Pottery Street** (壷屋やちむん道り; Tsuboya Yachimun-dōri). Formerly a lovely Okinawan teahouse, and before that a historic Ryūkyūan residence, Nuchigafū serves lunch and frothy *buku-buku* tea during the day and beautifully plated multicourse Okinawan dinners by night. Children aged 11 and older are welcome.

Yūnangi Okinawan ¥¥

(ゆうなんぎい; ☑098-867-3765; 3-3-3 Kumoji; dishes ¥750-1400; ⊗noon-3pm & 5.30-10.30pm Mon-Sat) You'll be lucky to get a seat here, but if you do, you'll be treated to some of the best Okinawan food around, served in traditional but bustling surroundings. Try the *okinawa-soba* set (¥1400), or choose from the picture menu. It's on a side street off Kokusai-dōri – look for the wooden sign with white lettering above the doorway.

Shanghai Wantan Rō Chinese ¥

(上海雲呑 樓; ☑098-943-4865; 2-21-21 Matsuyama; small plates ¥450-1080; ⊗8pm-5am) If you can hold out for this little late-night eatery, you won't be disappointed. The standouts of the drool-worthy menu (which is, incidentally, perfectly paired with ice-cold beer) are the juicy, deep-fried wonton dumplings and, if you're going to do it right, Shanghai *yaki-soba* (soba noodle stir-fry) and a side of steamed Chinese greens.

Ashibiunā Okinawan ¥

(あしびうなぁ; ☎098-884-0035; www.ryoji-family.co.jp/ryukyusabo.html; 2-13 Shuri Tonokura-chō; lunch sets ¥800-1280; ⊗11.30am-3pm & 5.30pm-midnight) Perfect for lunch after touring Shuri-jō, Ashibiunā has a traditional ambience and picturesque garden. Set meals feature local specialities such as *gōyā champurū*, *okinawa-soba* and *ikasumi yaki-soba*. On the road leading away from Shuri-jō, Ashibiunā is on the right, just before the intersection to the main road.

❶ INFORMATION

Tourist Information Counter (☎098-857-6884; Naha International Airport, 1F Arrivals Terminal; ⊗9am-9pm) At Naha airport's helpful tourism branch pick up a copy of the *Naha Guide Map* or the *Okinawa Guide Map*.

Naha City Tourist Information Office (那覇市 観光案内所; ☎098-868-4887; www.visit-okinawa.jp; 3-2-10 Makishi; ⊗9am-8pm) Located in the Tenbus Building, this gives out free maps and information.

❶ GETTING THERE & AWAY

Naha International Airport (那覇国際空港; Naha Kokusai-kūkō; OKA; ☎098-840-1151; www.naha-airport.co.jp/en) has direct international connections with Hong Kong, Seoul, Shanghai, Singapore and Taipei. Connections with mainland Japan include Fukuoka, Osaka, Nagoya and Tokyo; significant discounts (*tabiwari* on All Nippon Airways and *sakitoku* on JAL) can sometimes be had if you purchase tickets a month in advance.

As well as JAL and ANA, try searching these low-cost carriers, which may well have discount flights between Naha and your destination:

○ Jetstar (www.jetstar.co.jp)

○ Peach Aviation (www.flypeach.com)

○ Solaseed Air (www.solaseedair.jp/en)

○ Skymark (www.skymark.co.jp/en)

❶ GETTING AROUND

The Yui Rail monorail conveniently runs from Naha International Airport in the south to Shuri in the north. Prices range from ¥200 to ¥290;

Okinawan noodle dish

KENGO / SHUTTERSTOCK ©

Monorail

one- and two-day passes cost ¥700 and ¥1200, respectively. Kenchō-mae Station sits at the western end of Kokusai-dōri, while Makishi Station is at its eastern end.

Ishigaki

⊙ SIGHTS & ACTIVITIES

Fusaki Beach
Aqua Garden   Beach
(フサキビーチアクアガーデン; ☑0980-88-7000; www.fusaki.com/english; 1625 Arakawa; from ¥2000) Nonguests of the adjacent resort can pay to enter this massive 'aqua garden' complex with a beachfront pool, bar-restaurant, yoga lessons and a huge range of equipment rental options, from snorkels to stand-up paddleboards. Visitors can swim in the beach section without charge, though you may feel obliged to rent something from the vendors.

Club Med Kabira
Beach Visitor Pass   Outdoors
(☑0980-84-4600; www.clubmed.ca/r/Kabira-Ishigaki/y; Kabira 1; day/night passes from ¥14,000) While joining Club Med, the international fun-for-young-folks resort group, isn't for everyone, taking a day (11am to 6pm) or night (6pm to midnight) to join the fun and enjoy this excellent resort's pool, private beach and extensive drinking and dining facilities might be music to the ears of many. The deal is kept fairly hush-hush...enquire at the front desk. Passes include facilities use, food and limited beverages.

✖ EATING

Shima-no-tabemonoya
Paikaji   Izakaya ¥¥
(島の食べものや 南風; ☑0980-82-6027; 219 Ōkawa; small plates ¥580-1470; ⊗5pm-midnight Mon-Sat) This Ishigaki city favourite serves all the Okinawan and Yaeyama standards. The boisterous atmosphere and kitchen get top marks, although smokers detract from the experience. Try the *ikasumi chahan* (squid-ink fried rice; ¥700), *gōyā champurū* (¥750) or *sashimi moriawase*

Kerama Islands

The Kerama archipelago (慶良間諸島) is surrounded by reefs of diverse corals; their blue waters also provide sanctuary for breeding humpback whales and sea turtles. Several of the islands can be visited as a day trip from Naha, or you can overnight in an island *minshuku*.

Tiny Aka-jima (阿嘉島), 2km in diameter, has some of the Keramas' best beaches, including postcard-perfect Nishibama Beach (北浜ビーチ). A stone's throw from Aka-jima, Zamami-jima (座間味島) is slightly more developed with lovely beaches. Furuzamami Beach (古座間味ビーチ), approximately 1km southeast from the port (over the hill), is a stunning 700m stretch of white sand, fronted by clear, shallow water and a bit of coral. The beach is well developed for day trippers, with toilets, showers and food stalls; snorkel rental is ¥1000.

Zamami Village Office (座間味村役場; ☑098-868-4567) operates two high-speed ferry services per day on the Queen Zamami 3 (¥3140, 70 minutes) and one slower, daily service on Ferry Zamami (¥2120, 1½ hours) to/from Naha's Tomari Port. Make reservations by following the link from https://zamami touristinfo.wordpress.com/getting-here to the official ferry site. The Mitsu Shima motorboat also makes four trips a day between Aka-jima and Zamami-jima (¥300, 15 minutes). See also www.zamamienglishguide.com/ferries.

Clownfish in anemone, Kerama Islands
BUTTCHI 3 SHA LIFE / SHUTTERSTOCK ©

(sashimi assortment; depending on the size ¥750/1300/1800).

Look for the traditional front, with coral around the entry way and a red-and-white sign.

Oishiisā-gu Noodles ¥
(おいしーサー遇; ☑0980-88-2233; 906-1 Kabira; meals ¥600-1050; ☺11am-5pm, summer to 7pm; ℗) This sunlit soba place in Kabira serves local dishes like chilled *yomogi-soba* (mugwort soba) served in a conch shell, or *tebichi soba* (Okinawan soba topped with stewed pork trotters). Even better, follow your lunch with homemade gelato in flavours like Ishigaki beer, *gōyā* or black sesame and soybean.

ⓘ INFORMATION

Ishigaki-jima Tourism Association (石垣市観光協会; ☑0980-82-2809; Ishigaki-shi Shōkō Kaikan 1F; ☺8.30am-5.30pm Mon-Fri) Produces an English-language *Yaeyama Islands* brochure and operates a small-but-helpful information counter in the airport arrivals hall. Japanese readers find the *Ishigaki Town Guide* and the *Yaeyama Navi*.

Ishigaki-jima Rittō Ferry Terminal Offers an array of publications and other tourist information material.

ⓘ GETTING THERE & AWAY

Painushima Ishigaki Airport (南ぬ島石垣空港; ☑0980-87-0468; www.ishigaki-airport.co.jp; ☺7.30am-9pm) Has direct flights that travel to/from Tokyo's Narita Airport (Vanilla Air), Tokyo's Haneda Airport (JTA/ANA), Osaka's Kansai International Airport (JTA/ANA/Peach Airlines), Naha (JTA/ANA) and Yonaguni-jima (RAC).

Ishigaki-jima Rittō Ferry Terminal (石垣港離島ターミナル; ☑0980-82-0043; 1 Misaki) Serves islands including Iriomote-jima, Kohama-jima, Taketomi-jima and Hateruma-jima. Usually you can turn up in the morning and hop on the next ferry to your intended destination.

Ferry terminal, Ishigaki

ⓘ GETTING AROUND

While the island does have a limited bus service, your best bet is to rent a car or scooter to whiz your way around. There's a range of choices at the airport.

Ishigaki Rentacar (石垣島レンタカー; ☎0980-82-8840; 25 Ōkawa; ⊗8am-7pm) Located in the centre of Ishigaki city and has reasonable rates.

Gogoro Go Share (☎0980-87-5562; www. ridegoshare.jp/en; per hour from ¥1000) A new and unique-to-Ishigaki ride-share system for ecoscooters that are 100% battery operated. There are drop-off and recharge stations dotted around the island. Ask at any Gogoro station for the explanatory tour; there's also a location at the ferry terminal. Look out for the cyan-blue bikes.

KII PENINSULA

Kii Peninsula at a Glance...

The remote and mountainous Kii Peninsula (紀伊半島, Kii-hantō), which juts into the Pacific south of major Kansai cites Osaka, Kyoto and Nara, is a world away from the aforementioned urban sprawl. It's an excellent place to immerse yourself in Japan's ancient traditions and natural beauty – without having to work that hard. (Savvy local tourist boards have made it easy to book traditional accommodation online in English). Highlights of the region include the historic pilgrimage trails and onsen of the Kumano Kodō, Unesco World Heritage Sites, and the other-worldly mountaintop temple complex of Kōya-san, one of Japan's most important Buddhist centres.

Two Days in the Kii Peninsula

With just two days you have to make hard choices: either a night in Kōya-san, where you can sleep in a temple and spend the days exploring the mossy temple complexes, or head straight to Hongū, where you can walk a loop of the Kumano Kodō and visit Yunomine Onsen. Having a car helps to make the most of your time.

Four Days in the Kii Peninsula

With four days, you can start in Kōya-san and then head to Hongū, picking up the Kumano Kodō pilgrimage trail there and ending with the river boat ride down to Shingū. Alternatively you could spend the whole time walking the classic route from Tanabe. You'd need a whole week to fully immerse yourself in the charms of Kii.

Previous page: Nachi Taisha (p265)

Kansai International ✈ Airport
● Kaizuka
● Izumisano
● Sennan
Misaki ●
● Yoshino
● Shimoichi
● Gojō
Hashimoto
MIE PREFECTURE
Iwade
Wakayama ●
Wakayama ●
Gokurakubashi
**Kōya-san Cable
Car Station**
Garan
Kongōbu-ji
● Dorogawa
Sanjō-ga-take ▲ (1719m)
Oku-no-in
Tōrō-dō
Hakken-zan ▲ (1915m)
Hinode-ga-take (1694m)
Kami Kitayama
● Ōdai-ga-hara
● Kii-nagashima
● Kainan
Kōya-san
NARA PREFECTURE
▲ Shaka-dake (1800m)
● Shimotsu
Arida ●
Yuasa ● **Yuasa Station**
● Owase
🚉 Kii-yura
Gobō ●
● Ryūjin
● Tōtsukawa
Kumano Hongū Taisha
Kumano Hongū Heritage Centre
● Kumano Atashika
● Inami
Yunomine Public Bathhouse
Takijiri-🛕 Ōji
Tsubo-yu 🛁 Hongū
● Shiko
Sea of Kumano
● Atawa
🛕 Kumano Hayatama Taisha
Kumano Kodō
Kii-Tanabe Station
● Tanabe
Nachi-no-taki 🛕
Kumano Nachi Taisha
● Shingū
Shirahama ● **Shirahama**
Nachi-Katsuura ● Nachi
Tsubaki ● **Tsubaki**
Hiki ●
WAKAYAMA PREFECTURE
● Taiji
PACIFIC OCEAN
● Kushimoto
🧭 N
0   20 km
0   10 miles

Arriving in the Kii Peninsula

Kansai International Airport (KIX), south of Osaka, is convenient; you can pick up a rental car here. Alternatively, the JR Kinokuni line runs around the peninsula's coast, linking Shin-Osaka and Nagoya Stations (some to Kyoto Station). Special Kuroshio and Nankii *tokkyū* (limited express) trains can get you around the peninsula fairly quickly. Once you step off the express train, however, you're at the mercy of slow local trains and buses.

Where to Stay

The Kii Peninsula has fantastic lodging. A highlight of the region is getting to spend a night in a *shukubō* (temple lodging) in Kōya-san. The Kumano Kodō is lined with attractive *minshuku* (traditional guesthouses). Most guests spend a night in Hongū, the main hub of the pilgrimage route. Near Hongū, you have the option to stay in a ryokan (traditional inn) in Yunomine Onsen.

Nachi Taisha

Walking the Kumano Kodō

For over a thousand years, pilgrims have been following the Kumano Kodō, paths which link sacred sights throughout the forested Kii mountains. Trails have been expertly restored, leaving an authentic feel.

Great For...

☑ Don't Miss

Climb Nachi Taisha's steep steps for views to the waterfall and down to the Pacific.

History

From earliest times, the Japanese believed the wilds of the Kii Peninsula to be inhabited by *kami* (Shintō deities). When Buddhism swept Japan in the 6th century, these *kami* became *gongen* – manifestations of the Buddha or a bodhisattva – in a syncretic faith known as *ryōbu,* or 'dual Shintō'. Japan's early emperors made pilgrimages to the area. Over time, the popularity of this pilgrimage spread from nobles to *yamabushi* (wandering mountain ascetics) and common folk.

The focal points of worship are the Hongū Taisha, Hayatama Taisha and Nachi Taisha 'grand shrines', which are connected via trails, known today as the Kumano Kodō: the Kumano Old Road. The Kumano faith is not defined or standardised, and is

Hongū Taisha

ⓘ Need to Know

The classic route connects Tanabe with Shingū or Nachi. Walking is possible year-round.

✕ Take a Break

There is good accommodation en route; booking ahead is recommended.

★ Top Tip

See the Tanabe City Kumano Tourism Bureau (www.tb-kumano.jp) website for detailed information and maps of the routes and to book accommodation online.

open to reinterpretation by those who visit; it's a universal sacred site.

The Classic Route

Most visitors start in Tanabe, with an early-morning bus ride to **Takijiri-ōji** (滝尻王子; 859 Kurisugawa) **FREE**. One of five important Ōji shrines, Takijiri-ōji marks the beginning of the passage into the mountains. From here it is a two-day walk to Hongū, home to **Hongū Taisha** (熊野本宮大社; www.hongutaisha.jp; ⊙6am-7pm; **P**) **FREE**, dramatically perched on a tree-covered ridge, and the informative Kumano Hongū Heritage Centre (p269).

From Hongū you can board a bus for Hikari and then a traditional flat-bottomed boat that will carry you down the Kumano-gawa to Shingū. This is the traditional way to end the pilgrimage (well, minus

the bus), ending at **Kumano Hayatama Taisha** (熊野速玉大社; ☎0735-22-2533; 1 Shingū; ⊙6am-7pm; **P**) **FREE** here. The shrine dates from prehistory and celebrates Hayatama-no-Okami, the god said to rule the workings of nature and, by extension, all life. Meticulously maintained orange pavilions, some tied with impressively thick *shimenawa* (twisted straw ropes), stand in sharp contrast to the greenery all around, including what's said to be Japan's oldest conifer. In town there's a stone staircase, after which a 15-minute climb takes you to a large stone where it is said that the gods originally descended, at Kamikura Shrine.

Alternatively, you can keep walking from Hongū for two days more to **Nachi Taisha** (熊野那智大社; ⊙6am-4.30pm) **FREE**. Near the waterfall **Nachi-no-taki** (那智の滝), the shrine was built in homage to the waterfall's *kami*.

Buses serve key points along the route, so it is possible to do any of the above as a combination of walking and riding.

Kōya-san

◎ SIGHTS

The precincts of Kōya-san are divided into two main areas: **Garan (Sacred Precinct)** in the west, where you'll find interesting temples and pagodas, and **Oku-no-in**, with its vast cemetery, in the east.

A joint ticket (*shodōkyōtsu-naihaiken;* ¥1500) that covers entry to Kongōbu-ji, Garan's Kondō and Konpon Daitō, Reihō-kan and the Tokugawa Mausoleum can be purchased at the Kōya-san Shuku-bō Association office and the venues themselves.

Oku-no-in   Buddhist Temple

(奥の院; ◷24hr) **FREE** Oku-no-in, whose name means 'inner sanctuary', is perhaps the most intensely spiritual place in Japan. At its farthest reaches is the **Gobyō** (御廟), the crypt that Shingon Buddhism founder Kōbō Daishi entered to begin his eternal meditation. Spread out before it are some 200,000 tombs, creating Japan's largest cemetery, built during various historical eras by people, prominent and otherwise, who wanted their remains (or at least a lock of hair) interred close to the legendary monk.

Garan   Buddhist Temple

(伽藍; per bldg ¥200; ◷8.30am-5pm) The name of this temple, which is sometimes called Danjo Garan or Dai Garan, derives from the Sanskrit *saṅghārāma,* which means monastery. With eight principal buildings (temples, pagodas), the complex was the original centre for teaching established by Kōbō Daishi in the 9th century. It's still a teaching centre today, and you might see groups of saffron-robed novices making the rounds. The buildings have burned several times in the intermediate centuries and what you see today are almost entirely modern-day reconstructions.

Kongōbu-ji   Buddhist Temple

(金剛峯寺; ☏0736-56-2011; www.koyasan. or.jp; 132 Kōya-san; ◷8.30am-5pm) This is the headquarters of the Shingon sect and the residence of Kōya-san's abbot. The main gate is the temple's oldest structure (1593);

Oku-no-in

NEALE COUSLAND / SHUTTERSTOCK ©

the present main hall dates from the 19th century. It's free to enter the grounds, but costs ¥500 to enter the main hall, which has several *fusuma* (opaque paper sliding doors) adorned with landscape paintings by famed 17th-century artists, including those of the Kanō school. Many of the temple's statues and ritual implements are displayed at the Reihōkan.

Reihōkan   Museum
(霊宝館, Treasure Museum; ✆0736-56-2029; 306 Kōya-san; adult/child/student ¥600/250/350; ⊙8.30am-5.30pm May-Oct, to 5pm Nov-Apr) Several important artworks from Kōya-san's temples are collected here, most notably some Heian-era wooden sculptures of the Buddha and Fudō Myō-ō originally from Kongōbu-ji. Other works include scroll paintings depicting the life of Kōbō Daishi.

Tōrō-dō   Buddhist Temple
(燈籠堂, Lantern Hall; ⊙6am-5.30pm) **FREE** This large hall at the northern end of Oku-no-in is full of lanterns, which cover the walls and ceiling. Two of the large ones, at the back of the hall, are said to have been lit uninterruptedly for over 900 years. Other lanterns have been donated by dignitaries, including emperors and prime ministers.

✪ EATING

Bononsha   Cafe ¥¥
(梵恩舎; ✆0736-56-5535; 730 Kōya-san; lunch set menu ¥1200; ⊙6.30am-5pm, closed irregularly & late Dec-Mar; ✎) This chill spot – more Goa than rural Japan – with great wooden beams serves vegetarian dishes like tofu cheesecake that seem indulgent compared to temple food. Come after 11am for the daily lunch plate, only served until they run out. Good coffee and chai, too.

ℹ INFORMATION

iKoya (✆0736-56-2780; 357 Kōya-san; ⊙9am-5pm; 🛜) English-speaking staff and lots of local info; rent electric-assist bicycles here for ¥1000 per day (return by 4.30pm).

🛏 Sleep in a Temple

More than 50 temples in Kōya-san offer *shukubō* (temple lodgings), which serve *shōjin-ryōri* (Buddhist vegetarian cuisine).

The simplest rooms (starting at ¥9720 per person including two meals, usually with a surcharge for solo guests) are very basic, with shared facilities; many do not have air conditioning (though they offer space heaters in winter and fans in summer). Most have a variety of room styles, and for a higher rate you can get a room with a private bath and more amenities. Some have gorgeous rooms with garden views.

Shukubō have a fairly set routine. Most expect you to check in by 5pm, and some have a curfew. Monks usually perform a morning prayer service, which guests can observe. The service is followed by breakfast; the timing of this depends on the time of year, but expect it to be early. Communal bathing facilities are often only available between check-in time and 10pm.

You can reserve online (at least a week in advance) through the Kōya-san Shukubō Association, though many *shukubō* are now using popular online-booking sites. Peak travel times include April and October, during which you should book well ahead.

Japanese Buddhist cuisine at a Kōya-san temple
WISSUTA.ON / SHUTTERSTOCK ©

Kōya-san Shukubō Association (高野山宿坊協会; ✆0736-56-2616; www.shukubo.net; 600 Kōya-san; ⊙8.30am-4.30pm Dec-Feb, to 5pm Mar-Jun & Sep-Nov, to 5.45pm Jul & Aug; 🛜)

Kōya-san cable car

handles bookings for Kōya-san's *shukubō* (temple lodgings) and also temple meals; use its online system to book (you can just show up, but it's risky during peak periods like April and October). This office also has English info, including English-language audio guides (¥500) for major sights, and bicycle rental (¥1200 per day). It's in front of the Senjūin-bashi bus stop.

❶ GETTING THERE & AWAY

Access to Kōya-san is via the Nankai Railway from Osaka's Nankai-Namba Station; trains terminate at Gokurakubashi, at the base of the mountain. A cable car goes the rest of the way up the mountain. From the cable-car station, take a bus into town; walking is prohibited on the connecting road.

There are four daily (more frequent on weekends and holidays) reserved-seat limited-express Nankai Kōya line trains bound for Gokurakubashi (¥1650, 1½ hours); otherwise, the journey takes 10 to 15 minutes longer on a regular express (¥870).

Nankai's Kōya-san World Heritage Ticket (¥3400; www.nankaikoya.jp/en/stations/ticket. html) covers return train fare (including one-way limited-express fare from Osaka), buses on Kōya-san for two days and discounted admission to some sites. Purchase at any Nankai train station.

If you want to use a JR Pass, get to Hashimoto, on the JR Wakayama line, where you can connect to the Nankai line to Gokurakubashi (¥440, 45 minutes). This is most easily accomplished coming from Nara, via the JR Yamatōji line, with a transfer at Ōji for the JR Wakayama line (two hours plus transit time).

❶ GETTING AROUND

Buses run on three routes from Kōya-san Cable Car Station via the town centre (Senjūin-bashi bus stop; ¥290, 10 minutes), continuing either to Kongōbu-ji (Kongōbu-ji-mae bus stop; ¥290, 11 minutes) and Garan (Kondō-mae bus stop; ¥340, 15 minutes) or to Ichi-no-hashi (Ichi-no-hashi-guchi bus stop; ¥330, 14 minutes) and Oku-no-in (Oku-no-in-mae bus stop; ¥410, 16 minutes).

The bus office at the cable-car stations sells one-day bus passes (¥830), but once you're in town the sights are walkable.

Tanabe

😋 EATING

Shinbe
Izakaya ¥¥

(しんべ; ☎0739-24-8845; 12-45 Minato; dishes ¥300-2000; ⏰5-10.30pm Mon-Sat) In the warren of tiny restaurants called Ajikoji ('Flavour Alley') near Kii-Tanabe Station and the tourist-information centre, this boisterous, family-run *izakaya* is famous for its *ebi-dango* (shrimp-paste balls) and ridiculously fresh fish that the chef himself might have just pulled in from nearby waters. Sit at the counter for lots of local colour and tons of fun.

ℹ️ INFORMATION

Tanabe Tourism Information Centre

(田辺市観光センター; ☎0739-34-5599; www. tb-kumano.jp; ⏰9am-6pm; 📶) In front of Kii-Tanabe Station, with English-speaking staff and lots of local info, including a great map marked with restaurants that have English menus and bus schedules.

ℹ️ GETTING THERE & AWAY

The JR Kinokuni line connects Kii-Tanabe with JR Shin-Osaka Station (*tokkyū*, ¥4750, 2¼ hours). Buses running between Tanabe and Hongū (¥2060, two hours, from stop 2) stop at several places that serve as trailheads for the Kumano Kodō.

Hongū

◉ SIGHTS & ACTIVITIES

Tsubo-yu
Onsen

(つぼ湯; Yunomine; ¥770; ⏰6am-9.30pm) Right in the middle of Yunomine, this hot spring is inside a tiny wooden shack built on an island in the river. You can use it privately – it holds up to two people – on a first-come, first-served basis for up to 30 minutes. Rinse off at the tap before entering (no soap, shampoo or swimsuits allowed).

Admission includes entry to one of the baths at **Yunomine Public Bathhouse** (湯の峰温泉公衆浴場; regular bath ¥260, kusuri-yu ¥390; ⏰6am-10pm), which you can visit afterwards. For Tsubo-yu, first purchase a ticket at the public bathhouse; you'll be given a number card that indicates your place in the queue. When your number comes up, hang the card outside the bath; return it to the ticket counter when your time is up. Unfortunately, you can't pop into the public bathhouse while you're waiting.

Kumano Hongū Heritage Centre
Museum

(世界遺産熊野本宮館; ☎0735-42-0751; 100-1 Hongū; ⏰9am-5pm; 🅿) **FREE** Part museum, part visitor centre, this contemporary multimedia complex has exhibits about Kumano's culture and natural environment, plus English-speaking staff and resources for travellers.

😋 EATING

Cafe Bonheur
Vegan ¥¥

(カフェボヌール; ☎0735-42-1833; www. bonheurcompany.com; 436-1 Hongū; lunch mains ¥750-1000, dinner set meal ¥1200-3000; ⏰noon-3pm, dinner by reservation from 5pm, closed Wed; 🅿📶🍴) An unexpected treasure at Hongū's southern end is this vegan cafe in a former post office (with the wooden floors and clapboard walls to prove it). It does lunch plates with curry, tofu, salads, and bagel sandwiches. For dinner, ask your innkeeper to make a reservation.

ℹ️ GETTING THERE & AROUND

Hongū is served by infrequent buses from JR Gojō Station (¥3200, four hours) and Kintetsu Yamato-Yagi Station (¥3950, five hours and 10 minutes), both to the north; Kii-Tanabe (¥2000, two hours) in the west; and more frequent departures from Shin-gū (¥1500, 60 to 80 minutes) in the southeast.

Most Hongū buses also stop at Yunomine Onsen, but be sure to ask before boarding.

Autumn in Kyoto (p93)

In Focus

Ameya-yokochō (p42), Tokyo

Japan Today

Japan's stagnant economy and declining population may well be harbingers of the kinds of problems other developed nations will face as their populations shrink. And while many developed countries have recently focused inwards, Japan is taking tentative steps towards looking out. Will the country grow to embrace a new, yet-to-be-defined kind of cosmopolitanism, setting a model for others to follow?

A New Era

It caught everyone off guard when Emperor Akihito announced abruptly in 2016 – on TV, no less – that he wished to abdicate. The last abdication was in 1817, which was back in the days of the shogun. The modern constitution had no provision for what to do in this situation. For over a year, lawmakers debated whether or not Akihito, Japan's 125th emperor (according to the Imperial House Agency's record-keeping), should even be allowed to abdicate. Finally, a bill was passed that would allow the sitting emperor, just this once, to retire.

When Crown Prince Naruhito ascended the Chrysanthemum Throne on 1 May 2019, the Heisei era ended and a new one, the Reiwa era, began. Of course, the starts and ends of Japan's historic periods – in modern times determined by the passing of emperors – are determined by nature, yet they do seem to effectively bracket the culture's shifting moods.

belief systems
(% of population)

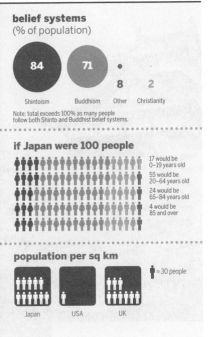

Shintoism 84 Buddhism 71 Other 8 Christianity 2

Note: total exceeds 100% as many people follow both Shinto and Buddhist belief systems.

if Japan were 100 people

17 would be 0–19 years old
55 would be 20–64 years old
24 would be 65–84 years old
4 would be 85 and over

population per sq km

≈ 30 people

Japan   USA   UK

Towards a More Open Japan?

Japan's population is famously shrinking and greying, and while the country is only on the edge of what is expected to be a precipitous fall, the labour market is already feeling the pinch. At the close of 2018, the national government passed an epoch-making immigration-reform bill that would allow a whole new class of foreign workers into the country, to spend between five and 10 years working in so-called 'low skill' jobs in construction, agriculture and the service industry.

It was the conservative majority government who pushed the bill, while the left-leaning opposition parties opposed it. There are legitimate reasons for concern: Japan already has an immigration loophole for low-skilled workers that has a history of misuse. The Technical Intern Training Program has been around since the 1990s, and is supposed to allow immigrants from developing countries to come to Japan to learn skills that they could then use to the benefit of their home countries. In reality, many wind up working in factories under conditions that violate labour laws. Between 2010 and 2018, 174 technical interns died. Critics of the new bill say there is still too much ambiguity to prevent similar exploitation happening.

The Tourists Are Here!

Japan has long hoped to boost its underdeveloped inbound-tourism industry. Then it got real by relaxing visa regulations for visitors from its Asian neighbours. Along with the periodically weak yen, this has resulted in a dramatic uptick of foreign visitors. Inbound numbers have more than doubled since 2010; in 2017 the country logged 28.7 million visitors, already overshooting the target of 20 million set for 2020 – the year Tokyo holds the Summer Olympics.

There is hand wringing, of course: How do we please these tourists? Where are we going to park all the tour buses? And will we ever be able to visit Kyoto in peace again?

But there is also intense fascination: What, exactly, do foreigners find interesting about Japan? There has been an explosion of TV shows trying to figure that out, interviewing tourists and even sending TV personalities to check out places listed in the Lonely Planet guide. The popular show *You! Ha nani shini nihon e?* (Why did you come to Japan?) sends cameras to Narita Airport to hunt out interesting subjects then follow them around. You've been warned!

Koriyama Castle in Nara (p133)

History

Japan has been shaped by both its isolation as an island nation and its proximity to the massive Asian continent (particularly Korea and China). During times of openness, the country has absorbed ideas and cultures from abroad; in times of retreat, it has incubated its own way of doing things. Together, these trends created the fascinating Japan we know today – as has its times of power struggle, aggression, defeat and resurrection.

mid-5th century
Writing is introduced into Japan by scholars from the Korean kingdom of Baekje (based on the Chinese system of characters).

710
Japan's first capital is established at Nara. By now, Japan has many characteristics of a nation state.

794
The imperial capital moves to Heian-kyō, renamed Kyoto in the 11th century.

Early Japan

The earliest traces of human life in Japan date to around 30,000 years ago, but it is possible that people were here much earlier. Until the end of the last ice age about 15,000 years ago, a number of land bridges linked Japan to the Asian continent. The first recognisable culture to emerge was the neolithic Jōmon, from about 13,000 BC. They lived a quasi-nomadic life in settlements along coastal areas, particularly in northeastern Japan, where they could fish, gather seaweed and wild mushrooms, and hunt deer and bear.

Sometime between 800 and 300 BC a new culture began to take shape, referred to as Yayoi. There remains much debate regarding the origin of this shift, whether it was brought about by settlers from China or Korea (or both); the earliest known Yayoi settlements were discovered in northern Kyūshū, close to the Korean Peninsula. The Yayoi introduced wet rice-farming techniques – a huge game changer, not just because it demanded more stable settlement but also because the labour-intensive practice was better suited to lowland areas, encouraging population growth in fertile basins.

Agriculture-based settlement led to territories and boundaries being established, and the rise of kingdoms, the most powerful of which was ruled by the Yamato clan in the Kansai region. The Yamato clan would go on to found the court in Nara and then later Heian-kyō (Kyoto) from where the imperial dynasty would rule for over a millennia.

The Rise & Fall of the Heian Court

In Kyoto over the next few centuries courtly life reached a pinnacle of refined artistic pursuits and etiquette, captured famously in the novel *The Tale of Genji,* written by the court-lady Murasaki Shikibu in about 1004. It showed courtiers indulging in diversions such as guessing flowers by their scent, building extravagant follies and sparing no expense for the latest luxury. On the positive side, it was a world that encouraged aesthetic sensibilities, such as of *mono no aware* (the bittersweetness of things) and *okashisa* (pleasantly surprising incongruity), which have endured to the present day. But it was also a world increasingly estranged from the real one. Manipulated over centuries by the politically powerful Fujiwara family, the imperial throne was losing its authority.

Out in the provinces powerful military forces were developing. Some were led by distant imperial family members, barred from succession claims – they were given new names and farmed out to provincial clans – and hostile to the court. Their retainers included skilled warriors known as samurai (literally 'retainer'). The two main clans of disenfranchised lesser nobles, the Minamoto (also known as Genji) and Taira (Heike), were enemies. In 1156 they were employed to help rival claimants to the Fujiwara family leadership, but these figures soon faded into the background when an all-out feud developed between the Minamoto and the Taira.

The Taira initially prevailed, under their leader Kiyomori (1118–81), who based himself in the capital and, over the next 20 years, fell prey to many of the vices that lurked there. In 1180 he enthroned his two-year-old grandson, Antoku. When a rival claimant requested

early 1000s	1192	1223
Lady of the court, Murasaki Shikibu, writes *The Tale of Genji*, considered one of the world's first novels.	Yoritomo takes the title of shogun from a largely powerless emperor, heralding the start of feudalism in Japan.	The monk Dōgen studies Chang Buddhism in China and later returns to found the Sōtō school of Zen Buddhism.

the help of the Minamoto family, who had regrouped, their leader Yoritomo (1147–99) was more than ready to agree. Both Kiyomori and the claimant died shortly afterwards, but Yoritomo and his younger half-brother Yoshitsune (1159–89) continued the campaign against the Taira. By 1185 Kyoto had fallen and the Taira had been pursued to the western tip of Honshū. A naval battle ensued, won by the Minamoto. In a well-known tragic tale, Kiyomori's widow leapt into the sea with her grandson Antoku (now aged seven), rather than have him surrender.

The Kamakura Shogunate

Yoritomo did not seek to become emperor, but wanted the new emperor to give him legitimacy by conferring the title of shogun (generalissimo), which was granted in 1192. He left many existing offices and institutions in place and set up a base in his home territory of Kamakura (not far from present-day Tokyo) rather than Kyoto. While in theory Yoritomo represented the military arm of the emperor's government, in practice he was in charge. He established a feudal system – which would last almost 700 years as an institution – centred on a loyalty-based lord–vassal system.

When Yoritomo died in 1199 (after falling from his horse in suspicious circumstances) his son succeeded him to the title of shogun. In truth though, the government was now ruled by the clan of Yoritomo's widow, the Hōjō, who acted first as regent before claiming the shogunate outright. It was during the Hōjō shogunate that the Mongols, under Kublai Khan (r 1260–94), twice tried to invade, in 1274 and 1281. On both occasions they were ultimately defeated by storms that destroyed much of their fleet. The typhoon of 1281 prompted the idea of divine intervention, with the coining of the term kamikaze (literally 'divine wind'). Later this term was used to describe Pacific War suicide pilots who, said to be infused with divine spirit, gave their lives to protect Japan from invasion.

Despite victory, the Hōjō suffered: their already depleted finances could not cover the payment promised to the warriors enlisted to fight the Mongols. Dissatisfaction towards the shogunate came to a head under the unusually assertive emperor Go-Daigo (1288–1339), who banded together with the promising young general Ashikaga Takauji (1305–58) to overthrow the Hōjō. Ashikaga claimed the mantle of shogun, setting up a base in Kyoto.

The Warring States

With a few exceptions, the Ashikaga shoguns were relatively ineffective. Without strong, centralised government and control, the country slipped into civil war as regional warlords – who came to be known as *daimyō* (domain lords) – engaged in seemingly interminable feuds and power struggles. The period from 1467 to 1603 is known as the Sengoku (Warring States) era. In 1543 the first Europeans arrived – another game changer – bringing with them Christianity and firearms. The warlord Nobunaga Oda (1534–82) was quick to apprehend the advantage of the latter. Starting from a relatively minor power base, his

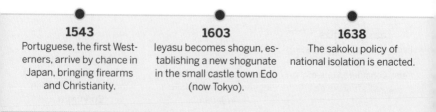

1543
Portuguese, the first Westerners, arrive by chance in Japan, bringing firearms and Christianity.

1603
Ieyasu becomes shogun, establishing a new shogunate in the small castle town Edo (now Tokyo).

1638
The sakoku policy of national isolation is enacted.

skilled and ruthless generalship produced a series of victories. In 1568 he seized Kyoto and held de facto power until, betrayed by one of his generals, he was killed in 1582. Another of his generals, Hideyoshi Toyotomi (1536–98), took up the torch, disposing of potential rivals among Nobunaga's sons and taking the title of regent.

Hideyoshi's power had been briefly contested by Tokugawa Ieyasu (1543–1616), son of a minor lord allied to Nobunaga. After a brief struggle for power, Ieyasu agreed to a truce with Hideyoshi; in return, Hideyoshi granted him eight provinces in eastern Japan. While Hideyoshi intended this to weaken Ieyasu by separating him from his ancestral homeland Chūbu (now Aichi Prefecture), the upstart looked upon the gift as an opportunity to strengthen his power. He set up his base in a small castle town called Edo (which would one day become Tokyo). On his deathbed, Hideyoshi entrusted Ieyasu, who had proven to be one of his ablest generals, with safeguarding the country and the succession of his

The Way of the Warrior

Samurai followed a code of conduct that came to be known as *bushidō* (the way of the warrior), drawn from Confucianism, Shintōism and Buddhism. Confucianism required a samurai to show absolute loyalty to his lord, possess total self-control, speak only the truth and display no emotion. Since his honour was his life, disgrace and shame were to be avoided above all else, and all insults were to be avenged. Seppuku (ritual suicide by disembowelment), also known as hara-kiri, was an accepted means of avoiding the dishonour of defeat. From Buddhism, the samurai learnt the lesson that life is impermanent – a handy reason to face death with serenity. Shintō provided the samurai with patriotic beliefs in the divine status both of the emperor and of Japan.

young son Hideyori (1593–1615). Ieyasu, however, had bigger ambitions and soon went to war against those loyal to Hideyori, finally defeating them at the legendary Battle of Sekigahara in 1600. He chose Edo as his permanent base and ushered in two and a half centuries of Tokugawa rule.

Tokugawa Rule

Ieyasu and his successors kept tight control over the provincial *daimyō,* who ruled as vassals for the regime, requiring them and their retainers to spend every second year in Edo, where their families were kept permanently as hostages – an edict known as *sankin kōtai*. This dislocating policy made it hard for ambitious *daimyō* to usurp the Tokugawas.

Early on, the Tokugawa shogunate adopted a policy of *sakoku* (seclusion from the outside world). Following the Christian-led Shimabara Rebellion, Christianity was banned and several hundred thousand Japanese Christians were forced into hiding. All Westerners except the Protestant Dutch were expelled by 1638. Overseas travel for Japanese was banned (as well as the return of those already overseas). And yet, the country did

1853–54	1859	1867–68
US commodore Matthew Perry's 'black ships' arrive off the coast of Shimoda, forcing Japan to open up for trade.	Five international ports are established in Yokohama, Hakodate, Kōbe, Niigata and Nagasaki.	The Meiji Restoration reinstates imperial authority; Japan's capital is moved to Edo, renamed Tokyo.

Traditional Samurai war helmet

not remain completely cut off: trade with Asia and the West continued through the Dutch and the Ryūkyū empire (now Okinawa) – it was just tightly controlled and, along with the exchange of ideas, funnelled exclusively to the shogunate.

Society was made rigidly hierarchical, comprising (in descending order of importance): *shi* (samurai), *nō* (farmers), *kō* (artisans) and *shō* (merchants). A class's dress, living quarters and even manners of speech were all strictly codified, and interclass movement was prohibited. Village and neighbourhood heads were enlisted to enforce rules at the local level, creating an atmosphere of surveillance. Punishments could be harsh, cruel and even deadly for minor offences. Yet for all its constraints, the Tokugawa period had a considerable dynamism. Japan's cities grew enormously during this period: Edo's population topped one million in the early 1700s, dwarfing much older London and Paris. Despite the best efforts of rulers to limit the growing merchant class, it prospered greatly from the services and goods required for *daimyō* processions to and from Edo. A new culture that thumbed its nose at social hardships and the strictures of the shogunate began to flourish. Increasingly wealthy merchants patronised the kabuki theatre, sumo tournaments and the pleasure quarters – generally enjoying a *joie de vivre* that the dour lords of Edo castle frowned upon.

The Meiji Restoration

In 1853 and again the following year, US commodore Matthew Perry steamed into Edo-wan (now Tokyo Bay) with a show of gunships – which the Japanese called *kurofune* (black ships), because they were cloaked in pitch – and demanded Japan open up to trade and provisioning. The shogunate was no match for Perry's firepower and agreed to his demands. Soon other Western powers followed suit. Japan was obliged to sign what came to be called the 'unequal treaties', opening ports and giving Western nations control over tariffs. Despite last-ditch efforts by the Tokugawa regime to reassert power, anti-shogun sentiment was high, particularly in the outer domains of Satsuma (southern Kyūshū) and Chōshū (western Honshū). Following a series of military clashes between the shogun's

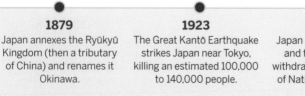

1879
Japan annexes the Ryūkyū Kingdom (then a tributary of China) and renames it Okinawa.

1923
The Great Kantō Earthquake strikes Japan near Tokyo, killing an estimated 100,000 to 140,000 people.

1931
Japan invades Manchuria and then dramatically withdraws from the League of Nations in response to criticism.

armies and the rebels – which showed the rebels to have the upper hand – the last sho-gun, Yoshinobu (1837–1913), agreed to retire in 1867.

In 1868, the new teenage emperor Mutsuhito (1852–1912; later known as Meiji) was named the supreme leader of the land, commencing the Meiji period (1868–1912; Enlight-ened Rule). The institution of the shogun was abolished and the shogun's base at Edo was refashioned into the imperial capital and given the new name, Tokyo (Eastern Capital). In truth, the emperor still wielded little actual power. A new government was formed, primarily of leading former samurai from Satsuma and Chōshū. Above all, the new leaders of Japan – keen observers of what was happening throughout Asia – feared colonisation by the West. They moved quickly to modernise, as defined by the Western powers, to prove they could stand on an equal footing with the colonisers. The government embarked on a grand project of industrialisation and militarisation. A great exchange began between Japan and the West: Japanese scholars were dispatched to Europe to study everything from literature and engineering to nation building and modern warfare. Western scholars were invited to teach in Japan's nascent universities. The Meiji Restoration also heralded far-reaching social changes. The four-tier class system was scrapped; after centuries of having everything prescribed for them, citizens were now free to choose their occupation and place of residence.

Rise of a Global Power

A key element of Japan's aim to become a world power was military might. Using the same 'gunboat diplomacy' on Korea that Perry had used on the Japanese, in 1876 Japan was able to force on Korea an unequal treaty of its own. Using Chinese 'interference' in Korea as a justification, in 1894 Japan manufactured a war with China; victorious, Japan gained Taiwan and the Liaotung Peninsula. Russia pressured Japan into renouncing the peninsula then promptly occupied it, leading to the Russo-Japanese War of 1904–05, won by Japan. When Japan officially annexed Korea in 1910, there was little international protest. Japan entered WWI on the side of the Allies, and was rewarded with a council seat in the newly formed League of Nations. It also acquired German possessions in East Asia and the Pacific.

Yet as the 1920s rolled around, a sense of unfair treatment by Western powers once again took hold in Japan. The Washington Conference of 1921–22 set naval ratios of three capital ships for Japan to five American and five British; around the same time, a racial-equality clause Japan proposed to the League of Nations was rejected. This dissat-isfaction intensified in the Shōwa period (1926–89; Illustrious Peace). In the fall of 1931, members of the Japanese army stationed in Manchuria, there to guard rail lines leased by China to Japan, detonated explosives along the track and blamed the act on Chinese dissidents. This ruse, which gave the Japanese army an excuse for armed retaliation, be-came known as the Manchurian Incident. Within months the Japanese had taken control of Manchuria (present-day Heilongjiang, Jilin and Liaoning provinces) and installed a puppet

1941	**1945**	**1972**
Japan enters WWII by strik-ing Pearl Harbor without warning on 7 December.	Hiroshima and Nagasaki become victims of atomic bombings on 6 and 9 August.	The USA returns adminis-trative control of Okinawa to Japan, but keeps many bases in place.

government. The League of Nations refused to acknowledge the new Manchurian government; in 1933 Japan left the league.

Skirmishes continued between the Chinese and Japanese armies, leading to full-blown war in 1937. Following a hard-fought victory in Shanghai, Japanese troops advanced south to capture Nanjing. Over several months somewhere between 40,000 and 300,000 Chinese were killed in what has become known as the Nanjing Massacre or Rape of Nanjing. To this day, the number of deaths and the prevalence of rape, torture and looting by Japanese soldiers is hotly debated among historians (and government nationalists) on both sides.

WWII & Occupation

Encouraged by Germany's early WWII victories, Japan signed a pact with Germany and Italy in 1940. With France and the Netherlands distracted and weakened by the war in Europe, Japan quickly moved on their colonial territories – French Indo-China and the Dutch West Indies – in Southeast Asia. Tensions between Japan and the United States intensified, as the Americans, alarmed by Japan's aggression, demanded Japan back down in China. When diplomacy failed, the USA barred oil exports to Japan – a crucial blow. Japanese forces struck at Pearl Harbor on 7 December 1941, damaging much of America's Pacific fleet.

Japan advanced swiftly across the Pacific; however, the tide started to turn in the Battle of Midway in June 1942, when much of its carrier fleet was destroyed. Japan had overextended itself, and over the next three years was subjected to an island-hopping counterattack. By mid-1945, Japan, ignoring the Potsdam Declaration calling for unconditional surrender, was preparing for a final Allied assault on its homeland. On 6 August the world's first atomic bomb was dropped on Hiroshima, killing 90,000 civilians. Russia, which Japan had hoped might mediate, declared war on 8 August. And on 9 August another atomic bomb was dropped, this time on Nagasaki, with another 50,000 deaths. Emperor Hirohito formally surrendered on 15 August. When NHK, Japan's national broadcaster, played the message, it was the first time the people of Japan had heard their emperor speak.

The terms of Japan's surrender to the Allies allowed the country to hold on to the emperor as the ceremonial head of state, but Hirohito no longer had authority – nor was he thought of as divine – and Japan was forced to give up its territorial claims in Korea and China. In addition, America occupied the country under General Douglas MacArthur, a situation that would last until 1952 (Okinawa would remain occupied until 1972).

The Boom Years

In the 1950s Japan took off on a trajectory of phenomenal growth that is often described as miraculous (though it was jump-started by US procurement for the Korean War). Throughout the 1960s, Japan's GDP grew, on average, 10% a year. The new consumer

1990
The so-called 'Bubble Economy', based on overinflated land and stock prices, finally bursts in Japan.

1995
The Great Hanshin Earthquake (magnitude 6.9) strikes Kōbe, killing more than 6000.

2005
Japan's population declines for the first year since WWII, a trend that will continue.

class, inspired by the images of affluence introduced during the American occupation, yearned for the so-called 'three sacred treasures' of the modern era (a play on the three sacred treasures of the imperial family: the sword, the mirror and the jewel) – a refrigerator, a washing machine and a television. By 1964, 90% of the population had them.

The 1964 Tokyo Summer Olympics, were seen by many as a turning point in the nation's history, the moment when Japan finally recovered from the devastation of WWII to emerge as a fully fledged member of the modern world economy.

Growth continued through the '70s and reached a peak in the late '80s, when wildly inflated real-estate prices and stock speculation fuelled what is now known as the 'Bubble economy'. These were heady times, when it seemed like all the hard work of the postwar decades had paid off; many Japanese went overseas for the first time, famously snapping up Louis Vuitton handbags by the armful. It seemed like things could only go up – until they didn't.

Heisei Doldrums

In 1991, just two years after the Heisei Emperor ascended the throne, the bubble burst and Japan's economy went into a tailspin. The 1990s were christened the 'Lost Decade', but that has since turned into two, and probably three, as the economy continues to slump along, despite government intervention. Long-time prime minister Abe Shinzō's so-called Abenomics plan, which included a devaluing of the yen, has had some positive effects on corporate gains – and also on in-bound tourism (making Japan a cheaper place to visit!) – and generated some 'Japan is back!' headlines, but ordinary people have seen little change. By now a whole generation has come of age in a Japan where lifelong employment – the backbone of the middle class – is no longer a guarantee.

There have been other disturbing troubles in Japanese society. In March 1995, members of the Aum Shinrikyō doomsday cult released sarin nerve gas on crowded Tokyo subways, killing 12 and injuring more than 5000. This, together with the devastating Kōbe earthquake of the same year, which killed more than 6000 people, signalled the end of Japan's feeling of omnipotence, born of the unlimited successes of the 1980s. The once proud brand of Japan Inc has been tarnished by successive corporate scandals. The 2011 earthquake and tsunami in northeastern Japan, coupled with the meltdown at the Fukushima Dai-ichi nuclear power plant, further underlined the nation's fragility.

With the abdication of the Heisei emperor in 2019, the era came to a close and so, many hope, will the malaise it came to symbolise.

2010	2011	2019
China surpasses Japan as the world's second-largest economy after the USA.	The Great East Japan Earthquake strikes off the coast of Tōhoku, generating a tsunami that kills many thousands.	Emperor Akihito, the first Japanese emperor of the modern age to abdicate, steps down on 30 April, ushering in a new era, Reiwa.

Shibuya crossing (p59), Tokyo

The People of Japan

The people of Japan are depicted as inscrutable. Or reticent. Or shy. They often can be, but often they're not. Japan is typically considered a homogeneous nation, and ethnically this is largely true (though there are minority cultures). But there are also deep divides between urban and rural, stubbornly persistent gendered spheres and growing social stratification. Increasingly, the Japanese are grappling with the problems faced by developed nations the world over.

Population

The population of Japan is approximately 126.5 million. That alone makes Japan a densely populated nation. But the population is unevenly distributed: about nine out of 10 people live in an area classified as urban. Roughly a quarter of the population (about 36 million) lives within the Greater Tokyo Metropolitan Area, which encompasses the cities of Tokyo, Kawasaki and Yokohama, plus the commuter towns stretching deep into the suburbs; it's the most heavily populated metropolitan area in the world. Another nearly 20 million live in the Kyoto–Osaka–Kōbe conurbation (often called Keihanshin). Japan has 13 cities in which the population exceeds one million.

But the population, in general, is shrinking and getting older: for the last two decades the country's birthrate has hovered consistently around 1.4 – among the lowest in the world. The population peaked at 128 million in 2007 and has been in decline since; the latest estimates see a decline of 20 million (roughly one-sixth of the total population!) in the next 25 years. Currently more than one in four Japanese is over the age of 65; in 25 years, if current trends hold, the number will be one in three and less than one in 10 will be a child under the age of 15.

Work Life

Over 70% of Japanese work in the service industry, a broad category that covers white-collar jobs, retail, care-giving and so on. A quarter of the population works in manufacturing, though these jobs are on the decline. Just 3.4% of Japanese today still work full-time in agriculture, forestry and fishing. It's a huge shift: until the beginning of last century, the majority of Japanese lived in close-knit rural farming communities.

For much of the 20th century, the backbone of the middle class was the Japanese corporation, which provided lifetime employment to the legions of blue-suited, white-collar workers, almost all of them men (nicknamed 'salarymen'), who lived, worked, drank, ate and slept in the service of the companies for which they toiled. Families typically consisted of a salaryman father, a housewife mother, kids who studied dutifully to earn a place at one of Japan's elite universities, and an elderly in-law who had moved in.

Since the recession of the 1990s (which plagues the economy to this day), this system has faltered. Today, roughly 37% of employees are considered 'nonregular', meaning they are on temporary contracts, often through dispatch agencies. In many cases they are doing work that once would have been done by full-time, contracted staff – only now with lower pay, less stability and fewer benefits.

Minority Cultures

Hidden within the population stats are Japan's invisible minorities – those who are native-born Japanese, who appear no different from other native-born Japanese but who can trace their ancestry to historically disenfranchised peoples. Chief among these are the descendants of the Ainu, the native people of Hokkaidō, and Okinawans.

Prior to being annexed by Japan in the 19th century, Hokkaidō and Okinawa (formerly the Ryūkyū Empire) were independent territories. Following annexation, the Japanese government imposed assimilation policies that forbade many traditional customs and even the teaching of native languages.

The number of Japanese who identify as Ainu is estimated to be around 20,000, though it is likely that there are many more descendants of Hokkaidō's indigenous people out there – some who may not know it, perhaps because their ancestors buried their identity so deep (for fear of discrimination) that it became hidden forever. There are maybe 10 native speakers of Ainu left; however, in recent decades movements have emerged among the younger generation to learn the language and other aspects of their culture.

Today's Okinawans have a strong regional identity, though it is less about their ties to the former Ryūkyū Empire and more about their shared recent history since WWII. The Okinawans shouldered an unequal burden, both of casualties and of occupation.

Another group is the *burakumin*. Racially no different from other Japanese, they were the disenfranchised of the feudal-era social hierarchy, whose work included tanning, butchering, the handling of corpses, and other occupations that carried the taint of death. Shunned, they lived in isolated settlements (called *buraku*). When the old caste system was abolished and the country modernised, the stigma should have faded, but it didn't: official household registries (often required as proof of residence when applying for a job) tied the ancestors of the *burakumin* to towns known to be former *buraku*.

Fushimi Inari-Taisha (p96), Kyoto

★ **Best Free Sights**

Fushimi Inari-Taisha, Kyoto (p96)

Nara-kōen, Nara (p140)

Hiroshima National Peace Memorial Hall for the Atomic Bomb Victims, Hiroshima (p179)

Shibuya Crossing, Tokyo (p59)

OLIVER FOERSTNER / SHUTTERSTOCK ©

Discrimination in work and marriage was once common, though negative feelings towards *buraku* descendants appear to be diminishing with each generation.

Though English is slim, the Liberty Museum in Osaka has exhibits on Japan's minority cultures and their struggles for social justice.

Religion

Shintō and Buddhism are the main religions in Japan. They are not mutually exclusive: for much of history they were intertwined. Only about one-third of Japanese today identify as Buddhist and the figure for Shintō is just 3%; however, many Japanese participate in rituals rooted in both, which they see as integral parts of their culture and community ties. Generally it is said in Japan that Shintō is concerned with this life: births and marriages, for example, are celebrated at shrines. Meanwhile, Buddhism deals with the afterlife: funerals and memorials take place at temples.

Shintō

Shintō, or 'the way of the gods', is the native religion of Japan. Its innumerable *kami* (gods) are located mostly in nature (in trees, rocks, waterfalls and mountains, for example), but also in the mundane objects of daily life, like hearths and wells. *Kami* can be summoned through rituals of dance and music in the shrines the Japanese have built for them, where they may be beseeched for a good harvest or a healthy pregnancy, for example; in modern times, this may be success in business or school exams.

Shintō's origins are unclear. For centuries it was a vague, amorphous set of practices and beliefs. It has no doctrine and no beginning or endgame; it simply is. One important concept is *musubi,* a kind of vital energy that animates everything (*kami* and mortals alike). *Tsumi* (impurities) interfere with *musubi* so purification rituals are part of all Shintō rites and practices. For this reason, visitors to shrines first wash their hands and mouth at the *temizuya* (font). Some traditional rites include fire, which is also seen as a purifying force. In the late-19th and early-20th centuries, Shintō was reconfigured by the imperialist state into a national religion centred on emperor worship. This ended with Japan's defeat in WWII, when Emperor Hirohito himself publicly renounced his divinity. It's unclear what those who today identify as Shintō actually believe.

Buddhism

By the time Buddhism arrived in Japan in the 6th century, having travelled from India via Tibet, China and Korea, it had acquired a whole pantheon of deities. More importantly, it didn't so much supplant Shintō as elaborate on it. Over time, Shintō *kami* became integrated into the Buddhist cosmology while many new deities were adopted as *kami;* those with similar aspects were seen as two faces of the same being.

Over the centuries, several distinct sects developed in Japan. Zen is the most well-known internationally, for its meditative practice *zazen* (seated meditation), but there are others, too, like the older esoteric Shingon sect (which shares similarities with Tibetan Buddhism) and the populist Pure Land sect (which has the greatest number of adherents). Regardless of sect, the most popular deity in Japan is Kannon, a bodhisattva who embodies mercy and compassion and is believed to have the power to alleviate suffering in this world.

Given its association with the afterlife, many turn to Buddhism later in life. (And because of its role in funeral rites, many young Japanese have a dour view of the religion.)

We Japanese

It's common to hear Japanese begin explanations of their culture by saying, *ware ware nihonjin,* which means 'we Japanese'. There's a strong sense of national cohesion, reinforced by the media which plays up images of Japan as a unique cultural Galápagos; TV programs featuring foreign visitors being awed and wowed by the curious Japanese way of doing things are popular with viewers. The Japanese, in turn, are often fascinated (and intimidated) by what they perceive as the otherness of outside cultures.

But, like Shintō, there are certain practices carried out by believers and nonbelievers alike. The Buddhist festival of O-Bon, in midsummer, is when the souls of departed ancestors are believed to pay a short visit. Families return to their home towns to sweep their gravestones, an act called *ohaka-mairi*, and welcome them. Only the most staunch nonbeliever could avoid the creeping sense that skipping such rituals would be tempting fate.

Women in Japan

Women have historically been viewed as keepers of the home, responsible for overseeing the household budget, monitoring the children's education, and taking care of the day-to-day tasks of cooking and cleaning. Of course this ideal was rarely matched by reality: labour shortfalls often resulted in women taking on factory work and, even before that, women often worked side by side with men in the fields.

As might be expected, the contemporary situation is complex. There are women who prefer the traditionally neat division of labour. They tend to opt for shorter college courses, often at women's colleges. They may work for many years, enjoying a period of independence before settling down, leaving the role of breadwinner to the husband and becoming full-time mums.

While gender discrimination in the workforce is illegal, it remains pernicious. And while there is less societal resistance to women working, they still face enormous pressure to be doting mothers. Most women see the long hours that Japanese companies demand as incompatible with child-rearing, especially in the early years; few fathers are willing or, given their own work commitments, able to pick up the slack. Attempts at work-life balance, such as working from home, can result in guilt trips from colleagues or bosses. Working women have coined the phrase 'maternity harassment' to describe the remarks they hear in the office after announcing a pregnancy, the subtle suggestions that she quit so as not to cause trouble. Six out of 10 women quit work after having their first child.

The World Economic Forum in its Global Gender Gap Report for 2018 has given Japan the damning rating of 110 out of 144 countries – in between Mauritius at 109 and Belize at 111. Far and away the lowest of any G7 nation, Japan scores particularly low in economic participation and opportunity and political empowerment.

On the upside: Japanese women have an average life expectancy of 89 years, second only to Monaco.

Izakaya in Ueno, Tokyo

Food & Drink

At its best, Japanese food is highly seasonal, drawing on fresh local ingredients coaxed into goodness with a light touch. Rice is central; the word for 'rice' and for 'meal' are the same: gohan. Miso soup and pickled vegetables often round out the meal. But from there Japanese food can vary tremendously; it can be light and delicate (as it is often thought to be) but it can also be hearty and robust.

The Japanese Restaurant Experience

When you enter a restaurant in Japan, you'll be greeted with a hearty *'irasshaimase'* (Welcome!). In all but the most casual places, the waiter will next ask you *'nan-mei sama'* (How many people?). Indicate the answer with your fingers, which is what the Japanese do. You may also be asked if you would like to sit at a *zashiki* (low table on the tatami), at a *tēburu* (table) or the *kauntā* (counter). Once seated you will be given an *o-shibori* (hot towel), a cup of tea or water (this is free) and a menu. More and more restaurants these days (especially in touristy areas) have English menus.

Often the bill will be placed discreetly on your table. If not, you can ask for it by catching the server's eye and making an 'x' in the air 'with your index fingers. You can also say *o-kanjō kudasai*. At some restaurants, you can summon the server by pushing a call bell on the table.

There's no tipping, though higher-end restaurants usually tack on a 10% service fee. During dinner service, some restaurants may instead levy a kind of cover charge (usually a few hundred yen); this will be the case if you are served a small appetiser (called *o-tsumami*, or 'charm') when you sit down. Payment is usually settled at the register near the entrance.

On your way out, if you were pleased with your meal, give your regards to the staff or chef with the phrase *gochisō-sama deshita,* which means 'It was a real feast'.

Izakaya

Izakaya (居酒屋) translates as 'drinking house' – the Japanese equivalent of a pub – and you'll find them all over Japan. Visiting one is a great way to dig into Japanese culture. An evening at an *izakaya* is dinner and drinks all in one: food is ordered for the table a few dishes at a time along with rounds of beer, sake or *shōchū* (a strong distilled alcohol often made from potatoes). While the vibe is lively and social, it's perfectly acceptable to go by yourself and sit at the counter. If you don't want alcohol, it's fine to order a soft drink instead (but it would be strange to not order at least one drink).

There are orthodox, family-run *izakaya,* often with rustic interiors, that serve sashimi (raw fish) and grilled fish to go with sake; large, cheap chains, popular with students, that often have a healthy (er, unhealthy) dose of Western pub-style dishes (like chips); and there are also stylish chef-driven ones with creative menus. A night out at an average *izakaya* should run ¥2500 to ¥5000 per person, depending on how much you drink. Chains often have deals where you can pay a set price for a certain amount of dishes and free drinks.

Kaiseki

Kaiseki is the pinnacle of Japanese cuisine, where ingredients, preparation, setting and presentation come together to create a highly ritualised, aesthetically sophisticated dining experience. It was born in Kyoto as an adjunct to the tea ceremony; though fish is often served, meat never appears in traditional *kaiseki*. The meal is served in several small courses, giving the diner an opportunity to admire the plates and bowls, which are carefully chosen to complement the food and season. It usually includes sashimi, something steamed, something grilled, soup and finishes with rice and then a simple dessert (though there may be many more courses).

At its best, it's eaten in the private room of a *ryōtei* (an especially elegant style of traditional restaurant), often overlooking a private, tranquil garden. This is about as pricey as dining can get in Japan, upwards of ¥20,000 per person, with advance reservations required. There are cheaper places though, and lunch can be a good deal – some restaurants do boxed lunches containing a small sampling of their dinner fare for around ¥2500 per person.

Sushi & Sashimi

Sushi (寿司 or 鮨) is raw fish and rice seasoned with vinegar and is a meal unto itself. Sashimi (刺身) is just raw fish and is usually a complement to a larger meal; *sashimi mori-awase* (刺身盛り合わせ; assorted sashimi) is a common dish to order at *izakaya*.

Sushi comes in many varieties: the most recognised kind is *nigiri-zushi*, the bite-sized slivers of seafood hand-pressed onto pedestals of rice. It can be very high-end, served piece

Miso ramen

SASAKEN / SHUTTERSTOCK ©

by piece at exclusive *sushi-ya* (sushi restaurants) where a meal of seasonal delicacies could run over ¥20,000 per person. It can also be very cheap, at *kaiten-sushi* (回転寿司), for example, where ready-made plates of sushi (about ¥200 each) are sent around the restaurant on a conveyor belt. Here there's no need to order: just grab whatever looks good.

At an average *sushi-ya*, a meal should run between ¥2000 and ¥5000 per person. You can order à la carte – often by just pointing to the fish in the refrigerated glass case on the counter – or a sampler set; the latter is a better deal (unless you are set on eating only your favourites). These usually come in three grades: *futsū* or *nami* (regular), *jō* (special) and *toku-jō* (extra-special). The price difference is determined more by the value of the ingredients than by volume.

Unless otherwise instructed by the chef (who may have preseasoned some pieces), you can dip each piece lightly in *shōyu* (soy sauce), which you pour from a small decanter into a low dish specially provided for the purpose. *Nigiri-sushi* is usually made with wasabi, so if you'd prefer it without, order *wasabi-nuki*. Sushi is one of the few foods in Japan that is perfectly acceptable to eat with your hands (even at high-end places!). Slices of *gari* (pickled ginger) are served to refresh the palate.

Though much is made of the freshness of the ingredients in modern sushi, the dish originated as a way to make fish last longer: the vinegar in the rice was a preserving agent. An older form of sushi, called *hako-zushi* or *oshi-zushi* ('box' or 'pressed' sushi) and more common in western Japan, is made of fish pressed onto a bed of heavily vinegared rice in a wooden mould with a weighted top. Left to rest, it acquires a slight tang of fermentation.

Ramen

Ramen originated in China, but its popularity in Japan is epic. If a town has only one restaurant, odds are it's a ramen shop. Your basic ramen is a big bowl of crinkly egg noodles in broth, served with toppings such as *chāshū* (sliced roast pork), *moyashi* (bean sprouts) and *negi* (leeks). The broth can be made from pork or chicken bones or dried seafood; usually it's a top-secret combination of some or all of the above, falling somewhere on the spectrum between *kotteri* (thick and fatty – a signature of pork-bone ramen) or *assari* (thin and light).

It's typically seasoned with *shio* (salt), *shōyu* or hearty miso – though at less-orthodox places, anything goes. Most shops will specialise in one or two broths and offer a variety of seasonings and toppings. Another popular style is *tsukemen*, noodles that come with a dipping sauce (like a really condensed broth) on the side. Given the option, most diners get their noodles *katame* (literally 'hard' but more like al dente). If you're really hungry, ask for *kaedama* (another serving of noodles), usually only a couple of hundred yen more.

Well-executed ramen is a complex, layered dish – though it rarely costs more than ¥1000 a bowl. Costs are minimised by fast-food-style service: often you order from a vending machine (you'll get a paper ticket, which you hand to the chef); water is self-serve.

Japanese Beef

Wagyū (Japanese beef) has cult status both in Japan and abroad, thanks to its rich marbling (which makes for very melty, tender meat). Most *wagyū* comes from a breed of cattle known as Japanese Black. Within that category there are a few premium brands that adhere to strict quality control and are prized as top-grade meat. These include Kōbe, Matsusaka and Ōmi. Kōbe, the most well-known brand, is limited to beef from cows raised in Hyogō-ken (the prefecture in which the city of Kōbe is located) and who are descendants of Tajiri-go, a famed (and prolific) bull from the 1930s.

Often the meat is seared at high temperature on a *teppan* (steel hotplate), diced and served with rice and miso soup. You can also grill strips of *wagyū* over coals at Korean barbecue-style places called *yakiniku*; eat it sukiyaki or *shabu-shabu* style; or order it at steakhouses paired with wine. All mention of premium Japanese beef comes with the following disclaimer: eat this, and you'll be spoiled for life.

Magic Words for Dining in Japan

If you're generally an adventurous (or curious) eater, don't let the absence of an English menu put you off. Instead, tell the staff (or ideally the chef), *omakase de onegaishimasu* (I'll leave it up to you).

This works especially well when you're sitting at the counter of a smaller restaurant or *izakaya*, where a rapport naturally develops between the diners and the cooks. It's best said with enthusiasm and a disarming smile, to reassure everyone that you really are game.

This isn't just a tourist hack: Japanese diners do this all the time. Menus might not reflect seasonal dishes and odds are the chef is working on something new that he or she is keen to test out on the willing.

It's probably a good idea to set a price cap, like: *hitori de san-zen-en* (one person for ¥3000).

Japanese Classics

Fugu (ふぐ) Poisonous pufferfish prepared by licensed chefs; a tasting menu usually consists of different parts of the fish prepared different ways.

Okonomiyaki (お好み焼き) Savoury pancake stuffed with cabbage plus meat or seafood (or cheese or kimchi...), which you grill at the table and top with *katsuo-bushi* (bonito flakes), *nori* (seaweed), mayonnaise and Worcestershire sauce.

Shabu-shabu (しゃぶしゃぶ) Thin slices of beef or pork swished briefly in a light, boiling broth then seasoned with *goma* (sesame-seed) or *ponzu* (citrus-based sauce).

Soba (そば) Thin buckwheat noodles, either *to-wari* (100% buckwheat) or cut with wheat; served in hot broth (flavoured with bonito and soy sauce) or with concentrated, room temperature broth on the side for dipping (the latter style is preferred by connoisseurs).

Sukiyaki (すき焼き) Thin slices of beef cooked piece by piece in a broth of soy sauce, sugar and sake at your table, then dipped in a raw egg.

Tempura (天ぷら) Seafood and vegetables deep-fried in a fluffy light batter, flavoured with salt or a light sauce mixed with grated *daikon* (radish).

Tonkatsu (とんかつ; 豚カツ) Tender pork cutlets breaded and deep-fried, served with a side of grated cabbage.

Udon (うどん) Thick white wheat noodles, served similarly to soba.

Unagi (うなぎ) Freshwater eel grilled over coals and lacquered with a rich, slightly sweet sauce. Note that *unagi* is listed as 'endangered' on the IUCN Red List.

Pouring sake

★ **Recommended Reading**

Sake Confidential: A Beyond-the-Basics Guide to Understanding, Tasting, Selection and Enjoyment (John Gauntner; 2014)

What's What in Japanese Restaurants: A Guide to Ordering, Eating and Enjoying (Robb Satterwhite; 2011)

Sake

What much of the world calls 'sake' the Japanese call *nihonshu* ('the drink of Japan'). It's made from rice, water and *kōji*, a mould that helps to convert the rice starch into fermentable sugars. Sake has existed for as long as history has been recorded in Japan (and odds are a lot longer). It plays an important part in a variety of Shintō rituals, including wedding ceremonies, and many Shintō shrines display huge barrels of sake in front of their halls (most of them are empty). Sake is always brewed during the winter, in the cold months that follow the rice harvest in September. Fresh, young sake is ready by late autumn.

Sake is classed by its *seimai buai* (精米歩合) – the amount of rice that is polished away before fermentation. As a general rule, the more polishing, the better the sake will be, as it is believed that sake made from the inner portion of the rice kernel is the smoothest and most delicious of all. Sake made from rice kernels with 40% to 50% of their original volume polished away is called *ginjō*. Sake made from rice kernels with 50% or more of their original volume polished away is classified as *dai-ginjō*. Sometimes the alcohol content is artificially regulated (either increased or reduced); unadulterated sake is known as *junmai-shu* (pure rice sake). On average the alcohol content of sake is around 15% (by law it can be no more than 22%).

If wine is defined by terroir then sake is defined by its water, usually mountain snowmelt that flows downstream through rice paddies picking up various minerals on the way. The variety of rice matters too, though many brewers buy rice from elsewhere in Japan (like Yamada Nishiki rice farmed in Hyōgō Prefecture and prized by brewers); there are also countless strains of *kōji* used in secret, proprietary blends. There are over 1500 *kura* (breweries) in Japan; almost everywhere has a *ji-zake* (local sake).

The taste of sake is often categorised as sweet *(ama-kuchi)* or dry *(kara-kuchi)*, though these are just starting points. Sake can also be *tanrei* (crisp), *hanayaka* (fragrant), *odayaka* (mellow) and much more. Naturally, it's the best pairing for traditional Japanese cuisine.

Green Tea

Japan is a treat for tea lovers. Here *o-cha* (tea) means green tea and broadly speaking there are two kinds: *ryokucha* (steeped with leaves) and *matcha*, which is made by whisking dried and milled leaves with water until a cappuccino level of frothiness is achieved. It's *matcha* that is served in the tea ceremony; it is quite bitter, so it is accompanied by a traditional sweet.

When you order *o-cha* in a Japanese restaurant (it's usually free, like water), you'll most likely be served *bancha* (ordinary tea). In summer, you might get cold *mugicha* (roasted barley tea) instead. After a course meal, restaurants often serve *hōjicha* (roasted green tea) which is weaker and less caffeinated. If you want to try out the more rarefied stuff, you'll have to seek out a teahouse or speciality shop. *Sencha* (煎茶) is medium-grade green loose leaf tea; *gyokuro* (玉露), shaded from the sun and picked early in the season, is the highest grade.

Eat Like a Local

All but the most extreme type-A chefs will say they'd rather have foreign visitors enjoy their meal than agonise over getting the etiquette right. Still, a few points to note if you want to make a good impression: there's nothing that makes a Japanese chef grimace more than out-of-towners who over-season their food – a little soy sauce and wasabi goes a long way (and heaven forbid, don't pour soy sauce all over your rice; it makes it much harder to eat with chopsticks). In Japan, it's perfectly OK, even expected, to slurp your noodles. They should be eaten at whip speed, before they go soggy (letting them do so would be an affront to the chef); that's why you'll hear diners slurping, sucking in air to cool their mouths.

Don't stick your chopsticks upright in a bowl of rice or pass food from one pair of chopsticks to another – both are reminiscent of Japanese funeral rites. When serving yourself from a shared dish, it's polite to use the back end of your chopsticks (ie not the end that goes into your mouth) to place the food on your own small dish.

Before digging in, it is customary in Japan to say *itadakimasu* (literally 'I will receive' but closer to *'bon appétit'* in meaning). It's considered bad form to fill your own glass. Instead, fill the drained glasses around you and someone will quickly reciprocate; when they do, raise your glass slightly with two hands – a graceful way to receive anything. Once everyone's glass has been filled, the usual starting signal is a chorus of *kampai*, which means 'Cheers!'.

Lastly, lunch is one of Japan's great bargains; however, restaurants can only offer cheap lunch deals because they anticipate high turnover. Spending too long sipping coffee after finishing your meal might earn you dagger eyes from the kitchen.

The Year in Food

Spring (March–May) The new growth of spring finds its way onto tables in the form of *takenoko* (bamboo shoots) and *sansai* (mountain vegetables). Especially good if you're in the mountains.

Summer (June–August) The season for cooling dishes like *reimen* (cold ramen) and *zaru-soba* (cold buckwheat noodles served on a bamboo tray). And nothing says summer like *kaki-gōri* (shaved ice topped with sweet syrup).

Autumn (September–November) The first sign of autumn is silvery *sanma* (Pacific saury) on menus. Other delicacies: *matsutake* mushrooms, ginkgo nuts, candied chestnuts and *shinmai,* the first rice of the harvest season.

Winter (December–February) Friends come together for steaming *nabe* (hotpot) dishes; this is also the season for *fugu* (puffer fish) and oysters.

Traditional painting depicting Samurai battle

Arts & Architecture

Japan has a sublime artistic tradition that has been influenced by the cultures of continental Asia and later the West. It has been shaped by a tendency to refine techniques and materials to an almost maniacal degree. Its traditional design aesthetic of clean lines, natural materials, heightened spatial awareness and subtle enhancement has long been an inspiration to creators around the world.

Traditional Painting

Traditionally, paintings consisted of black ink or mineral pigments on *washi* (Japanese handmade paper) and were sometimes decorated with gold leaf. Paintings of the Heian era (794–1185) depicted episodes of court life, like those narrated in Murasaki Shikibu's novel *Genji Monogatari* (The Tale of Genji), or seasonal motifs, often on scrolls. Works such as these were later called *yamato-e*; one of the most striking conventions of the form is the use of a not-quite-bird's-eye perspective peering into palace rooms without their roofs (the better to see the intrigue!). With the rise of Zen Buddhism in the 14th century, minimalist monochrome ink paintings came into vogue; the painters themselves were priests and the quick, spontaneous brush strokes of this painting style were in harmony with their guiding philosophies.

It was during the Muromachi period (1333–1573) that the ruling class became great patrons of Japanese painters, giving them the space and the means to develop their own styles. Two styles emerged at this time: the Tosa school and the Kanō school. The Tosa clan of artists worked for the imperial house, and were torch-bearers for the now classic *yamato-e* style, using fine brushwork to create highly stylised figures and elegant scenes from history and of the four seasons; sometimes the scenes were half-cloaked in washes of wispy gold clouds. The Kanō painters were under the patronage of the Ashikaga shogunate and employed to decorate their castles and villas. It was they who created the kind of works most associated with Japanese painting: decorative polychromatic depictions of mythical Chinese creatures and scenes from nature, boldly outlined on large folding screens and sliding doors.

With the Meiji Restoration (1868), when artists and ideas were sent back and forth between Europe and Japan, painting necessarily became either a rejection or an embracing of Western influence. Two terms were coined: *yōga* for Western-style works and *nihonga* for works in the traditional Japanese style. In reality though, many *nihonga* artists incorporated shading and perspective into their works, while using techniques from all the major traditional Japanese painting schools. There are many artists today who continue to create and redefine *nihonga*.

Wabi-sabi

Wabi-sabi is an aesthetic that embraces the notion of ephemerality and imperfection and is Japan's most distinct – though hard to pin down – and profound contribution to the arts. *Wabi* roughly means 'rustic' and connotes the loneliness of the wilderness, while *sabi* can be interpreted as 'weathered', 'waning' or 'altered with age'. Together the two words signify an object's natural imperfections, arising in its inception, and the acquired beauty that comes with the patina of time. It is most often evoked in descriptions of the tea ceremony, a kind of participatory performance art surrounding the ritual of drinking tea that came into vogue in the 16th century. Ceramics made for the tea ceremony – and this is where Japanese ceramics finally came into their own – often appeared dented or misshapen or had a rough texture, with drips of glaze running down the side. The teahouses too, small, exceedingly humble and somewhat forlorn (compared to the manors they were attached to) also reflected *wabi-sabi* motifs, as did the ikebana (flower arrangements) and calligraphy scrolls that would be placed in the teahouse's alcove.

Ukiyo-e (Woodblock Prints)

Far from the nature scenes of classical paintings, *ukiyo-e* (woodblock prints, but literally 'pictures of the floating world') were for the common people, used in advertising or in much the same way posters are used today. The subjects of these woodblock prints were images of everyday life, characters in kabuki plays and scenes from the 'floating world', a term derived from a Buddhist metaphor for life's fleeting joys. Edo's particular 'floating world' revolved around pleasure districts such as the Yoshiwara. In this topsy-turvy kingdom, an inversion of the usual social hierarchies imposed by the Tokugawa shogunate, money meant more than rank, actors were the arbiters of style, and courtesans elevated their art to such a level that their accomplishments matched those of the women of noble families. The vivid colours, novel composition and flowing lines of *ukiyo-e* caused great excitement in the West, sparking a vogue that one French art critic dubbed *japonisme*. *Ukiyo-e* became a key influence on impressionists (for example, Toulouse-Lautrec, Manet and Degas) and post-impressionists.

Shinjuku movie theatre, Tokyo (p35)

TOSHIAKI ONO / A.COLLECTIONRF / GETTY IMAGES ©

Superflat & Beyond

The '90s were a big decade for Japanese contemporary art: love him or hate him, Murakami Takashi brought Japan back into an international spotlight it hadn't enjoyed since 19th-century collectors went wild for *ukiyo-e*. His work makes use of the flat planes, clear lines and decorative techniques associated with *nihonga*, while lifting motifs from the lowbrow subculture of manga (Japanese comics); his spirited images and installations have become emblematic of the Japanese aesthetic known as *poku* – a concept that combines pop art with an *otaku* (manga and anime superfan) sensibility. As much an artist as a clever theorist, Murakami proclaimed in his 'Superflat' manifesto that his work picked up where Japanese artists left off after the Meiji Restoration – and this might just be the future of painting, given that most of us now view the world through the portals of two-dimensional screens.

Naturally, younger artists have had trouble defining themselves in the wake of 'Tokyo Pop', as the highly exportable art of the '90s came to be known. Some artists making a mark include Tenmyouya Hisashi, who coined the term 'neo-nihonga' to describe his works, which echo the flat surfaces and deep impressions of woodblock prints, while singing a song of the street; conceptual artist Tanaka Koki (named Deutsche Bank Artist of the Year in 2015); and the collective of irreverent pranksters known as Chim-Pom.

Kabuki

Around the year 1600, a charismatic shrine priestess in Kyoto led a troupe of female performers in a new type of dance people dubbed kabuki – a slang expression that meant 'cool' or 'in vogue' at the time. The dancing – rather ribald and performed on a dry riverbed for gathering crowds – was also a gateway to prostitution. A series of crackdowns by the Tokugawa establishment (first on female performers, then on adolescent male performers) gave rise to one of the most fascinating elements of kabuki, the *onnagata* (adult male actors who specialise in portraying women).

As kabuki spread to Edo (Tokyo), it developed hand in hand with the increasingly affluent merchant class, whose decadent tastes translated into the breathtaking costumes, dramatic music and elaborate stagecraft that have come to characterise the art form. It is this intensely visual nature that makes kabuki accessible to foreign audiences – you don't really have to know the story to enjoy the spectacle. (Tip: if you opt for the cheap seats, bring binoculars.) Over the course of several centuries, kabuki has developed a repertoire that draws on popular themes, such as famous historical accounts and stories of love-suicide, while also borrowing copiously from *nō* (stylised dance-drama), *kyōgen* (comic drama) and bunraku (classic puppet theatre). Formalised beauty and stylisation are the central aesthetic principles of kabuki; highlights for many fans are the dramatic poses (called *mie*) that actors strike at pivotal moments.

Golden Age of Japanese Cinema

The Japanese cinema of the 1950s – the era of international acclaimed auteurs Ozu Yasujirō, Mizoguchi Kenji and Akira Kurosawa – is responsible for a whole generation of Japanophiles. Ozu (1903–63) was the first great Japanese director, known for his piercing, at times heartbreaking, family dramas. Mizoguchi (1898–1956) began by shooting social realist works in the 1930s but found critical acclaim with his reimagining of stories from Japanese history and folklore.

Kurosawa (1910–98) is an oft-cited influence for film-makers around the world. His films are intense and psychological; the director favoured strong leading men and worked often with the actor Mifune Toshirō. Kurosawa won the Golden Lion at the Venice International Film Festival and an honorary Oscar for the haunting *Rashōmon* (1950), based on the short story of the same name by Akutagawa Ryūnosuke and staring Mifune as a bandit. Japanese cinema continues to produce directors of merit but has not emerged as the influential cultural force that its heyday seemed to foreshadow.

Temple or Shrine?

Buddhist temples and Shintō shrines were historically intertwined and centuries of coexistence means the two resemble each other architecturally; you'll also often find small temples within shrines and vice versa. The easiest way to tell the two apart though is to check the gate. The main entrance of a shrine is a *torii* (gate), usually composed of two upright pillars, joined at the top by two horizontal crossbars, the upper of which is normally slightly curved. *Torii* are often painted a bright vermilion. In contrast, the *mon* (main entrance gate) of a temple is often a much more substantial affair, constructed of several pillars or casements, joined at the top by a multi-tiered roof. Temple gates often contain guardian figures, usually Niō (*deva* kings).

Anime

Anime picked up where film left off, piquing the interest of subsequent generations and pointing them in the direction of Japan. Miyazaki Hayao (b 1941), who together with Takahata Isao (1935–2018) founded Studio Ghibli, is largely responsible for anime gaining widespread, mainstream appeal abroad. Thematically, his works are noteworthy for their strong female characters and environmentalism; *Nausicaä of the Valley of the Wind* (1984) is an excellent example. He was given an Academy Honorary Award in 2014.

Among the best-known anime is *Akira* (1988), Ōtomo Katsuhiro's psychedelic fantasy set in a future Tokyo inhabited by speed-popping biker gangs and psychic children. *Ghost in the Shell* (1995) is an Ōshii Mamoru film with a sci-fi plot worthy of Philip K Dick involving cyborgs, hackers and the mother of all computer networks. The works of Kon Satoshi (1963–2010), including the Hitchcockian *Perfect Blue* (1997), the charming *Tokyo Godfathers* (2003) and the sci-fi thriller *Paprika* (2006), are also classics.

One new director to watch is Shinkai Makoto: his 2016 *Your Name* was both a critical and box-office smash – the second highest-grossing domestic film ever, after *Spirited Away* (2001).

Contemporary Architecture

Since the 1980s a new generation of Japanese architects has emerged who continue to explore both modernism and postmodernism, while mining Japan's architectural heritage. Among the more influential ones are Andō Tadao (b 1941) and Itō Toyō (b 1941). Andō's works tend to be grounded and monumental, yet unobtrusive, with no unnecessary

Japanese bookstore in Ginza, Tokyo

★ Literary Classics

The Pillow Book (Sei Shōnagon; 1002)

The Narrow Road to the Deep North (Bashō Matsuo; 1702)

The Life of an Amorous Man (Saikaku Ihara; 1682)

Kokoro (Sōseki Natsume; 1914)

flourishes; he works in modern materials such as concrete and steel. He has many works in Tokyo and also on Naoshima.

Itō's designs are lighter and more conceptual, meditating on the ideas of borders between inside and outside, public and private. Among his signature works is the Sendai Mediatheque. Two of his protégés, Sejima Kazuyo and Nishizawa Ryūe, went on to form the firm SANAA. Their own luminous form-follows-function creations have also been influential. See their work at the 21st Century Museum of Contemporary Art in Kanazawa and the other-worldly Teshima Art Museum.

Another name to know is Kuma Kengo, who has received many high-profile commissions over the last decade, including the new stadium for the Tokyo 2020 Olympics. Kuma is famous for his use of wood, employing cutting-edge computer drafting technology to that age-old staple of Japanese construction.

Traditional Japanese Gardens

Gardening is one of Japan's finest art forms. You'll encounter four major types of gardens during your horticultural explorations.

Funa asobi Meaning 'pleasure boat' and popular in the Heian period, such gardens feature a large pond for boating and were often built around nobles' mansions. The garden that surrounds Byōdō-in in Uji is a vestige of this style.

Shūyū These 'stroll' gardens are intended to be viewed from a winding path, allowing the design to unfold and reveal itself in stages and from different vantages. Popular during the Heian, Kamakura and Muromachi periods; a celebrated example is the garden at Ginkaku-ji in Kyoto.

Kanshō Zen rock gardens (also known as *kare-sansui* gardens) are an example of this type of 'contemplative' garden intended to be viewed from one vantage point and designed to aid meditation. Kyoto's Ryōan-ji is perhaps the most famous example.

Kaiyū The 'varied pleasures' garden features many small gardens with one or more teahouses surrounding a central pond. Like the stroll garden, it is meant to be explored on foot and provides the visitor with a variety of changing scenes, many with literary allusions. The imperial villa of Katsura Rikyū in Kyoto is the classic example.

Onsen, Beppu

SEAN PAVONE / SHUTTERSTOCK ©

Onsen

Highly volcanic Japan has thousands of onsen (hot springs) scattered across the archipelago, which feed baths across the spectrum from humble to luxurious. The blissful relaxation that follows a good long soak can turn a sceptic into a convert and is likely to make you an onsen fanatic.

Taking the Plunge

Onsen water comes naturally heated from a hot spring, of which there are literally thousands scattered around the country. Some springs have developed into resorts, with strips of hotels and ryokan (traditional inns) housing elaborate bathhouses. Other onsen are hidden in the mountains or along undeveloped coasts; these humble baths may be no more than a pool in a riverbed blocked off with stones or a tidal basin beside crashing waves, in which case bathing is open-air, co-ed and usually free. (Unless stated otherwise, it's OK for a woman to enter rural, unattended baths in a swimsuit or with a 'modesty' towel.)

Shy bathers take heart: many resort inns offer what they call 'family baths' (家族風呂; *kazoku-buro*) or 'private baths' (貸切風呂; *kashikiri-buro*), small baths that can be used privately (solo, as a couple or as a family) for an hour. This may be free of charge or cost a few thousand yen. High-end inns might offer rooms with private hot-spring baths – the ultimate in luxury.

Snow-covered onsen, Takayama (p156)

ANUCHA PONGPATIMETH / SHUTTERSTOCK ©

Sentō, meanwhile, are old-school public bathhouses that date to the era when few Japanese homes had private baths. Most often the water in these baths comes from the tap but some use onsen water. As *sentō* are largely frequented by neighbourhood regulars, they can be a little intimidating – but they can also make for a great local experience. You'll need to bring your own towel and toiletries here, or rent/purchase them from the front desk.

In the lead-up to the 2020 Olympics and with the recent spike in inbound tourist numbers, a growing amount of onsen are upholding their right to refuse entry to people with tattoos of any kind, because of a historical and cultural association of tattoos with *yakuza* (Japanese mafia). There's nothing new about this rule, but in the past, it was seldom enforced, certainly with respect to the occasional lightly inked *gaijin* (foreigner). If an establishment has a policy against tattoos, it will be clearly stated at the entrance. If your tattoo is small enough to cover with a plaster, you may be able to get away with it. Unfortunately, it's a trend that doesn't seem to be going away.

If your body is a canvas, or a work of art, do keep this in mind before you drive all that way to your dream onsen in the Alps.

Onsen Etiquette

Bathing isn't just a pastime, it's a ritual – one so embedded in Japanese culture that everyone knows exactly what to do. This can be intimidating to the novice, but really all you need to know to avoid causing alarm is to wash yourself before getting into the bath. It's also a good idea to memorise the characters for men (男) and women (女), which will be marked on the *noren* (curtains) hanging in front of the respective baths.

Upon entering an onsen or *sentō*, the first thing you'll encounter is a row of lockers for your shoes. After you pay your admission and head to the correct changing room, you'll find either more lockers or baskets for your clothes. Take everything off here and enter the bathing room with only the small towel. That little towel performs a variety of functions: you can use it to wash (but make sure to give it a good rinse afterwards) or to cover yourself as you walk around. It is not supposed to touch the water though, so leave it on the side of the bath or – as the locals do – folded on top of your head.

Park yourself on a stool in front of one of the taps and give yourself a thorough wash. Make sure you rinse off all the suds. When you're done, it's polite to rinse off the stool for the next person. At more humble bathhouses you might have little more than a ladle to work with; in that case, crouch low and use it to scoop out water from the bath and pour over your body – taking care not to splash water into the tub – and scrub a bit with the towel.

In the baths, keep your head above the water and your splashing to a minimum. Whether or not you want to rinse off depends on you and the nature of the waters: some people want to keep the minerals on their skin; others prefer to wash. Before heading back to the changing room, wipe yourself down with the towel to avoid dripping on the floor.

Traditional Japanese ryokan

Ryokan

A hotel is a hotel wherever you go. And while some of Japan's hotels are very nice indeed, staying in traditional-style accommodation offers an added cultural experience. Sleeping on futons (quilt-like mattresses), soaking in an o-furo (Japanese-style bath, often communal) or starting your day with grilled fish and rice are all opportunities to connect a little deeper with Japan.

Choosing a Ryokan

There are a great variety of ryokan. Some are famous for their onsen baths, which may be indoors or outdoors – located along riverbeds or overlooking mountains; others are famous for their food, serving *kaiseki ryōri* (Japanese haute cuisine) that rivals the meals served in the best restaurants. (The priciest will excel in both.) Ryokan can be rambling old wooden buildings that look like they're straight out of a *ukiyo-e* (woodblock print) or they can be modern concrete structures. The latter are more likely to have an elevator, en suite bathrooms and a few rooms with beds (including a wheelchair-accessible room). Older inns may be draughty, with thin walls and shared toilets, but the atmosphere more than makes up for it.

Ryokan exist at all price ranges; note that rates are charged by person rather than by room. For a very nice experience, expect to pay between ¥12,000 and ¥20,000 per person, including meals. If you have food allergies or strong aversions, it's best to inform staff when making a reservation; many inns, especially those used to overseas guests, are accommodating.

The Ryokan Experience

For Japanese guests, a ryokan is a destination in and of itself and as a result most will check in as early as possible (usually 3pm). Most places expect you to check in by 6pm, unless you have arranged otherwise.

Leave your shoes at the entrance and put on the slippers set out for you. After signing in (yes, by hand), you'll be escorted to your room and perhaps given a basic tour of the inn on the way – to show you where the baths and dining rooms are located. Staff will most likely enter the room with you, to show you where the robes and towels are stashed. If you've reserved meals, the staff may then ask what time you would like them. Dinner is typically early, at 6pm or 7pm; breakfast is usually sometime between 7am and 8.30am. You can then make yourself a pot of tea – the supplies should be on the low table, along with some traditional sweets or snacks – and relax.

More on slippers: they shouldn't be worn on tatami mats (so slip them off before walking onto the tatami in your room). Separate slippers will be set out for use just in the toilet. There will also be outdoor slippers (either traditional wooden-soled *geta* or clunky plastic ones) in the entrance of the inn, if you need to pop outside. (Given all this sharing of slippers, most guests prefer to wear socks.) Rest assured, slipper etiquette is probably the most stressful thing you'll encounter.

All lodgings in Japan (save hostels) supply sleepwear and at a traditional accommodation this will be a *yukata* (light, cotton kimono-like robe). Don't be insulted if you're given one marked extra large – they're sized by length not by girth! Put it on over your underwear, left over right; women might want to wear a camisole, as the robes tend to creep open on top. Men typically tie the obi (sash) low on their hips while women tend to secure it snugly at the waist. You can wear the *yukata* anywhere around the inn, to and from the baths and during meals (though of course this is optional). At some onsen resort towns, guests wear them around town as well, while going from bathhouse to bathhouse.

Ryokan staff (often clad in kimonos) tend to be very doting. During meals they'll serve you course by course – and at some fancier inns meals can be taken in your room; during or after dinner, they'll come to lay out the bedding for you. After checkout, you'll be seen off with deep bows.

MADSOLAR / SHUTTERSTOCK ©

Survival Guide

Directory A–Z

Accessible Travel

Japan gets mixed marks in terms of ease of travel for those with disabilities. On the plus side, many buildings have access ramps, major train stations have lifts, traffic lights have speakers playing melodies when it is safe to cross, and train platforms have raised dots and lines to provide guidance for the visually impaired. You'll find most service staff will go out of their way to be helpful, even if they don't speak much English.

On the negative side, many of Japan's cities are still rather difficult to negotiate, with many narrow streets lacking pavements.

Major sights take great pains to be wheelchair

friendly and many have wheelchairs you can borrow for free. Note, however, that 'accessible' at traditional sights (such as castles and temples) might still mean steep slopes or long gravel paths. Often the accessible routes aren't obvious; telling staff (such as those at the ticket counter) that someone in your party is travelling in a wheelchair (車椅子; *kuruma-isu*) may, literally, open doors.

Train cars on most lines have areas set aside for people in wheelchairs. Those with other physical disabilities can use the priority seats near the train doors.

A fair number of hotels, from the higher end of midrange and above, offer a 'barrier-free' (バリアフリー; *bariafurii*) room or two (book well in advance). Larger attractions and train stations, department stores and shopping malls should have wheelchair-accessible bathrooms (which will have Western-style toilets).

Japan Accessible Tourism Center (www.japan-accessible.com) is a good resource. Download Lonely Planet's free Accessible Travel guide from http://lp travel.to/AccessibleTravel.

Book Your Stay Online

For more accommodation reviews by Lonely Planet authors, check out http://hotels.lonelyplanet. com/japan. You'll find independent reviews, as well as recommendations on the best places to stay. Best of all, you can book online.

Accommodation

Japan offers a wide range of accommodation. Western-style hotels can be found in most cities and resort areas. Even budget hotels

are generally clean and well serviced (though older ones might have smoky rooms). In the top-end bracket, you can expect to find the amenities of deluxe hotels anywhere in the world. For more information on staying in a ryokan (traditional inn), see p299.

Advance booking is highly recommended, especially in major tourist destinations.

Business Hotels

Functional and economical, 'business hotels' (ビジネスホテル; *bijinesu hoteru*) are geared to the lone traveller on business, but they're great for any kind of traveller – so long as you don't need a lot of space. The compact rooms usually have semidouble beds (140cm across; roomy for one, a bit of a squeeze for two) and tiny en suite bathrooms. Business hotels are famous for being deeply unfashionable, though many chains have updated their rooms in recent years. Expect to pay from ¥8000/12,000 for single/double occupancy (more in big cities like Tokyo).

Business hotels are usually clustered around train stations. Some reliable chains with huge networks include Toyoko Inn (www.toyoko-inn.com/eng) and Dormy Inn (www.hotespa.net/dormyinn/en).

Capsule Hotels

Capsule hotels (カプセルホテル; *kapuseru hoteru*) offer rooms the size of a single bed, with just enough headroom for you to sit up. Think of it like a bunk bed that has more privacy (and a reading light, TV and alarm clock). Prices range from ¥3500 to ¥5000, which usually includes access to a large shared bath and sauna. Personal belongings are kept in a locker room. Most capsule hotels only accept cash and do not permit guests who have visible tattoos.

Capsule hotels are commonly found in major cities and often cater to workers who have partied too hard

to make it back home or have missed the last train for the night. Most are men only, though some have floors for women, too.

Hostels

Japan has an extensive network of hostels. These include official Japan Youth Hostel (JYH; www.jyh.or.jp/e/index.php) properties as well as a growing number of independent, sometimes quite stylish, hostels. Among the more popular are the K's House (www.kshouse.jp/index_e.html) and J-Hoppers (www.j-hoppers.com) groups. Many

hostels are staffed by young travellers who often speak good English. Some, but not all, have kitchen facilities for guests.

Prices average around ¥3000 for a dorm bed. There will usually be some private and family rooms, too, costing about ¥1000 extra per person. Bedding is provided; towels can be hired for about ¥100. Basic toiletries (soap and shampoo) may or may not be supplied.

Customs Regulations

○ Japan has typical customs allowances for duty-free items; see Visit Japan Customs (www.customs.go.jp) online for more information.

○ Stimulant drugs, which include the ADHD medication Adderall, are strictly prohibited in Japan. To bring in certain narcotics (such as codeine), you need to prepare a *yakkan shōmei* – an import certificate for pharmaceuticals. See the Ministry of Health, Labour & Welfare's website (www.mhlw.go.jp/english/policy/health-medical/pharmaceuticals/01.html) for more details about which medications are classified and how to prepare the pharmaceuticals form.

Climate

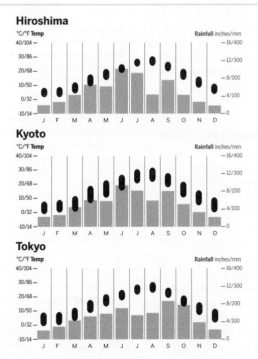

Hiroshima
°C/°F Temp   Rainfall inches/mm

Kyoto
°C/°F Temp   Rainfall inches/mm

Tokyo
°C/°F Temp   Rainfall inches/mm

Electricity

Tokyo and eastern Japan are on 50Hz, and western Japan, including Nagoya, Kyoto and Osaka, is on 60Hz.

Type A
120V/60Hz

Food

See the Food & Drink chapter (p286) for more information.

The following price ranges refer to a standard main meal:

¥ less than ¥1000 (less than ¥2000 in Tokyo and Kyoto)

¥¥ ¥1000– ¥4000 (¥2000– ¥5000 in Tokyo and Kyoto)

¥¥¥ more than ¥4000 (more than ¥5000 in Tokyo and Kyoto)

Health

Japan enjoys a high level of medical services, though unfortunately most hospitals do not have doctors and nurses who speak English. University hospitals should be your first choice; doctors are more likely to speak English and the level of care is usually highest. Larger cities, especially Tokyo, have clinics that specialise in caring for the foreign community; these will have doctors who speak English but they will be pricey. Most hospitals and clinics will accept walk-in patients in the mornings (usually 8.30am to 11am); be prepared to wait. Expect to pay about ¥3000 for a simple visit to an outpatient clinic and from around ¥20,000 and upwards for emergency care.

No vaccines are required for travel to Japan.

Medical Checklist

● Pharmacies in Japan do not carry foreign medications, so it's a good idea to bring your own. In a pinch, reasonable substitutes can be found, but the dosage may be lower than what you're used to.

● Though no prescription is necessary, thrush pessaries are only stocked behind the counter (you'll have to ask) and many pharmacies don't carry them.

Insurance

A travel-insurance policy to cover theft, loss and medical problems is essential. Worldwide travel insurance is available at www.lonelyplanet .com/travel-insurance. You can buy, extend and claim online anytime – even if you're already on the road.

Note that the only insurance accepted at Japanese hospitals is Japanese insurance. For any medical treatment you'll have to pay up front and get a reimbursement when you get home.

Internet Access

Many cities in Japan (including Tokyo, Osaka and Kyoto) have free wi-fi networks for travellers, though the system is still clunky in areas. To avoid frustration, heavy users might consider hiring a pocket internet device.

Most accommodation now has wi-fi. Hostels and business chain hotels are the most reliable for this; other places might only have a solid connection in the lobby.

Legal Matters

Japanese police have extraordinary powers. They can detain a suspect for up to three days without charging them; after this time a prosecutor can decide to extend this period for another 20 days. Police can also choose whether to allow a suspect to phone their embassy or lawyer, though if you find yourself in police custody you should insist that you will not cooperate in any way until allowed to make such a call. Your embassy is the first place you should call if given the chance.

Police will speak almost no English; insist that a *tsūyakusha* (interpreter) be summoned (police are legally bound to provide one before proceeding with any questioning). Even if you do speak Japanese, it's best to deny it and stay with your native language.

Note that it is a legal requirement to have your passport on you at all times. Though checks are not common, if you are stopped by police and caught without it, you could be hauled off to a police station to wait until someone fetches it for you.

Japan takes a hard-line approach to narcotics possession, with long sentences and fines even for first-time offenders.

LGBT+ Travellers

Gay and lesbian travellers are unlikely to encounter problems in Japan. There are no legal restraints on same-sex sexual activities in Japan apart from the usual age restrictions.

Some travellers have reported being turned away or grossly overcharged when checking into love hotels with a partner of the same sex. Otherwise discrimination is unusual (though you'll likely be given a hotel room with twin beds). One note: Japanese people, regardless of their sexual orientation, do not typically engage in public displays of affection.

Tokyo has the largest and most-welcoming gay scene, followed by Osaka. Utopia Asia (www.utopia-asia.com) has good recommendations for Japan.

Maps

Kodansha's *Japan Atlas: A Bilingual Guide* has maps labelled in English and kanji, though the road maps are not terribly detailed.

Media

Newspapers are sold at convenience stores, train-station kiosks and some hotels in major cities. Look for free mags at airports and hotels, and bars and restaurants popular with expats; many cities have expat-run online magazines, too.

Japan Times (www.japantimes.co.jp) Long-running English-language daily.

Time Out Tokyo (www.timeout.com/tokyo) Quarterly magazine on pop culture and events; look for its excellent mini city guides at tourist information centres around Japan.

Kansai Scene (www.kansaiscene.com) Free paper for Kansai's expat community.

Kyoto Journal (www.kyotojournal.org) In-depth articles on arts and culture from Japan and Asia.

Money

ATMs

Most Japanese bank ATMs do not accept foreign-issued cards. Seven Bank ATMs at 7-Eleven convenience stores (open 24 hours) and Japan Post Bank ATMs at post offices accept most overseas cards and have instructions in English. Most towns have one. Note that many banks place a limit on the amount of cash you can withdraw in one day (often around US$300).

Cash

Many places in Japan – particularly outside the cities – don't accept credit cards. Ryokan and smaller restaurants and shops are common cash-only places, so it's wise to keep cash on hand.

Credit Cards

Businesses that do take credit cards will often display the logo for the cards they accept. Visa is the most widely accepted, followed by MasterCard, American Express and Diners Club. Foreign-issued cards should work fine.

Exchanging Money

With a passport, you can change cash or travellers cheques at any Authorised Foreign Exchange Bank (signs are displayed in English), major post offices, some large hotels and most big department stores.

For currency other than US dollars, larger banks, such as Sumitomo Mitsui (SMBC), are a better bet. They can usually change at least US, Canadian and Australian dollars, pounds sterling, euros and Swiss francs.

MUFG Bank operates World Currency Shop (www. tokyo-card.co.jp/wcs/wcs-shop-e.php) foreign-exchange counters near major shopping centres in Tokyo, Kyoto and Osaka that exchange a broader range of currencies.

Note that you receive a better exchange rate when withdrawing cash from ATMs than when exchanging cash or travellers cheques in Japan.

Opening Hours

Some outdoor attractions (such as gardens) may close earlier in the winter. Standard opening hours:

Banks 9am to 3pm (some to 5pm) Monday to Friday

Bars From around 6pm to late

Department stores 10am to 8pm

Museums 9am to 5pm, last entry by 4.30pm; often closed Monday (if Monday is a national holiday then the museum will close on Tuesday instead)

Post offices 9am to 5pm Monday to Friday; larger ones have longer hours and open Saturday

Restaurants Lunch 11.30am to 2pm; dinner 6pm to 10pm; last orders taken about half an hour before closing.

Public Holidays

When a public holiday falls on a Sunday, the following Monday is taken as a holiday. If that Monday is already a holiday, the following day becomes a holiday as well.

Ganjitsu (New Year's Day) 1 January

Seijin-no-hi (Coming-of-Age Day) Second Monday in January

Kenkoku Kinem-bi (National Foundation Day) 11 February

Tennōno Tanjōbi (Emperor's Birthday) 23 February

Shumbun-no-hi (spring equinox) 20 or 21 March

Shōwa-no-hi (Shōwa Emperor's Day) 29 April

Kempō Kinem-bi (Constitution Day) 3 May

Midori-no-hi (Green Day) 4 May

Kodomo-no-hi (Children's Day) 5 May

Umi-no-hi (Marine Day) Third Monday in July

Yama-no-hi (Mountain Day) 11 August

Keirō-no-hi (Respect-for-the-Aged Day) Third Monday in September

Shūbun-no-hi (autumn equinox) 22 or 23 September

Taiiku-no-hi (Health-Sports Day) Second Monday in October

Bunka-no-hi (Culture Day) 3 November

Kinrō Kansha-no-hi (Labour Thanksgiving Day) 23 November

Practicalities

Smoking Japan has a curious policy: in many cities (including Tokyo, Osaka and Kyoto) smoking is banned in public spaces but allowed inside bars and restaurants. Designated smoking areas are set up around train stations. The number of smokers is declining every year; in Tokyo especially, an increasing number of restaurants and bars are banning smoking.

Weights & Measures Japan uses the metric system.

You will find intercity transport crowded and accommodation bookings hard to come by during the following high-season travel periods. Note that many shops and restaurants close for Shōgatsu and O-Bon.

Shōgatsu (New Year) 1 to 3 January

Golden Week 29 April to 5 May

O-Bon mid-August

Safe Travel

Japan is prone to natural disasters: earthquakes, tsunamis, volcanic eruptions, typhoons and landslides. Sophisticated early-warning systems and strict building codes do much to mitigate impact (but they are not foolproof, of course). Smartphone app Safety Tips sends notifications regarding weather alerts, tsunami warnings and impending seismic activity and also lists key phrases to help you get information in the event of an emergency.

Otherwise, the biggest threat to travellers is Japan's general aura of safety. Don't get too complacent: keep up the same level of caution and common sense that you would at home.

Taxes & Refunds

Japan's consumption tax is 8% (with an increase to 10% planned for October 2019). A growing number of shops offer tax-free shopping (noted by a sticker in English on the window) if you spend more than ¥5000. Passport required.

Since the tax is not charged at point of sale, there is no need to collect a refund when leaving the country; however, you should hand in a form affixed to your passport to customs officials when you depart. For details see www.enjoy.taxfree.jp.

Telephone

When dialling Japan from abroad, dial the country code (☎81), followed by the area code (drop the '0') and the number.

Mobile Phones

Japan operates on the 3G network, so overseas phones with 3G technology should work.

Prepaid SIM cards that allow you to make voice calls are not available in Japan. Data-only SIM cards for unlocked smartphones are available at kiosks at Narita, Haneda and Kansai airports and at large electronics stores (such as Bic Camera, Yodobashi Camera etc) in major cities. You'll need to download and install an APN profile; ask staff to help you if you are unsure how to do this (they usually speak some English).

Japan Helpline

English-speaking operators at Japan Helpline (☎0570-000-911) are available 24 hours a day to help you negotiate tricky situations. If you don't have access to mobile service, use the contact form on the website (www.jhelp.com/english/index.html).

There is a wide range of options, depending on your data and speed requirements (many cards will continue to work after the data usage has been exceeded but the speed will be very slow). B-Mobile's Visitor SIM (www.bmobile.ne.jp/english/index.html), which offers 14 days of unlimited data (the speed will be reduced for heavy users) for ¥2380, is a good choice.

Phonecards

Prepaid international phonecards can be used with any push-button phones, including regular pay phones. Look for the KDDI Superworld Card or the SoftBank Telecom Comica Card at convenience stores.

Time

All of Japan is in the same time zone: nine hours ahead of Greenwich Mean Time

(GMT). Sydney and Wellington are ahead of Japan (by one and three hours, respectively), and most of the world's other big cities are behind: New York by 14 hours, Los Angeles by 17 and London by nine. Japan does not have daylight saving time.

Toilets

○ You will come across both Western-style toilets and traditional squat toilets in Japan. When you are compelled to squat, the correct position is facing the hood, away from the door.

○ Public toilets are free. The *katakana* for 'toilet' is トイレ, and the kanji is お手洗い. Also good to know: the kanji for female (女) and male (男).

○ Toilet paper is usually provided, but it is still a good idea to carry tissues with you.

Tourist Information

Tourist information offices (観光案内所; *kankō annai-sho;*) can be found inside or in front of major train stations. Staff may not speak much English; however, there are usually English-language materials and staff are accustomed to the usual concerns of travellers (food, lodging and transport schedules). Many have free wi-fi.

Japan National Tourism Organization (JNTO; www.jnto.go.jp) is Japan's government tourist bureau. It produces a great deal of useful literature in English, which is available from its overseas offices as well as its **TIC** (☎03-3201-3331; www.jnto.go.jp; 1st fl, Shin-Tokyo Bldg, 3-3-1 Marunouchi, Chiyoda-ku; ⏰9am-5pm; ⊗; ⑤Chiyoda line to Nijūbashimae, exit 1) in Tokyo.

JNTO has overseas offices in Australia, Canada, France, Germany, the UK and the USA. See the website, which is also a useful planning tool, for more information.

Visas

Citizens of 67 territories, including Australia, Canada, Hong Kong, Korea, New Zealand, Singapore, the UK, the USA, and almost all European nations will be automatically issued a *tanki-taizai* (temporary-visitor visa) on arrival. Typically this visa is good for 90 days. For a complete list of visa-exempt territories, consult www.mofa.go.jp/j_info/visit/visa/short/novisa.html#list.

Japanese law requires that visitors entering on a temporary-visitor visa possess an ongoing air or sea ticket or evidence thereof. In practice, few travellers are asked to produce such documents, but it pays to be on the safe side.

For additional information on visas and regulations, contact your nearest Japanese embassy or consulate, or visit the website of the Ministry of Foreign Affairs of Japan (www.mofa.go.jp).

On entering Japan, all short-term foreign visitors are photographed and fingerprinted.

Women Travellers

Japan is a relatively safe country for women travellers, though perhaps not quite as safe as some might think. Crimes against women are generally believed to be widely under-reported, especially by Japanese women. Foreign women are occasionally subjected to some forms of verbal harassment or prying questions. Physical attacks are very rare, but have occurred.

The best advice is to avoid being lulled into a false sense of security by Japan's image as one of the world's safest countries and to continue to take the normal precautions that you would in your home country.

Transport

Getting There & Away

Air

Japan's major international airports include the following:

Narita International Airport (www.narita-airport.jp) About 75 minutes east of Tokyo by express train, Narita gets the bulk of international flights to Japan; most budget carriers flying to Tokyo arrive here.

Haneda Airport (www.tokyo-airport-bldg.co.jp) Tokyo's more convenient airport – about 30 minutes by train or monorail to the city centre – Haneda, also known as Tokyo International Airport, is getting an increasing number of international arrivals; domestic flights to/from Tokyo usually arrive/depart here.

Kansai International Airport (www.kansai-airport.or.jp) Serves the key Kansai cities of Kyoto, Osaka, Nara and Kōbe. Not as many direct international services as the Tokyo airports, but useful if you want to zero in on the Kansai area (or fly in from one and out of the other).

There are also many regional airports with short international flights to Asian countries, such as China, Korea, Hong Kong and Taiwan.

Getting Around

Air

Air services in Japan are extensive, reliable and safe. Flying is often faster and cheaper than *shinkansen* (bullet trains) and good for covering long distances or hopping islands. **All Nippon Airways** (ANA; ☏0570-029-709, in Osaka 06-7637-6679, in Tokyo 03-6741-1120; www.ana.co.jp) and **Japan Airlines** (JAL; ☏0570-025-121, 03-6733-3062; www.jal.co.jp/en) have the largest networks. All local carriers have websites in English to check prices and book tickets.

Tickets & Discounts

● Both ANA and JAL offer discounts of up to 50% if you purchase your ticket a month or more in advance, with smaller discounts for purchases made one to three weeks in advance.

● Foreign travellers can purchase **ANA Experience Japan Fare** one-way domestic tickets for the flat rate of ¥10,800. For details, see www.ana.co.jp/wws/th/e/wws_common/promotions/share/experience_jp.

● JAL's **Visit Japan Fare** offers a similar ¥10,800 flat-rate ticket for domestic routes to foreign travellers flying inbound on any Oneworld carriers. For details, see www.jal.co.jp/yokosojapan.

● JAL's **Okinawa Island Pass** (www.churashima.net/jta/company/island pass_en.html) is good for affordable island hopping; it's only available for foreign visitors and must be purchased abroad.

Budget Airlines

The recent proliferation of affordable airlines has brought previously

---

Climate Change & Travel

Every form of transport that relies on carbon-based fuel generates CO_2, the main cause of human-induced climate change. Modern travel is dependent on aeroplanes, which might use less fuel per kilometre per person than most cars but travel much greater distances. The altitude at which aircraft emit gases (including CO_2) and particles also contributes to their climate change impact. Many websites offer 'carbon calculators' that allow people to estimate the carbon emissions generated by their journey and, for those who wish to do so, to offset the impact of the greenhouse gases emitted with contributions to portfolios of climate-friendly initiatives throughout the world. Lonely Planet offsets the carbon footprint of all staff and author travel.

expensive and distant destinations like Hokkaidō and Okinawa within reach of budget travellers.

Air Do (www.airdo.jp) Connects Hokkaidō's New Chitose Airport with major destinations around Japan.

Jetstar (www.jetstar.com) Cheap flights from Tokyo's Narita Airport and Osaka's Kansai International Airport to Okinawa (Naha) and Sapporo (New Chitose).

Peach (www.flypeach.com) Good for flights out of Kansai.

Vanilla Air (www.vanilla-air. com) Cheap flights from Tokyo (Narita) to Okinawa (Naha) and Sapporo (New Chitose).

Bicycle

Japan is a good country for bicycle touring, and several thousand cyclists, both Japanese and foreign, traverse the country every year. Hokkaidō is a favourite cycling destination. Both KANcycling (www. kancycling.com) and Japan Cycling Navigator (www. japancycling.org) have tutorials on cycling Japan and trip reports.

Bus

Japan has a comprehensive network of long-distance buses. They're nowhere near as fast as the *shinkansen*, but a lot cheaper. Buses also travel routes that trains don't.

Japan Railways (JR) operates the largest network of highway buses in Japan; it tends to be a little pricier than other operators, but it's reliable. Buses tend to depart and arrive at train stations rather than bus stops elsewhere in the city. You can purchase these tickets from JR train stations.

Cheaper operators with large networks include **Willer Express** (☎050-5805-0383; www.willerexpress.com), which offers three-/four-/five-day bus passes. You can book seats on Willer and other buses through the company's Japan Bus Lines

service (http://japanbus lines.com).

Night buses are a good option for those on a tight budget without a Japan Rail Pass. They are relatively cheap and spacious – depending on how much you're willing to pay – and they also save on a night's accommodation. They typically leave at around 10pm or 11pm and arrive the following day at around 6am or 7am.

There are some truly bargain bus deals out there, but note that, while the government has been cracking down, cheaper operators have been known to skirt safety regulations (by overworking their drivers).

Car & Motorcycle

Driving in Japan is quite feasible, even for the mildly adventurous. Most roads are signposted in English; roads are in excellent condition; road rules are generally adhered to; and petrol, while

---

Baggage Forwarding

Baggage-courier services (called *takkyūbin*) are popular in Japan and many domestic tourists use them to forward their bags, golf clubs, surfboards etc ahead to their destination, to avoid having to bring them on public transport. The tourism bureau has been working to open this service up to foreign travellers; see its guide, Hands-Free Travel Japan (www.jnto.go.jp/hands-free-travel), for a list of luggage-forwarding counters, mostly at airports, train stations and shopping centres, set up for travellers.

This is a great service except for one caveat: in most cases, your bags won't get there until the following day. (So, for example, if you want to ship your luggage to or from the airport, you'll need a day pack with one night's worth of supplies.) On the other hand, this can free you from large luggage for a one-night detour to an onsen – just send your bags to the following night's destination.

Hotels can also often arrange this service for you (and the couriers will pick up the luggage from the lobby). Costs vary depending on the size and weight of the bag and where it's going, but is typically around ¥2000.

expensive, is not prohibitively so.

In some parts of Japan (most notably Hokkaidō and Okinawa), driving is really the only efficient way to get around. On the other hand, it makes little sense to have a car in the big cities, like Tokyo and Osaka, where traffic is thick, a preponderance of one-way streets makes navigation a challenge, and parking is expensive.

○ If you're a member of an automobile association in your home country, you're eligible for reciprocal rights with the **Japan Automobile Federation** (JAF; 📞emergency roadside help 0570-00-8139; www.jaf.or.jp), which has an office in Tokyo.

○ Driving is on the left. There are no unusual rules or interpretations of them and most signposts follow international conventions. JAF publishes a *Rules of the Road* guide (digital/print ¥864/1404) in English, which is handy.

Driving Licences

Travellers from most nations are able to drive (both cars and motorcycles) in Japan with an International Driving Permit (IDP) backed up by their own regular licence. The IDP is issued by your national automobile association.

Travellers from Switzerland, France and Germany (and others whose countries are not signatories to the Geneva Convention of 1949 concerning international driving licences) are not allowed to drive in Japan on a regular IDP. Rather, travellers from these countries must have their own licence backed by an authorised translation of the same licence. These translations can be made by their embassy or consulate in Japan or by the JAF.

Car Hire

○ Typical rates for a small car are ¥5000 to ¥7000 per day, with reductions for rentals of more than one day. On top of the rental charge, there's about a ¥1000-per-day insurance cost. Prices among major agencies are comparable.

○ Car-hire agencies are clustered around transit hubs: airports, major train stations and ferry piers. Those at the major international airports are most likely to have English-speaking staff.

○ Toyota Rent-a-Car (https://rent.toyota.co.jp) and Nippon Rent-a-Car (www.nrgroup-global.com) have large rental networks and booking in English is possible online.

○ Japanese law requires children under the age of six to ride in a car seat; rental car agencies provide them for a small extra fee.

ETC Cards

With an ETC card (www.go-etc.jp/english/guidebook/index.html) you can pass through the automated toll booths at 20km/h without stopping. The cards also save money: tolls for ETC users can be up to 30% less than standard tolls (depending on the time of day and distance travelled).

Rental cars have ETC card readers and major agencies will rent the cards for a small fee; you'll be presented with a bill for your tolls when you return the car. If you choose not to use an ETC card, or need assistance, staffed toll booths will be marked in green with the characters 一般 (*ippan*; ordinary).

Navigations Systems

Rental cars come equipped with satellite navigation systems that are generally very reliable; major agencies offer ones that have an English function. As Japanese addresses can be confusing, the best way to set your destination is by inputting the phone number. Many tourist organisations now also provide pamphlets with 'map codes' for major destinations, which you can key into car navigation systems.

Local Transport

Japan's larger cities are serviced by subways or trams, buses and taxis; indeed, many locals rely entirely on public transport. Note that all public transport except for taxis shuts down between midnight and 5am.

IC Cards

IC cards are prepaid travel cards with chips that work on subways, trams and buses in the Tokyo, Kansai, Sapporo and Hiroshima metro areas. They save you the trouble of having to purchase paper tickets and work out the correct fare for your journey. Each region has its own card, but they can be used interchangeably in any region where IC cards are used; however, they cannot be used for intercity travel.

The two most frequently used IC cards are **Suica** (www.jreast.co.jp/e/pass/suica.html) from JR East and **Icoca** (www.westjr.co.jp/global/en/ticket/icoca-haruka) from JR West; purchase them at JR travel counters at Narita and Haneda or Kansai airports, respectively. Cards can also be purchased and topped up from ticket-vending machines in any of the cities that support them. Both require a ¥500 deposit, which you get back when you return your card to any JR ticket window.

To use the card, simply swipe it over the reader at the ticket gates or near the doors on trams and buses.

Bus

The city where you will find yourself relying on public buses the most is Kyoto. Though the city has a subway train system, it is not convenient to reach all of the major Kyoto tourist sites.

Subway & Tram

Kyoto, Osaka, Tokyo and Sapporo have subway systems, which are usually the fastest and most-convenient way to get around the city. Stops and line names are posted in English. Kagoshima and Hiroshima have trams.

Fares are typically ¥150 to ¥250, depending on how far your ride (half-price for children). If you plan to zip around a city in a day, an unlimited-travel day ticket (called *ichi-nichi-jōsha-ken*) is a good deal; most cities offer them and they can be purchased at station windows.

Taxi

o Taxis are ubiquitous in big cities. They can be found in smaller cities and even on tiny islands, too, though usually just at transport hubs (train and bus stations and ferry ports) – otherwise you'll need to get someone to call one for you.

o Transit stations and hotels have taxi stands where you are expected to queue. In the absence of a stand, hail a cab from the street by standing on the curb and sticking your arm out.

o Fares are fairly uniform throughout the country and all cabs run by the meter.

o Flagfall (posted on the taxi windows) is around ¥600 to ¥710 for the first 2km, after which it's around ¥100 for each 350m (approximately). There's also a time charge if the speed drops below 10km/h and a 20% surcharge between 10pm and 5am.

o A red light means the taxi is free and a green light means it's taken.

o The driver opens and closes the doors remotely – full service indeed!

o Drivers rarely speak English, though fortunately most taxis now have navigation systems. It's a good idea to have your destination written down in Japanese, or better yet, a business card with an address.

Train

Japanese rail services are fast, frequent, clean and comfortable. The predominant operator is Japan Railways, commonly known as 'JR', which runs the *shinkansen* (bullet-train) routes. There is also a huge network of private railways.

o Most long-haul routes run local (called *futsū* or *kaku-eki-teisha*), express (called *kyūkō* or *kaisoku*) and limited-express trains (called *tokkyū*). Limited-express trains have reserved seats, with comfortable reclining chairs as well as toilets. All trains, save for a few *shinkansen* cars, are nonsmoking. Many different trains run on the same platforms, so be mindful of the signboards that note the schedule of departures.

○ Many long-haul trains have 'green car' carriages, which are akin to business class. Seats are a little more spacious and the carriages tend to be quieter and less crowded; they're also usually the last to sell out.

○ Tickets can be purchased from touch-screen vending machines in major train stations; most have an English function and those for *shinkansen* journeys accept credit cards.

○ If you are booking a series of journeys, have questions or just want the reassurance of buying a ticket from a person, major JR stations have what are called *midori-no-madoguchi,* which function as JR's inhouse travel agency; these days most staff speak enough English to answer basic questions. Private-line trains will have their own ticket windows.

○ Reservations can only be made for *tokkyū* liners and *shinkansen* services.

There are also unreserved *shinkansen* seats; the policy on limited-express trains varies by route and operator (some are all-reserved; others are not). Reserved-seat tickets can be bought any time from a month in advance to the day of departure.

○ It is generally not necessary to make reservations in advance except on weekends and national holidays and during peak travel seasons – such as Golden Week (late April to early May), Obon (mid-August) and the New Year period.

○ The website HyperDia (www.hyperdia.com) is useful for searching routes and travel times/costs in English.

Travel Passes

Rail passes, which range from the classic, countrywide Japan Rail Pass to a growing number of passes that zero in on specific regions, are excellent value. These passes are only available to foreign passport holders entering Japan on a tourist visa (station staff will check). Children between the ages of six and 11 qualify for child fares, while those under six ride for free.

Note that JR passes are valid only on JR services; you will still have to pay for private-train services. However, as the JR network is the country's largest, the coverage is good. The value is in getting to ride *shinkansen* and *tokkyū* trains, though of course you can use the passes on ordinary express and local trains, too.

New passes are being created all the time (and unpopular ones retired), so check websites for the latest information.

Japan Rail Pass

The Japan Rail Pass (www.japanrailpass.net) is perfect for first-time visitors who want to zip around to see the highlights. It covers travel on all *shinkansen* lines, though on some routes you may not be allowed to ride the very fastest trains (such as Nozomi and Mizuho). A 'green' pass is good for rides in 1st-class 'green' train cars.

A one-way reserved-seat Tokyo–Kyoto *shinkansen* ticket costs ¥13,910, so you only need make one round trip between Tokyo and Kyoto on the *shinkansen* to almost make a seven-day pass pay off. (Add a round trip between Narita Airport

Japan Rail Pass Costs

Duration	Regular (adult/child)	Green (adult/child)
7 days	¥29,110/14,550	¥38,880/19,440
14 days	¥46,390/23,190	¥62,950/31,470
21 days	¥59,350/29,670	¥81,870/40,930

and Tokyo and you're already saving money.)

The Japan Rail Pass must be purchased outside Japan. In order to get a pass, you must first purchase an 'exchange order' outside Japan at a JAL or ANA office or a major travel agency. Once you arrive in Japan, you must bring this order to a JR Travel Service Centre (in most major JR stations and at Narita, Haneda and Kansai international airports). When you validate your pass, you'll have to show your passport in addition to the exchange order.

When validating, you select the date on which you want the pass to become valid (starting immediately or on a later date). So, if you just plan to spend a few days in Kyoto or Tokyo before setting out to explore the country by rail, set the validity date to the day you start your journey outside the city.

Once you've validated your pass, you can make seat reservations from any *midori-no-madoguchi* ('green window' ticket counters) at JR train stations. You can also just show your pass at the ticket gates and hop on any unreserved train car (though you'd be wise to book ahead during peak travel times).

JR West Passes

JR West (www.westjr.co.jp) offers several regional rail passes useful for travellers who are giving Tokyo a miss. In addition to the routes outlined following, all Kansai area passes cover transport on JR lines to/from Kansai International Airport to Kyoto and Osaka.

Kansai Area Pass (one-/two-/three-/four-day pass ¥2200/4300/5300/6300, children half-price) Unlimited travel on all JR lines – except *shinkansen* lines – between major Kansai cities, including Himeji, Osaka, Kyoto and Nara. Perfect for exploring the Kansai region in depth.

Kansai Wide Area Pass (adult/child ¥8500/4250) Valid for five consecutive days; covers the same destinations as the Kansai Area Pass plus travel on the San-yō Shinkansen between Osaka and Okayama. Good for visiting Kansai with detours to Himeji and Naoshima (accessed from Okayama).

Kansai–Hiroshima Area Pass (adult/child ¥13,000/6500) Valid for five consecutive days. Good for everything covered in the Kansai Wide Area Pass, plus Hiroshima.

Kansai Thru Pass

The Kansai Thru Pass (two-/three-day pass ¥4000/5200; www.surutto. com) is a real bonus to travellers who plan to explore the Kansai area. It's good for travel on city subways, private railways and city buses in Kyoto, Nara, Osaka, Kōbe and Kōya-san, plus discounts at many attractions. It is available at the Kansai International Airport travel counter on the 1st floor of the arrivals hall and at the main bus information centre in front of Kyoto Station, among others.

Language

Japanese pronunciation is not difficult as most of its sounds are also found in English. You can read our pronunciation guides as if they were English and you'll be understood just fine. Just remember to pronounce every vowel individually, make those with a macron (ie a line above them) longer than those without, and pause slightly between double consonants.

To enhance your trip with a phrasebook, visit **lonelyplanet.com**. Lonely Planet iPhone phrasebooks are available through the Apple App store.

Basics

Hello.
こんにちは。 konnichiwa
How are you?
お元気ですか? o-genki des ka
I'm fine, thanks.
はい、元気です。 hai, genki des
Excuse me.
すみません。 sumimasen
Yes./No.
はい。/いいえ。 hai/ iie
Please. (when asking/offering)
ください。/どうぞ。 kudasai/dōzo
Thank you.
どうもありがとう。 dōmo arigatō
You're welcome.
どういたしまして。 dō itashimashite
Do you speak English?
英語が話せますか? eigo ga hanasemas ka
I don't understand.
わかりません。 wakarimasen
How much is this?
いくらですか? ikura des ka
Goodbye.
さようなら。 sayōnara

Accommodation

I'd like to make a booking.
部屋の予約を heya no yoyaku o
お願いします。 onegai shimas

How much is it per night?
1泊いくらですか? ippaku ikura des ka

Eating & Drinking

I'd like ..., please.
…をください。 ... o kudasai
What do you recommend?
おすすめは何 o-susume wa nan
ですか? des ka
That was delicious.
おいしかった。 oyshikatta
Bring the bill/check, please.
お勘定をお願い o-kanjō o onegai
します。 shimas

I don't eat ...
…は食べません。 ... wa tabemasen
  chicken 鶏肉 tori-niku
  fish 魚 sakana
  meat 肉 niku
  pork 豚肉 buta-niku

Emergencies

I'm ill.
気分が悪いです。 kibun ga warui des
Help!
たすけて! taskete
Call a doctor!
医者を呼んで! isha o yonde
Call the police!
警察を呼んで! keisatsu o yonde

Directions

I'm looking for (a/the) ...
…を探しています。 ... o sagashite imas
  bank
  銀行 ginkō
  ... embassy
  大使館 taishikan
  market
  市場 ichiba
  museum
  美術館 bijutsukan
  restaurant
  レストラン restoran
  toilet
  お手洗い/トイレ o-tearai/toire
  tourist office
  観光案内所 kankō annaijo

Behind the Scenes

Acknowledgements

Climate map data adapted from Peel MC, Finlayson BL & McMahon TA (2007) 'Updated World Map of the Köppen-Geiger Climate Classification', *Hydrology and Earth System Sciences*, 11, 1633–44.

Cover photograph: Mt Fuji above the clouds, iamlukyeee/Shutterstock©.

Illustrations pp44–5 and pp138–9 by Michael Weldon.

This Book

This 2nd edition of Lonely Planet's *Best of Japan* guidebook was researched and written by Benedict Walker, Ray Bartlett, Andrew Bender, Stephanie d'Arc Taylor, Craig McLachlan, Rebecca Milner, Kate Morgan, Thomas O'Malley, Simon Richmond and Phillip Tang. This guidebook was produced by the following:

Destination Editors James Smart, Laura Crawford

Senior Product Editor Kate Chapman

Product Editor Alison Ridgway

Regional Senior Cartographer Diana Von Holdt

Book Designer Wibowo Rusli

Assisting Editors Sarah Bailey, Andrew Bain, James Bainbridge, Judith Bamber, Samantha Cook, Lucy Cowie, Emma Gibbs, Carly Hall, Kate James, Kate Kiely, Jodie Martire, Lauren O'Connell, Gabbi Stefanos

Cover Researcher Brendan Dempsey-Spencer

Thanks to Naoko Akamatsu, Liese Bols, Jennifer Carey, Gwen Cotter, Liz Heynes, Campbell McKenzie, Virginia Moreno, Wayne Murphy, Kristin Odijk, Kirsten Rawlings, Clara Rocha, Brad Smith, Simon Williamson

Send Us Your Feedback

We love to hear from travellers – your comments keep us on our toes and help make our books better. Our well-travelled team reads every word on what you loved or loathed about this book. Although we cannot reply individually to postal submissions, we always guarantee that your feedback goes straight to the appropriate authors, in time for the next edition. Each person who sends us information is thanked in the next edition, the most useful submissions are rewarded with a selection of digital PDF chapters.

Visit lonelyplanet.com/contact to submit your updates and suggestions or to ask for help. Our award-winning website also features inspirational travel stories, news and discussions.

Note: We may edit, reproduce and incorporate your comments in Lonely Planet products such as guidebooks, websites and digital products, so let us know if you don't want your comments reproduced or your name acknowledged. For a copy of our privacy policy visit lonelyplanet.com/privacy.

Index

A

accessible travel 302
accommodation 302-3, *see also individual locations*
  children 32
  language 315
  ryokan 299-300
  temples 267
activities 20, *see also individual activities*
air travel 309-10
Akihabara 48-9, 71
Amerika-Mura 197
amusement parks
  Fuji-Q Highland 171
  Sky Circus 80
  Tokyo Disney Resort 80
  Tokyo Joypolis 80
  Universal Studios Japan 198-9
anime 295
aquariums 197
architecture 18, 295-6
area codes 307
art galleries 18, *see also* museums
  21_21 Design Sight 57
  21st Century Museum of Contemporary Art 158
  Asakura Museum of Sculpture, Taitō 43
  Benesse Art Site Naoshima 212-13
  Benesse House Museum 213
  Chichū Art Museum 213
  Ghibli Museum, Mitaka 57
  Kubota Itchiku Art Museum 168
  Kyoto International Manga Museum 109-10
  Kyoto National Museum 111
  Lee Ufan Museum 213
  National Art Center Tokyo 57
  SCAI the Bathhouse 43
  Sumida Hokusai Museum 53
  teamLab Borderless 64
  Ukiyo-e Ōta Memorial Museum of Art 59
  Yayoi Kusama Museum 60
arts 292-6, *see also* art galleries, courses, museums
ATMs 305
Atomic Bomb Dome 178-9
awamori 253

B

baseball 80
bathrooms 308
beaches
  Aka-jima 258
  Furuzamami Beach 258
  Fusaki Beach Aqua Garden 257
  Irimote-jima 251
  Nagata Inaka-hama 240-1
  Nishibama Beach 258
  Sunset Beach 248
  Zamami-jima 258
Benesse Art Site Naoshima 212-13
bicycle travel, *see* cycling
boat trips
  Iriomote-jima 251
  Kyoyo 114
  Osaka 199
  Tokyo 83
books 25, 296
Buddhism 284-5
budget 17
bunraku 198
bus travel 310, 312
bushidō 277
business hours 306

C

car travel 310-11
cash 305
castles & palaces
  Himeji-jō 206-7
  Hiroshima-jō 180
  Imperial Palace 56
  Kyoto Imperial Palace 107
  Matsumoto-jo 154
  Nijō-jō 106
  Osaka-jō 194-5
  Sentō Imperial Palace 107, 109
  Shuri-jō 254
Cat Street 39
cell phones 307
Central Japan 7, 147-59, **149**
  accommodation 149
  itineraries 148
  travel to/from 149
cherry blossoms 22
children, travel with 32-3
cinema 25, 294, 295
climate 16, 22-4, 303
costs 17
courses
  arts & crafts 63
  cooking 63, 117
  meditation 117
credit cards 306
culture 282-5
currency 305-6
custom regulations 303-4
cycling 310
  Kyoto 129
  Naoshima 215
  Osaka 199
  Tokyo 85

D

Daibutsu 136-7
Daisetsuzan National Park 222-3
dangers, *see* safety

Symbols & Map Key

Look for these symbols to quickly identify listings:

◎ Sights
❸ Activities
❸ Courses
❸ Tours
❸ Festivals & Events

❸ Eating
❸ Drinking
❸ Entertainment
❸ Shopping
❸ Information & Transport

These symbols and abbreviations give vital information for each listing:

🌿 Sustainable or green recommendation

FREE No payment required

☎ Telephone number
◷ Opening hours
Ⓟ Parking
㊋ Nonsmoking
❄ Air-conditioning
@ Internet access
📶 Wi-fi access
🏊 Swimming pool

🚌 Bus
⛴ Ferry
🚊 Tram
🚆 Train
🍴 English-language menu
🥗 Vegetarian selection
👪 Family-friendly

Find your best experiences with these Great For... icons.

Art & Culture
Beaches
Budget
Cafe/Coffee
Cycling
Detour
Drinking
Entertainment
Events
Family Travel
Food & Drink

History
Local Life
Nature & Wildlife
Photo Op
Scenery
Shopping
Short Trip
Sport
Walking
Winter Travel

Sights

🎨 Beach
🐦 Bird Sanctuary
☸ Buddhist
🏰 Castle/Palace
✝ Christian
☯ Confucian
🕉 Hindu
☪ Islamic
✡ Jain
✡ Jewish
🗿 Monument
🏛 Museum/Gallery/ Historic Building
🏚 Ruin
⛩ Shinto
☬ Sikh
☯ Taoist
🍇 Winery/Vineyard
🐾 Zoo/Wildlife Sanctuary
◉ Other Sight

Points of Interest

🏄 Bodysurfing
⛺ Camping
☕ Cafe
🛶 Canoeing/Kayaking
● Course/Tour
🤿 Diving
🍸 Drinking & Nightlife
🍽 Eating
🎭 Entertainment
♨ Sento Hot Baths/ Onsen
🛍 Shopping
⛷ Skiing
🛌 Sleeping
🤿 Snorkelling
🏄 Surfing
🏊 Swimming/Pool
🚶 Walking
🏄 Windsurfing
⊕ Other Activity

Information

🏦 Bank
🏛 Embassy/Consulate
✚ Hospital/Medical
@ Internet
⊘ Police
✉ Post Office
☎ Telephone
🚻 Toilet
❶ Tourist Information
● Other Information

Geographic

🏖 Beach
⊢ Gate
🏠 Hut/Shelter
🗼 Lighthouse
👁 Lookout
▲ Mountain/Volcano
🌴 Oasis
🌳 Park
)(Pass
🧺 Picnic Area
💧 Waterfall

Transport

✈ Airport
Ⓑ BART station
⊗ Border crossing
Ⓣ Boston T station
🚌 Bus
🚡 Cable car/Funicular
🚲 Cycling
⛴ Ferry
Ⓜ Metro/MRT station
🚝 Monorail
Ⓟ Parking
⛽ Petrol station
Ⓢ Subway/S-Bahn/ Skytrain station
🚕 Taxi
🚉 Train station/Railway
🚋 Tram
⊖ Tube Station
Ⓤ Underground/ U-Bahn station
● Other Transport

Stephanie d'Arc Taylor

A native Angeleno, Stephanie grew up with the west LA weekend ritual of going for Iranian sweets after *tenzaru soba* in Little Osaka. Later, she quit her PhD to move to Beirut and become a writer. Since then, she has published work with the *New York Times, Guardian, Roads & Kingdoms* and *Kinfolk Magazine,* and co-founded Jaleesa, a venture-capital-funded social impact business in Beirut. Follow her on Instagram @zerodarctaylor.

Craig McLachlan

Craig has covered destinations all over the globe for Lonely Planet for two decades. Based in Queenstown, New Zealand for half the year, he runs an outdoor activities company and a sake brewery, then moonlights overseas for the other half, leading tours and writing for Lonely Planet. Craig has completed a number of adventures in Japan and his books are available on Amazon. Check out www.craigmclachlan.com.

Rebecca Milner

California-born and living in Tokyo since 2002, Rebecca has co-authored Lonely Planet guides to Tokyo and Japan. She's also a freelance writer covering travel, food and culture. Rebecca has been published in the *Guardian,* the *Independent,* the *Sunday Times Travel Magazine,* the *Japan Times* and more.

Kate Morgan

Having worked for Lonely Planet for over a decade now, Kate has been fortunate enough to cover plenty of ground working as a travel writer on destinations such as Shanghai, Japan, India, Russia, Zimbabwe, the Philippines and Phuket. She has done stints living in London, Paris and Osaka but these days is based in one of her favourite regions in the world – Victoria, Australia. In between travelling the world and writing about it, Kate enjoys spending time at home working as a freelance editor.

Thomas O'Malley

A British writer based in Beijing, Tom is a world-leading connoisseur of cheap eats, dive bars, dark alleyways and hangovers. He has contributed travel stories to everyone from the BBC to *Playboy,* and reviews hotels for the *Telegraph.* Under another guise, he is a comedy scriptwriter. Follow him by walking behind at a distance.

Simon Richmond

Journalist and photographer Simon Richmond has specialised as a travel writer since the early 1990s and first worked for Lonely Planet in 1999 on their *Central Asia* guide. He's long since stopped counting the number of guidebooks he's researched and written for the company, but countries covered include Australia, China, India, Iran, Japan, Korea, Malaysia, Mongolia, Myanmar (Burma), Russia, Singapore, South Africa and Turkey.

Phillip Tang

Phillip Tang grew up on a typically Australian diet of *pho* and fish'n'chips before moving to Mexico City. A degree in Chinese and Latin American cultures launched him into travel and then writing about it for Lonely Planet's *Canada, China, Japan, Korea, Mexico, Peru* and *Vietnam* guides. Follow his writing at hellophillip.com, photos @mrtangtangtang and tweets @philliptang.

Our Story

A beat-up old car, a few dollars in the pocket and a sense of adventure. In 1972 that's all Tony and Maureen Wheeler needed for the trip of a lifetime – across Europe and Asia overland to Australia. It took several months, and at the end – broke but inspired – they sat at their kitchen table writing and stapling together their first travel guide, *Across Asia on the Cheap*. Within a week they'd sold 1500 copies. Lonely Planet was born.

Today, Lonely Planet has offices in Franklin, London, Melbourne, Oakland, Dublin, Beijing and Delhi, with more than 600 staff and writers. We share Tony's belief that 'a great guidebook should do three things: inform, educate and amuse'.

Our Writers

Benedict Walker

A beach baby from Newcastle, Australia, Benedict turned 40 in 2017 and decided to start a new life in Leipzig, Germany. Writing for Lonely Planet was a childhood dream and he has covered big chunks of Australia, Canada, Germany, Japan, USA, Switzerland, Sweden and Japan. Follow him on Instagram @wordsandjourneys.

Ray Bartlett

Ray Bartlett has been travel writing for nearly two decades, bringing Japan, Korea, Mexico, Tanzania, Guatemala, Indonesia and many parts of the United States to life in rich detail for top-industry publishers, newspapers and magazines. Ray currently divides his time between homes in the USA, Japan and Mexico.

Andrew Bender

Award-winning travel and food writer Andrew Bender has written three dozen Lonely Planet guidebooks (from Amsterdam to Los Angeles, Germany to Taiwan and more than a dozen titles about Japan), plus numerous articles for lonelyplanet.com. Andy also is a tour leader and tour planner for visits to Japan. Follow him on Twitter @wheresandynow.

More Writers

STAY IN TOUCH LONELYPLANET.COM/CONTACT

AUSTRALIA The Malt Store, Level 3, 551 Swanston St, Carlton, Victoria 3053
☑ 03 8379 8000, fax 03 8379 8111

IRELAND Digital Depot, Roe Lane (off Thomas St), Digital Hub, Dublin 8, D08 TCV4, Ireland

USA 124 Linden Street, Oakland, CA 94607
☑ 510 250 6400, toll free 800 275 8555, fax 510 893 8572

UK 240 Blackfriars Road, London SE1 8NW
☑ 020 3771 5100, fax 020 3771 5101

 twitter.com/lonelyplanet facebook.com/lonelyplanet instagram.com/lonelyplanet youtube.com/lonelyplanet lonelyplanet.com/newsletter